PUBLIC GOODS, PUBLIC ENTERPRISE, PUBLIC CHOICE

Public Goods, Public Enterprise, Public Choice

Theoretical Foundations of the Contemporary Attack on Government

Hugh Stretton

and

Lionel Orchard

St. Martin's Press

First published in Great Britain 1994 by
THE MACMILLAN PRESS LTD
Houndmills, Basingstoke, Hampshire RG21 2XS
and London
Companies and representatives
throughout the world

A catalogue record for this book is available
from the British Library.

ISBN 0-333-60724-4 hardcover
ISBN 0-333-60725-2 paperback

Printed in Great Britain by
Antony Rowe Ltd
Chippenham, Wiltshire

First published in the United States of America 1994 by
Scholarly and Reference Division,
ST. MARTIN'S PRESS, INC.,
175 Fifth Avenue,
New York, N.Y. 10010

ISBN 0-312-10742-0

Library of Congress Cataloging-in-Publication Data
Stretton, Hugh.
Public goods, public enterprise, public choice : theoretical
foundations of the contemporary attack on government / Hugh
Stretton, Lionel Orchard.
p.   cm.
Includes bibliographical references and index.
ISBN 0-312-10742-0
1. Public goods.   2. Social choice.   3. Government business
enterprises.   4. Economic policy.   I. Orchard, Lionel.   II. Title.
HB846. 5.O73   1994
338. 9—dc20   93-31621
                                                          CIP

to Sue

Contents

Part One

1 Motives

Western governments are supposed to contrive stable prices and full employment. They are supposed to restrain excessive inequalities of wealth and opportunity and see that everyone can achieve a basic standard of living. They currently wrestle with various effects of ageing population, and of women's changing rights, opportunities and stresses. Their environmental management is improving but still has far to go. Technical changes and imprudent deregulation have brought some of their financial systems near to anarchy. All these problems call for better rather than less government. None of them is soluble by unaided market forces.

The ex-communist governments of Eastern Europe and Asia face more fundamental problems of national purpose and institutional replacement. Before they learn how to manage a mixed economy they must first mix a manageable economy. Some talk as if efficient capitalism could be created simply by repealing the laws against it – but if they try that without care for the culture, the slow-built institutional structures and the intricate public regulation which characterize all the productive mixed economies, they will be in danger of running capitalism as disastrously as their predecessors ran socialism.

The once-poor countries which have managed to produce their way up from the third world have all done it with active government, variously productive and protective. The means vary with time and situation, but none of the remaining poor countries can expect to imitate the Asian tigers merely by passively exposing themselves to the world economy.

Thus the national economies of West, East and South all need intelligent government; but efforts to supply it are hindered by the widespread belief that governmental economic activity is by nature inefficient, its faults are incurable and it should therefore be minimized: 'least government is best government'.

This book has a simple purpose. Old and New Right are attacking the mixed economy's public sector. Among their weapons are 'economic theories of politics', now thirty or forty years old, which suggest that there can be no good ways to allocate public goods, manage public industries, arrive at collective social purposes, or govern democratically. We think these theories mistake some of the potentialities of both public and private enterprise. Because they simply recommend less of one and more of the other they discourage concerted efforts to improve either of them, or the

1

working relations between them. If believed, they reduce the possibilities of able, inventive government in societies which badly need such government. We think the world would do better without these persuasions. Other books explore the practical forces – class, business, political and other forces – which propel the general shift of opinion to the Right. This book deals only with its intellectual equipment: its theories.

Soon after the Second World War, as big government continued to grow, three young American economists – James Buchanan, Kenneth Arrow and Paul Samuelson, all since awarded Nobel prizes – published essays which used economic analysis to explain processes of political and social choice in democratic societies.[1] Those essays initiated what have come to be called public choice theory, social choice theory and theory of public goods. They joined older beliefs about motivation in government-owned firms which amount to a hostile theory of public enterprise. Arrow and Samuelson did not intend their work to be conservative, but many of their followers have made it so, and public choice theory was always so. Insofar as policies of tax-cutting, privatizing, deregulating and 'rolling back the state' have an intellectual basis, these theories supply it.

We will not treat the theories in all their nuances. That would be arduous for authors and readers alike. There are at least a thousand books and articles of social choice theory. The journal *Public Choice* has printed more than a thousand items in its first fifteen years. A number of reviews of the mature theories, mostly sympathetic, are in print[2] and offer comprehensive bibliographies. Our simpler aim is to criticize the theories in their essence, as clearly as we can, for readers in business and government and in other disciplines as well as the theorists' own.* We will argue that in most of

*Some scholars (and publishers) disapprove of writing thus about ideas 'in their essence' with minimal reference to their elaboration and repetition in the academic journals. We respect their reasons, but hope they will respect ours. There is a creeping effect of academic growth which calls for thought. As social theory accumulates, the requirement that each new contribution locate itself by summarizing the preceding state of the art forces a continuous shift of print (and time and cost) from new thought to recapitulation and scholarly apparatus. Some of that is useful (as in books whose whole purpose is to review the state of the art) but much of it is wasteful, and the waste is further encouraged by the promotional use of citation indexes. The shift – to text thickly encrusted with citations, footnotes and bibliography – also puts off non-academic readers. In other circumstances we might contrast 'books about life, written for the public' with 'books about other books, written for other academics', but this book is a hybrid. It is undoubtedly about other books, but it is about their relation to life and it is written for the public as well as our peers, so we have made it as readable and barnacle-free as we could.

their forms the theories have such incurable faults that they should simply be discarded.

The most widely read and influential of the newcomers are the public choice theorists. At the heart of their disagreement with traditional social thought is a disagreement about the motivation of people's public behaviour. Public choice theory is 'pure', built on formal premisses rather than observations of life, but its central premiss is an assumption about real-life motivation: the *homo economicus* assumption that in their political as well as their economic behaviour humans are the rational self-serving maximizers of economic theory, and what they want to maximize is material income or the satisfactions which they derive from it.

Some opposing ideas of community, and the social construction of freedom and individuality, are discussed toward the end of this book. Here at the beginning, before introducing the 'monomotivational' theories, this chapter sketches our own view of the mixed motivation of social behaviour. It is a traditional view, here merely to remind readers of the material and moral complexities of human purpose which they know in themselves and meet in daily life, and which have been main subjects of literature and moral and political philosophy since written history began.

CITIZENS' PURPOSES

Consider some ordinary people going about their daily business.

Our first example is a happy one. Her name is Ellie, she's thirty five and she's placed where she can look after her own interests without much harm to others. Many of the things she does are for her own benefit. She earns money, spends some of it on herself, lives in a house which she chose and decorated chiefly to suit herself. She has friends at work but competes with them when necessary: to look good, to get the interesting rather than the dull work, to get pay and promotion. Though friendly in manner she doesn't trust strangers very far: she locks her house and car, tells no one her bank number, picks up no hitchhikers, and is careful where she walks alone at night.

She also thinks of her own interests in the little she has to do with government. She claims all the tax allowances she's entitled to. She votes for Town Councillors who promise good services and zoning protection for her neighbourhood. In national elections she votes for the party which is generally supposed to represent the interests of her class.

At home she lives with husband and children. Her feelings about them may be mixed – they exploit her in all the traditional ways. But her behaviour towards them is unselfish – she cares for them in all the traditional ways.

Is she the selfish income-maximizer of economic theory – is her political and economic behaviour predictable by anyone who knows what her material interests are? Not entirely, for reasons of three kinds.

First, some of her public behaviour is positively unselfish. She votes for age pensions and other welfare benefits for which she's not entitled herself. She helps competitors at work to avoid mistakes. She wouldn't sell ill-chosen goods to unwary buyers even if her employer wanted her to. And so on – she looks out for herself, but not too greedily – she's a good sort in a culture which encourages her sort.

Second, some of her influence on the world is disinterested. Where her own interests are not at risk she still has a sense of justice and wants fair treatment for others besides herself. She joined a conservation group, originally for self-interested reasons when her own neighbourhood was threatened, but when that battle was won she stayed on, petitioning and letterboxing to preserve old buildings anywhere. Is that a generous gift of her time – or selfish because she likes the work and the friends she makes? It doesn't matter: either motive gets the good work done.

Third and most important, that last ambiguity is quite common: she gets a good deal of what she wants for herself by being helpful to other people: selfish purposes motivate generous behaviour. (Civilized institutions arrange a lot of that transformation.) At home Ellie happens to be the type who wants family life and love. From what we know of her and ourselves we suspect that she wants to love even more than to be loved – she continues to love her children through their odious phases, and her partner when his attention is on other things than love. But whether she does it from love or by way of trade, generosity to others often brings her things she wants for herself.

As at home, so at work. Ellie works for IBM, demonstrating new computing products and training their buyers to use them. This year the company has given a set of touch-screen machines to a political museum. Touch the screens in response to their screened instructions and they'll give you information about your political system. Summon the electoral map and touch your home address and you'll learn who represents you in national and local government, what party they belong to, their majority at last election and their voting record on major issues. Touch another option and a pie-graph tells how your tax dollar was spent last year, then touch a segment of the pie and you get a detailed breakdown of that segment of expenditure. The machine also offers to question *you*, testing your political knowledge with multiple-choice questions and answers. Why the gift to the museum? IBM regularly make public gifts for social or PR reasons. Many teachers bring their school classes to this museum. It's also visited by politicians including those who finance the schools. So the gift may boost sales of touch-screen gear to schools and other buyers.

When the machines arrive Ellie arrives with them, seconded for six months to teach the museum staff how to programme and manage them. That takes some doing: the programming is quite difficult and the staff are scarcely computer-literate when they begin. She finds she has to educate them as well as train them. They find her so clever and friendly that other branches of the museum bring computing problems to her. She helps with those because she's a helpful type, and thinks her employer wouldn't mind because it all helps the image. She is happy in her work because although she's in marketing she's not selling. There can be conflicts of interest in advertising or selling, and problems of conscience when you know that for some purposes a rival product is actually a bit better than yours. But demonstrating the latest ingenious gear to always-grateful people, and advancing womankind by doing it as a clever, helpful young woman in a cut-throat male world, together make for beautiful relations between conscience, ambition and fascinating work. Ellie wakes up each morning welcoming the day.

Not everyone in the workforce is so lucky – Ellie's balance of self-interest and generosity is not meant to be representative. But her experience illustrates a variety of relations between self-interested and generous motives and behaviour which can't be sufficiently understood, or predicted, by classifying all behaviour as either simply selfish or simply altruistic. In some activities – earning, shopping, defending her neighbourhood – Ellie looks after her own interests. It's in the nature of those activities that in some of them she helps herself, in some herself and family, in some (like defending the neighbourhood) herself and others. When she faces issues which don't touch her own material interests she still likes to see justice done – she bothers to go and vote, she doesn't neglect such issues as indifferent or none of her business. When she works for family or friends or the conservation group, gives to charity, votes for tax-financed welfare which will cost her more than it gets her, or helps more people at the museum than she's paid to help, she is genuinely unselfish. When she helps her bosses and fellow-workers at IBM and the customers she is paid to help, then her generosity to others gets her what she wants for herself: congenial work, pay and promotion, as well as the pleasure of being helpful and being liked for it. It may be that Ellie's good nature gets her the job at least as much as the job motivates the good nature. It may be otherwise with other people – self-interest alone motivates plenty of service to others – but the service may be doubly reliable if it has Ellie's double motivation.

As noted above, Ellie's motivation may be unrepresentative. But so is any other worker's – no one individual, or monomotivational model, can sufficiently represent the diversity of motives at work in business and government. Any large sample of working humanity is likely to show a spectrum of motivation from generous to acquisitive, with the generosity directed variously to employers, workmates, customers and passers-by. At the generous extreme are the volunteers who staff Meals on Wheels and other charitable services. At the other extreme are perhaps the banks' exchange gamblers, who deal with screened and telephoned information rather than people, buying and selling currencies minute by minute to gain or lose money without producing anything useful at all. Between the extremes are masses of people with ordinary mixtures of selfish, generous and disinterested purpose. Most of them work within the law and within informal codes of individual, professional and corporate behaviour. Some influence the laws and codes, by precept, example and voting. To dismiss economists' or other monomotivational theories of behaviour it should only be necessary to read the basic texts of modern psychology, industrial relations or management theory – or to reflect on one's own acquaintance within the two classes who between them do most of the world's work: domestic workers and wage-earners.

Very diverse motives get a third or more of all material production done by housework and other do-it-yourself labour. Some of it deserves to be called 'labour of love'. There is also simple self-help and subsistence; work done for the pleasure of doing it; some straightforward exchange of services between partners; much exploitation of women by men and children; housework done by women who would rather be out earning, and by other women who wish they didn't also have to go out and earn; and work bullied and coerced from women unable, because afraid, to escape it.

Most wage and salary earners want the rate for the job, whatever it is, but beyond that their wants vary. They range from people who chiefly want to put the world right, through those who chiefly enjoy the work itself or the company at work, to those who chiefly want the money. Some of course are equally interested in all four. At the money-hungry end of the spectrum are some each of the richest and poorest earners. There are people desperate for income – people with children and mortgages, or saving hard for houses or cars or travel, or deep in debt. There are rich professionals, corporate executives and others on the way to capital wealth. There are people chiefly interested in the money because nothing else about their work is very interesting – assembly-line hands, clerks, cleaners, labourers, burnt-out teachers, who don't much enjoy the work or (in some cases) the company that comes with it. There are casual workers stuffing envelopes, letterboxing, car-washing, clearing rubbish. Some at this dull end of the spectrum have fairly predictable 'labour market' responses to wage incentives alone – but even they have usually also got some ethical and aesthetic limits to what they're willing to do.

In varying proportions the motives of most of those people include some generosity, some disinterested morality, some customary acceptance of obligations to others, some interest in other rewards than money. There is also plenty of self-interested desire for material income, a desire so pervasive that every public and private institution must somehow harness or restrain it – the most self-sacrificing charity still needs independent, suitably motivated eyes to audit its books and monitor its uses of its resources. Virtue is no less genuine, and can be a good deal more reliable, when protected from temptation.

But although financial incentives and controls are a necessary condition of business and government, it does not follow that they are a *sufficient* condition of the *best* business or government, or a sufficient explanation of them. The universal coexistence of concern for self and concern for others in human behaviour is not best understood, or managed, by neglecting either one of the two.

We will next notice that theorists can mistake the effects of the selfish as well as the unselfish elements in the mix.

INSTITUTIONS' PURPOSES

Elements of generosity, disinterested morality and shared culture in people's public behaviour help to make 'monomotivational' public choice theory a bad predictor of their behaviour. But those are not usually the main causes of the theory's failure. Its main cause is a confusion about the operation of the self-interested motives on which the theory relies. In brief: the theory is uncertain or self-contradictory as to whether or not institutional arrangements (as opposed to market exchanges) can make people's self-interest motivate them to give good service to others. If they can, the theory fails, but it also fails if they can't, so the theorists' uncertainty is understandable.

Individual material self-interest is a powerful and pervasive motive in industrial societies and must somehow be disciplined and harnessed to good purposes. At first sight there seem to be two alternative ways of doing that: by market exchange, or by institutional means. At the heart of public choice theory is the belief that market discipline works better than institutional discipline. To understand why, compare the two:

Market discipline. When I bring my carrot crop to market the carrots will only fetch what they're worth to the buyers. (The buyers are disciplined too: if they offer too little, I'll switch to growing something else.) I don't need either generous motives or police supervision to get me to grow good carrots: the other dealers in the market induce me to do it. Thus they transform my self-interest: I do best for myself by growing the best carrots I can for them. Since this is the subject of one of the most famous passages of English prose, we had better quote it. In Book I, Chapter II of *The Wealth of Nations* Adam Smith observed that unlike other animals

> man has almost constant occasion for the help of his brethren, and it is in vain for him to expect it from their benevolence only. He will be more likely to prevail if he can interest their self-love in his favour, and show them that it is for their own advantage to do for him what he requires of them. Whoever offers to another a bargain of any kind, proposes to do this. Give me that which I want, and you shall have this which you want, is the meaning of every such offer; and it is in this manner that we obtain from one another the far greater part of those good offices which we stand in need of. It is not from the benevolence of the butcher, the brewer, or the baker, that we expect our dinner, but from their regard to their own interest. We address ourselves, not to their humanity but to their self-love, and never talk to them of our own necessities but of their advantages.

We will see that that passage actually offers market theorists less support than many of them claim. But first, compare the principle of market discipline with the common alternative to it.

Institutional discipline. Suppose I am a public servant – let's say an inspector for the Carrot Marketing Board. I'm employed to discipline the growers and protect the consumers by detecting carrot ingredients which buyers can't see for themselves: harmful levels of artificial colouring, hormonal stimulants, chemical fertilizer and insecticide, and so on. If I'm lazy or inept or take bribes from growers my superiors are supposed correct or sack me. But if I inspect the carrots with skill and integrity and make the consumers' interests my own I can expect to rise step by step to the top of my profession. Thus the institution which employs me transforms my self-interest: as with market discipline, I will get most for myself by doing my best for others.

Readers will scarcely need reminding of the celebrated virtues and vices of those two ways of disciplining conflicting self-interests. Markets let them discipline each other by voluntary exchange, leaving everyone to decide their wants and priorities for themselves; but markets can suffer well-known kinds of market failure and inequity. Institutions can coordinate complicated processes and embody principles of justice, but can suffer well-known kinds of bureaucratic oppression and inefficiency. We could have designed this book as a contribution to the debate between the two. Public choice theorists prefer market relations. Hard-line socialists prefer planned relations. Between those extremes, rejecting both their ideologies and approaching the subject with open minds, we could compare the 'market' and 'institutional' methods not just in general terms but in detail as each might work in the particular conditions of industry after industry and function after function of government. We might thus arrive at a best 'mix' for a mixed economy approaching the twenty-first century.

There is some sense in arguing like that and we will do it from time to time. But it can nevertheless be a deceptive way to perceive its subject, for two reasons. The minor reason is that it is not enough to see how alternative arrangements succeed in disciplining and serving opposing self-interests; systems should also be chosen for the other effects they have, including the scope and encouragement they offer to people's prudence, generosity and disinterested morality, as well as their self-interests. The major reason is that it is a mistake to see market relations and institutional relations as such distinct alternatives. First, markets themselves are institutions. They have to be organized and managed, and they can suffer as much bias or inefficiency as other organizations can. More important, most traders in modern markets are not individual carrot growers and consumers, they are firms. They are organized institutions, some of them employing tens or hundreds of thousands of people. They contain within them innumerable individual interests and conflicts of purpose. Most of what other institutions can do to harness their members' interests to their corporate purposes, firms can do – and much of what self-interested individuals can do to influence, evade or frustrate corporate purposes, the owners and directors and employees of firms can do. So as (say) raw materials pass from miners and processors to component makers, car makers and distributors and thence to car buyers there is about as much hierarchical organization, planning, and opportunity for organizational virtue and vice as there is in (say) the equally complicated provision of public education or health and hospital services. Both processes also include plenty of market relations, with opportunities for market efficiency or market failure. So as means of ordering conflicting individual interests, the simple contrast between market means and institutional means is in many respects a false contrast. Wherever, as in most modern business and government, activities require complicated organization and division of labour, there are not just two but many alternative ways of getting them done. All the alternatives are mixtures of organization and market exchange; and some further options may be concealed under those two labels – 'market' and 'organization' each stand for quite a range of devices for restraining, transforming, harnessing and enlisting self-interested motives to produce productive and socially acceptable behaviour.

We will argue later in this section that corporate organization, as an integral element of market systems, confronts public choice theorists with a dilemma. If firms can subordinate all their members' individual purposes to the corporate purpose of enriching the owners by pleasing the customers most, at least cost, two conclusions seem to follow. First, market systems don't ensure as much individual autonomy as they claim. Second, organizations *can* subordinate their members' purposes quite effectively to their corporate purposes, so the public choice theory of organizational behaviour must be false. Alternatively if public choice theory is right, and individual purposes commonly displace or pervert the ostensible purposes of organizations, two other conclusions follow. First, firms cannot be the single-minded maximizers of market theory, so market systems don't necessarily have the efficiency claimed for them. And second, organizations can serve, compromise and reconcile a lot of individual purposes. Together those conclusions leave no strong presumption that market relations are necessarily more free, fair and efficient than organized relations can be. In short, if firms can dragoon their workers' individual purposes, market relations are not so free – but if they can't, market relations are not so efficient – as market theories claim. And if they *can* effectively subordinate their members' interests and purposes to their corporate purposes, so presumably can other institutions, as public choice theory says they can't.

Meanwhile how exchange and institutional devices are mixed in particular activities of business and government can be important. It can have effects for good or ill on the quality of national life as well as the industries concerned. It is right to give careful thought to these issues. But it is usually wrong to decide them by simple ideological preference for market or institutional means without reference to the facts of each case. And it is usually wrong to design systems of motivation to run on material self-interest alone without enlisting any of the more generous, cooperative or principled impulses which can also contribute to good performance.

Profit-seeking business can't prosper, and police and other security systems can't cope, if most people – employees, customers, police – are willing to steal most of the time. Plenty of unimpeachably liberal, capitalist, non-socialist observers have noticed how systems constituted by profit-seeking firms and ostensibly motivated by self-interest alone actually depend on levels of inbuilt morality in most of the people most of the time:

morality which needs to be inculcated by the surrounding society and reinforced by the internal rules and culture of the profit-seeking corporations
themselves. We could cite liberal sources from Adam Smith's *Theory of
Moral Sentiments* (1759) through the nineteenth century works of J.S. Mill
and T.H. Green to Fred Hirsch's *Social Limits to Growth* (1976) which
notes with alarm the tendency of modern capitalism to erode the communal
morality on which it itself depends. Instead of those, we will refer to some
classical sources of modern management theory.

Sixty years ago three books appeared which are a watershed in the study
of individual motivation in business government organizations.

In *The Modern Corporation and Private Property* (1932) Adolf A. Berle
and Gardner C. Means measured the separation of ownership from control
in the growing number of firms which had no dominant shareholder. Those
firms' directors must keep them profitable to survive, but beyond that Berle
and Means thought that directors could, should, and increasingly did,
manage with a balanced regard for the interests of shareholders, employees, customers, and society at large. That assumed and encouraged some
disinterested concern for others in the directors' motivation. The more that
concern came to be recognized as proper and desirable, and a qualification
for appointment as director, the more the directors' benevolence could be
reconciled with their self-interest and reinforced by it.

In *The Human Problems of Industrial Civilization* (1933) Elton Mayo
reported a number of investigations of industrial psychology and management including the famous Hawthorne experiments. In those, a group of
workers with measurable output were monitored while their wages and
conditions of work were one by one improved. With each improvement,
output increased. Then the improvements were one by one taken away, and
output continued to increase. For that unexpected effect the investigators
identified two causes. The workers were encouraged by the unusual attention and respect being paid to them, and among themselves they became a
coherent and happy working group. Material conditions and rewards were
only some, and not always the most important, among the causes of their
motivation and performance. The human relations school of management
was born and has since developed to get more attention in most management schools and corporate practice than the economists' rival theories
whose simple view of motivation is expressed in the concept of a labour
'market' where workers sell work, and employers buy it, as a commodity
like carrots.

Four years later in *The Functions of the Executive* (1937) Chester Barnard,
an executive of the Bell Telephone Company, offered a new understanding of
the nature and motivation of organized work in business and government.

Barnard saw formal organization, including the organization of business corporations, as a mode of cooperation. 'Organization comes into being when two or more persons begin to cooperate to a common end.' If the common purpose requires that work be coordinated by the giving and taking of orders, the people cooperate in that. So even if their role includes giving orders, bosses necessarily lead rather than command. If they have authority, give orders, and the orders are obeyed, that is still by consent. Attracting and maintaining that consent – that willingness of everyone in the organization to cooperate for common purposes – is the leaders' central task.

Conventional incentives operate – the fear of the sack, the exchange of work for wages. But by themselves they can't usually motivate reliably good performance – 'where conformance is secured by fear of penalties, what is operating is not the moral factor in the sense of the term used here, but merely negative inducements of incentives'. Especially for leaders and managers, 'only the deep convictions that operate regardless of either specific penalties or specific rewards are the stuff of high responsibility'.

Though he stressed the cooperative element in organized work, Barnard also saw that it was shot through with actual and potential conflicts. His first originality lay in the way he related the cooperation to the conflicts and perceived, in the relation between the two, the main function of leadership. His second originality lay in seeing most of the conflicts as both material and moral, so that to do their job properly leaders need both technical and moral capacities. They need to be clever and good, or at least sensitive to others' goodness, and each of the two qualities is likely to be useless – or worse – without the other.

Barnard was not an academic theorist. He claimed that his practical executive experience had convinced him that economists had overemphasized the element of rational economic calculation in people's behaviour. It was wrong to think that 'man is an "economic man" carrying a few non-economic appendages'. In real life, including corporate life, economic and non-economic motives constantly mix. Also, motives conflict. The conflicts are not only between person and person, they are often between one motive and another within one person's mind. Barnard depicted those actual and potential conflicts in the following way.

Each of us has a number of roles in life: parent and child, spouse and lover, friend, neighbour, employee, and so on. Each of us belongs to a number of organizations: a family, a firm, perhaps a church, some clubs and associations. Within each organization we may have a number of relationships: with superiors, with subordinates, with fellow-workers, with a firm's suppliers and customers. For each relationship we tend to have a code of conduct. We know how to treat (and what treatment to expect from) spouse, children, employers, workmates, and so on. The code for each relationship may be imposed on us by social rules, or by our own choice – there may be more choice about some of the codes than about others. Some of an individual's codes may be highminded, enjoining honesty and generosity. 'Be kind to old people, don't cheat children, pay your lawful debts.' Some may be the opposite. 'Pay the least tax you can, strangers are fair game, never give a sucker an even break.'

Because they often conflict, we have to order the codes. Barnard concocted a memorable example:

Mr A, a citizen of Massachusetts, a member of the Baptist church, having a father and mother living, and a wife and two children, is an expert machinist employed at a pump station of an important water system. For simplicity's sake, we omit further description. We impute to him several moral codes: Christian ethics, the patriotic code of the citizen, a code of family obligations, a code as an expert machinist, a code derived from the organization engaged in the operation of the water system. He is not aware of these codes. These intellectual abstractions are a part of his "system", ingrained in him by causes, forces, experiences which he has either forgotten or on the whole never recognized. Just what they are, in fact, can at best only be approximately inferred by his actions, preferably under stress. He has no idea as to the order of importance of these codes, though, if pressed, what he might say probably would indicate that his religious code is first in importance, either because he has some intellectual comprehension of it, or because it is socially dominant. I shall hazard the guess, however, that their order of importance is as follows: his code as to the support and protection of his own children, his code of obligations to the water system, his code as a skilled artisan, his code with reference to his parents, his religious code, and his code as a citizen, For his children he will kill, steal, cheat the government, rob the church, leave the water plant at a critical time, botch a job by hurrying. If his children are not directly at stake, he will sacrifice money, health, time, comfort, convenience, jury duty, church obligations, in order to keep the water plant running; except for his children and the water plant, he cannot be induced to do a botch mechanical job – wouldn't know how; to take care of his parents he will lie, steal, or do anything else contrary to his code as a citizen or his religious code; if his government legally orders him to violate his religious code, he will go to jail first. He is, however, a very responsible man. It not only takes extraordinary pressure to make him violate any of his codes, but when faced with such pressure he makes great effort to find some solution that is compatible with all of them; and because he makes that effort and is capable he has in the past succeeded. Since he is a very responsible man, knowing his codes you can be fairly sure of what he will do under a rather wide range of conditions.

The Functions of the Executive, pp. 267–8

Within any big firm Mr A's number of potentially conflicting codes is likely to be multiplied many times by the number of material interests and moral and social concerns possessed by all the people who must cooperate in the firm's work. Their individual purposes, and the codes which go with their diverse trades and professions and organizational roles, must somehow be reconciled with or subordinated to the purposes of the enterprise; and individual purposes are reconciled or coordinated most effectively if the individuals feel that they are members of the enterprise and share its purposes. They can't be simply deceived or coerced into feeling that: the common purposes must have some genuine interest, material or moral or both, for them.

How can that be achieved when the potential conflicts are so many? Executives have to cope with personal conflicts between individuals; conflicts of interest between owners, managers, workers, customers, creditors and community concerns; conflicts within some of those groups – between some shareholders and others, some managers and others, one labour union and another; and conflicts between short and long term interests of some of those groups. And the conflicts of interest tend to be expressed as moral conflicts as each interest asserts the code which seems to justify its claims.

Executives exist to resolve such conflicts. It is their main function. When they face conflicts between interests and between codes they respond (Barnard observed) in one of three ways. Some can't make up their minds. They can't bear to disappoint any of the parties, they won't face the problem, they put it off, it paralyses them. These executives are no good. A second group, who see themselves as tough and effective, make cutting decisions one way or another, upholding one of the codes and breaking one or more of the others. That weakens the broken codes and upsets the people who believe in them, live by them and may gain by them. Most of the codes are there for good reasons so the morale of the enterprise is likely to suffer. Third, there are good executives. They are inventive in one or both of two ways. They find a course of action which as nearly as possible satisfies all the relevant codes. Or they persuade people to modify the codes themselves in ways which preserve their necessary virtues but reduce their conflicts. If they succeed by the first method 'all the codes are strengthened by the experience; but such a solution frequently requires imaginative and constructive ability'. So does the second approach, in which leaders must persuade people to respect each others' codes and where necessary amend their own. In that process there may be a fine line between honest moral reasoning and self-interested hypocrisy. Barnard was well aware of that, and always argued on the honest side of the line. Executives were not there to make everyone slave exclusively for the shareholders. Even if they were, the shareholders' interests would not usually be well served until they were reconciled with the reasonable material and moral requirements of all concerned.

We need not follow Barnard's detailed exploration of executives' functions in business and government. His analysis is here only as a celebrated and enduring expression of a general way of understanding organized behaviour. Besides some generous instincts and some disinterested altruism, most people most of the time pursue the self-interests which they think are justifiable and not those which are not. They do so partly because they respect and often strongly support the relevant codes, and partly because they know that other people are likely to enforce them. Together the codes are a large part of any culture – of society as a whole, a social class, a corporation or institution of government, a trade or profession. Our final concern, in this opening chapter about motivation, will be with the culture from which people derive most of their ideas of right and wrong and fair dealing, their obligations to each other and their claims on each other.

But before turning to that subject, notice that Barnard's understanding of corporate behaviour and management has the deadly implications for public choice theory that were foreshadowed earlier. If firms can effectively discipline or transform all their members' purposes, so presumably can public institutions; and market systems don't offer as much individual autonomy and choice as market theories claim. If on the other hand firms' purposes have to incorporate many of their members' purposes, reconciling or adjudicating their conflicts as fairly as possible, then many individual demands are being met satisfactorily by institutional rather than market means; and market systems may not have much of the particular kind of efficiency which is claimed for systems of exchange between individual 'maximizers'.

CULTURE AND MOTIVATION

We return to Adam Smith. Did he really see all service to others as necessarily motivated by self-interest? On the contrary, he scorned attempts to reduce all motives to one, all measures of welfare to one, or all virtues to one. He specially scorned 'a propensity ... which philosophers in particular are apt to cultivate with a peculiar fondness, as the great means of displaying their ingenuity, the propensity to account for all appearances from as few principles as possible'.[3] The famous passage quoted earlier does not say that when a man wants service from others 'it is in vain for him to expect it from their benevolence'. It says 'it is in vain for him to expect it from their benevolence *only*'. Amartya Sen, a leader in social choice theory, summed up Adam Smith's general understanding of human motivation:

> The basic pluralism of Smith's position comes out sharply in his discussions of various virtues – prudence, humanity, justice, generosity, public spirit, etc. – to all of which intrinsic importance is attached.

A natural human sympathy with others, which takes pleasure in others' pleasure and suffers with others' pain, is the basic source of the virtues. But they are defined and strengthened by social means:

> Smith ... emphasizes the importance of "rules of conduct" in influencing people's behaviour and the positive role that such rules can play: "Those general rules of conduct when they have been fixed in our mind by habitual reflection, are of great use in correcting misrepresentations of self-love concerning what is fit and proper to be done in our particular situation."
>
> Amartya Sen, 'Adam Smith's prudence', in Sanjaya Lall and Frances Stewart (eds) *Theory and reality in development* (1986)

Self-interest is strong, especially in economic life, but even there it works by means and within limits set by collective rules and individual morality. Much can depend on the quality of the rules and the morality, and on the outcome of efforts to change them for better or worse.

History has since done a good deal to confirm Smith's balanced view of sympathy and self-interest. By Act of Parliament in 1847 British factory workers got a 10 hour day. They did not get it by industrial bargaining (strikes were unlawful) or by electoral numbers (scarcely any of them had votes). They got it when humanitarian reformers persuaded a majority in parliament, and probably in the class which parliament then represented, that it was cruel, unnecessary and imprudent to treat them as their employers were doing. Self-interest prompted some of the votes, but certainly not enough to pass the Act. Reformers had achieved a cultural change: a change in the prevailing morality.

Through the following century women have made some progress toward political, economic and domestic equality. Once again the progress has not been achieved chiefly by industrial muscle or market bargaining. Getting the vote has helped, but only when enough of both men and women voters were persuaded not to resist the economic and domestic changes as they had done in the past. Changes in formal and informal rules – institutional changes – have followed and then reinforced changes in the prevailing morality, and the two together have altered the motivation of a great deal of public and domestic behaviour.

The nineteenth and twentieth centuries – the centuries of industrial capitalism and democratic government – have seen scores of changes of that general kind, both in the rules with which behaviour has to comply and in the 'internalized' conceptions of self-interest, and ideas of right and wrong and mutual obligations, which are inculcated by prevailing cultures and shape many of the motives of their members.

SUMMARY

Selfish intentions don't always hurt others and unselfish intentions don't always help them. (Self-interest can prompt me to grow excellent carrots for market; altruistic charities, or moralists, have sometimes done more harm than good to those they tried to help.) We can summarize our commonsense view of motivation in a formal way by listing a range of motives from selfish to unselfish, each with a range of effects it may have. Since these are individual motives it is convenient to express them in the first person singular.

I serve myself at others' expense when I cheat, steal, compete for scarce resources, exploit others' labour, win at gambling, buy cheap and sell dear.

I serve myself without affecting others' interests much when (living alone) I do my own shopping and housework and choose what channels to watch.

I enrich myself by growing good carrots for others, as in most exchange business and wage employment. (Both have the usual market ambiguity, which is why they belong in two places on this list. I both help others by growing good carrots for them, and gain at their expense by getting the highest price I can.)

I serve my own interests in ways which unavoidably help others too, as when I defend the interests of my household, neighbourhood, class or nation.

I help or hurt others without affecting my own material interests, for example as a middle-income voter who supports tax transfers from rich to poor, or as a man voting for measures which only affect relations between women.

I help others because I enjoy doing it, and would suffer private guilt if I didn't.

I help others because I'm proud to, or expected to, and would suffer public shame if I were seen not to.

I help others from genuine concern for them when it doesn't affect my interests.

I help others from genuine concern for them when it costs me some self-sacrifice.

I act towards others, or vote for measures which affect others, on moral principles some of which are not concerned with selfishness or altruism – murder is always wrong whatever its motives or social effects. The moral principles on which I act sometimes accord with my material interests, sometimes don't, and are sometimes neutral to them. (Notice that there may often be differences between the social value of my behaviour and what many would see as its moral value. If I help others for my own pleasure I may deserve no moral credit, but still be a social benefactor. Notice, also, that such 'self-interested generosity' is likely to defeat theories and predictions which assume that self-interested behaviour is always materially acquisitive.)

Besides individual behaviour I also have some selfish, some disinterested and some self-sacrificing wishes about the kind of society that would be good for me and for others to live in. Given sufficient income, my desire for more is at least equalled by my desire that societies – mine and others – be just, peaceful, equal, affectionate, inventive, artistic, interesting; I don't want them to be unjust, violent, excessively unequal, greedy, unloving, dull. These desires focus on two aspects of societies' patterns of motivation: the values and wants which they instil into their people, and the extent to which their culture and institutions then harness those motives to produce productive and sociable behaviour.

We have thus summarized three diversities. A range of motives, of which material acquisitiveness is only one, can be found in every individual and every society. The cultural and institutional shaping of people's motives varies widely between (say) Sweden or Hungary and (say) Haiti or South Africa. And societies vary, and change over time, in the ways in which they harness particular motives to produce particular kinds of behaviour.

Given those real-life diversities, why do our new theorists want to insist that political and economic behaviour is best understood by assuming that its motivation is single-purposed, acquisitive, and unchanging? It may be partly for ordinary conservative or self-interested purposes – the theories tend to be used to defend inequalities, to free business from government, to argue for cutting taxes and welfare. If those class or political purposes are at work they are the business of other books. But there is also an intellectual, theoretical purpose, as follows.

THEORISTS' PURPOSES

In Lisa Peattie and Martin Rein, *Women's Claims: A study in political economy* (1983), there is a perceptive account of the processes of cultural and motivational change which have accompanied the progress of the women's movement. Their study led Peattie and Rein to link a particular practical hindrance to *reforming* social behaviour to an intellectual hindrance to *understanding* it:

> Every movement for social reform comes up, sooner or later, against the barrier of the natural: that which cannot be changed because it is in the order of things, outside the span of intervention. [An example is the 'natural' division of labour between men at work and women at home.] Since there is evidently no use arguing about what should be done about things which are beyond our control, which are properly part of the natural order, the boundary between natural and artificial is important in setting off the area for political argument and policy analysis from that of the order of nature which must be [merely passively, uninterferingly] understood. This line of course may be, and is, set differently in different societies and in different periods. . . . the boundary between the natural and the artificial is not settled but continually being renegotiated. In particular, we argue and conduct research around the issue of whether a given phenomenon is properly placed on one side or the other of the boundary.
>
> *Women's claims*, pp. 1–4.

Behaviour which is seen as natural looks unchangeable. Science can merely understand it, passively. With behaviour which we see as artificial or optional, on the other hand, we can study the options, argue for new ones, and work for change. But some disciplines can do so more readily than others. Orthodox economists aspire to theory of a kind which can only work with stable subject-matter. They need economic behaviour to have a motive force as simple and unchangeable as the gravitational force on which Newtonian physics relies. By contrast political or institutional economists try to choose theories and methods appropriate to understanding behaviour whose motivation varies with its political and social context and may well be open to deliberate change. As Peattie and Rein contrast the two approaches, 'the analytic conventions of economics are in search of models of phenomena treated as natural ones. In contrast political economy points to the role of social and political institutions in shaping economic outcomes. Thus political economy is, in effect, either arguing for some actual shift in the position of the boundary between natural and artificial, or – which may be just as important – drawing attention to the fact that this boundary is, in principle, shiftable' (p. 4).

Considering the length and depth of the intellectual tradition which sees human purposes as complex, variously selfish and unselfish, and changeable, public choice theorists may be seen as attempting an unusual shift, an opposite shift to those achieved by most reformers. They want to take a phenomenon long perceived as wilful and changeable and remove it to the realm of the natural and unchangeable: to persuade people that material greed is, and will inescapably remain, the single, natural, dominant motive of their political, economic and social behaviour.

We disagree. Theory should adapt to life, not imitate scientific models developed for quite different subject-matter. Material self-interest is strong and pervasive in the motivation of people's public behaviour. But it is open to many institutional transformations, and even in its pure form we do not believe that it dominates other impulses so regularly or completely that the behaviour can be predicted from knowledge of the material interests alone. One need not be religious oneself to agree in a general way with the understanding of human psychology to be found in the world's major religions and literatures: good and evil, selfish and generous, loving and hating, interested and disinterested, sympathetic and indifferent impulses coexist and contend with one another in individuals and in the principles embodied in the cultures and institutions which individuals inherit and shape, and which in turn do much to shape them.

In that complexity reformers should work to encourage the better potentialities and discourage the worse. But we believe that opposite effects – degrading effects – are more likely to follow from the theories which we now attack.

2 A Very Short History

This short history indicates which theories are our subject, when and by whom they were introduced, and some relations between them.

AN AGE OF INNOCENCE

James Buchanan

In 1949 in 'The Pure Theory of Government Finance: A Suggested Approach'[1] Buchanan contrasted two views of the state. In the first, 'the state, including all the individuals in it, is conceived as a single organic entity. In the second, the state is represented as the sum of its individual members acting in a collective capacity'. Buchanan thought that the theory of public finance tended to muddle the two. What government does was usually considered in the first way: government acts, or is urged to act, to maximize 'the public interest'. But how to pay for public goods had usually been considered in the second way: taxes were designed with their individual distributional effects in mind. While there might be practical reasons for thinking in that sloppy way, Buchanan argued that a rigorous theory ought to relate the individual distribution of public costs to the individual distribution of public benefits. Only then could one know whether particular policies, or state activity as a whole, were increasing inequalities, leaving them as they were, or reducing them. Progressive taxes might not reduce inequality if the benefits which they financed were distributed regressively. Regressive taxes might not increase inequality if the benefits they financed were distributed progressively. And so on – only by 'individualizing' both sides of the ledger could the net distributional effects of state activity be known.

Most of the later concerns of public choice theory were nascent in that article. Politics might consist chiefly of individual and group efforts to get most benefits from government and pay least tax. That activity might divert time and resources from productive uses. Not only by what it did, but also by the unproductive things which its operations tempted private individuals and groups to try to do, government might thus reduce production, the more so the more it tried to increase or redistribute it. So 'least government is best government'.

Buchanan did not develop any of those arguments in his 1949 paper. He merely called for consistent accounting to relate the individual distribution of public costs to the individual distribution of public benefits. Except in

21

formal theories of public finance that was an unoriginal idea at the time. The democracies were three or four years into a reformist phase in which the individual and class distributions of public costs and benefits were incessantly related to each other. In designing new health and welfare services and incomes for the unemployed, policy makers not only connected the two distributions in their own debates, but did their best to see that those who paid and benefited would connect them too. British and European governments presented as many as possible of their welfare arrangements not as free handouts from consolidated revenue but as contributory schemes, in the spirit of Buchanan's requirement that 'Ideally, the fiscal process represents a *quid pro quo* transaction ... a market-type relationship exists between the individual and the government'. Many of the new levies were called insurance contributions rather than taxes, to persuade people that they were getting their money's worth. On the other side of the ledger many of the policy makers were aware of other winners besides the users of the services. Where the planners were competent, public housing subsidies went to the tenants rather than the suppliers from whom government bought the necessary land and building services. Health planners were as careful of doctors' rewards as of patients' benefits. European governments' practical attention to the unintended as well as the intended beneficiaries of public activity was a decade or more ahead of the attention which American public choice theorists eventually paid to the same subject. Buchanan's paper could have served as a report of much existing practice rather than as a call for something new.

Kenneth Arrow

The above quotation from Buchanan was truncated: he actually wrote of transactions between government and 'all individuals collectively considered'. The individualist view of the state does not deny the need for public goods of the kind that cannot be retailed to individual buyers. But how should the citizens collectively, or their government on their behalf, decide *what* public goods to produce? Some welfare economists had hoped for a market-like way of doing it. If all the citizens recorded their individual preferences, could not a most-preferred collective choice be derived, by a suitable process or 'social welfare function', from those preferences? In 1950 in 'A Difficulty in the Concept of Social Welfare'[2] and the following year in *Social Choice and Individual Values*, Kenneth Arrow proved that it could not be done. In any likely democratic political conditions there is no logical way, without the possibility of internal contradictions, to derive a best collective choice from disagreed individual preferences. Democracies must therefore continue to make the best of majority rule. Through many later publications Arrow defended majority rule and debated how to civilize it, especially by encouraging appropriate liberal values and collective morality. Others, as we will see, took social choice theory (as it came to be called) in a different direction as they developed an odd, sterile, self-sustaining industry which simply proliferated impossibility theorems.

In 1954 Buchanan responded to Arrow's argument in two articles: 'Social Choice, Democracy and Free Markets' and 'Individual Choice in Voting and the Market'.[3] He questioned the very idea of 'social rationality'. Recalling his distinction between individualist and organic views of society, he argued that to be consistent, the organic view must suppose that society is an entity which has values which may be independent of its members' values. So Arrow was mistaken in trying to derive social values from individual preferences. If 'the individual is the only entity possessing ends or values … no question of social or collective rationality may be raised. A social value scale as such simply does not exist'. Alternatively if a social value scale does exist, it must have been arrived at by a social entity, not by individual preferences, and the rationality of the society's behaviour can only be tested by reference to the society's ends and values, not its members' ends and values. (Buchanan then complicated the argument by adding that a social entity capable of having ends and values might choose to base them, partly or wholly, on its members' ends and values.)

So, first, Arrow should not try to derive social preferences from individual preferences, or judge them to be contradictory by reference to individual preferences. Second, Buchanan thought Arrow had confused two purposes. When Arrow sought 'a process or rule which, for each set of individual orderings, … states a corresponding social ordering', process meant one thing and rule meant another. Buchanan argued that decision-making processes might produce consistent collective choices even though (as Arrow rightly insisted) the choices could not be logically derived from the initial individual preferences. A double defence of majority rule followed. First, majorities and their decisions tend to be temporary: what one majority enacts today a reshuffled majority may repeal tomorrow. Majority rule is acceptable 'because it allows a sort of jockeying back and forth among alternatives, upon none of which relative unanimity can be obtained … In this way, majority decision-making itself becomes a means through which the whole group ultimately attains consensus, that is, makes a genuine social choice. It serves to insure that competing alternatives may be experimentally and provisionally adopted, tested, and replaced by new compromise alternatives approved by a majority group of ever-changing composition'. (But we will notice a later argument that constitutional and tax laws should be reserved from majority rule and subjected to minority veto.) Buchanan's second objection to Arrow's argument was also a practical one. To derive social choices from individual preferences by logical inference rather than political process, one must assume that the individual preferences are (for the moment, at least) fixed. But 'the definition of democracy as "government by discussion" implies that individual values can and do change in the process of decision-making'[4] and it is desirable that they should be free to do so.

Two defences of majority rule were thus, in an odd way, at war with one another. The difference is best understood by bringing together Arrow's proof that a best social choice could not be derived from individual preferences, and some later theory about rational individual behaviour in systems of majority rule. Any majority can be seen as a coalition of interests – whether selfish or not makes no difference. A group excluded from the majority can replace a group within it by offering its support to other members of the majority on better terms. It will often be worth while for excluded groups and majority members to do such deals – which then become vulnerable to more offers of a similar kind. So if people behave as the theory assumes they do, there will be incessant changes of majority membership and policy. Theorists see cycles, and call the activity cycling. Because cycling is predictable, the composition and policies of the majority are not. Since most groups' programmes include some policies which need time to be effective, the chronic instability may get most people less than they could get by stable alliances based on kept promises, party discipline or other stabilizers. Arrow and many like-minded political scientists observed that over much of the democratic world outside the United States comparatively stable majorities and policies were achieved on a dual basis of compatible material interests and shared conceptions of justice, social purpose and good government. Hence Arrow's lifelong interest in those shared beliefs and the means by which they are developed. With no presumption that people's concerns are all predictably selfish, and with as much concern for the social goods as for the individual goods achieved by political association, this branch of social choice theory rejoined the mainstream of political theory and analysis (and accordingly ceases to be part of our subject). Meanwhile Buchanan and like-minded public choice theorists, unwilling to allow such force or importance to shared ideals or loyal alliances, defended majority rule *because* of its instability: shuffling majorities would tend to give everyone some share of power and benefit, off and on, over time.

Paul Samuelson

Samuelson's 'Pure Theory of Public Expenditure'[5] appeared in 1954. Public goods have to be financed from taxation because their users can't be charged individually for their use. That leaves an awkward independence between the real demand for the goods and the effective demand for them. The effective demand for public goods is the amount of tax the people vote to pay. But optimists can hope to get more than their share of the goods but pay less than their share of the tax. That freeloading possibility tempts people to vote for low taxes, each hoping nevertheless to get more than his dollar's worth of public goods. It follows (Samuelson argued) that democracies have a chronic tendency to supply themselves with less public goods than their people would buy if they had to pay for them individually as market goods. In 'Why the Government Budget is too small in a Democracy' (1960)[6] Anthony Downs (whose work is noticed below) reached the same conclusion by a different route. People's imperfect knowledge of what they give and get from government can encourage both under-spending and over-spending on public goods; Downs expected the underspending to predominate and leave a net shortage of the public goods which the citizens would vote and pay for if they knew what they were doing.

Four thoughtful economists had thus drawn attention to some political problems of public financial policy-making. Each message related both to method and to policy. Buchanan wanted people to relate the distribution of taxation wherever possible to the distribution of the benefits which it financed. That would clarify the actual distributional effects of alternative policies. With the citizens and policy-makers thus enlightened, Buchanan trusted majority rule to arrive over time at equitable policies and to educate all concerned in the process. Arrow showed that those democratic processes could not be replaced by any more mechanical way of deriving collective policies from individual preferences; and to Buchanan's confidence in majority rule he added a traditional concern for the quality of prevailing public and political morality. Samuelson and Downs noticed some reasons why democracies tend to undersupply their public sectors. Regardless of any charitable or socialist considerations, collective self-interest should rationally shift them some way to the Left.

To political theorists and other non-economists most of that was already familiar. Samuelson's perception was correct but one-eyed: politicians can attract votes by undertaxing, but also by concealing taxation, by oversupplying public goods, and by other means: Samuelson's is only one of the tendencies that may be at work, variably in varying circumstances. Politicians know the tactical possibilities of exposing or concealing the distributions of burdens and benefits which Buchanan, like all virtuous thinkers, wanted to expose. Nobody except a few welfare economists had ever supposed it possible to do what Arrow showed to be impossible. Beyond the usual economists' assumption that people look to their economic interests in their economic behaviour, none of the contributors proposed any radical simplification (or truncation) of human nature or political analysis. Ideologically, in Truman's and Eisenhower's America, none of them strayed far from the middle of the road.

That innocence ended with the proposal that people do, and perhaps should, seek *nothing but* individual gain in their political activity. Anthony Downs, a Chicago economist, introduced it but thought better of it. Gordon Tullock, a lawyer/bureaucrat at the University of South Carolina, seized it and stayed with it. Inspired by those two, Buchanan adopted it.

INDIVIDUAL GAIN AS THE ONLY POLITICAL MOTIVE

Anthony Downs

In 1957 Downs published *An Economic Theory of Democracy* and foreshadowed it in 'An Economic Theory of Political Action in a Democracy' in the *Journal of Political Economy*.[7] We read those works now with joy and horror: horror at what they say, but joy at how clearly they say it, and at Downs' remarkably constructive response to criticism of them. *An Economic Theory of Democracy* is the first full exposition of what many practitioners still see as the essentials of public choice theory. Five years later in an article on 'The Public Interest: Its Meaning in a Democracy' Downs acknowledged what was wrong with the earlier work and developed the essentials of much of the criticism of public choice theory (including ours) which has appeared since. The original argument and the correction were so thorough, so lucid, and came so early in the history of public choice theory that they are worth quoting at some length. In 1957,

> In spite of the tremendous importance of government decisions in every phase of economic life, economic theorists have never successfully integrated government with private decision-makers in a single general equilibrium theory. Instead they have treated government action as an exogenous variable, determined by political considerations that lie outside the purview of economics. This view is really a carry-over from the classical premise that the private sector is a self-regulating mechanism and that any government action beyond maintenance of law and order is "interference" with it rather than an intrinsic part of it.
>
>   Most welfare economists ... implicitly assume that the "proper" function of government is to maximize social welfare ... [But] even if social welfare could be defined, and methods of maximizing it could be

agreed upon, what reason is there to believe that the men who run the government would be motivated to maximize it?

[M]ost attempts to deal with government in economic theory ... do not really treat the government as part of the division of labor. Every agent in the division of labor has both a private motive and a social function. For example the social function of a coal-miner is removing coal from the ground, since this activity provides utility for others. But he is motivated to carry out this function by his desire to earn income, not by any desire to benefit others. Similarly ... I present a model of government decision-making based on this approach.
[The model is built on axioms of which the important two are:]

1. Each political party is a team of men who seek office solely in order to enjoy the income, prestige and power that go with running the government apparatus.
2. Every agent in the model – whether an individual, a party or a private coalition – behaves rationally at all times; that is, it proceeds toward its goals with a minimal use of scarce resources and undertakes only those actions for which marginal return exceeds marginal cost.

[It follows that] political parties in a democracy formulate policy strictly as a means of gaining votes. They do not seek to gain office in order to carry out certain preconceived policies or to serve any particular interest groups; rather they formulate policies and serve interest groups in order to gain office. Thus their social function – which is to formulate and carry out policies when in power as the government – is accomplished as a by-product of their private motive – which is to attain the income, power and prestige of being in office.

This hypothesis implies that, in a democracy, the government always acts so as to maximize the number of votes it will receive. In effect, it is an entrepreneur selling policies for votes instead of products for money ... We cannot assume a priori that this behavior is socially optimal any more than we can assume a priori that a given firm produces the socially optimal output ...

Because the citizens of our model democracy are rational, each of them views elections strictly as means of selecting the government most beneficial to him ... [8]

Most people however don't know how to vote for their own interests, and it would cost them too much to find out. Their ignorance has important effects.

First, it makes opportunity for persuasion. 'Persuaders are not interested per se in helping people who are uncertain become less so; they want to produce a decision that aids their cause'. They do it chiefly by offering false or biased information. Because they can influence votes, they acquire disproportionate political influence. Because influence is expensive (for research, media costs, etc.) bribery is encouraged.

Second, to save time, voters demand ideologies and parties supply them. People vote for the ideology which seems friendliest to their interests.

Third, political ignorance is rational for most people. The only purpose of voting is individual gain, and the gain from a single vote is always likely to be less than the cost of keeping well-informed. But lobbyists for particular firms or industries can profit by being well-informed. In politics, therefore, knowledgeable producers confront ignorant consumers, and usually win, so government has a regular bias in favour of producers and against consumers. This is not a result of foolish apathy on the part of the consumers. It is because all the parties act rationally. For that and other reasons 'democratic political systems are bound to operate at less than maximum efficiency. Government does not serve the interests of the majority as well as it would if they were well informed, but they never become well informed. It is collectively rational, but individually irrational, for them to do so; and, in the absence of any mechanism to insure collective action, individual rationality prevails'.[9]

Perhaps Downs' mistake was to generalize to the rest of the democratic world the Chicago city politics of the 1950s. In later chapters we will criticize elements of the theory as they were taken up, and to further extremes, by other theorists. But Downs long ago anticipated us. In response to criticism by Gerhard Colm and other political theorists he published in 1962 an article on 'The Public Interest: Its Meaning in a Democracy'.[10] Instead of the 1957 axioms there are familiar liberal political theorists' assumptions about the social conditioning and mixed motivation of political behaviour. Downs agrees with his critics that some 'crucial political decisions ... are made by men acting for the common good instead of their own'. People do have and act on conceptions of 'the public interest'. Downs now assumes 'that all citizens who adhere to a democratic system agree that the proper function of government is to act for the greatest benefit of society as a whole, even though they may disagree widely about what actions are best for it in any given circumstances'. Ideas of the public interest serve as criteria for judging government performance; they persuade people to accept policies which conflict with their individual interests; they guide officials when they lack specific electoral or governmental instructions. Whatever officials' real motives may be, they have to defend their actions as good for the welfare of society as a whole. 'The necessity of defending himself in this manner checks each public official from totally disregarding the welfare of potential questioners. It also forces him to develop a concrete concept of the public interest which may serve him as a guide when other rules are not sufficient to determine the best action at a given moment'.

Though ideas of the public interest vary, they all overlap in 'the minimum consensus necessary for the operation of a democratic society'. Though commonly expressed as formal and informal rules of behaviour, the consensus also includes some vision, however vague, of a good society. The vision and rules are ultimately derived from ethical values, originally linked to religious beliefs or ideas of natural law. These canons of behaviour 'are part of the basic culture that is passed on from generation to generation and constantly reinforced through schools, family life, churches, and other institutions engaged in enculturation and social control. In essence these rules constitute a "social contract" analogous to that which classical political theorists assumed to be at the root of each society although this "contract" is only implicitly "signed" by each person as he absorbs its values in the process of growing up and living in the society'. The word 'absorb' is not casually chosen: though good economic behaviour may be sufficiently ensured by self-interest and law enforcement, good political behaviour depends on civic values being internalized to become in some degree the citizen's own. A minimum consensus, with rules of behaviour and a vision of a good society, is a condition of democracy's survival. Commitment to it 'implies that each citizen is willing to sacrifice his short-run interests to at least some extent if those interests require behavior or policies detrimental to the survival of the system. His commitment is not necessarily based on altruism, it can be simply an expression of long-term self-interest'. But 'self-interest is not narrowly defined; it can include highly altruistic behavior that an individual believes he ought to undertake, even at his own expense'. That contradictory definition of self-interest, to which public choice theorists resort when their backs are to the wall, abandons the chief originality, and any predictive power, of the theory they employ.

Downs offers some speculation about the conditions in which citizens and officials may be inclined to pursue their own or their society's interests; and a subtle and interesting discussion of some effects of economic growth, through increasing division and specialization of labour, on people's perceptions of their own interests, the public interest, and relations between the two. Downs suspects that despite some countervailing effects these trends make it harder to maintain democratic consensus and public-spirited behaviour. To offset that trend, a democratic society must continuously indoctrinate its citizens with the values contained in its basic minimum consensus. They must be taught sufficiently similar intermediate values that their behavior, by and large, is consistent with the system. Such behavior must include willingness to make personal sacrifices to keep the system from perishing, adherence to a few basic moral rules, observation of the political constitution, and agreement on a vague set of policy principles. These values must be given enough moral force in the mind of each person that he usually overcomes the temptation always faced by every member of an organization: the desire to break the rules in order to procure some short-run personal advantage at the expense of furthering the long-run purposes of the organization, which are themselves ultimately beneficial to him. Men naturally tend to weight short-run considerations more heavily than long-run ones, and their own preferences more heavily than the preferences of others. These tendencies must be so resisted by moral suasion, backed by the threat of reprisal, that the basic rules predominate in the operation of the system, thus making behavior tolerably predictable.

Any description of a democratic system which does not include some mechanism for self-perpetuation is an incomplete description. It does not explain why people keep obeying the rules that make it possible. This omission is, in my opinion, the biggest single failing of my own economic theory of democracy.

The 1962 article was meant to repair the 1957 *Economic Theory* for continuing use. It is our opinion, not Downs', that what it actually did was to restate a standard liberal political theory of democracy, while still emphasizing, as most liberal theorists do, that economic self-interest is a strong one among the diverse motives at work in democratic politics. We suggest later that Arrow's 1951 book should have stopped rather than started the social choice theorists' proliferation of impossibility theorems. For similar reasons Downs' 1962 article could appropriately have ended the public choice theorists' search for an exclusively economic theory of exclusively selfish political behaviour. None of the distinctive aims or assumptions of that pursuit are compatible with Downs' 1962 conclusion, with which we happily concur:

As social scientists we should analyze the world realistically so that, as ethical men, we can design social mechanisms that utilize men's actual motives to produce social conditions as close as possible to our ideal of "the good society". Failure to be realistic about human nature would lead us to design social mechanisms that do not achieve their desired ends. Conversely, abandoning ideals leads to cynical nihilism. I hope my amended model will provide greater insight into how to go about making the real world more like the ideal one.[11]

Gordon Tullock

Tullock has been the most insistent and persistent believer that people act selfishly in most things and certainly in politics. In 1959 in an article on 'Problems of Majority Voting'[12] he argued that majorities would maltreat minorities without limit or misgiving if the majorities were stable; fortunately individuals can often gain by changing sides, so vote-trading (log-rolling) not only establishes majorities, it also shuffles their membership over time. This prevents the worst treatment of minorities. But all the alternative individual tactics under majority rule have worse results for most of the citizens, most of the time, than an ideally efficient allocation of resources could give them.

Is it wicked for people to trade votes for exclusively selfish purposes? It is characteristic of Tullock that he answers only the first half of the question, as if the second half were not worth asking. 'Ethical systems vary greatly from culture to culture, and I do not wish to rule out the possible existence somewhere of an ethical system which could bar log-rolling, but surely the American system does not … all our political organizations bargain in this fashion'. If they did not, people would always vote against gains for others (Tullock cannot imagine helping others *except* for one's own gain) and the results would be worse for everyone. Without log-rolling permanent minorities would be permanently exploited, and many of the majority's individual interests would also be frustrated. With log-rolling the costs and benefits are distributed more widely, but are too big: government taxes and spends too much. Although it is better than despotism, 'the system of majority voting is not by any means an optimal method of allocating resources … It seems likely that careful analysis of the process would lead to the discovery of improved techniques and a possible increase in governmental efficiency'.[13] The truth and logic of this argument were attacked by Downs 'In Defence of Majority Voting' (1961):[14] some of the theorised effects do not occur in the real world, majority voting is not the cause of those that do, and only majority voting can guarantee that every vote will have the same weight as every other vote.

Tullock was already associated with Buchanan, and the 'careful analysis' he had called for appeared in 1962 in their joint book, the most celebrated of all public choice texts, *The Calculus of Consent: Logical Foundations of Constitutional Democracy*. Of their respective contributions to it Buchanan has said that 'my own emphasis was on modelling politics-as-exchange, under the acknowledged major influence of Knut

Wicksell's great work on public finance. By comparison ... Gordon Tullock's emphasis (stemming from his own experience in, and his reflections about, the bureaucracy) was on modelling all public choosers (voters, politicians, bureaucrats) in strict self-interest terms'.[15] In *The Calculus of Consent* they argue for politics as a species of market exchange, with *homo economicus*, the rational egoist utility maximizer, as model citizen. Their version of methodological individualism allows no social judgements, for example of the justice of particular property rights or distributions, or the outcomes of government actions (though we think they smuggle some in); individuals can merely judge how well they do by particular exchanges or under particular decision rules.

Principles are proposed for deciding what government should do (it should ideally do nothing but facilitate whatever mutually advantageous exchanges the citizens cannot make in economic markets), and for choosing decision-making rules. If politics is to simulate voluntary exchanges decisions should ideally be unanimous, and in a Tullock world they will only be unanimous if everyone gains from them. '"The social contract" is of course vastly more complex than market exchange, involving as it does many individuals simultaneously. Nevertheless the central notion of mutuality of gain may be carried over to the political relationship. When it is translated into individual behavior, mutuality of gain becomes equivalent to unanimous agreement among the contracting parties. The *only* test for the presence of mutual gain is *agreement*'.[16] Most real-life decisions create winners and losers, but the winners can buy the losers' consent by compensating them. If a policy will increase wealth sufficiently to allow everyone thus to gain, there can be unanimous support for it. But if winners can't afford to compensate all losers because their gains total less than the losers' losses, the policy must be net destructive of wealth and a unanimity rule will ensure its rejection.

Decision-making rules should accordingly be designed with two opposing tendencies in mind. The bigger the required majority (the nearer to unanimity), the higher the costs of negotiating agreement and compensating losers: call those decision costs. The smaller the required majority (the further from unanimity), the bigger the losses which majorities can force on minorities: call those external costs. As the required majority increases, the decision costs rise and the external costs decline. It is rational to require the majority at which marginal decision costs equal marginal external costs. That is to say it might be rational for an individual to vote for such a rule before he knows how it will affect his particular interests in the future. In the year in which Buchanan and Tullock began writing their *Calculus*, the philosopher John Rawls published the thought that people might agree a constitution more readily if they did it behind a 'veil of ignorance', not knowing what their particular situations and capacities would be in real life. Rawls expected that, being risk-averse, all would agree on rules fair to all including the least fortunate. He intended his veil of ignorance as a mental device. Buchanan and Tullock thought it could be real: when people choose constitutions they may be uncertain enough about their long-term fortunes to *all agree* on the rules which should thereafter govern the making of their *disagreed* decisions about day-to-day policies. The constitutional agreement could be unanimous, or nearly so; post-constitutional decisions might be governed by the above marginal cost considerations, which might require majorities of (perhaps) 66 per cent.

Those majorities, with changing composition, would be put together on issue after issue by log-rolling legislators. People could trade their votes on issues which concerned them less for support on issues which concerned them more intensely. Thus everyone could have a share of power and use it to best advantage: votes *should* be like dollars, to be spent as their owners prefer. But the authors still expected the trading to produce excessive taxing and spending, as people voted themselves excessive benefits hoping to load their costs onto others. Where Samuelson and Downs expected people's freeloading ambitions to reduce the taxes (and thus the public goods) they would vote for, these authors expected them to vote for excessive public goods (and therefore taxes). Much of Buchanan's later writing has argued for constitutional provisions to remove taxation from majority rule.

In 1896 Wicksell, fearing that majorities might exploit and discriminate against minorities, had suggested that tax laws should require unanimous support. But he added two provisos. Buchanan and Tullock accepted the first proviso, that a unanimity rule should not be so strict as to allow a few dissenting individuals to hold out for unreasonable compensation, so it should merely require some very large majority. Second, laws which affect distributions of wealth and income should be required to be unanimous only if existing distributions are just. Wicksell was explicit: 'justice in taxation tacitly presupposes justice in the existing distribution of property and income'. If the distribution is unjust, 'society has both the right and the duty to revise the existing property structure. It would obviously be asking too much to expect such revision to be carried out if it were to be made dependent upon the agreement of the persons primarily involved'.[17] That proviso Buchanan rejects. In principle he doesn't believe there can be any valid judgement that a distribution is just or unjust. In practice 'we start from here, not from somewhere else'. A main purpose of a unanimity rule is to *protect* existing distributions, whatever they are and however come by, against changes which would disadvantage *anybody*. It is interesting to think of the relation between this rule and Buchanan's evident values if his recommendation were applied now to the new constitutional democracies in East Europe, to enable a few unrepentant apparatchiks to veto any changes to government powers, property rights or asset ownership.

Different readers have seen different themes in *The Calculus of Consent* as the most important. At the time, Buchanan emphasized 'politics as exchange'; in retrospect he has emphasized the idea of a contractual constitution. One reviewer at the time (James Meade) and another later (Charles Rowley) focused on the relation between the two. Meade did not think it possible to separate them as Buchanan wishes, i.e. to incorporate all decisions about distribution into the constitution, so that day-to-day 'post-constitutional' politics could consist of nothing but mutually advantageous exchanges. Questions of structural change inevitably continue to arise in day-to-day politics. When they do, existing distributions cannot be assumed always to be just, and should not be protected by a winners' power to veto any change. For such issues Meade thought simple majority rule appropriate. Rowley, writing twenty five years later of public choice theory as it had been developed by Downs, Tullock, Niskanen, Mueller and others, praised Buchanan's constitutional vision as a sole source of hope and sanity for public choice theorists. 'Powerful though the insights of this burgeoning literature undoubtedly are, they are driven by the most pessimistic vision of mankind. So pervasive is the emphasis ... on the utility and wealth destruction imposed by self-seeking agents, that few scholars of public choice escape completely untainted by cynicism, if not despair, concerning the prognosis for democracy through the remaining years of the twentieth century. [I]n aggregate, what appears ... is little less than the mathematics of unmitigated misery. Worse still, the cynicism encouraged by this mounting evidence of self-mutilation undoubtedly has imposed ... costs upon society, as political agents eagerly ape the behaviour ascribed to them by scholarship'.[18] Yet progress is a fact, and Rowley ascribes most of it not to the usual causes but to constitutional constraints on self-seeking behaviour, as explained in *The Calculus of Consent*. The comment seems odd, because many national constitutions have no distributional constraints – the British parliament can lawfully nationalize anything, with or without compensation – and the main constitutional proposal in *The Calculus of Consent* is in effect for a ban on *any* distributional changes. But however awkward, the reliance on constitutional constraints is necessary to the public choice faith. If mutually destructive self-interested behaviour has been restrained by anything else – for example by elements of mutual care, ethical consensus or conceptions of public interest or social justice – the public choice assumptions about political motivation must be wrong.

Anthony Downs' review[19] praised the book highly for extremely useful insights. 'These include why bicameral legislatures make sense, why men who disagree about concrete issues can rationally agree on constitutional rules, which types of activities should be "collectivized" under government control and which should not, why a federal government structure minimizes political bargaining costs, the nature of "log-rolling" and when a requirement for a special majority is the most efficient decision-making rule'. On the other hand their extreme individualism blinded them to the problem of coordinating government policies, and the book 'does not allow for coalitions and parties in its scheme, it does not pretend to offer a cohesive model of the entire democratic process, and it contains numerous errors in logic and several conclusions which I believe are wrong'. A footnote listed disagreements about effects of majority voting, relations between compensation payments and external economies, and the logic of talking about 'society's welfare' in a strictly individualist argument.

Mancur Olson[20] was glad that 'economic theory has come to be considered as a general theory of rational behavior', and welcomed Buchanan's and Tullock's 'stimulating addition to this new literature'. He reproved their right-wing bias but forgave it for its originality. ('In scholarship it is not perhaps necessity, but prejudice, that is the mother of invention'.) He retailed, without much comment, their argument for unanimity. He thought their treatment of economies of scale, externalities and unexploited profits 'absurd'. And against their liking for voluntary organization he offered a simple objection which he presently expanded into an influential book.

Mancur Olson

In *The Logic of Collective Action* (1965) Olson made further use of the idea of freeloading. Collective action for common ends on a voluntary basis is never rational, so will never happen, because each individual (unless psychologically disturbed) will decide to leave the action to others then freeload the benefits; so contributing has to be compulsory. But the usual forms of compulsion tend to hinder competition and free exchange, so they restrict output and everyone gets less than they might. In *The Rise and Decline of Nations* (1982) Olson argued that coercive, restrictive, selfdefensive organization is thicker on the ground, and economic efficiency and growth are accordingly less, the longer a country has enjoyed stable, uninterrupted democratic government. This explains the postwar decline of the English-speaking countries and the economic progress of Germany, Japan and the Asian tigers. The reasoning, its merits and its relation to real history are discussed below in Chapter 3.

FACTUAL VERSUS AXIOMATIC ACCOUNTS OF BUREAUCRACY

Anthony Downs' *Economic Theory of Democracy* had a certain amount to say about government. Politicians want the fruits of office and seek office by trading policies for votes. In *The Calculus of Consent* Buchanan and Tullock did not take that theme much further: they were chiefly interested in voters' pursuit of their interests and politicians' pursuit of votes. Neither book probed far into the internal organization of government or the motivation of its employees. Tullock and Downs presently explored that subject, Tullock in *The Politics of Bureaucracy* (1965) and Downs in *Inside Bureaucracy* (1967). Both were pessimistic, after experience of American bureaus, but wrote broadminded books in the tradition of organization and management studies. Downs acknowledged debts to Max Weber, and one reviewer thought his 'section on the inevitability and necessity of bureaus and other non-market organizations in society presents a lucid, welfare-economic discussion of the appropriate role of government in a market society'.[21] His bureaucrats are rational maximizers and do what they can to expand their budgets, but most of them have other purposes besides self-advancement: besides 'purely self-interested employees' there are also conservers, zealots, advocates, statesmen. Tullock's message claimed three kinds of balance. (1) Many of the problems of bureaucracy afflict private as well as public business. (2) Organizations have corporate purposes; their members have private interests; good organizational design and leadership consist in contriving the least conflict and most identity between the two. This is not the same as Chester Barnard's account of corporate leadership but is compatible with it. (3) Bureaucracy is necessary for many public and corporate purposes and has good as well as bad potentialities. Both authors suggest ways of encouraging better rather than worse, especially by localizing bureaucratic tasks wherever possible. Tullock admires the local independence which successful empires used to allow their provincial and colonial governors.

Tullock's introduction asserts that 'There are important areas for which the economists' assumptions are clearly inapplicable, notably the governmental bureaucracy [to which] the analysis of markets has relatively little application'. Thus he distances his study from public choice assumptions. In a preface to the book Buchanan tries to reduce the distance, suggesting that however sharply Tullock distinguishes political from economic behaviour, he still offers 'an economist's understanding' of the political behaviour. Mueller prefers to increase the distance: both editions of his *Public Choice* dismiss Tullock's and Downs' books on bureaucracy from consideration because however 'insightful', they do not theorize bureaucracy 'from a public choice perspective'. The approved public choice theorist of bureaucracy is William Niskanen.

Niskanen limits the scope of *Bureaucracy and Representative Government* (1971) by defining bureaus as 'non-profit organizations which are financed, at least in part, by a periodic appropriation or grant'. That excludes most private corporate bureaucracies, and public enterprises which pay their way entirely by sale of their services. Niskanen models bureaucratic behaviour on certain assumptions. Though the original demand for public services may come from all or some of the public, it is a monopolist (government) which effectively demands them, and usually another monopolist (a bureau) which supplies them. Government knows what it demands, and may know although it cannot always measure what is supplied; but only the bureau which supplies the service knows its true cost schedule, and how efficiently or wastefully it is operating. When government allows the supply to be monopolized in that way – rather than putting it to competitive tender by rival bureaus or private suppliers – it usually denies itself any independent information about the efficiency of the supply, or alternative sources of supply. Government may create monitoring agencies, but their effect varies with the nature of the business, and they also are bureaus.

These conditions allow wide scope to the bureau managers. As to how they are motivated, Niskanen is not consistent. On p. 34 any bureau within his definition 'will usually be quite indifferent to the interests of its customers, even if a large proportion of the total financing is from the sale of services'.[22] On p. 36 'bureaucrats are people who are, at least, not entirely motivated by the general welfare', and on page 37 'there are probably some elements in [a bureaucrat's] utility other than the general welfare and the interests of the state'. On p. 39, although 'some bureaucrats, by either predisposition or indoctrination, undoubtedly try to serve (their perception of) the public interest ... it is *impossible* for any one bureaucrat to act in the public interest, because of the limits on his information and the conflicting interests of others, regardless of his personal inclinations'. On p. 36 public interests weigh only if serving them earns rewards: 'Among the several variables that may enter the bureaucrat's utility function are the following: salary, perquisites of the office, public reputation, power, patronage, output of the bureau, ease of making changes, and ease of managing the bureau'. The first six always vary, and the last two sometimes do (Niskanen asserts), with the size of the bureau's budget, so for scientific and reformist purposes it will suffice to assume that expanding his budget is every bureaucrat's only purpose: 'budget maximization should be an adequate proxy even for those bureaucrats with a relatively low pecuniary motivation and a relatively high motivation for making changes in the public interest'. (p. 38)

On those assumptions Niskanen composes a mathematical model which purports to predict the size of bureaus' budgets and the whole government budget under various conditions, and their relation to the ideal budgets which would most nearly meet the citizens' real demands for public services, and distribute their tax costs (in a rough class way) proportionally to the benefits which different classes of people derive from them. We do not think the model has much useful relation to life or to the historical and technological reasons for modern government growth, but interested readers can find the mathematics on pp. 45–123 of *Bureaucracy and Representative Government*, or some bare essentials of it on pp. 252–7 of Dennis Mueller's *Public Choice II* (1989).

Niskanen's conclusion is that 'a better government would be a smaller government. This conclusion accepts as given the demands for public services as expressed through our political processes and is based on the consequences of the bureaucratic supply of public services, majority rule, and proportional taxation'. To improve performance he would shift as many services as possible from central to local government; get more services from competitive public or private suppliers; reconstruct senior bureaucrats' incentives; require two-thirds majorities for all or some appropriation bills; and reduce taxation but make it more progressive. 'A competitive supply of public services combined with a progressive tax system ... would generate a nearly optimal level of public services and a nearly general agreement on the size of government'. (pp. 228–9)

RENT-SEEKING

In 1967 in 'The Welfare Costs of Tariffs, Monopoly and Theft'[23] Gordon Tullock attacked an accepted way of estimating the economic costs of tariffs and monopolies. When a tariff or monopoly raised the price and reduced the consumption of a commodity, most welfare economists saw only the lost consumption of that commodity as a loss to the economy as a whole. What the producers gained from the higher price was merely an income transfer from some citizens to others, not a further reduction of the whole output. Viewed in that way the loss caused by tariffs and monopolies appeared to be less than one per cent of United States consumption, and accordingly unimportant.

Tullock had four objections to that reasoning. In ascending order of importance:

Collecting tariffs has unproductive public and private costs for customs officers, customs agents, etc.

Gains from high prices sustained by tariffs are not income transfers. Goods are being produced inefficiently where efficient imports are available, so the excess of protected domestic prices over import prices is a social loss arising from inefficient use of resources.

Gains from monopoly pricing are income transfers, but they are social losses if they are then wasted. If they are spent to acquire or maintain the monopoly, gains from monopoly pricing are wasted and represent social loss.

Finally – and the foundation for a new branch of public choice theory – the firms and industries which enjoy tariff or monopolist advantages are not the only ones which have tried to acquire those advantages. Many may try where only a few succeed. The lobbying and other costs of those who don't succeed, plus any government costs (for example in anti-trust activity) to prevent them from succeeding, also waste resources. Tullock illustrated his theme vividly from the social cost of theft. Successful and unsuccessful burglars equip themselves to burgle. Their efforts compel householders to invest in locks and screens and private security, and the state to devote resources to police, courts and jails. These unproductive costs may be many times greater than the income transfers effected by theft, and they should count as lost consumption. 'The total social cost of theft is the sum of the efforts invested in the activity of theft, private protection against theft, and the public investment in police protection.' (p. 231)

As with theft, so with tariffs and monopolies. 'The budget of the anti-trust division and the large legal staffs maintained by companies in danger of prosecution would be clear examples of the social cost of monopoly, but presumably they are only a small part of the total. That very scarce resource, skilled management, may be invested to a considerable extent in attempting to build, break, or muscle into a monopoly. Lengthy negotiations may be in real terms very expensive, but we have no measure of their cost. Similarly, a physical plant may be designed not for maximum efficiency in direct production, but for its threat potential . . . [P]robably much of the cost of monopoly is spread through companies that do not have a monopoly, but have gambled resources on the hopes of one . . . [so] the total costs of monopoly should be measured in terms of the efforts to get a monopoly by the unsuccessful as well as the successful' (p. 232).

Except for blurring some differences between tariffs and monopolies, this article, like Tullock's book on bureaucracy two years earlier, was neutral about government. By departing from free trade, government as villain encouraged industries to seek tariffs. By its anti-trust activities, government as hero tried to prevent monopoly and deter attempts to achieve it, and the more effective its activities the less of both wasteful monopoly and wasteful seeking there would be. Though Tullock did not say so explicitly, the social waste which he identified clearly arose from two alternative causes: there was the pursuit of monopoly by unaided capitalist means, and there was gain-seeking (chiefly from tariffs) which depended on favours from government.

Economists continue to explore these social costs in various ways with the same impartiality, in the United States under the general label of 'directly unproductive profit-seeking'. Public choice theorists have mostly confined their attention to activities and social costs for which they believe they can blame the government rather than the parties who seek favours from government. 'Rent-seeking' has become the accepted term for these activities. Theorists detect them in tariff and trade policies, in most industrial and commercial regulation, in the registration and licensing of skilled tradespeople and professionals, in competition for office, campaign funds and other gains within and between political parties, in committee behaviour, in tax, welfare and environmental policies, in government procurement, tendering and contracting, in corporate chartering and company lawmaking, in international aid policies and in the design of national constitutions. It is a large and expanding literature. It has its extremists whose theories of predatory government insist that the *only* purpose of *any* government is to create opportunities for unproductive private gain. In Charles Rowley, Robert Tollison and Gordon Tullock (eds) *The Political Economy of Rent-Seeking* (1988), Tullock suggests that the chief remaining shortcoming of rent-seeking theory is its inability to measure the quantities of rent-seeking waste. 'In the existing literature there is not a single direct measure of rent-seeking cost' (p. 465). Developing satisfactory methods of measurement should be the next theoretical task.

COMING OF AGE: THE STATE OF THE ART IN 1971

With Tullock's rent-seeking contribution and Niskanen's theory of bureaucracy the basic ideas of social choice and public choice theory were in being. In the shortest shorthand: people are assumed to have the same purposes in their political and economic activities. They mostly act to maximize their wealth, though other purposes sometimes intrude. In economic markets they buy goods with dollars. In political markets they exchange votes, influence, campaign contributions or bribes for public goods. Government has some intrinsic inefficiencies, so public action is not justified by market failure alone, but only where it actually improves on market performance. Each citizen should ideally buy exactly what he or she wants from government. Where that is impossible because the goods are indivisible, the schedule of public goods should ideally be derived, logically or by voting procedures, from the citizens' individual preferences. Though both those methods of deciding an optimum public supply are strictly impossible, government should ideally approximate them as nearly as it can in its decision-making.

But government is not ideal. Individuals, groups, firms, politicians and bureaucrats all do their rational best to enrich themselves from government, freeloading benefits and offloading costs onto others. Many of the winners' gains waste resources and reduce welfare, and there is further waste in the unsuccessful rent-seeking of the losers. Though most social choice and public choice theorists agree that self-interested political behaviour (unlike self-interested economic behaviour) tends to reduce economic efficiency, there is some disagreement about how it does so: most public choice theorists think the contending political forces produce too much taxation and government, while Samuelson, Downs and some other economists think they produce too little. Mainstream economists (whose contributions to social choice or public choice theory are not their main work) also tend to pay more attention to the productive effects of complex organization and coordination in government and corporate business, while public choice specialists concentrate on the social costs of organization and especially of government.

Some theorists do and others don't continue to distinguish social choice from public choice. Insofar as there is any difference, social choice theorists tend to theorize about the logical and voting procedures likely to come nearest to deriving public policies from individual preferences, including preferences for general social qualities as well as individual gains; and some have written about the necessary role of moral rules and aspirations in civic and political life. Public choice theorists tend to focus on self-interested motivation and on individual and group gains and losses from government activity. But these differences are not distinct and there is no clear boundary between the two schools of thought.

Since 1971 the basic ideas have been refined, elaborated, applied and occasionally tested in a great many case studies, mostly of federal, state or local politics in the United States. The journal *Public Choice* was founded in 1976. A brief sketch follows of some main concerns of the literature since 1971, but readers who want a proper account of it should read Dennis Mueller's *Public Choice II* (1989) or one of the other surveys listed earlier.[24]

EMPIRICAL STUDIES OF PRIVATE GAINS FROM GOVERNMENT

Many case studies have been designed to show the predictive or explanatory power of axiomatic economic theories of political behaviour.

Studies of regulated industries try to estimate the private gains and social
costs from regulation, and how they are distributed between producers,
consumers and regulators. Most of the studies are confined to financial
effects – they don't notice the effects of regulation on safety, quality of service, professional competence or ethics, the solvency of banks, truthful
labelling or other information services. Most of the financial effects are
necessarily notional because they have to depend on estimates of what perfectly competitive (or other alternative) prices might be, and what unregulated monopoly prices might be. Some researchers estimate the gross gains
to regulated firms; some subtract the transaction and lobbying costs of
influencing the politicians who legislate the regulation and the bureaucrats
who administer it. Some estimate the consumers' gains from regulation.
Some theorize that regulators will set prices at which the electoral support
(campaign contributions, propaganda, etc.) attracted by the last dollar of
the permitted price equals the electoral support (consumers' votes) lost by
that dollar. Since neither effect is measurable, or of interest to the regulators if they are bureaucrats rather than politicians, the theory is not testable.
Some thinkers prefer an earlier (but also untestable) theory that there is
often a better alternative than government intervention. Ronald Coase
argued[25] that where regulation is occasioned by externalities like pollution,
it could often be replaced by private contract: if one of the troublesome and
troubled parties (it does not matter which) pays the other to change its ways
or go away, that should achieve a socially optimal use of the relevant
resources. In most real-life cases – with transaction costs, large numbers of
diversely affected parties including some too poor to buy off their oppres-
sors, and technical uncertainties about who is causing what (whose
exhausts are meeting which other emissions to trigger the photosynthesis
which contributes how much of the pollution in whose air?) – the theory is
agreed to have little practical application.

Trying with varying success to cope with these difficulties there have
been case studies of trade regulation by tariff, quota and price support
schemes, stock exchange and anti-trust regulation, and the regulation of
hospitals, air and water quality, waste disposal, the depletion of fish, timber
and other renewable and non-renewable resources, wilderness, landscape
and architectural conservation, and the certification and licensing of skilled
trades and professions. There are comparisons of alternative methods of
regulation, for example of taxation and standard-setting as means of regu-

lating environmental quality. The studies typically report gainful/wasteful activities and either suggest, or lament the absence of, theories capable of explaining them. The case studies have plenty of practical interest but collectively they do not support the axiomatic *homo economicus* core of public choice theory. There is lots of material self-seeking, but in different ways and degrees in different cases, and in diverse combinations with purposes of other kinds.

Some contributors review some of the diversities. In a 1990 article on 'The political economy of environmental regulation'[26] Robert W. Hahn finds among other things that no theory can yet explain *what* gets regulated; there are exceptions to most theories which try to predict how regulatory instruments are chosen; most environmental regulations are very inefficient methods of 'redistributing revenues from less powerful to more powerful groups', which some theories assume to be the primary purpose of regulation; the main beneficiaries of regulation 'seem to vary from case to case'; some regulation increases and some reduces profit; and theorists should stop trying to generalize from single cases. This review reads rather like a historian's list of objections to trying to fit such variable behaviour to any generalized, monocausal theory. Hahn's own theoretical proposal is that 'the outputs of environmental policy emerge from a struggle between the interest groups'. But the groups range from exclusively wealth-seeking to exclusively ideological and the outcomes of their struggles are rarely predictable. Thirty years of theory don't seem to have improved on the historians' approach to the subject.

On a larger scale there are continuing disagreements about the effects of political self-seeking on the size of government, and its relation to the size and scope of government that the citizens really need. Most public choice theorists expect freeloading voters and budget-maximizing politicians and bureaucrats to raise more taxes than necessary, to supply more public goods than the citizens would be willing to pay for in a market way, and to have those goods produced less efficiently than market goods are produced. Samuelson and Downs expected an opposite effect on taxation and allocations to public goods, and in 1976 Cotton M. Lindsay theorized that public managers tend to produce goods more cheaply (by sacrificing quality) than profit-seeking managers do. In the US, public veterans' hospitals keep death and disease at bay as effectively as private hospitals, at lower cost. (The savings are at the expense of the patients' comfort and peace of mind, which Congress doesn't monitor, rather than their physical health, which Congress does.)

All the self-interested motives modelled in these contradictory theories are present in actual behaviour – but as usual in varying degrees, and in conjunction with varying amounts of disinterested and dutiful motivation. The theorists differ partly because they generalize from too few cases, but also because many of them apply an unusual interpretation of Occam's Law.

EXPLANATION, PREDICTION AND OCCAM'S RAZOR

Where the factual evidence is neutral between alternative hypotheses, William of Occam (c.1300–1349) recommended trying the simplest: 'don't multiply entities beyond necessity'. Moderns also aspire to 'parsimonious' theory. Public choice theorists invoke the principle, often naming Occam, to allow three devices we doubt he intended:

(1)   Where a number of conditions have to be present to produce an effect, it may be explained by reference to only one of them. Thus:
(2)   Where a number of motives converge to prompt an action, any one of them may sufficiently explain the action.
(3)   Where we cannot penetrate other minds we may properly ascribe to them any motive which *plausibly could* prompt the behaviour to be explained.

The third principle comes in weak or strong form. Weak: When action is consistent with either selfish or dutiful purposes, ascribe it to selfish purposes. Strong: When action is plainly altruistic and could not be anything else, it may be presumed to yield self-satisfaction or 'psychic income'. and thus be self-interested for theoretical purposes.

To illustrate, all but the last variant of the principle are at work in William Landes' and Richard Posner's theory and historical explanation of judicial independence.[27] Readers may first reflect on the reasons why it is generally thought to be desirable that judges should not accept bribes or political instructions. Landes and Posner think one reason is enough. Legislators sell laws for 'campaign contributions, votes, implicit promises of future favors, and sometimes outright bribes'. They want the best prices they can get. The market prices are higher if the buyers can expect that their purchases won't be spoiled, perhaps quite soon, by hostile interests buying or bullying hostile interpretations from the courts. So the politicians who framed the US Constitution and the First Amendment are presumed to have provided for judicial independence simply to raise the prices they could thereafter get for their legislative decisions.

These 'Occamish' devices allow complex causation and diversely motivated behaviour to be explained after the event as monocausal and monomotivational, and to support monocausal, monomotivational public choice

theory. But for obvious reasons their use also accounts for the theory's failure to generate reliably true predictions. At prediction, which is the appropriate test for it, it continues to be less reliable than the relevant branches of
mainstream political science, or experienced common sense.

There remain two large bodies of work, one with distinct public choice
character and the other without. Formal analysis of voting systems and
decision-making rules is done much as political scientists have always
done it. But distinctive assumptions and values shape the public choice
proposals for tax and constitutional reform.

DIRECT AND REPRESENTATIVE DEMOCRACY

Majority rule is an imperfect way to protect minorities and decide on
public goods. Theorists discuss alternative voting systems. There are
demand-revealing games – iterative voting procedures which compel players to vote honestly for the public goods they are actually willing to pay
for. Point voting allows each voter to spread a number of votes over a
number of issues or concentrate them on one or a few issues, as either positive or negative votes, thus reflecting both the voter's preferences and the
intensity with which they are held. Public goods can be supplied only to
those happy to pay for them if clubs or cooperatives supply them to their
members. And instead of bringing the goods to the people, people can
move to the goods: there are studies of the extent to which Americans
migrate to states, cities, or suburbs whose local taxes and services suit them
best. Advocates call this voting with the feet and critics call it segregation.

Those discussions are really *all* about clubs, in that their only practical
application is to groups small enough, with purposes simple enough, for
their members to decide their policies one by one. Real government may
decide occasional issues by plebiscite but most of it is necessarily representative. Public choice and social choice theorists don't differ much from
other political scientists as they analyse the formal qualities of unicameral
and bicameral legislatures, American and Westminster relations between
executive and legislature, two-party and multi-party systems, and so on.

Nor do their empirical studies in this field differ very much. Public
choice theorists seek but rarely find empirical proof of their theories. Plenty
of behaviour accords with the theories but plenty does not, and from the
1970s there has been some shift from the quest for proofs to case studies in
the muckraking tradition whose conclusions support cynical views of
American government rather than rigorous theories of all government. A
dozen researchers in the 1970s discovered the political business cycle

(governments inflate employment before elections and deflate after them), often unaware that the Left Keynesian economists Balogh and Kalecki had predicted it in the 1940s. But 'although there exists clear evidence that some governments in some countries at some points in time have behaved as the political business cycle model predicts, the evidence is not strong enough to warrant the conclusion that this type of behavior is a general characteristic of democratically elected governments'.[28] Studies of Congressional behaviour find plenty of pork-barrelling, log-rolling and campaign financing that accord with theory but also principled behaviour that belies it. On tax and welfare issues the poorer half of voters should theoretically vote for income transfers from rich to poor, the richer half should vote for poor-to-rich transfers, so the median voter should rule, and allow no transfers unless he can generate a coalition for transfers from both ends to the middle. There exist theories which depict each one of those patterns as dominant, and traces of each are discernible in most democracies' policies, but no country's voters have been found to be as single-minded or as uniformly selfish as such theories predict. Nor are all legislators the pure self-seeking power-brokers of 'hard' theory. Dennis Mueller's review of the literature comes to the unsurprising conclusion that 'the results to date are strong enough to sustain the plausibility of the hypotheses that (a) candidates spend money to win votes, and (b) contributors give money to obtain more preferred political outcomes'. But 'more preferred' need not mean selfish. People contribute generously to campaigns for many good causes, and 'evidence also exists that a representative's ideological position has an independent effect on his voting'.[29] After twenty years or so of empirical research none of the original and distinctive elements of public choice theory can be said to be proven, or to be more reliable predictors than the political theories they purport to replace.

THE SIZE OF GOVERNMENT

At the other extreme from detailed case studies are James Buchanan's and others' proposals about the contractual justification of government, the need to limit its growth and ways to limit it.

In *A Theory of Justice* (1971) the liberal philosopher John Rawls suggested as a basis of government a kind of social contract whose implications are at once individualist and egalitarian. Some public choice theorists have welcomed this modern revival of a social contract view of government (as a ground for limiting its powers), and have welcomed Rawls' individualism. But they dispute the egalitarian elements of his argument, which among other things plainly empower democratic governments to distribute and redistribute wealth. These arguments are discussed below in Chapters 6 and 8.

There is more practical argument about the general role of government in Geoffrey Brennan's and James Buchanan's *The Power to Tax: Analytical Foundations of a Fiscal Constitution* (1980). Government is depicted as an exceptionally powerful economic monopolist. The primary purpose of the politicians and bureaucrats who command it is to maximize its (and their own) revenue. The citizens have scarcely any influence over government, and electoral, party-political competition does not restrain its budget or activities. Only constitutional provisions can limit its growth, by limiting what it can spend, and then only if they are entrenched against majority rule.

The constitution should therefore be enacted as nearly as possible with unanimous consent, and entrenched against amendment by anything but near-unanimous agreement. It should dispose of divisive questions about the distribution of wealth by giving the existing distribution constitutional status. And – decisively – it should limit the government's power to tax, to borrow, and to print money. Government should be required to balance its budget; and to ensure political backing for the constitutional tax limits, the common conservative principle that taxation ought to be broad-based and flat should be reversed: taxation should instead be narrow-based and progressive, so that the most powerful citizens will resist it most vigorously.

When the constitution has thus entrenched the distribution of wealth and limited the amount that government can spend, ordinary majority rule with its vote-buying and log-rolling and shuffling coalitions can decide how to allocate the spending to particular public goods.

PUBLIC ENTERPRISE

Unlike public choice and social choice theory, opinions about the efficiency of governments and their business enterprises are neither new nor in most people's minds very theoretical. They have always been influential as governments and their electors determine, by many small and occasional large decisions, the mix of their mixed economies; and prevailing opinions are now likely to have special force in the reconstruction of the ex-communist economies.

Although there has of course been theoretical writing about public and non-profit enterprise, and voluminous writing about public administration, our chapter on public enterprise is addressed not to particular theorists but to widely held public opinions on the subject. The everyday criticism of public efficiency tends to focus on four main shortcomings and ascribe them to four main causes. Public enterprises are thought to neglect their customers' wants, to allocate resources inefficiently, to produce inefficiently at unnecessary cost, and often to be stuck in their ways, resisting necessary modernization or replacement. These inefficiencies arise because administrative planning is a poor substitute for the customers' market demands; public investors and managers lack profit-seeking discipline and incentives; public employees can use industrial muscle to get more pay for less work than market-disciplined employers could afford; and governments can and do finance inefficient and unnecessary activities to continue when market discipline would reform or close them down.

Most economic theorists of government share these beliefs and some contribute to them, but it is chiefly in their popular, unacademic forms that they are discussed in Chapters 4 and 7.

CRITICS

Forty-four papers critical of public choice or social choice theory are listed in a note.[30] Some of them express internal disagreements within or between the two schools. Public choice theorists dislike the social choice theorists' insistence that collective policies have to be judged by other tests than their accord with individual preferences: Gordon Tullock has asserted 'The General Irrelevance of the General Impossibility Theorem'. Many, led by Downs himself, have qualified the simplicities of his original economic theory of democracy. Voters are not all rational egoists, and ideas of public interest are conceded to weigh with some politicians and bureaucrats. There are claims which incorporate concessions – for example the claim that public choice theory remains useful as a method of electoral analysis however altruistic people may prove to be and however social rather than individual some of their goals are. In recent years Olson, Brennan and others have conceded that some governmental redistribution from rich to poor may be good, and campaigning for it should not count as wasteful rent-seeking.

Outsiders' criticism, mostly from political science, economics, law and philosophy, has had half a dozen main targets: the truth and testability of the theories; the assumption of rational egoist motivation; the hostility to ideas of public interest; the fitness of market models of political activity; and the nature and concealment of the theorists' values.

Some of the comparisons of public and private efficiency are disputed on factual grounds. Voters are found to vote otherwise and for other reasons than the theories assume. They do not appear to have the stable set of mutually independent 'goals' that axiomatic general theories of their behaviour need to assume. Nor is there the one-way causation which many of these particular theories depict. People's wants are partly-social creations, and the institutions and processes which shape them are among the subjects of their political activity. People's private interests both affect and are affected by their moral beliefs and conceptions of public interest and social good. The convictions which impel their political activity are often developed and changed in the course of the activity. And they are observed to vote for varying combinations of private interest, others' interests, qualities of their societies which affect their interests, and qualities which don't.

There are related objections to understanding government as a marketplace for individual exchanges. How are the traders and the traded goods produced? Critics think that property rights, in personal capacities as well as material assets, owe so much to past and present government that they cannot rightly be seen as exogenous, wholly owned items which are merely *exchanged* in the political marketplace; many are generated or acquired there. 'Market equilibrium' signifies a set of agreed prices and mutually beneficial transactions, but political 'equilibrium' may be a misleading euphemism for any degree of class or other domination over subjects too weak to resist. Meanwhile the market model blinds its users to the expressive, educational and unifying functions of political activity.

There are compound objections to the theorists' way with values. Critics think the theorists' distinctions between 'positive' and 'normative' theory are deceptive because both are value-structured. Concepts of methodological individualism and Pareto optimality, and distinctions between public and private goods, between constitutional and post-constitutional decisions and between political processes and outcomes all have value premises and prescriptive implications which ought to be explicit but rarely are. When exposed, the values are those of a libertarian conservatism which would entrench the wealth of the rich against democratic taxation or redistribution. In one critic's words, 'honoring tastes expressed in the marketplace is freedom; honoring those expressed in the voting booth is repression. We have the further question of freedom from what? Or freedom for what? The answer to the first is consistently simple: freedom from government. The answer to the second is equally simple but rarely stated: freedom for those who have, to have more, and for those who do not have, to continue in this state'.[31]

Two critics write with special power, and we gratefully acknowledge our debt to their work. Kenneth Arrow and Amartya Sen are distinguished economists in other fields, as well as leaders of the social choice school.

One of Arrow's contributions has been to the formal theory of public investment in a mixed economy. How should the amount and composition of public investment be decided? Apart from any crude public choice desire to minimize public investment, there is an orthodox presumption that the optimum pattern of public investment must be the one which equates rates of return in the public and private sectors. That belief cannot survive the argument of Kenneth Arrow and Mordecai Kurz in *Public Investment, the Rate of Return, and Optimal Fiscal Policy* (1970). Though it relates directly to neoclassical economic theory rather than to public choice theory, the argument is worth noticing for its rigorous demonstration that public investment needs distinctive principles of its own.

The authors first remind us of some standard objections to aiming at equal rates of return to public and private investment. There are diverse market rates of return: which of them should public investors try to copy? Where futures markets don't exist and future prices are unpredictable, present rates of return may not prompt efficient allocation. It may not be reasonable for public investors to treat risk as private investors do. Some of the returns to public investment accrue to private investors and many of the returns have to be guessed at, often arbitrarily, so any equation with private rates may be unreliable. Both the rates of return and the recipients of the returns can vary with the way in which public investments are financed. And many people believe that government, as a trustee for generations unborn, should *not* apply the present generation's time preferences and social discount rates to its long-term investment decisions. But even if these familiar difficulties are assumed away, the heart of Arrow's and Kurz's argument is a formal demonstration that 'the relation between investment and present and future rates of return is complex . . . [T]he optimal level of investment, apart from normal growth, is not determined by the rate of interest but primarily by its future changes'. Effects vary with the way in which public investment is financed. Neither in theory nor in practice can market rates of return sufficiently indicate optimum levels of public economic activity: 'specialized criteria are needed to guide the investment decisions of the public sector' (pp. xx–xxv, 1).

When they write about public choice theory *Arrow and Sen* do so courteously (unlike Samuelson, who has called proposals for constitutional tax limits 'fiscal fascism'). Having proved that 'best' policies (in any useful sense) cannot be derived from individual preferences alone, they discuss how free citizens with diverse values and interests *should* arrive at common policies. Both insist on the importance of the citizens' values, and their judgements of social as well as individual good. In many papers over many years Arrow has dwelt on the functions of social norms and moral codes in economic as well as political behaviour, and as aids to efficiency as well as equity – reductionist accounts which ascribe behaviour to rational self-interest alone can't adequately explain the behaviour. As with government, so with social science: 'The discussion of any important social question must involve an inextricable mixture of fact and value'. Practical papers cited in Note 30 to this chapter indicate the general intent of his own values: 'Taxation and Democratic Values: A Case for Redistributing Income' (1974), 'A Cautious Case for Socialism' (1978), 'Two Cheers for Government Regulation' (1981). He does not forget the millions of unemployed in the Great Depression, or the economists who said their unemployment was their own choice (and are saying it again now).

Sen does not forget childhood in Calcutta. Among other things he is a development economist, deeply concerned with the problems of the very poorest countries, and as intolerant as Arrow is of expert pretensions to moral neutrality. Users of the concept of Pareto efficiency think it allows them to order economic conditions as better or worse without employing any value judgements of their own: their judgements purport to rest on the citizens' preferences alone. But the citizens' preferences run to others' behaviour as well as their own, so in 'The Impossibility of a Paretian Liberal' (1970) Sen showed that judgements of Pareto optimality can be internally contradictory or perverse, so they don't test what they purport to test. In 'Rational Fools: A Critique of the Behavioural Foundations of Economic Theory' (1977) he unpacked economists' notions of revealed preferences and rationality. People (he observed) may act for their own advantage, for others' advantage from sympathy with them, or (sometimes against their personal preferences) from commitment. The commitment may be to universal ethical rules, or to the interests of 'particular others': family, neighbourhood, class. With changing combinations of those motives in action, their 'revealed preferences' may reveal little, some of it misleading, about their purposes and their rationality. A behaviourist economic science which looks only to people's actions without trying to understand their thoughts is defective even for its own purposes. So – by implication – are the versions of public choice theory which impute exclusively self-serving purposes to all behaviour. (From that axiom, Sen deduces: "Can you direct me to the Railway Station?" asks the stranger. "Certainly" says the local, pointing in the opposite direction to the Post Office, "and would you post this letter for me on your way?" "Certainly" says the stranger, resolving to open it to see if it contains anything worth stealing.) What we call mixed motivation in this book is analysed more precisely by Sen to expose its implications for economic theory, and for discussions of welfare and rationality in particular.

Sen has also added to Arrow's demonstration that the best policies cannot be derived logically from individual preferences, and come to similar conclusions: one cannot contribute to policy-making in any but a blundering or plundering way without resort to values, and to judgements of how people experience the effects of policies – i.e. to 'interpersonal judgements of well-being'. The value of the policies must usually depend on the substantive, constitutive values they express, as well as on their technical qualities and the procedures by which they are decided.

This chapter has identified the bodies of theory which are our subject. From now on we try to focus on the ideas themselves, citing particular works and authors only as necessary to exemplify the ideas or expound them fairly in their authors' terms. As we said at the outset, what follows is not a review of the literature. There are already a number of those. Our different purpose is to consider the theoretical ideas themselves, their merits, and their relation to life and policy.

Part Two

3 Public Goods

Mixed economies need both public and market goods. The amount and kind of public goods have to be determined by political choice. This chapter argues that those choices are not likely to be improved by the use or the common misuses of public goods theory or social choice theory.

PUBLIC GOODS THEORY

National defence, law and order, lighthouses, streets and street lighting are examples of goods which are called 'public' because they can't be supplied to anybody without being available to everybody, and their individual users can't be made to pay for them. Next there are goods which it is possible but unusual to charge each user for: highways, bridges, weather forecasts, public libraries, national parks. Finally there are goods which can quite well be supplied in a market way but which many governments choose to supply to some or all of their citizens free or below cost: education, health services, public transport. For some analytical purposes economists define as 'public' only those goods, like lighthouses, which cannot be supplied on any user-pays basis. But the subjects of this chapter are theories about the political decisions rather than the nature of the goods, so for present purposes we will treat as public goods all those whose supply is determined not by individual market demand but by collective political choice, i.e. any goods and services which governments decide to supply free or below cost to their users.

The argument of Paul Samuelson's 1954 'Pure Theory of Public Expenditure'[1] can be put into plain language, and into its context in neoclassical economic theory, as follows. An ideally efficient market economy would allow individuals to get the best available return for their contributions to production, then spend their incomes as they liked best, thus maximizing their satisfaction or 'utility' as far as their individual wealth and earning capacities allowed. The system as a whole would allocate resources to meet the pattern of individual preferences revealed in the people's market demands, so that (given the existing distribution of endowments, and a number of other conditions) the market mechanism or 'hidden hand' would ensure that the population as a whole made the most satisfying possible use of its resources.

But nobody wants private goods only. Everybody – including firms producing private goods for market – needs some public goods too. So firms' and individuals' demands for goods need to include the public as well as the private goods which together will do most for their utility. In the light of their individual means and preferences each should want to spend so many dollars on a particular basket of market goods and so many dollars on a particular basket of public goods.

But it is in the nature of public goods that individuals can't usually get exactly their money's worth, no less and no more, of exactly the public goods each wants. So as self-interested maximizers people are motivated to take advantage of that awkward inefficiency: they try to pay as little tax as they can, while grabbing as many public goods as they can. That behaviour causes three inefficiencies. First, most people won't succeed in getting exactly the public goods which they want, and which they would be willing to pay for if they had to, if the goods could only be obtained as market goods. Second, there are opportunities for plunder as some get more than their tax-paid shares of public goods and others get less. Third – the main burden of Samuelson's argument – when asked how much public goods they individually want to pay for (i.e. what tax they're willing to pay) people are motivated to understate their wants, each hoping to get the goods they want at less than cost, i.e. at other taxpayers' expense. But the effective demand for public goods is the total amount of tax the population votes to pay. So with everyone understating their wants, i.e. resisting sufficient taxation to supply their real wants, there must be a chronic under-supply of public goods.

That last conclusion had radical rather than conservative conclusions – far from taxing and spending too much, government was misreading real public demand and taxing and spending too little. Samuelson's warning, being in algebra in the *Review of Economics and Statistics*, did not alarm the masses. But a few years later John Kenneth Galbraith made a best-seller of the same theme in *The Affluent Society* (1957). Driving their private Cadillacs down pot-holed, uncleaned, unpoliced public streets, Americans were misjudging their proportions of public investment and private spending to produce national conditions of 'private affluence and public squalor'. Galbraith's persuasions and the educational influence of Samuelson's middle-of-the-road textbook were among the intellectual supports of the leftward shift of opinion in the 1960s, and the Kennedy and Johnson round of welfare initiatives.

But careless or more conservative readers could draw different conclusions from Samuelson's theory.

First, taxing, public spending and public goods make opportunities for freeloading which can make the allocation of resources both immoral and inefficient. It seems to follow that the higher the proportion of resources that are allocated in a market way, where there's no escape from paying for what you get and getting what you pay for, the more just and efficient the economy is likely to be.

Second, some of the freeloading in practice shifts resources from poorer to richer. That frustrates the humane intentions of welfare measures, and increases inequalities in unproductive ways which do nothing to enhance work incentives as inequalities should.

For the second complaint there was some solid evidence. In Britain, Richard Titmuss[2] was the first of a number of researchers who found that middle-class people were getting more than their share of health and educational services simply by being smarter at getting them. As most of the politicians and public servants who designed the welfare measures belonged to that class, they may even consciously or unconsciously have designed the measures to serve their own class interest. (Public choice theorists would expect them to do that, as we will see.)

What would Left thinkers do about such upward transfers? For example when education is free, middle class children continue to get more than their numerical share of it. On average, whether from heredity or family environment, more of them climb higher up the educational ladder than, on average, working class children do. If you were a Left reformer or voter when that was discovered, what should you do? Three responses were possible.

First, you could justify the upward transfers. In a competitive world a national community has an economic as well as a social and cultural interest in educating its people to the limit of their capacity. However small the working class share of the education, that class can still be richer the better educated, and therefore more productive, the population as a whole is. And if working class children can't have equal educational opportunities without some net transfer of income to the middle classes, that price is worth paying because the educational opportunities are so valuable.

Second, you could think how to retain the new equalities without the upward transfers. You could charge for education but give vouchers to the children of means-tested parents; or if that would reduce total education undesirably, and discriminate unfairly between the children of mean and generous parents within the middle class, you could adjust the progressive income tax to charge the richer class more than the cost of its disproportionate share of free education.

Third, you could take the opportunity to move from Left to Right. We doubt if upward welfare transfers alone have driven many people to do that, but if you want to go for other reasons the upward transfers allow you to claim unselfish egalitarian reasons for going. The claim may be spurious or mistaken – the total tax and welfare measures of the postwar decades in fact did more to reduce than to increase inequalities. But a selective eye could find exceptions, beginning with America's urban renewal programmes and Britain's free health and educational services. From those it was possible to generalize a belief that it is in the nature of all public goods to allow affluent freeloading and greater inequality than before. However mistaken, that belief made a 'bridge of disillusion' over which numbers of the young radicals of the 1960s passed to become the middle-aged conservatives of the 1980s.

Thus although Samuelson's theory plainly implied that the democracies needed more public goods and services than they were voting themselves, some of his reasoning could be misused for the opposite purpose of arguing that they would do better with less. So also could some uses and misuses of the social choice theory which developed from Kenneth Arrow's paper 'A Difficulty in the Concept of Social Welfare' (1950)[3] and his book *Social Choice and Individual Values* (1951). It is convenient to introduce social choice theory before discussing the persuasive effects of the two theories together.

SOCIAL CHOICE THEORY

Leading social choice theorists claim to be broadly concerned with the relation between citizens' individual judgements and their collective social decisions, a subject which has occupied political philosophers since Plato, more intensely since the seventeenth century, and most intensely since the development of modern democracy. But in practice most economists' social choice theory has not addressed the questions which troubled Locke and Rousseau and John Stuart Mill. Instead it has been narrowly concerned with some logical qualities of sets of individual preferences, and with the impossibility of deriving collective preferences from them by mathematical procedures.

Some welfare economists had thought it possible to index welfare – to devise a formula such that given some statistical information about nations' economic systems it would be possible to calculate and compare how good they were (in some specified sense) for their members. Governments could then compare the effects of alternative policies in order to decide between them. Societies could be compared at different dates to see whether they were progressing. For those purposes some theorists thought (for example) that it might do to have a formula which gave independent weight to income per head, and the equality with which it was distributed. But 'social welfare functions' of that kind would have to incorporate value judgements, for example of the relative importance of total income and its distribution; and there must probably be more value judgements or psychological guesses, or both, in judging that an additional dollar could do more for one person's welfare than for another's. (In economists' jargon, someone would have to make interpersonal comparisons of utility.) So it occurred to those who wanted economic science to be strictly neutral and objective and make no value judgements, that in a democracy it ought to be possible for the citizens themselves, rather than their economists or government, to judge their own 'utilities' and decide what values should be built into any formula for collective social welfare. The citizens could not be expected to be unanimous. They would always have some conflicts of interest and belief. But if all possible alternative uses of society's resources could be listed, and if every citizen would number them in order of his or her preference, it should be possible to calculate mathematically which alternative would most nearly satisfy most preferences and should therefore be the collective choice. That exercise might be substantial, to arrive at the society's most preferred economic system, or distribution of income, or other government policies. It might be constitutional, to arrive at the society's most preferred procedure for arriving at collective choices. It might be moral, to arrive at the society's most preferred moral rules, or mixtures of mutual obligation and permissible self-interest. There might then be an objective democratic basis for ideas of the 'national interest', the 'common good', and society's 'common values', 'collective purposes' and 'general will'.

If economists could derive social choices from individual preferences by formula in some such way, that would have philosophical and political interest. Philosophically they could dream of deriving 'ought' from 'is' by discovering what democratic governments ought to do on a basis of objective facts (about the citizens' preferences) without any need for ethical or value judgements by governments or their economists. We will criticize that philosophical ambition later. Here we are concerned with the practical possibility that as neutral 'technicians of democracy' economists might discover a democratic society's most-preferred policies in that uninterfering way.

By elegant mathematical reasoning in his 1950 paper 'A Difficulty in the Concept of Social Welfare' Kenneth Arrow proved that it could not be done. In the conditions in which it would normally have to be attempted there is no consistent way, without the possibility of internal contradictions, by which a single social choice can be derived from disagreed individual preferences. As long as three or more citizens are able to rank three or more alternatives, they either agree (in which case nothing further is needed) or disagree (in which case no purely logical or mathematical procedures can be relied on to yield a consistent, non-contradictory result).

There the business ought to have ended. A positivist mistake had been corrected. When expert scrutiny found no serious fault with Arrow's reasoning the search for an objective social welfare function or 'consensus machine' should have simply ceased.

Instead, an extraordinary thing happened. The search for a consensus machine did effectively cease, but forty years and a thousand books and articles later, scores of economists are still writing variations of Arrow's work.[4] Instead of one impossibility theorem there are now hundreds of them: hundreds of ways of proving that a purely logical or mathematical consensus machine is impossible. It is as if the joy of proving that the world was round had generated a continuous industry in replicating, elaborating and multiplying the proofs that it couldn't be flat. We do not really understand why it happened, but the following is *how* it happened.

Arrow's theorem said that a social welfare function, i.e. a formula or procedure to derive social choices from individual preferences, was impossible in what he called 'natural' conditions. He called the conditions natural because anyone who wanted a democratic social welfare function at all was likely to want it to fulfil these conditions. He originally specified five, then revised them to four, as follows. Individuals should be allowed to rank any number of alternatives in order of preference. If people prefer (say) alternative x to alternative y, that preference should not change because of changing preferences for other things. If every individual prefers x to y, society must do likewise. And there must be no dictator – no one whose preferences can command or override everyone else's preferences. (Short titles for those conditions were: unrestricted domain; independence of irrelevant alternatives; a 'Pareto' rule that any unanimous preferences should prevail; and no dictatorship.) What Arrow proved was that no consistent, non-contradictory social welfare function could comply with all four of those reasonable requirements.

What social choice theorists have chiefly done since is to explore the logical effects of varying the conditions. Discard any one of Arrow's conditions and there is now an impossibility theorem which does without it. There are impossibility theorems for more than a hundred other sets of conditions. Some of them are replicated for different meanings and interpretations of the same conditions. Theorists have devised mathematical notation for elements of liberty so that they could model procedures for deriving collective rules about liberty from individual votes about it, in order to prove *their* impossibility. There has also been some modelling of alternative voting systems and practices, for example strategies to frustrate other voters' preferences by mis-stating one's own.

Meanwhile there have been very few possibility theorems. The few are of two kinds. They have implausible or undesirable conditions, like dictatorship; or they incorporate interpersonal judgements of utility. The latter deserve notice because the whole social choice industry arose in the first place from a desire to avoid making interpersonal judgements of utility.

The theories which Arrow showed to be impossible, and most of the impossibility theorems themselves, are concerned with attempts to arrive at social policies without considering their effects. Why not consider their effects? Because if you want to compare the social effect of one policy with the social effect of another, you must first decide what weight to give to their effects on different people. You must decide whether an additional loaf of bread is likely to do more good for a starving child than for a well-fed millionaire. If you think it might, you may need to decide whether it is right to tax the millionaire to feed the starving child. And you may need to decide whether 'right' should have a utilitarian or a moral meaning. You must make both interpersonal judgements of utility, and moral or value judgements.

We will argue later that value judgements are inescapable in any serious discussion of social policy, and are concealed in all social choice and public choice theorizing. But some welfare economists don't believe that, and want to offer society a politically and morally neutral expertise. They may agree that social policies have to arise from interpersonal comparisons and value judgements, but they think those judgements should be made by the citizens themselves without interference by social scientists or governments. Hence the search for a formula or procedure which could derive policies directly and sufficiently from the citizens' preferences alone. Arrow proved that to be impossible in logic. But it should already have been obvious to common sense that it was anyway impossible in practice.

How could individual preferences in practice produce workable public policies? If the policies are derived one by one from the citizens' votes on one issue after another the policies won't hang together and government must collapse from incoherence. So – as social choice theorists have always insisted – what each citizen must rank in order of preference must be whole, coherent sets of policies which promise 'whole' social futures. But that is absurd: the technical planning, budgeting and coordination which now strain the resources of elaborate public services would have to be designed instead by each voter as she registered her preferences. The detailing of policies and the day-by-day judgements which adapt them to changing conditions involve politicians and public servants in incessant moral choices and comparative judgements of people's welfare; those also must somehow be supplied by daily mathematical processing of the citizens' individual preferences. If on the other hand welfare theorists merely want the citizens to express preferences for broad principles and directions of development, to be implemented in detail by politicians and public servants, that describes what happens now and offers no advance on it. Arrow proved to be logically impossible a dream that was already impossible in practice.

We think, perhaps more contentiously, that the dream was also morally undesirable. Its pretence of moral neutrality is false; it merely replaces better moral principles by worse. Instead of saying 'cruelty is wrong and a good culture does not teach people to enjoy it' the expert says 'as far as our profession is concerned the only wrong is frustrating the people's choices'. Thus the political scientist abandons the political philosopher's traditional tasks of considering which social principles are best, and studying how people's principles and preferences are formed. If what most people like best is to watch lions eat a few Christians every Saturday, political scientists need only check that the votes are correctly counted or – better still – recommend privatization and admission charges so that the entertainment will meet a precise market demand with no freeloading. We need not labour the point: no democrat should be indifferent to the wants which a democracy generates or allows to be satisfied. And just as it is right to defend minorities, it may also be right to defend majorities from themselves. If tobacco advertisers with millions to spend on mass persuasion can persuade a majority to smoke, and can further persuade them to forbid any public spending on smoking research or anti-smoking education, we believe that doctors and researchers and reformers should still divert any public resources they can lay their hands on to persuading the majority to have more sense: they should not be deterred by respect for majority rule, or by accusations that they are elitist or paternalist because they profess to know the people's interests better than the people themselves do. There will always be conflicts between principles of democratic government and principles of good behaviour, and between moral ways and utilitarian ways of deciding what behaviour is good. Those are problems for later chapters. Meanwhile they cannot be resolved by pretences of moral abstinence or political neutrality.

Those are the logical, practical and moral reasons why we think the economists' social choice industry has become a sterile mathematical recreation which should have ceased thirty years ago. Arrow's original proof was useful to correct a mistake by some welfare economists and to head off any further waste of effort in that direction. But since then the industry has become a self-generating and self-serving one, with no helpful and some harmful reference to real social life. Some people think its conclusions strengthen the case against public goods; and its habits of mind can positively blind its practitioners to the real life under their noses.

A good example is the question of majority rule. Arrow's own response to his logical discovery, as a scholar with common sense and a social conscience, has generally been to see majority rule as the best approach, however rough and ready, to good democratic government. Mathematical procedures should help to design voting systems to elect politicians, rather than to choose policies. Anthony Downs, another early 'economic theorist of politics', put the two together to suggest that people choose the politicians they believe will think, act and respond to changing circumstances as their electors would wish them to do.[5] Downs had been anticipated by Sir Robert Peel, British Prime Minister in the 1840s. The Reform Act of 1832 brought the beginnings of a mass electorate. Party organizations were formed to woo it. Leaders began to promise voters specific policies in their election manifestos. But how binding were those promises? Should every policy and act of government be put to a vote and have the prior approval of the public or the party before it could be implemented? Peel argued that that would be impossible. Nobody – public, party or politician – could foresee the problems a government would face, sometimes at short notice, through its seven-year term. Party and public should elect leaders whose judgement they trusted, perhaps better than they trusted their own: leaders who shared their values and general social purposes and could be expected to act accordingly, as far as practicable, in all circumstances foreseen and unforeseen. A century later Arrow and Downs agreed. But in other minds, perhaps keener on doing maths than understanding government, rigorous unrealism persists. A number of social choice theorists have offered this knock-down objection to majority rule: if a society of three members distributes its income by majority rule, it will be rational for any two members to divide the income between them and leave none for the third member.

What is wrong with that reasoning? It relies on one motive only, and one numerical characteristic, of majority rule. It mistakes their effects. And it neglects many other relevant characteristics of majority rule. We will list eight of those other characteristics, not so much to prove the theorists wrong about majority rule as to illustrate what is wrong with theorizing about *any* social behaviour in this abstract, axiomatic, mono-motivational way.

One: If, as is normal, the three who must divide the society's income also produce it, it is likely that their division of labour and economies of scale enable them to produce more than three times as much as any of them could produce alone. If two take all the income the third must die or emigrate, cutting output by more than a third and leaving the majority poorer, not richer, than before. As Amartya Sen has observed, the rational egoists of economic theory would often be self-defeating 'rational fools'. Logically (but just as unrealistically) the three egoists of this theory should divide the income equally, because any minority has a decisive bargaining advantage against any majority: she can reduce their income by withdrawing her labour. That holds for each of them, so if they are rational the highest income available to any of them is an equal third.

But perhaps the third member of the theorists' society is too young or too old to be a producer? Either handicap is one which members of the majority must also suffer in the course of their lives. To secure their own whole-life incomes they need to establish a reliable rule or agreement for the support of dependants, and pay the present dependant accordingly. But if they are ruthless enough, can they make provision for old age because that is still ahead of them, but not for childhood because that is now behind them? No – if there's no support for children there will be no new workers to replace old ones and produce output to support them in old age.

Two: In real life the two egoists, not being social choice theorists, will foresee the above effects and give the third member at least enough to keep her alive and at work. How much that takes may depend on her sense of justice and her opportunities to emigrate, as well as her material needs; and if the majority remember Chester Barnard's analysis they may allow for the minority's moral codes as well as her material needs when deciding how much to pay her, even if their only purpose is to maximize their own incomes.

Three: It follows that the offending theory can only apply at best to the distribution of surplus value, i.e. output above whatever must go to the producers to keep them producing. Here it is history that contradicts the theory. In all democracies majorities have power to strip rich minorities of their capital wealth, and no democracy has done it. Democracies have often been justly accused of neglecting or exploiting *poor* minorities, but those have so little to lose that rich minorities would always offer more plunder to majorities of rational egoists. But all democracies allow rich minorities to keep their wealth and much more than their pro-rata share of income, even when ruled by majorities of middling and poor. That may be because other kinds of power prevail over majority rule, or because majorities think they get more by cooperating with the rich minorities than by plundering them; but whatever the reasons, the practice of democratic majorities everywhere belies the theorists' expectations.

Four: Real societies have more than three members and so do their majorities. Majorities are rarely homogeneous, or unanimous on all issues.

Most members of majorities on some issues find themselves in minorities on others, so prudence dictates some mutual forbearance, and perhaps some laws to protect minorities. Democratic winners may often take unfair shares but it is rarely in their interest to take all.

Five: Another characteristic of divided and changing majorities is that they act together for purposes, and within limits, which are bargained and agreed among themselves. On some issues at least, majorities commonly have members, and sometimes substantial internal minorities, who have bonds of sympathy, obligation or material interest with the 'external' minorities against whom the majority's will prevails. The need to hold wavering members then constrains the majority's policies and limits the damage its members allow it to do to those outside its ranks; far from using its numbers to plunder its opponents to the limit, forbearing behaviour is a condition of the majority's own existence and power. (Moderate conservatives won't let their harsher colleagues abolish free health services; moderate socialists won't let their harsher colleagues confiscate capitalist property.)

Six: Whatever their internal restraints, democratic majorities are never free to do what they like. They live under laws, and formal and informal rules of behaviour, many of which they support for prudent reasons, which put a great many constraints on winners taking all even if winners want to.

Seven: Some of the rules are moral rules, part of the shared culture. Even in the greediest societies it usually happens that a majority on any particular issue is composed of some members who have material interests in that issue and others who don't. The latter, being disinterested in the matter at issue, may have both greedy and altruistic reasons for restraining the greed of their self-interested colleagues. Greedy reasons: the power to plunder may need to be used sparingly if each use of it makes more enemies and disgusts more swinging voters; so members may not want to waste the power on issues from which they won't personally profit. At the same time it costs the disinterested members nothing to show some altruism by doing what they can, for good moral reasons, to restrain their plundering colleagues. The moral and immoral motives may reinforce each other as those who want to plunder other victims next week, but also want to think of themselves as decent people with reasonably generous standards of behaviour, use moral arguments to restrain their colleagues from plundering *these* victims *this* week.

Eight: Besides their conflicting interests and beliefs democratic people also have common interests and shared beliefs, including moral beliefs, which help to restrain them, much of the time, from treating one another too badly.

Those factors don't suffice to protect minorities from misrule by majorities in the Balkans or in Ulster, or until lately in the ex-slave states of the US. But those exceptions cannot be explained by any economic theory of politics. On the contrary the religious, racial and communal hatreds which drive those oppressive majorities serve to confirm, by contrast, what mere greed does *not* impel normal majorities to do.

Meanwhile the eight listed above are among the reasons for doubting that anything new or useful will be discovered about real political life or majority rule by the use of a formal model of two egoists electing to starve a third to death. More generally we doubt that any axiomatic reasoning or mathematical procedures of this kind will discover much about people's motivation or behaviour in their political activity, or about the policies which they or their governments would do best to choose. That should have been obvious a generation ago. We think that most social choice theorists in most of their work are wasting talents for which the world has better uses.

THE THEORIES TOGETHER

Samuelson's theory of public expenditure is not much known except to economists. Even among economists we suspect that social choice theories are read chiefly by social choice theorists. Neither theory is cited much in discussions of economic policy outside the profession. But there have been attempts to popularize them in books in plain language, and we cannot know what indirect influence they may have through whatever they contribute to economists' general attitudes to public and private goods. Whatever their force, the persuasions are usually to the effect that choices and allocations of public goods lack any rational democratic basis and are consequently open to pork-barrelling and freeloading, and likely to be less efficient for their ostensible purposes and for the economy as a whole than market choices and allocations would be. Not much is heard these days of Samuelson's and Downs' warnings about the undersupply of public goods.

Both beliefs should be tested for fit with the facts of political and economic life. But there are first some theoretical objections to them.

Samuelson's theory expects politicians to buy votes by restraining taxes. There was some ground for that when the theory was written in the immediate postwar years, when people wanted high wartime rates of income tax to come down as fast and far as possible. There has again been ground for it in the taxcutting climate of the 1980s. But votes can be bought equally by negative or positive means – by offering to cut taxes or increase benefits to the voters. Through the 1960s politicians were commonly suspected of increasing taxation, often by the painless method of 'bracket creep' as growth and inflation together shifted taxpayers from one marginal rate up to the next, and of using the gains to finance real wage rises for public employees and a steady expansion of welfare benefits. Both could be seen as principled social improvements or as sectional vote-buying; it was often because they *were* both that they could attract wide enough support to get enacted. And just as the taxcutting mood of the postwar years was reflected in Samuelson's theory that public goods tend to be undersupplied, so the spending mood of the 1960s was reflected (as we will see) in public choice theories which predicted that public goods would tend to be oversupplied: politicians and public servants would raise as much revenue as possible and use it to buy votes for the politicians and to increase bureaucrats' pay by enlarging their departments.

We need not labour this simple theme. In real life politicians can compete for support by taking less, by giving more, or by clever mixtures or pretences of both; and those purposes coexist a good deal of the time with more principled purposes in the minds of politicians, public servants and electors. Put simply: votes can be attracted by giving, by not taking, and by governing well. It is stupid, and quite unpromising for purposes of understanding and prediction, to build deductive theory on any one only of the three propensities. Intelligent analysis must always be alert for all three. The selective blindness of public goods theory, public choice theory and theories of perfectly benevolent government are equally silly.

Samuelson's theory suggested that democracies need more public goods than they generally vote themselves. Arrow and Sen have never suggested that they need less, and when writing on other subjects than social choice theory they have both argued for many progressive policies and active roles for government. Both also argue that as policies cannot be sufficiently derived from individual preferences their foundations should include moral considerations. But in coming to these progressive conclusions the three leaders have few followers among public goods and social choice theorists, most of whom – if they link their work to policy at all – come to more conservative or 'radical Right' conclusions. A common theme is that the provision of public goods allows so much freeloading and self-interested contrivance by powerful groups and individuals that societies do well to make do with as few taxes and public goods as possible. An influential leader of that school of thought is Mancur Olson, and to sample it we can sketch the argument of his books *The Logic of Collective Action: Public goods and the theory of groups* (1965) and *The Rise and Decline of Nations* (1982).

The curious argument of *The Logic of Collective Action* is this: because freeloaders can gain more from collective action than the collective actors can, collective action is never rational. Suppose that I ply a trade whose members could gain by acting together to lobby government, raise prices, or raise or lower wages. Acting together costs the actors time and money, so to maximize my gains I leave the action to others. But so do they, because they're rational too, so the action never happens. Olson's rational maximizers are extreme examples of Amartya Sen's rational fools.

Why do people nevertheless act together for common or generous purposes in real life? If they do it willingly Olson says they are irrational, by which he means driven by ideology or 'psychological disturbance or disequilibrium'. (Voluntary military service, ambulance driving, surf life-saving, mountain rescue, school crossing service, meals on wheels, prevention of cruelty to children and animals?) But most cooperators are not volunteers, they are coerced or rewarded to take part, by means designed to make sure that those who benefit *do* contribute to the costs. Thus in a society of egoists, groups who could gain by collective action have two options. They can do nothing and gain nothing, as rational fools. Or they can act together by means which prevent freeloading. Those means range from compulsory taxation and military service through industrial and commercial regulation, oligopoly, closed shop unions and other kinds of coerced or contractual cooperation, to the licensing of skilled trades and professions. Those are normal and often effective conditions of acting together, just as laws against murder and theft are necessary conditions of living together. So far, the theory has said nothing new. But the heart of Olson's argument is his belief that most ways to prevent freeloading also reduce the efficiency of the economy as a whole. *That* is why the freeloading problem is a serious one.

Thus on its own assumptions the theory can be discarded if taxation, regulation and other cost-sharing methods can be reconciled with general economic efficiency. But there are also better reasons for discarding it. The only gains which Olson allows his rational egoists to seek are things they can acquire, i.e. items of property external to the people who acquire them. He assumes that the activity of acquiring them is always unwelcome: a cost to be avoided if possible. In this miserable conception of what it is to be human, people never enjoy interesting or challenging or sociable activity for its own sake. They may be coerced by rules of good behaviour but never welcome them or enjoy behaving well. If they act together it is never because acting together is more enjoyable than idling alone. If they act in sympathy with others, for the good of others, to enjoy teamwork in common causes, to improve their society's justice or quality of life, or merely to keep boredom at bay, it can only be because they are psychologically disturbed. Olson may allow convivial, expressive, affectionate, non-acquisitive behaviour in the separate realm of leisure and consumption, but never at work or in government. His is an extreme example of the definition of rationality which has long prevailed in the positivist or Chicagoan branches of American social science: rational means seeking money for oneself; arational means seeking anything else for oneself; irrational means seeking anything good for other people. Thus a word which used to describe a relation between means and ends has come to describe ends instead: rational no longer means 'logically related' or 'effective for its purpose', it means 'having no other purpose than individual greed'.

To summarize: Olson argues that freeloading possibilities make straightforward collective action irrational for the individuals concerned. So people who can gain by acting together develop various kinds of group action, often coercive, to ensure their own freeloading gains or to prevent others'. Such group action (by monopolies, trade unions, licensed trades and professions, industrial and commercial lobby groups and so on) tends to distort the allocation of economic resources, entrench restrictive practices, hinder innovation and growth, and thus reduce national economic efficiency. But there can rarely be collective action without such damaging behaviour. Conclusion: the most efficient economy will be the one with least collective action and therefore least public goods. Government should encourage market efficiency by enforcing strict anti-trust laws, but should otherwise do as little as possible.

In *The Rise and Decline of Nations* (1982) Olson used the theory to explain the rates of economic growth of the leading capitalist countries after the second world war, as follows. Wherever public goods are provided, including public regulation of private production and exchange, there is likely to be group behaviour of the kind described above which will distort the allocation of resources, discourage innovation, and divert talent away from producing goods and services to regulating, politicking and other unproductive activity. Olson focuses on two characteristics of the group behaviour. Concentrated interests (such as the firms or unions in a particular industry) can usually exert more influence than can the larger, more dispersed groups (such as the industry's customers, or the society's consumers) who may have more claim to represent the society as a whole. And people are generally slow to perceive the benefits they might get by group action, and slow to organize and act to get the benefits; so restrictive institutions and practices accumulate quite slowly over time. It follows that countries with long histories of stable government have the largest number of entrenched group interests and therefore the most cluttered, distorted and slow-growing economic systems.

That is the theory which Olson uses to select the causal factors that he will include in his historical explanations. Factors modelled in the theory are included, others (however potent they may have been) are not. The effects to be explained are the slow economic growth of the English-speaking countries since the second world war and the faster growth of Germany, Japan, Taiwan and South Korea. In the US and UK the accumulation of entrenched interests and restrictive practices continued in the normal way and allowed comparatively slow growth. Germany and Japan differed in two respects. Their own dictators had smashed the unions and other self-defences of labour. And entrenched capitalist groups lost their influence when after World War Two the victors purged some of the owners and managers who had been close to the old governments, and created new 'cleanskin' democratic governments with no inherited obligations to either side of industry. It was because market forces were thus freed to work unhindered (Olson concludes) that they worked the German and Japanese economic miracles.

That is an incompetent historical explanation. Even if the market freedoms were as Olson represented them their effect could not be estimated without also estimating the effects of half a dozen other factors which were also at work. Germany and Japan had much physical damage to repair and replace. For a decade or more they were scientific and technical borrowers, rebuilding an established technology or (especially in Japan) continuing to catch up with the world's technical leaders. Those conditions commonly allow faster growth than mature economies can achieve. Both countries got substantial international aid, mostly at American expense. Both had unusually intense motivation. The victor countries had triumphs to remember and many of their people could feel that they had earned some right to relax after six years of superhuman effort. By contrast the defeated had more than damaged cities and industrial capacity to rebuild; they had disasters to forget and damaged cultures and self-respect to rebuild. There was powerful appeal in the idea of hard work to restore lost standards of living, and to win through from military failure to economic leadership. Without armed forces or defence industries they could devote all their resources to useful production while the victors bled each others' economies with an escalating arms race and some millions of their healthiest young workers wasted in 'military unemployment'.

All those conditions contributed to the German and Japanese performance. To attribute it to a single factor is a mistake, and Olson's single factor of 'less group action' is anyway exaggerated. The ownership of German and Japanese industry was almost as concentrated after the war as before. It was not significantly less monopolistic than British or American industry.

In Japan it was subject to stronger public planning and direction than British and American industry were, and there were independent sources in Japan's modern history for her remarkable output of entrepreneurs. Both countries' occupation governments then their own democratic governments encouraged the development of labour unions, and their level of industrial cooperation may have owed as much to the psychology of national recovery as to union weakness. Finally it is difficult to believe that least collective action, least public goods and 'youngest' government regularly cause greatest productivity if the national comparisons are extended to the leading Western countries. Among OECD countries the US has the smallest public sector and the least union membership and power. Sweden has the biggest public sector, the most union membership and power, and a longer history of settled and stable government than the US. Yet by most standards through many of the relevant years those opposites were the world's richest countries, richer than any of those which operated between their extremes. They are rich for partly similar, partly different, partly unique reasons, complex reasons very few of which are noticed in Olson's analysis or could be predicted by the type of theory he uses.

The conservative impulses which Olson sees obstructing change in the mature economies do nevertheless exist. Robert Reich, reviewing Olson's work,[6] distinguished three kinds of response to economic innovation. The first is as Olson describes: potential losers from change combine to block it, so economic growth is slow. The second response is also as Olson describes. In Taiwan, South Korea, Singapore and Japan the losers have often been defenceless and have suffered a good deal from changes they were powerless to prevent. Taiwan and South Korea killed or jailed any who offered serious resistance; Singapore and Japan had gentler but still effective ways of preventing resistance, especially resistance by the lower ranks of low-paid and insecure labour. 'Rapid industrial change', Reich observed, 'is relatively easy to achieve when the leaders who plan it have no serious worries about politics, when economic planning is made by stable elites who simply need not take account of how the burdens of economic change are borne by the less advantaged.'

The third approach to change is to enlist those it will affect in planning it, to see that its costs and benefits are distributed in ways which most people see as fair. From shop-floor participation in decisions about plant and working conditions, through union representation on corporate boards, to cooperative retraining schemes and tripartite negotiation of national price and income policies and development objectives, elements of economic democracy are helping much of north-western Europe to rival the performance of the more confrontationist English-speaking countries.

However harsh Japan is to its lower ranks of insecure workers, its performance gains much from the depth of consultation with its upper ranks of
secure workers. Australia's economic growth surged through the first five
years of its successful, union-based incomes policy. British trade unions
missed a chance of that sort of cooperation when they spurned the Wilson
government's invitations to join in an incomes policy.

Dictatorial brutalities are rarely possible and never desirable in mature
democratic economies. That leaves two options for the interest groups
whose influence Olson fears. They can confront one another and try to
manipulate government to block or distort what change they can, as some
of them do in the US and UK. Or they can bargain and cooperate with government and one another to plan changes as equitably as possible, as
increasingly in western Europe. If the US and UK are losing ground it may
be from too little public planning and economic democracy rather than too
much. But those possibilities will not be noticed by historians who allow
Olson's theory to guide their search and selection of the causes and effects
of economic development.

THE USES OF PUBLIC GOODS

Here follows a reminder of what these theories leave out: a brief list of
reasons why modern mixed economies need public goods and need not be
deterred from providing them by the difficulty of deciding about them.

First, many of the decisions are easy. In societies which can afford them
it is not hard to decide to have piped water, sewerage, money, weights and
measures, road and rail and power and telephone networks, weather forecasting, lighthouses and radio beams, police, law and order, schooling for
all children, public health services, and public regulation of waste disposal,
noxious trades, work safety, and the labelling of dangerous drugs and anything else which endangers life if falsely labelled. It is true that there are
wide variations in the efficiency, honesty and equity with which those
goods are provided in different societies. But where there is good government the provisions can often be as efficient, and more equitable, than are
provisions of market goods to people with unequal incomes. Where the
provisions are bad the need is usually to improve them, not reduce them – a
poor water supply doesn't reduce thirst, crooked police don't make policing less necessary, bad roads are better than none, and so on. The reasons
for improving rather than reducing inefficient provisions of necessary
public goods are much the same as the reasons for improving rather than
reducing inefficient provisions of necessary market goods.

Many public goods go to produce other goods. Industry can't function without quite complex public services and infrastructure. Private agriculture, medicine, engineering and electronics are only a few of the many industries which have learned a great deal from public scientific research. Most of the skill in a modern economy is built on a base of public education. Wherever public goods are not separate retail items (like free concerts or national parks) but are inputs to the production of market goods or public necessities, cutting public investment is not likely to increase private output or improve national efficiency. Switching off the public navigational beams won't cause private air or sea transport to grow. Letting the roads rot won't expand private road transport. Closing the public schools won't increase private skills or productivity. And so on – the need is to get the mix of productive factors right, as in any productive process which has to combine numerous inputs in correct proportions.

In that mix the relations between public investment and private performance can be quite complex. (i) Public investors commonly buy private products and stimulate investment in their production. Only in fully employed conditions need that merely crowd out equivalent private activity. (ii) Public investment creates skills and services which determine many private costs and efficiencies, and many of those effects are cumulative as high or low levels of annual public investment build up sufficient or insufficient, up-to-date or out-of-date public capital and services for private use. (iii) Where public investment increases national income, some additional private saving and investment are likely. These relations were explored by Kenneth Arrow and Mordecai Kurz in *Public Investment, the Rate of Return, and Optimal Fiscal Policy* (1970) cited earlier, and more recently by David Alan Aschauer and others.[7] Aschauer's empirical observations and theoretical modelling of relations between public non-military investment, private profitability, private investment and the growth of private productivity suggest that a shortfall in public investment has accounted for much of the decline in US economic growth since 1970. 'If the United States had continued to invest in public capital after 1970 at the rate maintained for the previous two decades, we could have benefited in the following ways:

● Our chronically low rate of productivity growth could have been up to 50 per cent higher – 2.1 per cent per year, rather than the actual rate of 1.4 per cent;
● Our depressed rate of profit on nonfinancial corporate capital could have averaged 9.6 per cent instead of 7.9 per cent;

- Private investment in plants and equipment could have increased from the sluggish historical rate of 3.1 per cent, to 3.7 per cent of the private capital stock.[8]

The better Japanese and German performance through the same years was supported by between twice and three times the US rate of non-military public investment.

Where the public and private products are not joint but are independent, there can still be synergy between them. Public museums and national parks stimulate privately profitable tourism. Public art schools and galleries encourage both producers and buyers of private art. And there are other relations where the public services contribute not to the production but to the acceptability of private products. Public inspection and licensing tell people which drugs are safe, which nighties are nonflammable, which doctors are respectably qualified – and probably increase demand for those goods and services. Finally many public goods are bought from private producers. The net effect of these interrelations is that public and private investment tend to vary together rather than inversely. Over time there is more 'crowding in' than 'crowding out'. Except for a few lines of public investment that can be turned on or off countercyclically, boom and slump signify too much activity in both sectors or too little in both.

Next, it is a mistake to suppose that people – even exclusively self-interested people – want only the public goods which they use themselves. Looking only to my own self-interest (any rational egoist may say) I want a great many public goods to be supplied to other people. I want to live in a rich, productive society, so it must provide public infrastructure to all its industries, not just the one I happen to work in, and it must see that all its people, not just me, acquire as much education and skill as possible, with as much public provision as it takes. I want to live in a cultivated and interesting society. So I want good public provisions for those of the creative arts that need public help, not just the one I happen to practise myself, and I want as much intellectual and artistic life and fire and invention as possible to be built into the common culture and the individual people of the society in which I live. Besides good highbrow culture I also like good lowbrow culture, which also uses some public goods: sports arenas, picnic grounds, community centres, and the public broadcasters whose soaps and sitcoms have so far averaged at least as funny and moving as their incessantly interrupted commercial competitors. Outdoors I don't enjoy streets lined with beggars and alcoholics and homeless children – or muggers and pickpockets – so I want sufficient, intelligent, effective welfare provisions for those who need them. Finally (if my egoism is of the weak-minded, comfort-loving kind) I want to enjoy life self-indulgently but with as little guilt, shame or other internal unease as possible, so I would like my country to be generally regarded as one of the more equal of the democracies, in which my pleasures don't have to cause much pain to others. For all these selfish reasons I am probably not the only one (our representative egoist might say) who would rather live with one happy lover in the upper reaches of one of the more progressive Western democracies, paying half my income for public goods, than live tax-free with a submissive harem as a super-rich, super-powerful oil sheik, he being these days the human who possesses the most of what neoclassical economic theory, public goods theory and public choice theory assume that humans most desire. Rising numbers of the sheiks themselves live abroad in welfare states these days.

There is a further, more important effect of the difference between better and worse cultures. Cultures not only satisfy people's wants, they also do a good deal to form them. Later chapters will argue that the worst shortcoming of liberal philosophy in general and its economic variants in particular is that they assume a world of fully formed adults and won't consider what forms them: what makes the difference between (say) a society with a democratic majority for substantial equality between the sexes, and another whose men enslave its women in a regime of patriarchy, purdah and female circumcision. In Western countries public goods and services make a good deal of the difference between better and worse culture, and consequently between better and worse government. The quality of public education, broadcasting, religion and subsidized arts, and the kinds of morality and social purpose which they help to instil into people, have direct effects on everyone, and powerful indirect effects as they help to determine the quality and social values of the people who are recruited into the influential trades: politics, public service, research, education, journalism, broadcasting and the arts. Meanwhile other public services – in housing, welfare and income support – affect the kind of upbringing and independence that households with low incomes are equipped to give their children.

As to how cultures form people, especially influential people, there have been odd contrasts in the thinking of Right and Left. Conservatives have traditionally been most concerned about the influences which form people's character and values. In movements like 'the moral majority' they still are. But although they have been more paternalist than others, and happy to see elites govern, they have commonly worried more about the morals of lower than upper classes. Left thinkers on the other hand insist that power is unequally distributed and that democracies are dominated by rich minorities, but – perhaps because they hate to admit that any capitalist regime is better than any other – they have been least concerned about the quality of elites and the cultures which form them. That has meant, para-doxically, that the critics who ought to have been most concerned have commonly been least concerned about the different quality of the rulers and the different experience of the ruled in (say) Scandinavia, Argentina and South Africa.

Public education and arts are not all good, and profit-seeking education and arts are not all bad. Anyone educated chiefly by TV commercials is likely to value innocent fun, family life and human diversity as well as fast cars and personal freshness. But with increasingly monopolist ownership and political misuse of the most penetrating media, with much of the best literary and artistic talent in advertising, and with market forces exposing children (it is said) to moving pictures of forty thousand violent deaths by the time they are twenty-one, the chances for high social purposes, for independent critical and creative thought, for uncommercial or anticom-mercial social research, and for a peaceful, intelligent, compassionate cul-ture to prevail, must depend a good deal on the public contributions to mass and class education. And it costs nothing to keep those services public: we pay the same for them one way or the other, through taxes or the price of soap.

Besides affecting a society's culture public goods also affect, for better or worse, its distribution of real wealth and income. Samuelson regretted that users can't be made to pay for 'pure' public goods. There are also many goods – like education, child care, hospital services – which users can be made to pay for but which many governments choose to finance from taxes and supply free or below cost to some or all of their users. That separation of the costs from the benefits makes opportunity for the free-loading and allocative inefficiency of which public goods theorists com-plain. But with many taxes and services freeloading can be prevented, and where it can, the separation of costs from benefits can have positively good uses. To sketch some of them, we can accept the conservative presumption that when government wants to help its poorer citizens it should normally do it by transferring income to them. That leaves them as free as everyone else to judge their own wants and spending priorities. We agree: for those who need it, the age pension is the simplest and best of all welfare meas-ures. Only when income transfers function badly, or other measures can work better, are other measures justified. Here follow half a dozen exam-ples of circumstances in which public goods or services may do more good than equivalent money could.

Public services may serve better than income when people need kinds of protection which they can't buy individually. That applies broadly to most law and order and specifically to the regulation and inspection of the growing number of market goods and services whose quality or safety consumers can't judge for themselves: the purity of packaged foods and drugs, the safety of electrical appliances and things made of poisonous or inflammable plastics, the solvency of banks, and so on.

Some income transfers are thought to harm the work incentives of those who provide the income, those who receive it, or both. If employers are required to pay their employees child allowances, or fares to work, they may discriminate against workers with children who live beyond reach of the factory smoke. Though they bring other problems, tax-financed child allowances and subsidized child-care and public transport may be preferable. If high progressive taxes finance a generous dole to large numbers of unemployed, that may deter some rich from investing and some poor from seeking work. Retraining schemes and public employment in useful services may be less expensive and more productive than those income transfers.

Goods and services may be better than income if they are harder to divert from their intended users. Public child-care may take better care of some children than their parents would buy for them if they had to pay for it. Most societies have some households whose women, children or aged dependants need protection from breadwinners who spend too much of the bread on drink, drugs, gambling or other recreations, or who simply disappear. Secure tenure of public housing and access to free schools, medical services and women's and children's shelters may do more for them than money which may be seized by the cause of their troubles.

Goods and services may do more than income to help people who would be weak bargainers in hard markets. If government wants to help hard-up people to house themselves, rent allowances may look cheapest in the short run, but aids to home purchase and a stock of well chosen and managed public housing can house people more securely and cost households and taxpayers less in the long run.

There are services which volunteers will provide to needy people if they have public or charitable rather than profit-seeking organizers. Without their public status and subsidy there would be fewer Meals on Wheels and they would cost the taxpayers more, directly in paying wages for home services or indirectly in hospitalizing people for want of home services.

Two final arguments about public goods may be noticed here though their main exposition belongs in the next chapter. Freeloading counts against public goods only if there is a better alternative – if market supply prevents freeloading. All public goods theorists assume that it does. The belief has two bases, both disputable. First it rests on a moral judgement which defines freeloading as getting what you have not paid for. Why not getting what you have not earned? Anyone with less capitalistic morals can see that unearned incomes from rent, interest, dividends and capital gains are just as freely loaded as any public goods are. On that basis private freeloading is on much grander scale than public freeloading is, and the way to reduce it is to shift more of the means of production, especially the sources of rent, into public, cooperative or non-profit ownership. Second, even on capitalist assumptions private freeloading is large and probably increasing. Business gains from externalities, monopoly and other market imperfections are free gains. So are many executive gains which are greater than any available in honest public service: many times the highest public salaries, with share options, cars, expense accounts, opportunities for tax avoidance and insider trading, and other bonuses. Insofar as there are market prices for executive services, the rates are set by the prevailing business culture, not by bargaining between employer and employed with opposing interests – when directors fix directors' rewards, employer and employed are the same people. There are no effective legal or market limits to how much of their firms' earnings corporate directors can take from their shareholders.

There is finally an argument about the mode of production of public goods. People who believe that public enterprise is less efficient than private enterprise think that public goods get some additional inefficiency, over and above their freeloading inefficiencies, from their mode of production. There are two objections to that belief. The evidence does not always support it – public and private enterprise have had different efficiency at different times, in different industries and in different countries, but research has not revealed any general superiority of one over the other. And public goods are not all produced by public producers. Public and private goods are often produced by similar mixes of public and private enterprise. Armies, police and public services get most of their buildings and equipment from private producers, while (for example) public producers until recently supplied about half the inputs to the production of Europe's private cars. So even if it were true that private production was more efficient than public it would still take research to discover whether public or private goods in mixed economies incorporate the bigger proportion of private 'value added'. Meanwhile the comparative efficiencies of public and private production are subjects of the next chapter.

SUMMARY

This chapter has argued that most economists' social choice theory is sterile, and that relations between public goods theory and real life are as follows.

Mixed economies need public goods for many purposes: to supply necessary goods and services whose nature prevents their being supplied as market goods; to supply necessary inputs to private and domestic production; to give people education and skills which it is in other people's interest as well as their own that they should have; to transmit and enrich common culture to improve the quality of individual and social life; to help share tastes and preferences by giving people better rather than worse wants and beliefs and social purposes; and to improve the distribution of wealth and real income, especially where in practice that can't be achieved, or not as well, by the distribution of money income.

For those purposes public goods are ordered and allocated by mixtures of political, administrative and market choice. (Public and market choices mix, for example, when users shop for partly subsidized or differentially taxed goods.) Though many of the political and administrative choices are in practice made by governing groups or individuals, most are open to majority rule and conform to its general directions. In stable democracies without serious racial or religious conflicts, majorities tend to have continuously changing composition. They treat minorities tolerably for a variety of self-interested and benevolent reasons. Nevertheless government is not always fair or beneficent. Rich groups and classes can acquire disproportionate influence over it. Public goods can be under- or over-supplied. They can be ill-chosen, inefficiently produced, maldistributed, wasted. Freeloaders can get more than they pay for. By a variety of inducements, manipulators can get politicians, administrators, and voting groups to help them to more public goods than they deserve. Democratic control over these processes can be negligent, corrupt, oppressive or otherwise imperfect. A main activity of democratic reformers for two centuries past has been to develop the beneficent potentialities of government and restrain its sins, by all means from research and persuasion, through enfranchising and organizing the voters, to designing better policies and institutions.

Most of those diverse potentialities of government have been apparent since government began, and studied by political scientists at least since Aristotle. So have the mixed motives which produce government's performance. But faced with those familiar facts of history and politics, what the economic theorists of government do is this: they select one only of the many motives at work, and imagine a world animated by that one alone. They imagine it incompetently, because the efficient organization of production and the efficient market relations which they envisage actually depend on the presence of law, culture and morality which their selected motive alone could never produce or sustain. They thus theorize a system with an unworkable contradiction at its heart. The theories are consequently hopeless predictors. Instead of systematic empirical tests their authors are reduced to drawing attention to their occasional fit with real life, as some industrial lobby gets what it wants, or as Samuelson's theory fits the tax-cutting mood of the 1980s.

In practice the theories have three other uses. They occupy academic time and publications in what hostile critics see as ritual or recreational rather than useful activity. They mislead researchers in the way we have described: the theory advises researchers to search any social system or process for its elements of individual greed and to be satisfied when they find them. They are thus encouraged to neglect the system's other conditions and causes, however necessary and potent those may be, and whatever opportunities they may offer for management or reform. Finally the theories moralize: despite false pretences of objectivity they persuade people to want less public goods and less government, to believe that individual greed is natural and is more rational, so by implication more to be preferred, than other purposes in life.

4 Public Enterprise

It is widely believed that public enterprises tend to neglect their customers' wants; to allocate productive resources inefficiently and use them inefficiently; and to resist reform or closure when those are needed. Together the four beliefs compose what may be called a theory of public incompetence.

The public shortcomings are thought to have four main causes. For deciding what to produce, planners' choices are poor substitutes for people's market demands. Public investors and managers lack the personal financial incentives which profit-seekers have. Private employees endanger their jobs if they achieve pay and conditions their employers can't afford, but there is no such market limit to what organized, hard-bargaining public employees can extract from the taxpayers. And inefficient private enterprises are automatically eliminated by market forces but governments can and do allow inefficient or unnecessary public activities to continue.

This chapter argues that some of those beliefs have been well founded, others less so; that public enterprises do face some distinctive temptations, but so do private enterprises; and that many of the virtues and vices of the two modes are not fixed but changeable. Governments should approach questions of economic structure with open eyes for the facts and issues in each case, and with open minds about the means of action in each case, rather than with fixed preferences for public or private ownership. The communist belief that governments should own all capital and plan all economic activity no longer has serious defenders so there is no need to attack its theoretical basis. But the opposite faith, that economic systems do better the less public enterprise they have, still has believers and their reasons are this chapter's concern.

FACTS

Our subject is the theories which lead people to expect public enterprise to be less efficient than private. But first, which is more efficient in fact? It is surprisingly difficult to know. Public and private enterprises rarely produce the same goods in the same conditions with the same purposes to make exact comparisons possible. Even when they do, the results vary widely enough to allow no knock-down conclusion. Many comparisons were attempted through the 1960s and 1970s and we can report some general conclusions from one German-American and one British review of them.

Thomas E. Borcherding, Werner W. Pommerehne and Friedrich Schneider contributed 'Comparing the Efficiency of Private and Public Production: The Evidence from Five Countries' to Supplement 2 (1982) of *Zeitschrift für Nationalökonomie/Journal of Economics* pp. 127–56. They found that 36 of the 43 studies they surveyed showed private enterprises with lower costs than their public equivalents. But they concluded that some of the comparisons had neglected the public costs occasioned by private production, or had failed to relate the higher public costs to the public producers' additional products or purposes, so that taken together the comparisons did not justify a general shift to 'more market and less government'.

In 'The comparative performance of public and private ownership' in Lord Roll of Ipsden (ed.) *The Mixed Economy* (1982) pp. 58–93, Robert Millward surveyed some of the same American and a number of other British and American examples. He found a number of public producers with lower unit costs than their private equivalents. Like the American reviewers he found wide variations within as well as between the sectors. Other conditions (scale, input prices, the nature of the industry, the presence or absence of competition) often seemed to affect performance more than public or private ownership did. On stronger grounds than those of the German-American reviewers Millward came to similar conclusions: judgements of comparative efficiency vary with the chosen criteria of efficiency, but by any of the commonly used tests 'there seems no general ground for believing managerial efficiency is less in public firms' (p. 83).

Public choice theorists have drawn different conclusions from much the same evidence. Reviewing the same studies and some others on pp. 261–6 of *Public Choice II* in 1989, Dennis C. Mueller concluded that 'the evidence that public provision of a service reduces the efficiency of its provision seems overwhelming'. The first three overwhelming items were these:

(1) An Australian private airline is said to have had 'efficiency indices 12–100 per cent higher' than its public competitor. Mueller does not disclose that the (unsubsidized, profitable) public airline had previously competed the private line to the brink of insolvency. The conservative government wanted the private line to survive. R.M. Ansett took it over, ordered some Lockheed propjets for it because he did not believe its pilots could convert straight from piston engines to pure jets, then persuaded the government to do four things for him. It forced its public airline to exchange some existing aircraft with him, to his advantage. It blocked the import of the fast French jets the public airline was about to buy. It allowed the import of Ansett's slower propjets. It forced the public airline to buy the

same propjets, some way behind Ansett in the delivery queue. And it forbade any future competition between the two in either aircraft type or fares. Those were the conditions, unmentioned by Mueller, in which Ansett recorded higher profits for a while. Whether they actually indicated greater efficiency is doubted by some critics: Ansett's corporate accounting makes it difficult to compare like with like, i.e. a segment of a diversified transport conglomerate with a single-purpose public airline.

(2)   The same airlines are compared again six years later with the same result. Mueller does not report that often since that time, and continuously for some years up to his publication date, the public airline has been more profitable than the private. A year after Australia deregulated its air traffic the public airline was still posting steady profits and the private airline frequent losses. The multinational owners of the private line have been trying to sell it, without success. The government is selling both its lines – the successful domestic competitor and the international Qantas which in its 70 years of life, 50 in public ownership, has been unsubsidized, consistently profitable, and alone among the major internationals has never lost a life.

(3)   A 1982 study compares one public with one private Australian bank. Mueller reports that 'sign and magnitude of all indices of productivity, response to risk, and profitability favor private banks', unobtrusively generalizing from his one case to 'banks'. The 'productivity and response to risk' of the one private bank in the study have since landed it with many millions more bad debts than its public competitor. During 1992 its share price fell by a third, its chief executive and half its board resigned, and it was for a time under investigation for suspicion of unethical practice. We await Mueller's next edition with interest, to see which public banks (French? Swedish? Norwegian?) he selects for comparison with the deregulated performance of America's private Savings and Loans institutions.

Mueller's first three items probably misrepresent the quality of the rest, many of which (though too often selective) are by competent investigators. The truth is that public and private efficiencies are not fixed facts of life, they change. We will notice that British coal and steel producers have been at different times among the least profitable and the most profitable in western Europe, and the transformations from worst to best were effected by public owners. Public Renault's and private Fiat's sales have leapfrogged more than once over the years. And so on.

If the facts reveal no intrinsic superiority, does it follow that theories about the comparative efficiency of public and private enterprise are useless? Not necessarily. If theories draw attention to distinctive potentialities and hazards of each mode they may encourage the improvement of each, and of relations between them. The worst effect of a rigid belief in the superiority of either mode is that it encourages reformers to concentrate on shifting activity from one mode to the other, rather than on improving the quality of either. Socialists concentrate on nationalizing, liberals on privatizing, each accepting the characteristics of public and private enterprise as given and unimprovable. In real life both modes vary from excellent to terrible, and theories about their distinct potentialities can be useful if they focus on ways and means of improving each, and on questions about the best role for each in mixed economies in particular circumstances and with particular social purposes. The purposes may matter as much as the circumstances do. For example Hungarians, Swedes and Americans, wanting different social effects, may well vote for different mixtures of public and private enterprise – but may all benefit from improvements in each mode.

It may therefore be worth while to explore the reasons why people expect public and private enterprise to have different efficiencies and inefficiencies.

QUESTIONS

If private ownership is thought to be better than public, is it better at what, for whom, by what criteria? If (for example) public bus services break even serving everybody, while private services have lower costs, make profits, but fail to serve some residents at awkward locations, which is more efficient? A government clothing factory makes service uniforms which could be imported a little cheaper. It employs women in a steel town which has few other jobs for them. Without it the nation would have more unemployed, less output and a worse balance of payments. Is it an inefficient investment?

Is the argument about ownership – so that government ownership of Renault Motors or (from time to time) British Steel makes them public enterprises? Or is the argument about profit-seeking – so that Renault and British Steel count as private enterprises whoever owns them? (If so, could a whole capitalist system operate without private owners?)

Or is the argument about market relations, i.e. about the difference between producers like Renault and British Steel which charge their customers for their products and tax-financed producers like public hospitals and schools which don't?

Is the argument about individual enterprises' performance, or the performance of whole economic systems with different proportions of public ownership?

Finally are these sensible questions to ask in such general terms, expecting answers true for all cases? British Steel has been Europe's worst and then its best steelmaker; the richest countries include the United States and Japan with the smallest public sectors and Sweden with the biggest; so why should we expect *any* simple generalizations about public and private performance to be reliable over time, or from industry to industry, or from country to country?

This chapter will review some popular and some theoretical reasons why people expect public enterprise to be less efficient than private. What kinds of efficiency are meant? Why are public enterprises expected to be unresponsive to their customers' wants? Why are their work incentives expected to be poor? Why should slack public enterprises be harder to reform or replace then slack private ones? And what sort of theory about public and private enterprise might serve mixed economies best?

CRITERIA OF EFFICIENCY

Investigators of the efficiency of public enterprises face two initial difficulties. First, efficiency is not matter-of-fact, it is a slippery, value-structured concept – but to say so can look like an attempt to evade simple, commonsense tests of efficiency. Second, public enterprises often have multiple purposes and ought to be judged by the efficiency with which they serve all their purposes, not just one of them – but that argument also can be misused to excuse poor performance, for example to dismiss valid comparisons with private enterprises which serve the same purposes at less cost. We should resist those tricks – but at the same time remember that they misuse arguments which are valid when used honestly. Efficiency *is* a word with alternative meanings, all value-structured. Public enterprises *do* often and rightly have multiple purposes. In what follows, both themes should be understood in their honest, not their evasive, usages.

We will try to clarify the subject in a 'Yes, but ...' way. (Begin with the simplest idea of efficiency. Yes, but notice its limitations. They suggest alternative, more complex concepts of efficiency. Yes, but notice *their* shortcomings. And so on.)

First, efficient can mean at least cost. This is the commonest and for many practical purposes the best test of efficiency. If rival producers compete to make steel, to build the same model of house, to provide the same rubbish removal service, or to can the same tonnage of peaches, the least-cost performer is the most efficient. If the industrial conditions are such that all the competitors have to use the same inputs at the same prices, those who achieve the lowest costs must do so by 'pure' efficiency, i.e. by the methods which get most output from given resources with least waste of time, effort or materials.

But such pure comparisons are rare. In practice products are not exactly comparable (lower costs may mean poorer quality) or producers don't all face the same input prices. The world's steelmakers pay a wide range of prices for their coal, iron ore and labour. Among house-builders one may do best because he manages to pay his workers less. One rubbish remover may do best because he uses cheap old trucks. One fruit canner may do best because she owns her business free of debt and has no interest to pay. The builder is using cheaper labour than his competitors, the dustman is using cheaper equipment, the canner is using cheaper money; you have to discount those advantages before you can judge the pure efficiency with which they use their resources.

But a profit-seeking producer may not want to discount those advantages: low costs may look efficient however they're achieved. In any case it may be efficient management which gets the cheaper inputs. A good builder may use quite a lot of apprentice labour (helping the apprentices and the economy, as well as his costs, by training them). A rational dustman chooses cheap old rather than smart new trucks. A prudent food processor finances her cannery with equity rather than debt capital. Efficiency can apply to the choice and procurement of productive resources as well as their use.

But cheap inputs can alternatively come by luck or misbehaviour: East Asian dictatorships make their steelworkers work longer hours for less pay than West European democracies do. A housebuilder may cut costs by using unqualified tradesmen. A rubbish contractor's defective old trucks may afflict his workers and the neighbourhoods they serve with grit and dust. A cannery may be debt-free by inheritance rather than good management. Low costs don't *necessarily* signify efficient production.

There is similar ambiguity in relations between efficiency and market strength. Marketing can be done more or less efficiently. Efficient marketing may in turn improve productive efficiency if it increases volume and economies of scale. If it builds market strength, it may encourage directors to risk more investment in research and development, which may add to the efficiency of the firm and the economy as a whole. But market strength may also allow big producers to underpay their suppliers and overprice their products, efficiently for their owners but inefficiently for everyone else.

When production has multiple purposes there may be double trouble. It is usually easier to judge how well it serves some purposes than others; and judgements of its overall efficiency depend on social judgements – value judgements, likely to be disagreed – about the relative importance of the various purposes. Analysts may be tempted to give most weight to things like costs and profits which can be readily measured, and least to things like environmental quality or workers' job-satisfaction which are harder either to measure or to agree about.

In real life these difficulties are often complicated, but they can be illustrated by a simple example. There was a time when Sweden, Norway and Australia staffed their suburban trams or trains as follows: each Swedish and Australian vehicle carried a driver only, each Norwegian vehicle also had a conductor. The Norwegian conductor cost more than the Swedes' and Australians' alternative methods of collecting fares; Sweden paid the highest wages; so the order of cost per vehicle mile ran from Norway (dearest) to Australia (cheapest). The order of costs per passenger journey and per passenger mile was different because of the countries' different urban patterns. Australia had big, sprawling cities with a low density of population; that made for long journeys, long walks from home and workplace to the nearest transport stop, infrequent schedules, and a strong preference for private motoring. Norway had similar problems on different scale with its pattern of medium and small-sized cities. Sweden's train services were in a few densely populated cities which made for efficient public transport routes, frequent services, short distances from transport stops to home and workplace, and heavy use of the service. Sweden had the lowest costs per passenger journey and passenger mile; Norway came next per passenger journey, Australia per passenger mile. There were other differences in the quality and equity of the services. In Sweden and Australia some aged and handicapped people and some young children could not use the transport because there were no conductors to help them. That had worse effects in Australia than in Sweden – Swedish passengers were as well-behaved without conductors as Norwegians with them, but Australian trains without conductors were often vandalized and sometimes dangerous at night, so others besides the physically handicapped were afraid to use them. That was an effect of different cultures rather than management, though the Australian managers should perhaps have adapted better to the culture with which they had to work. At providing transport accessible to everyone the Norwegians were most efficient and the Australians least.

Economists who distinguish 'efficient' from 'effective' might prefer to call the Norwegian service the least efficient but most effective. That makes efficient mean cheapest – but even that can be ambiguous, depending on whose efficiency is noticed. Nationally, the Norwegian conductors were not as expensive as they seemed. Sweden and Australia had very full employment at the time, so hiring conductors might well have reduced output in other industries – but Norway had some unemployment, so the conductors weren't depriving other industries of labour. Sacking them would put some of them on the dole and increase other welfare costs, so the cost of their useful services was actually less than their wages.

Thus to compare the efficiency of those services it is necessary to get the facts right, but also to take sides in a number of conflicts of interest and social purpose. The multiple purposes of public transport services don't excuse any inefficiencies, but they do make some of the efficiencies difficult and contentious to measure and compare.

Notice that the difficulties are not peculiar to public enterprises. There is a sense in which all enterprises are multi-purposed. Profit-seeking firms have to serve many of their workers' and customers' purposes in order to serve their own, and the law requires them to serve many communal purposes. A firm which cuts its own costs by unloading them onto workers, neighbours or government services may be efficient for its owners but not for the economy as a whole; if its directors or hard-bargaining workers manage to preempt the gains it may not even be efficient for its owners. Suppose that some improvement in the 'pure' efficiency of (say) material-handling allows gains which all go to higher wages, leaving the firm's unit costs of production the same as before. Do you conclude that there has been no gain in overall efficiency – or that efficiency has improved and allowed some better distribution of income? (Or worse distribution, depending on your idea of distributive justice.) The argument is back where it began, asking 'efficient at what, for whose purposes?'

Judgments of efficiency are vital. Business and government can't work without them. The available tests range from hard to soft, objective to subjective, certain to uncertain. But the hard tests don't necessarily measure the most important qualities, and the choice of measures and tests is always a social choice – value-structured, advantaging some people and purposes more than others, open to honest disagreement.

CONSUMER SOVEREIGNTY

Many public enterprises – oil, coal and steel producers, carmakers, airlines and others – have paid their way in competitive industries. They concern this section only as practical disproofs of the belief that public ownership necessarily kills competitive purpose and performance. What follows relates only to the (many) public activities which *can* survive without treating their customers properly. That kind of enterprise is rightly condemned when it is insensitive to the proper wants of the people it is meant to serve.

When public suppliers neglect their customers' preferences, mostly wrongly but sometimes rightly, it is for reasons of five general kinds. The suppliers are lazy or incompetent. They are selfish, arranging their work for their own rather than the customers' convenience. They are doing their duty, rightly refusing demands for things the customers are not entitled to. They can't do the work properly because mean politicians afraid of mean taxpayers won't finance them properly. Or they are reformers who believe they know the customers' or the society's interests better than the customers do. Not all of the last is bad – it may often be right to supply people with better education, research and information, public health, building safety, fire protection, water quality or women's shelters than they thought they wanted.

The theories which we oppose should be confronted at their best, and where their supporting evidence is strongest. Some of the best (i.e. worst) examples of public defiance of customers' interests can be found in some British, American and Australian public housing provisions of the 1950s and 1960s, and they led some experts, notably Alice Coleman whose work is cited below, to condemn all public housing as unnecessary and unlikely to help its tenants much. Most of the sins listed above – ignorance, bureaucratic self-service, mistaken good intentions – contributed to producing dreadful public housing, some of which began to be demolished within a decade or two of being built. It is scarcely necessary now to spell out what was wrong with segregating large numbers of hard-up households and stacking them into massive towers and wall-blocks of identical apartments. None of those barracks' intended residents were consulted about their design; most were offered no alternative to them if they wanted public housing at all. The public recoil from the new estates was correct: the bigger the developments, the more uniform and anonymous the apartments, the more apartments served by each entrance, lift, corridor or balcony, the more alternative exits and entrances there were, the more bridges from block to block, and the more ambiguous land there was, neither clearly private nor clearly public, for parking and recreation, the more the residents suffered from crime, vandalism, truancy, drug abuse, illness, domestic violence, family breakdown, unemployment, debt and measurable unhappiness. The authorities responsible for the developments never monitored those effects, and when others did, most of the authorities continued to deny that the housing forms had anything to do with the bad behaviour. But the evidence was at length conclusive, especially for New York in Oscar Newman's *Defensible Space* (1972) and for London and Oxford in Alice Coleman's *Utopia on Trial* (1985): bad design can, and in those communities did, increase some people's bad behaviour and many people's unhappiness.

The authorities had also neglected the taxpayers' interests. Less land or money or both could often have housed the tenants better. The British towers used more land and subsidy per resident than the more popular housing forms they displaced. The costs of the Melbourne towers could have bought their tenants capacious houses and gardens in middle-class suburbs.

What prompted such blunders? Untested theories, mostly by architects and town planners who read no social theory and did no social or economic research, led bureaucrats to delude themselves and their politicians about the physical, financial and social costs of their proposals. Some British bureaucrats wanted to increase house-building by using some heavy constructive capacity as well as the country's cottage-building capacity. They may have been influenced by the big builders who alone could bid for the big contracts. Some may also have liked the way the big projects both magnified and simplified their tasks. All those errors depended on the initial sin of ignoring the customers' preferences.

If those were unalterable characteristics of public enterprise its critics would be right enough. But they are not. Even in public housing they are not. In Britain the offending policies were never adopted by Buckinghamshire and some other local authorities. While the Melbourne towers were building, the other Australian states continued to build the cottage forms their public tenants preferred. Through the same decades West European governments gave massive aid to house-building in the forms which were traditional and popular in their cities. So even in their heyday the giant Anglo-American-Australian mistakes were exceptions rather than the rule in the Western world. The mistakes have been researched, lessons learned, policies reversed and many of the relevant officials replaced. Meanwhile before and since, the Western world has continued to have many good public landlords. They leave no excuse for bad ones, or for theories that all public landlords must be bad. But their good performance is not automatic. The lessons that have been learned need to be built into the educational curriculum and kept in mind by politicians, public landlords, press and public.

Even at their best, public landlords have one group of dissatisfied customers of theoretical interest: those who don't get the housing they want because the landlord thinks they are not entitled to it, or other customers have prior rights or more urgent needs for it. So customers are frustrated for the third and most respectable of the reasons listed earlier: there's not enough of the resource to satisfy them all. The effect may be unavoidable wherever public supplies not only improve the supply of necessary goods but also change the principles of distribution and the customers' expectations; it is quite possible to create both better housing and greater 'housing dissatisfaction'. The dissatisfaction may be re-directed rather than new. Hard-up ill-housed people who used to blame themselves or rapacious landlords or impersonal market forces for not housing them satisfactorily now blame the government. The shift from market to administrative allocation creates the presumption that the alloca-tion of the goods ought to be fair. That is not a bad presumption to create, but the principles of fairness and some of their individual applications are likely to be disagreed. That is a common cost of resorting to administrative allocation. The disputes may give public enterprise a bad name, but leaving hard-up customers to the cruelties of the market may be a worse neglect of their needs and preferences.

When public suppliers maltreat their customers *without* good reason, the misbehaviour often owes more to monopoly than to public ownership. Both public and private operators can exploit natural monopolies – fran-chised private utilities and their public equivalents have both included good, bad and indifferent performers. The bad public ones don't justify privatizing them all, any more than the bad private ones justify nationaliz-ing them all – it is more sensible to improve both modes. Some public monopolies – in transport, health, education, research, policing, air traffic control, weather forecasting, rescue work and other necessary services – have been positively inventive in responding to their customers' needs. Designers and reformers of such services should study the good performers at least as carefully as the bad.

An enterprise's sensitivity to its customers' wants generally depends, like other elements of its efficiency, on conditions of which its type of own-ership is only one and not necessarily the most important. Is it a monopolist or a competitor? Are its customers other firms and tough bargainers, or are they consumers and if so are they experienced shoppers, or once-only homebuyers or first-time carbuyers? Do they have much market strength or political influence? Does the nature of the work tempt workers to maltreat their customers, or inspire them to treat them well? The attention to cus-tomers' wants – both face-to-face, and in strategic allocative and produc-tive decisions – depends on many other things than merely the type of ownership; and among public enterprises it can vary widely with the nature of the industry and the work, the quality of management and staff, the available resources and the relevant policy decisions.

All that is or ought to be common knowledge. But prejudices for and against public employment persist so obstinately that it may be worth emphasizing the range of behaviour to be found within the public sector by citing two limiting cases. The first is a regional water board whose employees' unions enforced a rule that to turn a stop-cock out of working hours took four men: one to turn the tap, a driver to get him there, a security officer to open and close the relevant gates, and (because any three require it) a fourth to supervise, all at penalty rates. At the other end of the spectrum is an elderly professor of history whom we know well. He is close to retirement, and also to finishing a distinguished book on a hot subject. He has nothing material to gain or lose by the quality of his teaching through his remaining years. It could be boring or perfunctory without penalty. He has exactly the lack of material incentive that market theorists fear in public employees. But his teaching continues to be exceptionally gifted, inventive and productive, and he would regard with amused contempt any banal economist who wondered why. Market theorists should keep the professor in mind; socialist theorists should remember the regional Water Board; the public sector's customer-care ranges all the way from the one to the other – but not in any regular way which could be predicted from axiomatic theory about public ownership. Neither of those limiting cases was predetermined, each was a choice: there are also slothful academics, and excellent public utilities.

Finally, although public monopolies neglect their customers' wants worse and oftener than competitive private enterprises do, they rarely do them as much active harm as the worst private enterprises do. Public banks and businesses don't fail to pay. Public enterprises don't sell gullible customers gold bricks – shares in fraudulent companies, building blocks on swampland, used cars with cracked engine blocks and gearboxes full of sawdust, useless therapies, flammable nighties, violent pornography. In advertising and other efforts to shape rather than serve the customers' preferences, public enterprises probably do less harm than the worst private operators do. So some at least of the unresponsiveness of the stodgier public services is worth having, including their discouragement of the customers' more anti-social or self-destructive desires.

To summarize:

Plenty of public enterprises which market their goods and services are as attentive to their markets as their private equivalents are.

Public monopolies with some choice about how they treat their customers vary as widely as private enterprises do, though in partly-different directions. Some of the best public services can plan further ahead, risk more research and development, and respond more inventively to their customers' needs than competitive profit-seekers can afford to do. But many public monopolies have been less responsive to their customers' wants – especially to changing wants – than market-disciplined enterprises, public or private, can afford to be. But public enterprises are rarely as predatory or dishonest with customers as the worst private operators are.

Many other things besides the type of ownership and the degree of monopoly contribute to the responsiveness of public enterprises to their customers' wants. As with other elements of their performance, much depends on the motivation of the public employees.

INCENTIVES IN THEORY AND PRACTICE

The theory that directors and workers in public enterprises have poorer incentives than their private equivalents has two main bases. First, because they don't have to seek profits or fear losses as private owners do, public managers can be lazy and unenterprising; and because they can, some will. Second, public employees can bargain for more pay for less work at tax-payers' expense so there is no necessary link between how well they work and how much they earn, whereas private firms' employees must bargain for shares of market earnings which depend partly on their own per-formance, so there is both an incentive to work well and a market limit to the amount the workers can expect to get.

Most argument about those beliefs is practical, as ours will be. But first, they have obvious flaws as deductive theories. If owners' incentives are what matter, the theory should compare enterprises which are managed by their owners with enterprises which are not. It would then expect small owner-managed firms to be efficient, but big private as well as public enter-prises – all those with salaried directors – to be equally *in*efficient. If (to avoid that implication) it is assumed that the usual institutional arrange-ments – competitive appointment and promotion, bonus and other incen-tive payments, etc. – will induce salaried directors to make their owners' interests their own, that also should be equally true in public and private enterprises. So the argument must return to the nature of the owners' incen-tives. As to them, the theory simply cheats by smuggling in a 'vacant set': its premise is that private owners have a profit-seeking incentive which public owners do not have. That could only support the ensuing deductions if there were a further premise that profit-seeking is the only incentive there is, or the only way owners can benefit materially from owning. In practice that is false. In principle the theory should compare like with like: the incentives one group *has* with the incentives the other group *has*. Its rea-soning could then compare the behaviour to be expected of profit-seekers with the behaviour to be expected of politicians, or perhaps the electors to whom politicians owe their pay and prospects, with their different incen-tives. If theorists assume that the two groups are similarly self-interested it is not clear why they are expected to behave very differently: profit-seekers have to compete by motivating their managers to produce better goods at lower market prices, while politicians have to compete for votes by motivating their managers to produce better public goods at lower tax prices. In theory each seems as likely as the other to want best goods at least cost and to select and reward their managers accordingly.

There is a similar flaw in the theory that workers can extract better pay and conditions from public employers because government has more resources than market-disciplined firms have. Here the concealed assumption is that superior resources will always be used to meet workers' demands, never to fight them. But public resources which can afford losses in unprofitable enterprises can equally afford losses from industrial conflict. Faced with strikes or hard bargainers, government can afford to hold out for longer and can mobilize more kinds of anti-strike action than most private employers can. Without any stated premise about how resources will be used, the theory leaves government as likely to underpay its employees as to overpay them.

Executives however are different. The private sector commonly pays more – nowadays much more – at the top. Whatever that does to executives' performance once they're hired, it makes it likely that the private sector has more than its share of the best talent. The executive rewards may not have much effect on initial recruitment, when rates of pay are much the same in both sectors and private employment may be less secure. There is a surer indication in the disproportionate flows between the sectors later on. In the English-speaking countries many more middle and upper managers move from public employment to private than from private to public. Various attractions and preferences keep *some* of the very best in the public sector; but when allowance has been made for that, and for the unequal flows to be expected because of the unequal size of the sectors, it still seems likely that the private sector attracts more than its pro-rata share of the highest executive talent. The imbalance is hard to correct. Government has some good reasons for restraining its executives' pay. There may be a case for introducing some public restraints on private pay. We will return to the problem below, under 'Directors' incentives'.

On incentives generally, practice is usually a better guide than theory. Public services do include examples of all the incentive problems and consequent bad performance that their critics allege. Public policy-makers and managers should be aware of them, design systems to minimize them, take all possible precautions against them. Nevertheless the incentive problems don't justify a general distrust of public enterprise, for a number of reasons. First, they only afflict some activities; many other activities go as well in either sector, some go best in the public sector. Where the problems are, they are not all incurable; we will presently instance some once-poor public enterprises which have revolutionized their performance. The public hazards should anyway be weighed against the incentive problems of the private sector when considering the best mix for a mixed economy. Finally the motivation of work is actually so complex, and can vary so widely from culture to culture, industry to industry and job to job, that intelligent chiefs in both sectors have learned to design quite intricate 'incentive mixtures' *within* their industries and enterprises. The simple belief that insecurity, competition and fear of the sack motivate all the best work including most of the work of the private sector, while security and seniority motivate all the worst work including most of the work of the public sector, has never guided the directors of either Toyota Motors or the National Health Service, whose incentive arrangements we will presently sketch. To grasp their reasons it will be convenient to compare some incentive problems first of workers in the two sectors, then of directors in the two sectors.

WORKERS' INCENTIVES

We need not repeat our earlier discussion of the complexity of work incentives and motivation in the real world. Employees' behaviour is affected by the prevailing cultures of the society and the enterprise, by individual personality, by the scale of the enterprise and the amount of bureaucratic coordination that it necessitates, by the ease or difficulty and the interest or tedium of the work, by the human relations which the work entails, by the quality of management, and by other conditions, as well as by the standard material incentives of desire for money, hope of promotion and fear of the sack. Critics of public enterprise, like economists, generally focus on the last three. Two of them – desires for pay and promotion – don't necessarily differ from sector to sector: the workers did not suffer a personality change each time a British car manufacturer passed from private to public ownership or back to private. There are many occupations in which, because of the nature of the work, the ordinary sticks and carrots work as well (or badly, if badly managed) in either sector. There is rarely much difference between the performance of signalmen on public and private railroads, drivers of public and private buses, tellers in public and private banks, pilots and technical staff in public and private airlines, nurses in public and private hospitals, musicians in public and private orchestras, performers and technicians in public and private theatre, opera and ballet companies; and so on. There are also occupations which go better in public than in profit-seeking employment: politicians, judges, police, soldiers and some others need to be protected from material temptations; social workers, educators and researchers are expected to serve other purposes as well as, or instead of, enriching themselves by giving their customers exactly what they want.

There remain two large groups of public employees who have often enough earned public employment its bad name. There are masses of clerical and other public servants whose work is dull (so it is hard to inspire them) and often also difficult to measure, or supervise closely (so it is hard to discipline them). They may start late and finish early, with much sociable chatter and private telephoning and long tea-breaks; they may be rude, oppressive or inattentive to customers; they may misuse rights to overtime, flexitime, living and travelling allowances, study leave, sick leave and invalidity and pension entitlements. Some adventurous spirits have even run private enterprises – escort agencies, bookmaking, research and consultant services – from their public offices with generous use of public equipment and services. The second unpopular group – sometimes with reason, sometimes not – have been workers in industries like British steel and coal and some public utilities, in which strong unions have sometimes enforced staffing levels and work practices which unreasonably restrict productivity.

Most abuses of the first kind afflict public activities which in practice can't be privatized, so the question is not whether profit-seeking alternatives would be better but whether and how the public performance can be improved. It can usually be improved. There are good models – public services have many hardworking and effective divisions and individuals. Some of the branches of government which allowed a lot of bad behaviour were old, unmodernized and under-educated when they offended. Some others were recent creations with inexperienced designers and managers. Experience has prompted reviews, reconstructions and better performance. There are higher educational standards, more competition for entry and promotion, provisions for continuing study and retraining. Working rules, measures of performance and accountability have been improved. Employees' confidential dossiers, which were originally opened to them at their behest for their protection, now shame some sinners into better behaviour. Some bureaucracies have been humanized a little with flatter structures, more consultation, a friendlier culture within the service and a cultivated 'culture of service' in customer relations. Organizational changes produce smaller, more coherent working groups and give them more responsibility. Many of these developments aim to improve incentives and job satisfaction for people doing intrinsically dull work. The effects are not always measured, or measurable. Our own experience in public offices and trading enterprises, and our reading of the growing literature of public management, suggest that there has been a good deal of improvement. A lot of stodgy public service continues but (in democracies with developed economies) culpably lazy, inefficient or unnecessary public activity is rarer than it was.

The second much-criticized group has been organized labour in some public industries. As in the private sector, by no means all union action has harmed the industries' efficiency. It has often improved health, safety, working conditions and industrial cooperation in wholly desirable ways. Where it has enforced more secure employment, that has sometimes improved efficiency as well as justice. Wage pressures have encouraged modernizing investment. And so on. But there have also been uses of union power which were undoubtedly hostile to the employers' (i.e. the taxpayers') interests, to productivity and technical progress, and sometimes to other workers, notably women. From those experiences also, lessons have been learned.

We invite attention to one lesson from which we believe that people Left of centre have learned less than they should. Through the 1970s the British government starved its steel and coal producers of capital and – partly because they valued full employment more than higher pay – those industries' unions resisted some of what little modernization the government did attempt. That did not justify any general conclusions about union behaviour in public industries – public miners across the Channel were welcoming modernization, private miners in the US were getting higher pay and less underground work than public miners anywhere. But what some called 'the British disease' did encourage conservative critics to depict the government's and the unions' short sight as a normal effect of public ownership. Ironically it was then by believers in that theory that it was dramatically falsified. Through the 1980s the government revolutionized both industries by forceful means including what the press called 'smashing' the miners' union. Perhaps the union was foolishly led. Certainly its ordeal and defeat had grievous consequences for tens of thousands of miners, their families, and the life of some of the towns their industry had sustained. It was understandable that the anger and compassion of the Left should focus on those effects. With hindsight many now agree that the industries had to be modernized somehow, some day, and that unions willing to negotiate the changes could have won better terms for their members than they got by fighting to the death. What has not been as widely celebrated as it deserves to be, *especially* on the Left, is the death of the theory of public incompetence. A public owner turned Western Europe's least profitable steel producer into its most profitable. It has always had one or a few extremely efficient, up-to-date plants: its poor overall performance arose from using them for limited hours (or sometimes not at all) while keeping old plant going, under government or union pressure, for regional and employment purposes. But when the revolution came in the 1980s, none of the theorized hindrances prevented it. The unions failed to block it. The government financed expensive, forward-looking modernization. And far from perpetuating inefficient or unnecessary activities it closed outdated steelworks and coal pits quite ruthlessly. Government can learn – and when it does, its direction of its productive enterprises can be more single-minded, far-sighted and effective than either the mostly-powerless shareholders or the self-perpetuating boards of directors of many big private corporations have managed to be.

For the theory that unions would always be stronger against public than against private employers there was never much evidence outside Britain and Australia. There is even less since the 1980s saw the British government defy some of the strongest unions, and the Australian government negotiate, through its 'Accord' with organized labour, nine years' continuous reduction of real wages in both sectors of the economy. In its assumptions about union strength, both halves of the theory of public incompetence are often wrong. Politicians have strong competitive incentives to cut costs and improve services wherever they can. And private employers' capacity to pass costs on to their customers can also vary: it can be elastic if the firms or their workers have some monopolist strength, if the demand for their products is inelastic, if they can persuade government to tax or protect them differently, and so on.

A final error in the theory is its assumption that public employment is secure and bureaucratic while private employment is insecure and competitive. In fact there is a wide variety of tenures in both sectors, and much of the best performance in both is achieved by contriving deft 'incentive mixtures'. Some of the public 'mix' takes deliberate account of the incentive difficulties the critics of public enterprise have in mind. For example it is true that public enterprises have rarely managed to build economically, so sensible governments get most of their building done by competitive tender by private contractors. Within each sector some work is done best by securely employed people, some by more casual or competitive workers, some by self-employed suppliers of goods and services. To illustrate how 'dappled' the incentive patterns of the best public and private enterprises can be, we conclude this section with sketches of the incentive arrangements for workers in Britain's National Health Service, and for the workers who make Toyota cars.

The National Health Service employs most of its hospital workers on much the same terms as private hospitals do. Nurses and other service staff are salaried. Cleaners are salaried by the hospitals or by their cleaning contractors. Repairs and maintenance are usually done by independent tradespeople. The significant differences between modes of employment in public and private health services are almost all in the employment of doctors and some other professionals.

Where health services are private, doctors have commonly charged fees for service: so much for each visit, each specialist consultation, each therapeutic procedure. That might be thought to limit their fees to what their patients can afford, but it does so only indirectly. Hospital and specialist services can be so expensive that most users of private health services insure against their costs. The cost levels determine the insurance premiums, but it is by the insurance companies rather than the patients that any direct market discipline has to be applied to doctors' fees. If they take a business view, insurers don't have to keep their premiums within everyone's capacity to pay: high rates from two thirds or three quarters of the population may well yield more than whatever basic rate the whole population could pay. Up to the point at which higher premiums would lose more revenue than they gained, the insurers will make more money the more the doctors charge and the more over-servicing they do; and when patients have paid their premiums they too may have no strong incentive to limit their demand for services. Fee levels established in those conditions then influence the terms on which governments must, by one means or another, engage doctors to attend the uninsured poor. Where private medicine prevails in affluent societies, doctors do well and health costs take a comparatively high percentage of national income.

The British service provides uneven hospital services but medical services comparable with the best, at unusually low cost: about 7 or 8 per cent of national income, compared with America's 12 or more. Part of the saving comes, regrettably, from under-financing Britain's hospitals. The rest comes from effects of the National Health Service on doctors' incomes and doctors' and patients' incentives. The arrangements have been much modified since their introduction in 1948, but they still offer three basic ways for doctors to earn their livings. Private practice, setting their own fees, is open to any doctors and patients who want it. Within the national service, financed from taxation, family doctors are paid capitation, i.e. an annual rate for each patient on their list, adjusted to encourage them to accept an optimum number, neither too few nor too many. Third, there is a national structure of salaried hospital and specialist jobs, for which doctors apply (and compete) as vacancies occur. The capitation fees for family doctors, and the salary scales for everyone from hospital interns to eminent heads of clinical teams and departments, are negotiated nationally.

Many modifications to those basic arrangements have been designed to refine the doctors' and patients' incentives. Examples: for some services which family doctors can alternatively do themselves or refer to specialists, capitation may encourage the use of specialists; to reduce that expensive bias a little but not too much, some fees for service are available as supplements to capitation. When compulsory 'apprenticeships' were introduced for general practitioners, doctors who took pupils earned supplements. Other supplements reward seniority and higher qualifications, service in some sparsely populated and some inner city districts, and some specific standards of preventive medicine. As it became harder for doctors to afford the capital costs of the premises which the best practice was coming to require, the government began to build and let (to those who wanted them) health centres in which doctors could practice under the same roof with paramedical and welfare services.

There is some light external discipline. There are tribunals to which patients can complain about their doctors. (They can also change doctors, so there is some each of administrative and market discipline.) Doctors and patients with no contrary incentives sometimes choose expensive treatments where cheaper ones would do, or (from ignorance) worse treatments where better ones are available. So the Health Service monitors some statistics of its members' practices, and may question any that look questionable, medically or financially.

Through all the fine tuning, and bargaining over pay and conditions, the basic incentive principles persist. Specialists who get their work from other doctors are salaried. They also get their appointments and promotions from committees chiefly of other doctors. Doctors who get their work directly from the public, so have to be chosen by patients rather than by other doctors, are paid chiefly for the number of patients they care for rather than the number of things they do or prescribe for them. Incentive considerations are delicately balanced in that arrangement. It leaves doctors and patients free to choose one another, while encouraging doctors to accept plenty of patients. Because patients get free care a few are inclined to demand too much of it. If the government were paying fees for each service, doctors might be tempted to comply; capitation ensures that their principles are reinforced by their self-interest in avoiding unnecessary work. (In theory, doctors wanting to attract more patients to their lists might be over-indulgent – but in practice patients who demand unreasonable time and attention are not worth the capitation they bring.) Capitation encourages preventive care: both parties benefit if doctors teach patients to keep healthy.

There has been some replacement of market incentives by administrative controls. There are now re-training requirements, restrictions on part-time doctoring, financial rewards for specified standards of preventive medicine and for doctors who do their own night visits. Some of the changes may not be worth their costs: they irritate doctors who were practising well without them, they divert doctors' time from medicine to record-keeping, they have substantial accounting costs.

But those changes are marginal. The original principles of the Health Service survive. Its incentive arrangements for doctors tend to be negative or neutral – they chiefly avoid encouraging bad practice, or interfering with the doctors' independence as clinicians. They still offer comparatively little in the way of positive sticks and carrots or bureaucratic accountability. How can public employees in a vast national institution be allowed such independence? The fact is that doctors are specially adaptable to public management because they need so little of *any* management. Whether salaried or self-employed they combine unusual individual independence with an unusual capacity to supply their own quality controls, in quite tough and effective forms. To most who choose it, their work is attractive and satisfying, in human and professional ways. Together with hot competition and high qualifications for entry, that fills the profession with able people who enjoy their work. The divisions of labour which happen to be functionally efficient – between patients, nurses, pharmacists, paramedicals, general practitioners, specialists, and in a number of those occupations between partners, seniors and juniors, members of teams – happen also to ensure expert mutual scrutiny, direct or indirect, of most of the work. A strong professional culture encourages independence and candour, mostly accepted as uninsulting, in consultant opinions which are often, necessarily, opinions about other doctors' work. Thus doctors supply most of their own discipline, accountability and quality control. In the National Health Service they do it with fewer contrary temptations than they might face in private practice. Their professional autonomy is reinforced by the secure tenure which most of them achieve. Their tenure, autonomy, and comparative freedom from bureaucratic management are important conditions of their good, low-cost performance, and testify to the intelligence with which this exceptionally efficient public institution was designed, nearly half a century ago, to give its customers such value for money: more for less than from any other national medical system, public or private, in the affluent world.

With the incentive mix in that public service, compare the mix employed by a supremely successful private manufacturer. About a third of the workers who make Toyota cars are securely employed, usually for their working lifetimes, by the company. In return for its commitment to them the company expects strong commitment *from* them – to each other, the product and the company. That sort of commitment is powerful in itself, and it reduces the need for more expensive incentives, including supervision: the more the productive workers can be their own and each other's quality controllers, the better.

Why do secure lifetime employment and respect for seniority, condemned by almost all critics of public services, serve some of the world's most competitive private enterprises better than the flexible, anxiously competitive 'labour market' of economists' imagination? There are two main reasons. First, complex design and manufacturing operations, like other activities which demand high skills and continuous innovation, use many skills which are specific to particular products, processes, and directions of product and process development. Market leaders stay ahead at least as much by continuous marginal improvements as by occasional 'great leaps forward'. Such skills tend to be developed over time on the job, and are not quickly replaceable. Once developed, it is in everybody's interest that they be retained and nurtured in the enterprise which developed them. Secure salaried employment, with welfare and pension benefits, is appropriate; and with it, as much as possible of interest in the work, pride in the company and its products, and mutual respect and consultation within the organization.

Second, two kinds of cooperation are important in such enterprises. People and departments with diverse functions and skills must cooperate with each other. That is not helped by personal insecurity and competition for promotion, with people trying to make themselves look good and others look bad, to hog the credit and shed the blame for joint achievements. They cooperate better if they deal with colleagues as secure as themselves, with a long-term interest in cooperating well. And as noted above, a good deal of skill has to be learned on the job, much of it from fellow workers and immediate seniors rather than from owners or managers. Imparting skills to young people is often a pleasure. Having them then use the skills to supplant you is not. Seniors won't willingly equip juniors to steal their jobs or prospects of promotion. So as well as a need for secure tenure, as much promotion as possible may need to be by seniority. Effective trust between fellow workers needs comparatively *un*competitive conditions, or conditions in which team competes with team or company with company, rather than worker with worker. The hotter the competition between firms, the more need there may be for willing cooperation within them.

But not for everyone. Why does only a third or so of Toyota's (and Japan's) workforce enjoy the security of the celebrated 'Japanese labour system'? There are organizational and exploitive reasons. Demand for Toyota cars fluctuates and it suits the company to use *some* workers who can be put on and off accordingly – but they must not be workers to whom the company is committed. Quite a lot of the manufacturing work can be done by insecure workers, some low-skilled and low-paid, if they can be closely supervised. Profit-seeking owners tend to watch and exploit their workers more zealously than salaried managers do, so the work is best done in small owner-managed firms and workshops. And the more components Toyota can buy from such suppliers, the less bureaucratic supervision and corporate welfare it has to pay for. So two-thirds or so of each car is made by independent suppliers: old-style capitalist exploitation joins with the modern principle of devolving as much responsibility as possible as close to the workplace as possible. Within the small firms there is less welfare, less security, often lower pay; but face-to-face relations and a common interest in getting and keeping the Toyota work can often generate a degree of solidarity and respect for seniority. Thus not much of the workforce as a whole fits the old stereotype of the monster corporation supervising and exploiting tens of thousands of frightened, insecure employees.

(Toyota did not invent the idea of designing then assembling components mostly made by others. The practice is at least as old as the car – William Morris especially developed it from 1910. It can be compared with the organizational and incentive mixes which public enterprises use when – for example – a public oil corporation has twenty or thirty specialist private subcontractors on its North Sea oil rig, or a public housing enterprise has bureaucrats finance its houses then collect their rents, but private architects design them, private contractors build them and private tradespeople repair and maintain them.)

It can be seen that our representative public health service and private manufacturer have a good deal in common. They tailor incentives to particular jobs and the types of people who do them. They encourage as much as they can of self-direction and mutual quality control by their workers. Both of them enlist a good deal of professional and corporate pride, and commitment to shared purposes. Those 'soft' incentives are reinforced by 'hard' arrangements for pay and promotion and, where necessary, supervision and accountability. The proportions of soft and hard vary with circumstances and the nature of the work, but a good deal of both operate in most good public and private enterprises. The public sector may have more benevolent purposes and less market discipline than the private sector, but those differences have a certain balance: if some public activities go slack from lack of financial pressure, others get their benevolent work done for less pay with more generous commitment than profit-seekers can usually expect of their employees. But the differences are in degree rather than kind – there are vision and commitment at Toyota too. Remember Chester

Barnard's imaginary waterworks engineer, 'Mr A', well paid, securely employed, living and working by his seven codes of conduct. Barnard did not say whether the waterworks had public or private owners. It need not matter, provided both have able, well-motivated directors. But that is an important proviso.

DIRECTORS' INCENTIVES

Mixed economies have many activities whose ownership is not really in question. On the one hand the traditional activities of government can only be public. On the other, most of what small business does is best left to small business, much of it run by its owners. In most of the industries in which public and private ownership are real alternatives the scale of operation is so large that the typical firms are big public companies with individually powerless shareholders, run not by their owners but by self-perpetuating boards of directors. Public business enterprises are likewise run by directors, with the difference that government has an effective owner's power over them. For present purposes the useful comparison is therefore a three-cornered one, between the incentives of politicians, public directors and private directors.

Politicians' behaviour belongs in the following chapter on public choice theory. Here we can briefly notice the chief temptations they face as public investors. They may invest in a pork-barrelling way to buy local or sectional votes. To attract votes by cutting taxes they may starve public industries of resources. Or they may sell them, to meet some of the current costs of government, improvidently, by spending capital instead of raising revenue. When they do that the economic effects are different from those of private takeovers, which pass cash to shareholders who usually reinvest most of it. When the government sells assets and hands the proceeds to consumers it reduces the economy's available investment funds by the amount those consumers don't save. It is as if it sold bonds, i.e. borrowed private capital, to finance consumer spending – a variant of the short-sighted, tax-hating behaviour which Paul Samuelson characterized in his pure theory of public expenditure. With the conservative shift of opinion through the 1980s the political temptation was strong. The British, Japanese, Australian and New Zealand governments sold many enterprises.[1] European governments meanwhile held on to most of their mines, steelworks, airlines, harbours and canals, water and power supplies, telecommunications, a carmaker, a national oil corporation and other productive enterprises, unmoved by theorist Samuelson or Minister Walsh.[1] Far-sighted public investment helped greatly to rebuild and unify western Europe's economy after 1945. There and elsewhere, politicians have attracted support by undertaking great public works, or lost it by letting public services run down, at least as often as they have won votes by tax-cutting. Financing the current costs of government by running down or selling off productive enterprises has been an unusual, not a usual, device of modern governments; the recent British aberration does not support a general theory of public improvidence. And the same British government showed how decisively government can reform and transform public industries if it wants to.

Public business directors differ from private directors much less than politicians differ from private shareholders. Increasingly, public and private executives are the same sort of people, or indeed the same people – public enterprises recruit executives from the private sector, private corporations recruit larger numbers from the public services. Most of both are nowadays on term contracts. Their styles grow more alike as they pass through the same management schools and as governments want their enterprises to be, and look, businesslike. Competition for the top jobs with the top pay in their industries, and ambitions to distinguish themselves, are common to both sectors. Between the public and private incentives there are only two general differences. They arise from the multiple purposes of some public enterprises, and from their executives' different relation to government.

Many public enterprises exist to serve a number of purposes at once. When the purposes conflict or compete for resources there can be uncertainty and conflict about their priorities. What extra costs or reduced profits are justified to treat public employees better than a ruthless private employer might treat them? to locate work where most unemployed need it or where women need it? to give sheltered employment to handicapped workers? to supply apprenticeship or other training cheaper than public trade schools can supply it? to run power, telephones, transport, postal services – or adult education, counselling, legal services, women's and children's shelters – to remote and sparsely settled communities? What cross-subsidizing from some customers to others should public services do? The capacity to reconcile or balance conflicting purposes *without* recourse to a decisive 'bottom line' is a valuable one. It is one decisive advantage of public ownership. It complicates the choice and training of executives and the assessment of their performance, and it can be misused to excuse poor performance, but it can also allow powerful motivation, and the most effective use of resources. Meshing and balancing diverse purposes requires (among other things) conscious moral considerations. When ordinary ambitions to rise, win, excel, earn the highest pay and drive the finest car are superimposed on a passion to be good as well as clever – to do justice, cure cancer, discover the mechanisms of biological mutation, protect threatened children, house hard-up households, double the use of public libraries especially by the least educated people, conserve natural resources for future generations – the compounding incentives can be very powerful.

Private corporations may of course serve broad social purposes, because their directors believe they should or because government pays or requires them to do so. But they may also have conflicts with the society around them. Theorists – even the most conservative – list many ways in which profit seekers may reduce rather than increase the efficiency of the economy as a whole, for example by monopolist or oligopolist misbehaviour, predatory pricing and other unfair trading, insider trading, tax avoidance by means which reduce productive efficiency, physically dangerous products and processes, and many and various kinds of environmental degradation. Many of those sins have also been committed by public enterprises, whose misbehaviour is sometimes easier and sometimes harder to correct. It is a detailed question, varying from industry to industry and culture to culture, whether those kinds of misbehaviour are best prevented by market forces, public regulation or public ownership.

Those are typically conflicts between owners' or enterprises' interests and public interests. They do not necessarily involve conflicts between the enterprises and their own directors. But the latter conflicts are increasingly important, and the second basic difference between public and private directors' incentives to which we wish to draw attention is in the different success with which government has been able to keep them honest. Private executive loyalty to firms and their owners has always depended to some degree on company law and its enforcement. That dependence has increased dramatically since the separation of ownership from corporate control introduced substantial conflicts of interest, actual or potential, between directors and the owners who employ them.

Business people tend to imagine the market economy as a natural system of exchange with which government can choose whether or not to interfere. But there is nothing natural about the firm. Its distinctive powers – corporate entity, joint stock and limited liability – are pure government creations. They are critically important: the firm is the device which allows the efficiencies of complex, large-scale organization to coexist with the efficiencies of the market. But the firm's necessary powers are also potentially dangerous. Their misuse has occasioned a steady growth of regulation, much of it at the behest of business itself. However no government has yet limited the whole amount of reward which directors can lawfully take from their firms. When the corporate powers were first developed there did not seem to be any need to do that. The owners would normally direct their firms or, if they hired managers to do it, self-interest would motivate them to keep a sharp eye on the managers and pay them no more than market wages. But the twentieth century has seen a huge increase in corporate size and a famous separation of ownership from control. Few big firms now have a dominant owner or shareholders' organization. Boards have become self-perpetuating – directors are chosen by other directors rather than by the owners who notionally employ them. Directors decide one another's pay, and in doing so they have direct conflicts of interest with their firms' owners and sometimes with their workers and customers. What those conflicts owe to public policy is best illustrated in the American history of corporate regulation.

The US Constitution empowered the states rather than the federal government to charter (i.e. register) companies. The first general chartering acts were passed during the Jacksonian years of populist democracy when there was widespread suspicion of corporations, especially big ones. The acts were severely restrictive, especially of corporations' size. They limited the amount of share capital a corporation could raise, and the amount it could borrow. Takeovers were blocked because corporations were not allowed to own other corporations' shares. They must stick strictly to the purposes and types of business specified in their charters. Some states chartered them for limited terms so that they must periodically get their charters renewed. Some would only charter corporations owned by their residents. Some restricted them to doing business within the state which chartered them.

Business which needed to be big found various unsatisfactory ways around those constraints, sometimes circumventing the law and sometimes breaking it. But the constraints were more onerous as the scale of business grew through the nineteenth century, and in the 1890s the State of New Jersey led the way to a permanent solution: if you can't beat 'em, join 'em. If a state legalized what the big corporations wanted to do it could charge a lot for its charters and cut its other taxes accordingly. By 1896 New Jersey had revised its charter law to allow corporations to be as big as they liked; to operate anywhere; to be owned by residents of any state or nation; and most important, to own other corporations. Standard Oil and US Steel led such an influx of corporate customers that New Jersey was able to abolish almost all its other taxes. Other states soon competed. Delaware, especially, strengthened big owners by allowing shares with unequal voting rights, and pyramiding through holding companies. For many years the Ford family controlled its motor company while owning less than five per cent of it.

Other states competed for the business and Delaware's share of it declined just as New Jersey's share had done. But Delaware made a triumphant comeback in 1967 by exploiting the separation of corporate ownership from control which Berle and Means and others had noticed from the 1930s onward. Why compete to attract corporate owners when it was now not owners but directors who decided where to charter most big corporations? The Delaware politicians changed sides. Their 1967 Corporations Law deliberately strengthens directors against their owners. Shareholders can no longer propose changes to a Delaware corporation's charter; only directors can. (Directors can thus block shareholders' attempts to improve their control of directors' rewards.) Directors can lawfully vote on schemes from which they can derive loans, stock options, bonuses and other 'incentive compensations'. They can have their corporations indemnify them for any civil or criminal penalties they suffer for misbehaving as directors. (Among other things that makes some federal efforts to discipline them less effective.) And as far as the state law is concerned, most of what they take for themselves need no longer be disclosed to shareholders, press or public; any disclosure is an effect of federal law or Stock Exchange rules.

Within seven years of the 1967 revision half of the hundred biggest American corporations and nearly half of the thousand biggest were chartered in Delaware. Most of the biggest hundred and many of the rest now pay their chief executives ten or fifteen times as much as state governors or the President or Chief Justice of the United States are paid. Some pay fifty times as much. In one recent year the President and Chairman of the Walt Disney corporation between them took $72m, mostly in realized stock options.

British directors have followed the American lead. Through the 1980s their earnings grew at about twice the national average rate. In real terms after tax and discounted for inflation, directors of the top group of British companies gained 31.5 per cent in the tax year 1988–9 while the corresponding gain for 'senior managers' was 4.7 per cent. At Coloroll, Lonrho and Hansons, Chairmen's salaries trebled. British law allows directors to take share options to the value of four times annual salary; in a rare shareholders' revolt Burtons cut their Chairman's salary from £1.36m to below £1m chiefly to block his attempt to take £8m of share options.

In Australia the biggest disclosed director's salary in 1989 was A$5.3m, the next biggest $1.9m, and about fifty directors were believed to be taking $1m or more, only six or eight times the Prime Minister's salary. But if Australian directors lag behind American salaries, Australian company law has allowed them to be pioneers of the directors' private company which exists to prey on the public company which they direct. The private company may borrow from the public company, sell its directors' services to it, acquire its shares by various means. Some directors use the device to borrow more than they would be allowed to borrow directly from their public companies, some chiefly milk income from the public company, some chiefly transfer its capital ownership to themselves. Many of those activities are corrupt in any moral or business sense of the word but broke no Australian laws in the 1980s.

Some theorists expected the takeover boom to discipline directors because takeovers can restore control by a dominant shareholder. But takeovers don't restore dominant *owners*: the directors of the target firms, the directors of the raiding firms and the directors of the banks which stake them are all directors using other people's money. They have directors' rather than owners' interests. None of them stands to lose anything and most stand to gain if they over-pay each other.

We think the directors' modern powers are important not because of their occasional scandalous misuse but because of their normal lawful use, and because of a widespread misunderstanding of their nature. Directors are wrongly believed to be earning market rates for their services. Where there is no dominant owner or shareholders' organization the relation between a firm and its directors cannot be a market one and their rates of pay cannot be market rates in the usual meaning of the words. Prevailing rates do exist but they reflect group gains moderated by collective prudence. The rate at which they draw ahead of other earned incomes cannot be explained like the price of corn by the forces of supply and demand: the suppliers and demanders are the same people. If a board does occasionally head-hunt, and bargain for a particular executive's services, the directors who bargain as employers will usually take more themselves the more they agree to pay to newcomers; there is no bargaining between opposed interests as required for genuine market prices. Most directors' rewards are not bargained at all, they are self-chosen within limits set only by prudent attention to the prevailing business culture. Directors largely shape that culture. One of its functions is to legitimize their gains. 'Firms get what they pay for', say business spokesmen. Economists, some in think-tanks financed by corporate directors, agree: they theorize as if directors and those who employ them were different people. Thus what directors decide to take from their firms is professionally misrepresented as the efficient market price of their services.

Compare what limits top pay in the public sector. Politicians limit what they take from well-founded fear of electoral backlash fuelled by a vigilant press. They apply similar limits for similar reasons, and for broader tax-cutting, cost-cutting reasons, to their bureaucrats' and public business executives' pay, and they have effective means of enforcing the limits. Thus political self-interest, as well as any higher purposes which the politicians share with their electors, has kept public leaders' pay reasonable in all the respectable democracies. The public sector can still keep its directors' fingers out of the till. The private sector can't.

Freeing the private directors from owners' control has flawed the efficiency as well as the morality of their incentives. To show how, we may begin by contrasting three views of their incentives. Traditionally directors were owners, or their owners made sure they served owners' interests exclusively. (Only if they do so and thus optimize the use of the owners' capital can Adam Smith's hidden hand be supposed to work properly to give the market economy its theoretical efficiency.) Next, the New Deal generation of Berle and Means and Chester Barnard hoped that the separation of ownership from control would free directors to civilize capitalism by attending more impartially to all the interests affected by their actions: owners' interests could now be balanced against the interests of workers, consumers, neighbours, communal and national concerns. (Theorists might perceive some sacrifice of efficiency for greater equity.) But third, directors can use their freedom to get whatever the law allows them to get for themselves, leaving others including a great many powerless owner/shareholders to look out for themselves as best they can, as everyone else in a capitalist economy is expected to do. Elements of all three principles are probably present in the minds and motives of most modern directors. But the third seems to be gaining on the other two, with unpleasant implications for private and public efficiency and some widely held social values.

Wholly selfish directors who decide their own rewards *can* serve their owners' interests well. They must usually keep their firms in profit, and the more their firms earn, the more they may hope to take for themselves without provoking hostile press or political notice or shareholders' revolts. But that is not a reliable harmony of interests. The more the directors take, the less there is for others. They don't always have to keep their firms in profit to enrich themselves – some of the biggest plunder, some of it lawful, has been from failing firms. They may do well out of debt-financed takeovers which switch most of their firms' earnings from dividends to debt service. They do not always share their owners' interest in steady growth by producing and trading. The best strategies for directors are by no means always the best strategies for owners.

Are these conflicts overcome if directors' rewards are performance-linked? No: directors can take excessive rates of bonus and profit share just as they can take excessive salaries or penthouse perquisites. Nevertheless if they take only from their firms' owners (through bonuses, profit shares, cheap share options, etc.) there is a certain moral and economic case for letting them do it. The argument is rarely stated explicitly but it deserves some sympathy from both Left and Right. In a capitalist society, why should capital wealth come only by inheritance, or by success in a few arts like professional sport, popular music or film acting? Or all too rarely from businesses which start so small that shoestring entrepreneurs can keep hold of them as they grow? Many executives of big firms do more for national wealth and growth than most of their shareholders do. Why shouldn't the best directors earn enough to become substantial capital owners themselves? There is a common interest in having a society's capital in the hands of able investors, and able investors are more likely to be recruited by executive competition than by inheritance or championship golf or pop-singing. If the executives' gains are at shareholders' expense, i.e. are transferring capital from passive rentier owners to proven business leaders, so much the better.

The trouble with that appealing argument is that other winners – public executives and bureaucrats, leading scientists and artists and educators, in whose creativity there is also a common interest, would want similar rewards, both to be fair and to enable their professions to go on attracting talented recruits. If the argument has merit it ought to apply to all exceptionally productive people. In practice moreover the directors' gains don't come only from owners; directly or indirectly as they raise their firms' costs, extend their inequalities and divert some of their productive energies they take resources from workers, consumers and taxpayers as well as owners. So the argument for directors taking more from their owners extends to an argument for steeper inequalities throughout society.

Some of that process is already under way – some other people are sharing the directors' gains. Big firms use more lawyers and accountants than they used to do. Besides reducing the firms' liability to corporate taxation they design the directors' packages. So, increasingly, do consultants who specialize in the work. Seeing what they are enabling the directors to take, these aides demand comparable rewards and the directors cause their firms to pay them. Leading corporate lawyers take so much that governments are having trouble finding judges. More than half of all new luxury cars now go into corporate ownership but private use; the carmakers' and car-leasing directors price the cars up accordingly, and reward themselves accordingly. Most metropolitan four- and five-star hotels exist to serve customers spending other people's money. Conservative rhetoric pillories politicians and bureaucrats for spending other people's money, but business chiefs now spend much, much more of it, more luxuriously, on themselves than any democracy's public leaders do.

It is wrong for any group in society to be able to take other people's money without private consent or public discipline. But moral objections to directors' misuses of their powers are not the most important objections to them. What is most important is to recognize that a fundamental social control has broken down. The breakdown threatens ill effects of three kinds. First it raises some costs and subjects the direction of 'big' business to some perverse motivation: the incentives which should theoretically harness directors' energies to owners' interests, and through them to the productive interest of society as a whole, are less reliable than they used to be. Second, public enterprise is exposed to one or both of two ill effects. Public business executives can guess that privatization will double their pay if they have recommended privatization and see them sacked if they have opposed it, so their advice about it can't be disinterested. At the same time governments are having to pay their executives some at least of the increases the private directors are taking; and public directors' gains have a stronger tendency than private directors' gains to spread downward through the managerial ranks, and sideways to comparable levels of the public service bureaucracy. Thus the private directors' behaviour is increasing some costs and income inequalities and corrupting some incentives in both sectors, with no reason to believe that the change is motivating any higher productivity than would have occurred without it.

But – as a third ill effect – the increase in peak pay is for some occupations only. It goes to directors of big firms, to lawyers and accountants whose clients are directors of big firms, to some of the luxury trades on which those winners spend their firms' money, and by competitive imitation some lesser increases go to public business executives, bureaucrats and judges. In the private sector not many of the gains filter down to the plant managers, engineers, product developers and designers who contribute at least as much to productivity as most directors do. Nor are the gains shared elsewhere in society by many people in small business, scientific and social research, the highbrow arts, or the rank and file of journalists, teachers, public servants, nurses and welfare workers. It is fortunate that talented young people usually have other things as well as money in mind when they choose their occupations, but they can't all resist the magnetism of the new business and financial opportunities. The authors' universities have seen substantial shifts of talent away from engineering, science, arts and humanities into law, accountancy and business studies. There is no reason to believe that the shift of talent into big business, and especially into its financial rather than its productive branches, is good for anyone but the winners – or that most of it is market-demanded in the theoretically productive meaning of the term.

It would be wrong to exaggerate or generalize too far from these trends. Plenty of business continues to be directed efficiently, for reasonable rewards, by people with appropriate incentives. Plenty of invention and innovation continues to come from firms of all sizes, with or without dominant owners. And with and without dominant owners plenty of private firms operate with care for their workers and customers and neighbours, with commendable social responsibility. But we believe the direction of change is as we describe, and – without its hedges and fences – our argument can be summarized as follows.

In the English-speaking democracies the directors of most of the biggest private corporations are using their freedom from either market or legal restraint to take steadily more of their firms' money for themselves. They also cause their firms to pay increasing rates to the lawyers and accountants they use, and to pay for many more luxury cars and hotels than would exist if their users had to pay for them from their own taxed incomes.

The private directors' and associates' excessive takings can harm the public sector in various ways. By competing for talent at ever higher rates they force public employers to pay their executives more, increasing their costs and internal inequalities. Many more managers and administrators still pass from the public to the private sector than move the other way. The high private pay also tempts public directors to favour or oppose privatization for reasons irrelevant to its merits.

Occupational incentives must tend to become less efficient as corporate direction, company and tax law, accountancy, financial services and advertising attract more high talent and leave less for engineering, manufacturing and process management, technology, the natural and social sciences, education, public services and some of the creative arts. The shift – or inducement to shift – is not from less productive to more productive occupations, or from easier to more difficult or disagreeable ones, it is simply to the occupations with easiest access to other people's money. Manufacturing declines in the English-speaking world as financial services expand, many of them unnecessary, some purely predatory.

These trends seem likely to degrade, rather than improve, economic efficiency and social well-being. The trends are propelled by the corporate directors who decide their own rewards without effective control by anyone else. The occasional scandal may do less harm than the steady growth, over time, of the rewards of the group as a whole. In some countries their temptations have been intensified by measures of deregulation. Some governments are deterred from stricter regulation by the fear that they may drive corporate headquarters offshore – the old competition between New Jersey and Delaware for the directors' favour begins to operate internationally. In the

European Community on the other hand most member countries began with different corporate structures which allowed better internal control of executive behaviour. Until recently some member countries had a good deal of their heavy industry in public ownership. They are all now required to adopt the Community's uniform code of corporate regulation, which is increasingly detailed and strict. Though they have had some scandals, their directors seem on the whole to be better behaved than others.

It goes without saying that the private sector still has plenty of good directors and managers, just as the public sector does. Most of the best in both sectors operate with other purposes besides making money for themselves. But as long as some private directors continue to generate financial scandals and most private directors continue to increase their own rewards as they are currently doing, their material incentives cannot be *relied on* to motivate the most productive or socially valuable performance. Material incentives are not the only incentives, but even if they were, the private directors' worse temptations, and the ramifying social effects of their escalating pay, need to be offset against the productive effects of their higher pay in any comparison of their incentives with those of public directors.

If this argument is conceded, the champions of private enterprise may still prefer it wherever possible because they believe that poor private performance tends to be eliminated by market forces while poor public performance tends to persist. Those beliefs (with which we partly agree) are our next subject.

DEATH, TAKEOVER, REFORM

Theory: Market forces ensure efficiency by eliminating inefficient private firms, while government often allows inefficient public activities to continue.

Both processes certainly happen. But they do not always or necessarily happen. This section expresses four reservations about them: (i) market forces don't eliminate *all* inefficient or socially harmful firms; (ii) the failure of inefficient firms can have economic and social costs which public enterprises can usually avoid; (iii) if public enterprises are inefficient at socially necessary tasks which private enterprise cannot do at all, that does not constitute a case against public enterprise; and (iv) governments vary widely in their efforts to keep their enterprises efficient, and the rest should learn from the best.

All economists know a standard list of conditions in which, in theory and sometimes in practice, inefficient firms can survive: if they are monopolists or uncompetitive oligopolists in industries which have long lead times or are difficult for newcomers to enter for any other reason; if they are in industries with continuous returns to scale; if high costs or other inefficiencies are imposed on them by government or industrial action; if government protects, franchises or subsidizes them; if in serving their own purposes efficiently they impose external costs or inefficiencies on others; if they are in marginal or declining industries or other situations which don't attract competitors; if they have such assets that they can survive losses for long periods by dissaving, or if despite inefficient trading or technical insolvency they can continue to attract funds or credit from imprudent suppliers, banks, bond buyers, share buyers, depositors or other suckers. And as noted in the previous section, wherever there is effective separation of corporate ownership from control it may be possible for performance which is efficient for directors' purposes to be inefficient for owners' or others' purposes. How prevalent any of those conditions are and how much inefficiency they encourage are practical questions to which answers vary with time and circumstance. For our present purposes it is enough to note these well-known shortcomings of the theory that market forces automatically keep firms efficient.

Two other shortcomings deserve notice. They relate to the first and third of three steps of reasoning: (i) competition ensures efficiency by eliminating less efficient firms; (ii) competition motivates people to do their best; and (iii) competition is the main or sufficient cause of productive efficiency.

For pure theorists the first proposition suffices. It sufficiently explains why market systems are as efficient as possible. Nothing is implied or need be known about the causes which make some firms more efficient than others; it is enough to know that those who survive must be the most efficient, not the least efficient or a random selection of better and worse.

To be content with that, one must assume that bankruptcies, voluntary liquidations and asset-stripping takeovers are beneficent processes without costs, or that their benefits exceed their costs. But business failures do impose losses which add up to social or system losses: they signify wasteful uses of resources with opportunity costs, and in practice most of them dissave, i.e. waste or consume some capital. The theory also appears to assume that failure is punctual and instantaneous, whereas in life it can be agonizingly slow and wasteful. It is said (we have not researched it) that only one new enterprise in five survives five years. Many of the other four are wound up without insolvency, but most have lost money or failed to earn much for their founders. If we must assume some inefficiency in eighty per cent of enterprises under five years old, it can't ever be true that only efficient firms are at work. Of course this argument should not be pushed too far. Most new ventures, especially those that don't survive, are small ones – family businesses, shops or workshops or service partnerships. The newcomers under five years old may do a small percentage of the business of the whole private sector. Nevertheless they do include inefficient performers failing from causes which new *public* enterprises (whatever their other sins) rarely suffer: inadequate capital, skill, experience or market knowledge; too much debt; too many bad debts. There can also be severe social costs, for example in local unemployment, forced migration and wasted public and domestic capital, when big firms fail, or improve their efficiency by closing or relocating less efficient plant. If public infrastructure or private housing lose use and value because of business failures, the public and domestic losses should be offset against any business gains in estimating net effects on national economic efficiency. The net effects may often be positive, as the theory expects. Many business failures do indeed see better performers replacing worse. When the changes occur in reach of diversified labour markets rather than at remote locations or in company towns, the public and domestic effects may not be great and may not all be negative. But a theory linking business failure to economic efficiency should direct attention to all its effects on efficiency, not just one of them.

Our second proposition – that besides negatively eliminating poor performers, competition may positively motivate good performance – may also be true in many cases. But the surer you are of that, the more you may be tempted to fall for the third proposition, that competition is a *sufficient* cause of efficient performance. There are theoretical, practical and political objections to that. As theory, it needs a clause about the conditions in which it holds. Moreover the clause it needs is not the usual *ceteris paribus* to indicate a determinate relation, i.e. that a change in competition will always cause a corresponding change in efficiency as long as other conditions don't meanwhile change, or have countervailing effects. What is needed is the *in*determinate proviso 'in some conditions but not in others'. The effect of competition on efficiency does not depend on other conditions not changing or countervailing the effect of competition, it depends on what the other conditions *are*. In some conditions competition increases efficiency, in other conditions it may reduce efficiency, in others again it may extinguish whole industries or keep poor countries poor.

The practical objection follows from that. Not only is the proposition sometimes false (some monopolies are efficient, competition can sometimes reduce efficiency, and so on) but efficiency has many other necessary conditions besides competition. So governments wishing to encourage efficiency may need to attend to many other conditions besides the state of competition. Hence the political objection to a proposition which tells government that all they need do to make their industries prosper is expose them to global competition: a level playing field with no favours will make champions of them, or if not, nothing will. Some politicians believe it. Others find it convenient to say that they do when what they actually want is to oblige business by deregulating, and oblige other taxpayers by cutting public investment in education, health, research, industrial safety and the public infrastructure and services on which efficient industries depend. In reality national economic efficiency has many necessary conditions including many which only government can contrive. Most governments know it and act accordingly, whatever their rhetoric of the moment, though some have lately been taking rather short-term, improvident views of the task.

A good example of long sight, together with quick responses to immediate conditions, can be found in the Japanese government's role in Japan's modernization, which is worth notice here for its theoretical as well as practical interest. In *Governing the Japanese Economy* (1993) Kyoko Sheridan identifies successive policy cycles or changes of direction in the government's economic policies through the century of Japan's industrialization, and explains them as follows. In broad terms economic growth requires a dozen or so enabling conditions to be present, including for example natural resources; an educated, hard-working, cooperative population; law and order; various financial and commercial institutions; a rate of saving or other source of capital; available technology or a capacity to invent it; entrepreneurs; a public infrastructure of ports, roads and bridges, rail and telecommunication networks; access to world trade; and so on. When its modernization began Japan had a few but not many of those items. The government which initiated the modernization did its best to develop all the missing ones, with varying success. Some took longer to develop than others. Some had to be started by government but could then be continued by private owners. When some were achieved, others could develop in a market way. After a time, when most of the necessary conditions were in place and private industrial development was under way, it became possible to identify bottlenecks: the one or two necessary conditions whose provision was least adequate, and was therefore limiting the rate of economic growth to less than the other conditions would collectively allow. Having identified the limiting conditions government would concentrate on expanding or reforming them until – having succeeded – other conditions became the 'limiters', and attention switched to those. There were substantial changes of that kind at intervals of twelve to twenty years, or oftener when wars or earthquake damage required. The conditions perceived as 'limiters', at different times included education, elements of culture, the supply of entrepreneurs, the financial system, the rate of saving, foreign exchange, access to certain raw materials, steel output, public compliance with taxation, peasants' and workers' tolerance of harsh living and working conditions, and – interestingly for our present purposes – too much competition in the 1950s, and too little in the 1870s and 1970s. (Through the 1950s the government actively encouraged the development of oligopolistic firms big enough to compete internationally, while for the time being protecting them from import competition. When those giants had the international success they were designed for, but began to misuse their market strength at home, government began to apply the legal and 'anti-trust' requirements by which most advanced democracies try to keep such monsters efficient for their customers as well as themselves.)

The policies which thus led Japan from feudal seclusion to parity with the most advanced industrial economies were not all lovable. They included false starts and mistakes, military follies and brutalities, and ruthless priorities which imposed harsh living and working conditions for long periods on a great many Japanese people. But given the purposes and priorities of the economic policy-makers they were exceptionally intelligent and successful in contriving a single effect (economic growth) which depended on sets of conditions which changed with each phase of growth and with changing international circumstances, and which included some necessaries which only government could supply, some which could safely be left to the market, and some which needed different amounts and kinds of public action at different times. The heart of the policy-makers' skill was their capacity to understand not what each necessary condition would cause if the others were absent or stable, but how each interacted with each in the changing set which propelled the economy's growth.

The chief bearers of the skill were committed, observant, adaptable bureaucrats. Most were not academic economists and did not make much use of formal Neoclassical or Marxist economic theories. From home, school and university they had learned national ideals, some Confucian philosophy, and professional education in law, engineering or other fields. The leaders had risen in the service chiefly by demonstrating a capacity to think strategically about the economy and translate strategies into effective policies. Sheridan describes them as 'elite generalists'. Their idealism was not socialist or social-democratic – they never doubted that it was a capitalist economy they were shaping, and it was the capitalist economy itself – rather than separate public welfare arrangements – which should be developed to meet most of the needs of the Japanese people. They were practical, not ideological, about the capacities and roles of public and private enterprise. From comparatively small public budgets they were comparatively large public investors, but they were quick to end public activities which had served their purposes. They understood economic performance as a product of political, cultural and educational conditions as well as strictly economic conditions. Most of their ambitious but pragmatic political economy they learned from their superiors, from each other, and from direct observation of their country's economic activity. Kyoko Sheridan, an able Japanese economist, is entirely serious in ascribing the 'Japanese miracle' in part to Japan's having had through most of the relevant decades no management schools (so management was taught with 'hands on' the business to be managed) and very few economists among her economic policy-makers (so they had to study how the economy actually worked, rather than relying on axiomatic or monocausal theories about the sources of efficiency and growth). That judgement of Sheridan's is neither anti-intellectual nor anti-theoretical. Managers and bureaucrats alike were highly educated in demanding disciplines in the best universities – but in more principles than the axiomatic laws of supply and demand.

The Japanese example serves to introduce the second subject of this section, the tendency of public activities which escape market discipline to persist when they are no longer efficient or no longer needed. The tendency is not apparent in Japan's modern history. Many Japanese enterprises and some whole industries were created by government to meet national needs then readily privatised when private owners were willing and able to run them. There were radical rounds of privatization in the 1880s and 1980s and individual cases at various dates between; there was also public conscription and direction of private industry in wartime. In the 1960s MITI stopped much of its detailed resource-rationing and in the 1970s it stopped most of its detailed industrial guidance, and promptly reduced its divisions by more than half. In those and many other ways Japanese government has shown a fairly reliable propensity to close down, sell off or reform any inefficient or unwanted public activities, and also any efficient ones which (for purposes of economic growth) could as well be continued in private ownership.

Some modern British governments have tolerated 'inertial inefficiency' in their public enterprises, but – spectacularly – others have not. Railways, coal and steel prospered better after their original nationalization than before it, and rail efficiencies were further improved by drastic network cuts in the 1960s. When the British-owned private car-makers failed, public owners took them over and put most of them back into profit. Governments of both parties had British steel maintain a good deal of old plant, because of its location and employment effects, along with (at every date) some of Europe's most advanced and efficient plant. Coal was allowed to lag further behind its technical possibilities, partly for employment reasons and partly because British governments began starving some of their enterprises of capital from the 1960s. Some people defended that: low pay for all in under-capitalized, over-manned industries was perhaps better, all things considered, than technical progress to yield high pay for some, unemployed doles for others and higher taxes to finance the doles. But however humane, that 'industrial museum' could not survive the dwindling protection which came with Britain's EEC membership. One after another the car, steel and coal industries were revolutionized not by market forces or private profit-seeking incentives but by forceful directors appointed and backed by determined governments. As we argued earlier, Left objections to the ruthlessness and social costs with which some of the changes were enforced should not blind us to the central fact that it was by public owners, after private management had failed, that these major industries were transformed.

Those were showy achievements. It is more important in the long run that democratic governments of advanced economies have developed, as permanent elements of government, elaborate and reasonably effective means of keeping their public sectors honest and efficient, just as they earlier developed the elaborate corporate and commercial law and enforcement, and other public infrastructure, which keep their private sectors reasonably honest and efficient. Big public sectors are comparatively recent growths. It has taken a generation or two to identify their distinctive problems and develop regular means of coping with them. It took rather longer, and still probably costs government rather more, to civilize the modern private sector. The practical comparisons cited earlier suggest that the disciplines have roughly equal success.

Most democratic governments nowadays are under steady political, press and public pressure to economize their resources and keep their enterprises as efficient as they can. Tax resistance has tempted some of them to starve their enterprises of capital, but there is growing awareness of that danger and public industries continue to be much more highly capitalised, on average, than private. Public activities are routinely audited, monitored by Organization and Methods offices, reviewed from time to time by private sector management firms, and investigated by parliamentary committees. Some (banks, airlines, steel-makers, car-makers, publishers) compete in open markets. For many of those which don't, detailed performance standards and indicators have been devised. Some work in the knowledge that governments could close or privatize them. Most are required to have much more transparent planning and accounting than are required of private corporations – public owners can generally know much more about their enterprises than most private shareholders can. Finally there is accumulating experience of the ways in which public and private efficiencies can be affected by their interrelation, i.e. by the detailed mix of the mixed economy. Governments and their managers learn what public enterprises must do for themselves, what they can do better than private firms can, what they can best have done by competitive private tender, what inputs are best bought from private suppliers, and what tasks can *not* safely be entrusted to private profit-seekers.

Of course the results are rarely faultless. Some activities are still difficult to discipline. Some politicians and public managers continue to be lazy, corrupt or less than competent. Depending on who wins elections, national economic systems may be deliberately biased to favour private capital, public sector labour unions, the social class to which bureaucrats belong, or other minorities. Waste and venality persist where the standard safeguards don't all apply, chiefly in 'secret' defence industries. But the developed democratic world now has regular means of keeping most public enterprises efficient. The means are widely known. Most governments have strong incentives to practise them. Increasingly, electors and critics of government insist that they be employed. The days are gone when significant numbers of seriously inefficient or unnecessary public services could lumber on like Dickens' Office of Circumlocution, secure against closure, privatization or effective reform.

ENTERPRISE AND SYSTEM

Beliefs about the efficiency of public and private enterprise are linked – sometimes carelessly – to beliefs about the productive and allocative efficiency of economic systems.

With productive efficiency the link is simple. If private enterprise is believed to be more efficient than public, economic systems should be more efficient the more the goods which the people want are produced by private rather than public enterprise. (*Not* '... the more private and the less public enterprise there is'. Productive efficiency won't be improved by cutting the public services which are necessary for private efficiency.)

There are links between 'sector mix' and productive efficiency, but they are not as simple as that. Private enterprise has not been shown to be generally more efficient than public – but there are particular industries and services at which one mode or the other is generally better. Mixed economies can accordingly have more efficient or less efficient mixes, independently of the relative size of the sectors. (If you doubt it, imagine an economy in which private profit-seekers own all the hospitals, blood services, primary schools, universities and judges, and the government owns all the houses, shops, fashion industries, newspapers and racehorses.) It is also true that each mode does best in the presence of the other. They trade with each other, each thus getting the benefit of what the other does best. Private enterprise is more efficient with reliable law and order and public infrastructure than without them. The uncompetitive activities of government can benefit from the competitive environment around them, which offers models of customer-responsive service and produces alert critics of unresponsive public services. Performance standards for natural monopolies and other uncompetitive activities can sometimes be set by reference to competitive industries. Rightly used, public ownership can sometimes increase rather than reduce competition, as when public producers, proof against takeover, compete with what would otherwise be private monopolies. Thus to be as productive as possible, economic systems need an appropriate mix. But that is consistent with a wide range of sector sizes and proportions, because of the wide range of industries in which public and private ownership can be equally efficient.

There are more intricate relations between the mix of public and private enterprise, the mix of market allocation and planned allocation of resources, and the allocative efficiency of economic systems. Market economies are better than planned economies at meeting consumers' market demands, for three reasons. The customers' spending tells producers what customers want more reliably than government planners can usually do. Markets convey that information more quickly and cheaply than planners and administrators can usually do. And market discipline constrains the producers to respond to the customers' demands as planners do not always do. But we should beware of the careless conclusions that are sometimes drawn from those truths. (i) The 'administrative parsimony' of market systems is exaggerated; plenty of planning and market research are done by producers for market. (ii) Plenty of market competitors are publicly owned, so the extent of market allocation of resources is not necessarily related to the extent of public ownership. (iii) Many public monopolies are or can be made as market-responsive as equivalent private monopolies are. (iv) It is not true that consumer sovereignty and allocative efficiency are better the more resources are allocated by market and the less by planning. Neither is well served by 'private affluence and public squalor', by the undersupply of public goods predicted by Samuelson's pure theory of public goods, or by forcing people to substitute worse or dearer private provisions (private police, commercial television, profit-seeking schools, unsafe banks) for better public provisions. The work of David Alan Aschauer and others, noticed earlier, suggests that inadequate *public* investment has been a main cause of American's declining rates of *private* productivity and growth since the 1970s. (v) It is not true that the proportions of market and public goods dictate the proportions of private and public production, or vice versa. Plenty of market goods are produced by, or with inputs from, public producers; plenty of public goods, though paid for by government, are produced by, or with inputs from, private producers.

To summarize: The theory that the efficiency of firms and of economic systems is assured by the automatic extinction or takeover of inefficient enterprises needs all the standard exceptions for imperfect competition, externalities, distributional effects, etc. It needs exceptions for the types of takeover which pass control of efficient and inefficient firms alike to directors who intend to plunder them, to the bidders who most need their tax losses, or to the bidders and bankers who are willing to load them with most debt. It needs qualification for the processes of business failure and their economic and social costs. Above all it needs attention to all the other interrelated conditions, many of which government has to supply, which are necessary for the efficient allocation of resources and the efficient production of goods – conditions without which the extinction of inefficient producers may simply keep poor economies poor, as it does through much of the third world, rather than ensuring their economic efficiency or growth.

This chapter might now conclude by listing the good purposes which public enterprises can serve, the conditions in which they can be efficient, and the considerations which might therefore guide decisions about the desirable mix of public and private activity in mixed economies. But those decisions are made by governments, so people who believe that public and private enterprise can be equally efficient might nevertheless opt for the biggest possible private sector and the smallest possible public sector if they distrust the politicians and public servants who must make the sector choices and give directions to the public elements in the mix; i.e. it is possible to distrust public enterprise not because you expect it to be inefficient but because you expect governments to misuse it. Public choice theory encourages that expectation so we discuss that body of theory next, before arriving at conclusions about the desirable mix of mixed economies in Chapter 7.

5 Public Choice: The Attempt

THE THEORY

Most public choice theory rests on four assumptions: (i) individual material self-interest sufficiently motivates most economic behaviour, which (ii) is sufficiently understood by the use of neoclassical economic theory; and since (iii) the same individual material self-interest sufficiently motivates most political behaviour, (iv) that also may be sufficiently understood by the use of the same neoclassical economic theory. We dispute all four assumptions but lest our account of them be thought unfair, here is how a wholly sympathetic surveyor of public choice theory introduces it:

> Public choice can be defined as the economic study of non-market decisionmaking, or simply the application of economics to political science. The subject matter of public choice is the same as that of political science: the theory of the state, voting rules, voter behavior, party politics, the bureaucracy, and so on. The methodology of public choice is that of economics, however. The basic behavioral postulate of public choice, as for economics, is that man is an egoistic, rational, utility maximizer.[1]

A simpler summary might say that economics now has two branches: one explains how *market* goods are demanded and supplied and the other (public choice) explains how *public* goods are demanded and supplied.

In Chapter 2 we listed the main applications of the idea that people try to maximize the same things in their political and economic life, so that political activity can be sufficiently understood and predicted as driven by rational individual self-seeking. Government is a market-place where citizens trade taxes for public goods. Between citizens and politicians it is an exchange of support (votes, propaganda, campaign contributions) for benefits. But if government is thus a market-place it is riddled with market failure. Wherever they can, people freeload public goods, and their successful and unsuccessful efforts to do so waste a lot of resources. Some extremists think that freeloading rather than market exchange is the main political motive and that all government activity is actual or attempted plunder – 'legitimate theft'. Theorists disagree about the desirability and likely effects of particular voting systems, and of majority rule and other decision rules; but most agree that politicians', bureaucrats' and public business managers' performance cannot be affected by trying to improve the quality of the people who achieve office, it can only be affected by subjecting their self-seeking to effective constitutional and other constraints. There is accordingly much academic discussion of what those constraints should desirably be.

The usual way to learn more about political life is to study it, including how it varies over time and from culture to culture. But public choice theory aspires to be very pure theory. From simple postulates about an invariable human nature the theorists deduce how people must be expected to respond to any situation: to the need for government, to particular constitutions and voting rules, to each others' behaviour, to opportunities to gain at each others' expense, and so on. Why theorize so artificially when political life is accessible to more direct study? From studying the theorists' activity we have come to believe that many of them chiefly want to discredit government, but that for many a main purpose is to develop theory of a certain formal kind for its own sake, and to debate and elaborate its internal forms as an acceptable academic activity. Of course that is not what the theorists themselves say about their purposes. Axiomatic theory has an honourable scientific history. In 1979 the Introduction which was quoted above continued:

> Not surprisingly the recent efforts to explain and predict political behavior with highly simplified and abstract models have been challenged by some of those traditionally charged with that task. The political scientists's view of man the voter or politician is, in general, quite different from that assumed in the public choice models. The environment in which these characters interact is usually assumed to possess an institutional richness far beyond that implicit in these abstract models. To many political scientists the public choice models seem but a naive caricature of political behavior.
>
> The public choice theorist's answer to these criticisms is the same as the answer economists have given to the same criticisms as they have been raised against their 'naive' models of economic behavior down through the years. The use of the simplified models of political behavior is justified so long as they outperform the competitors in explaining political behavior. At this point, the degree to which economic models of democracy offer superior explanatory power is still in doubt. Much effort has been devoted recently to testing various aspects of the public choice model of democracy, however, and an appraisal of its relative merits should soon be possible.
>
> Dennis C. Mueller, *Public Choice* p. 5

When that hopeful expectation appeared the political scientists' criticisms which it cited were already fifteen and twenty years old. The theories had not passed any convincing tests through those years, and they have not passed any since. Most of the few 'proofs' offered in the journals do not arise from systematic attempts at disproof, or surveys of the theory's performance with whole sets or categories of political behaviour; they merely record individual cases, almost all from American federal, state or local government, in which facts are found to fit the theory. When Mueller's book reappeared (as *Public Choice II*) in 1989, all reference to empirical testing had been deleted from the Introduction. Some positive, some negative and some inconclusive tests are reported on a few later pages, with the conclusion that 'As so often in the social sciences, a bold new theory loses much of its shine as it is dragged through the muddy waters of empirical analysis' (p. 271). On the central question which divides public choice theory from other disciplines and traditions of social inquiry – the question whether political motivation is mixed as traditionally understood, or exclusively selfish – Mueller reports continuing empirical confirmation not of public choice theory but of the traditional view. The clearest test is the redistributive activity of government. On public choice assumptions all transfers should be from the weakest to the strongest contenders, and selfishly motivated. But in practice

> the narrow self-interest model of voting does not explain well the voting behavior of many individuals. Nor does it explain all redistribution activity. Social insurance programs, like old age and survivors' insurance and unemployment compensation, appear to have widespread popular support that goes beyond the rational decisions of a selfish individual calculating her retirement needs or the probability of losing her job ...
>
> The rational, self-interest models of redistribution predict a sharp division between groups over government policies. If redistribution is from rich to poor, then all those with incomes above the median should vote against the redistribution policies, all of those with incomes below the median should vote in favor. But survey results again do not indicate such a clear dichotomy. Income is not closely related to voting behavior ...
>
> On the other hand, many expenditures, subsidies, regulations, and tax measures can best be explained as the rewards to better organization and lobbying efforts by some groups. Although the self-interest model does not explain all redistribution activity of government, it certainly explains some. The best model of redistribution is one that combines elements of both the normative and positive public choice theories of distribution ...

A programme of means-tested aid to families with dependent children has attracted both kinds of support. There are benevolent taxpayers; and as most political scientists would have predicted, 'the selfish interests of the poor get greater weight in states in which interparty competition is more intense. Variables related to both hypotheses turn out to be significant, implying that both the willingness of taxpayers to pay and the ability of the poor to take explain differences in the levels of aid across states' (pp. 456–7).

Thus this most encyclopaedic, sympathetic and up-to-date survey of public choice scholarship concludes that 'The patterns that we have observed ... might be explained as a modest amount of rich-to-poor redistribution for altruistic or impartial insurance motives and an indeterminant amount of selfishly motivated redistribution with no clear directional impact'. Political life turns out to be not as public choice theory assumes it to be, but as mainstream political theorists and researchers have always understood it to be.

This chapter suggests reasons why public choice theory failed. The next notices how those who persist with it accommodate to the failure.

THE DEFENCE OF *HOMO ECONOMICUS*

Many public choice theorists now concede that as a description of political motivation and behaviour the theory is false. 'There may be good reason to believe that *homo economicus* may be descriptively somewhat less relevant in the political setting than in economic markets'.[2] (Some unease is evident in the need to translate 'untrue' into 'descriptively somewhat less relevant'.) 'And as research results have indicated, *homo economicus*, as an all-purpose explanatory model, runs into some apparent difficulties. Analysts are hard put to explain such behavior as individual voting in large-number electorates, individual volunteers in defense of the collectivity, and voluntary payment of income taxes'.[3] Similar acknowledgements by Anthony Downs are quoted on page 131 below.

Why persist with assumptions which are neither true nor helpful to prediction? There is a respectable argument that although self-seeking may not be a sole or even dominant human purpose, it is the element of human motivation and behaviour which makes government necessary, and which in turn makes it necessary to constrain government. In David Hume's famous words, 'In constraining any system of government and fixing the several checks and controls of the constitution, every man ought to be supposed a knave and to have no other end, in all his actions, than private interest'. We share Hume's prudent concern but think he threw the baby out with the bathwater. Besides restraining the anti-social manifestations of self-interest, rules should at the same time be designed to enable and protect the productive and cooperative elements of human nature, including the many opportunities to create common interests and enlist self-interest in cooperative activities. Public choice theorists should know that better than most – rules to restrain bad behaviour can all too easily distort or block good behaviour, as any critic of unnecessary red tape knows. (Legislators could eliminate car accidents by banning automobiles, eliminate corporate fraud by abolishing companies, reduce pornography by outlawing books and films, and so on.) A central task and skill of government is to contrive ways to prevent bad behaviour without also preventing good, and ways to enable and protect good behaviour without protecting bad. That problem for government arises directly from the complexity of human intentions, the traditionally understood propensities to good and evil of which readers were reminded in Chapter 1. So although Hume's defence of the law-maker's assumption of *homo economicus* is a respectable one, we think he was wrong, or was writing carelessly that day. He should have advised law-makers to assume that every man is 'a *potential* knave, as capable of evil as of good if opportunity offers'.

Other, more slippery, defences have been raised for the assumption that people have 'no other end ... than private interest'. While Mueller in 1979 was still hoping for empirical proof that political man is no different from economic man, others were offering other reasons for persisting with the assumption. Brennan and Buchanan offer three.

> First, if one insists on a comparison of *homo economicus* with alternative behavioral models *of roughly equal levels of abstraction and generality,* many of the grounds of debate are swept away. Models of behavior that are psychologically richer may be rejected because of their failure to meet the implicit austerity test. (Our emphasis.)

What is wrong with the *homo economicus* assumption is that (i) it models only one motive, whereas real motivation is complex, and (ii) it generalizes, whereas real motivation is variable. It is absurd to defend those mistakes because any other assumptions that made the same mistakes ('met the same austerity test') would be as bad.

Second, although Mueller defines *homo economicus* as maximizing 'an objective function ... defined over a few well-defined variables' and Buchanan has often defined him as maximizing net wealth, his defenders can always shift their ground:

> *Homo economicus* is not well defined, and the would-be critic may find that his quarry has disappeared, only to reemerge in another guise. In specifying *Homo economicus* as a net wealth maximizer, for example, one may fail to explain much of what can be observed, but the observations

may not be definitive because the defender of the model may resort to changes in the specification of the choosers' utility functions. In other words, the defender of *Homo economicus* deflects the criticism of the content of preferences by the claim that the structure of preferences rather than content is the central element of the model.

That says that public choice theorists need not assume that people are wealth maximizers, or selfish, or prone to prefer private advantage to social justice; all one need assume is that people seek whatever they are observed to seek. This empties the model of any meaning or predictive power whatever. Christ, Mother Teresa and the kamikaze pilots are all *homines economici* if it means no more than doing whatever you choose to do, for your own benefit or others'. Brennan and Buchanan think to evade this criticism by saying that for their purposes it is only necessary that 'individuals consider their own interests, whatever these may be, to be different from those of others'. If they are merely different by definition because they belong to different individuals the defence is pointless. If the real interests are assumed to differ, we are back with the objection to over-generalizing. Some interests differ, others don't; some of the things I want I want for my benefit, others for yours. Christ's, Mother Teresa's and the kamikaze pilots' purpose was precisely to subordinate or identify their interests with those of others. (So, in varying degrees, do the virtuous and affectionate propensities in all of us aspire to do, in our opinion.) The important thing for theoretical purposes is to grasp the effect of the switch which increasing numbers of public choice theorists are making, from assuming that people want to maximize their wealth to assuming that people vote their generous or disinterested social preferences as well as their individual interests. With that assumption the theory ceases to have any testable predictive power because it is explicitly ignorant of *what* motivates people's behaviour. Nevertheless it is still used as a conservative persuader, just as neoclassical theory is by some economists: it suggests that whatever people are currently getting must be the option they prefer of the options open to them by voluntary exchange – unless government action has frustrated or distorted the exchanges.

Brennan's and Buchanan's third defence, of the *homo economicus* assumption which they now concede to be of indeterminate content and unreliable for prediction, is the most remarkable. It is called 'the argument for symmetry'. It deserves to be quoted at length:

> On the basis of elementary methodological principle it would seem that the *same* model of human behavior should be applied across different institutions or different sets of rules. If, for example, different models of

human behavior were used in economic (market) and political contexts, there would be no way of isolating the effects of changing the institutions from the effects of changing the behavioral assumptions. Hence, to insist that the basic behavioral model remain invariant over institutions is to do no more than apply the ceteris paribus device in focusing on the question at issue.

If an individual in a market setting is to be presumed to exercise any power he possesses (within the limits of market rules) so as to maximize his net wealth, then an individual in a corresponding political setting must also be presumed to exercise any power he possesses (within the limits of political rules) in precisely the same way. If political agents do not exercise discretionary power in a manner analogous to market agents, then this result must follow because the rules of the political game constrain the exercise of power in ways the rules of the market do not, which is to say that the constraints are not comparable in the two settings. Otherwise, there must be an error in analysis or observation. No other conclusion is logically possible, given the invariance of the behavioral model across institutions.

This procedure does not, of course, rule out the possibility that actual behavior in differing institutional contexts will be different. What it does exclude is the introduction of behavioral difference as an analytic assumption. If behavioral differences are attributable to differences in rules, it must be possible to link the rules in some way to the behavioral patterns they generate, without resort to separate fundamental models of behavior, which can do nothing but guarantee emptiness in any attempted institutional comparison.

Summarily,

> The symmetry argument does nothing to establish *Homo economicus* as the appropriate model of human behavior. Alternative models may be introduced. The symmetry argument suggests only that whatever model of behavior is used, that model should be applied across all institutions.
>
> *The Reason of Rules* pp. 48–50

A first response to that might be to accept it, but substitute a better psychological model, for example of humans who maximize net wealth in their economic activities, safety and freedom in their political activities and love and the welfare of others in their household activities (though that would be almost as simplistic as the model it replaced). But that would not meet the objection that the effects of the psychology and of the different institutions' rules could not be separated analytically by the method of paired comparisons with *ceteris paribus*. What the quoted passage requires to make any sense at all is not that the same human nature operate under the different institutional rules, but that it be assumed to seek exactly the same thing, or pattern of things, in its political, economic and household activities.

The method is wrong for its purpose. The basic differences between public choice theory and traditional social thought are two: that public choice theorists use a single-purpose model of man, and expect it to explain all his behaviour, political as well as economic. In the passages quoted above, the Laureate of the movement concedes that the relevant model of man may well be false, and that using it to explain political as well as economic behaviour is justified not by observations of life but by methodological convenience. What is the convenience? Recall, from the passage already quoted:

> If ... different models of human behavior were used in economic ... and political contexts, there would be no way of isolating the effects of changing the institutions from the effects of changing the behavioral assumptions. Hence, to insist that the basic behavioral model remain invariant over institutions is to do no more than apply the ceteris paribus device in focusing on the question at issue.

The 'ceteris paribus device' is a wrong device – a useless device – for 'the question at issue'. If I assume that motivation is uniform, I must conclude that all observed differences between political and economic behaviour are caused by the different rules of the political and economic institutions. What is wrong with that as a scientific procedure should be obvious, but it may be spelled out by reversing the device. If I choose instead to assume that the rules of political and economic institutions are identical, I must conclude that all observed differences between political and economic behaviour arise from the different motivation of political and economic behaviour. The choice of assumption chooses the conclusion. The argument for 'symmetry' seems absurd.

In real life nature, culture, institutional structures and rules, and wilful individual decisions *interact* to determine behaviour. They are not independent forces whose aggregate or net effects constitute behaviour. Motives operate differently in the presence of different rules. Rules have different effects in the presence of different motives. They affect each other. Their interaction and effects cannot be discovered by 'holding' one and therefore ascribing all differences to the other. But the theorists' longing for that sort of science is obstinate:

... we do not take into consideration the whole personality of each individual when we discuss what behavior is rational for him. We do not allow for the rich diversity of ends served by each of his acts, the complexity of his motives, the way in which every part of his life is intimately related to his emotional needs. Rather we borrow from traditional economic theory the idea of the rational consumer ... We assume that he approaches every situation with one eye on the gains to be had, the other eye on the costs, a delicate ability to balance them, and a strong desire to follow wherever rationality leads him ... Empirical studies are almost unanimous in their conclusion that adjustment in primary (social) groups is far more crucial to nearly every individual than more remote considerations of economic or political welfare. Nevertheless, we must assume men orient their behavior chiefly toward the latter in our world; otherwise all analysis of either economics or politics turns into a mere adjunct of primary-group sociology.

A. Downs, *An Economic Theory of Democracy* (1957)

There are many empirical disproofs of conclusions derived from the *homo economicus* assumption. They are not the main concern of this book but we can mention some of the best known. A great many studies of voters' beliefs and behaviour show many of them voting for reasons of ideology, self-expression, family and party affiliation and racial, religious or national sentiment as well as, or often enough instead of, individual material advantage; and many do vote when rational maximizers would not. Many theorists have followed Niskanen[4] in assuming that bureaucrats' pay varies with the budget or number of employees the bureaucrats command, so they work to expand their empires and this explains the excessive growth of government. If that were general enough for reliable prediction it would be hard to explain why Sweden's government handles twice the proportion of GNP that Japan's government does, or why Australia and some other countries reduced their public sector shares through the 1980s. To a systematic inquiry into their beliefs in 1985/6, three quarters or more of Australia's central public service leaders said government was too big and ought to be reduced, public anxieties about its growth were justified, and its excessive growth had done more harm than good to efficiency and welfare.[5] Their beliefs appeared to owe more to their education in 'dry' economics than to their age, seniority, or class or individual economic interests; and they were indeed reducing government, including their own numbers and the real income of many public employees, significantly. In fact few governments have ever paid their biggest employers (commonly military chiefs and heads of health, welfare and educational services) as much as they pay their judges, auditors-general, consultant cost-cutters and heads of President's, Prime Minister's, Cabinet and Treasury departments which have high importance but command comparatively small numbers and departmental budgets. Some bureaucrats have certainly risen by expanding their operations as the theorists assume, but in recent years there have probably been more personal rewards for public managers who cut numbers and costs than for those who inflate them. Peter Self observes that even if strictly egoistic, 'the bureaucrat may place more weight on having a quiet life or a cautious security (surely the best choice in some institutional settings), or ... he may maximise his personal gains by controlling or dismantling other parts of government. Also relevant would be the nature of his career structure, peer influence and opinion, institutional and group rivalries, and even perhaps the bureaucrat's own sense of public service'.[6]

A second reason why few of the theories pass predictive tests is that, unlike the natural-scientific theories they try to imitate, most of them are not designed to be testable. Honest theorizing of the axiomatic deductive kind searches for postulates from which testable predictions can be deduced. Most public choice theorists stick to their distinctive postulates about motivation, and spend their time elaborating the deductions which can be derived from them, however untestable those deductions may be. There is much reasoning to the effect that 'if people are rational maximizers, it follows that their activities under particular freedoms or constraints must be affording them this or that degree of satisfaction, which however we cannot measure, because satisfactions are subjective and incapable of interpersonal aggregation'. Alternatively actual political effects are ascribed, wherever it seems at all plausible, to the postulated motivation alone. Such theorizing seems to be judged (by journal editors and referees, and academic appointment and promotion committees) not for its performance in any useful social or scientific sense but for its elegance, originality, fidelity to the original articles of faith, and (with some editors) the density of algebra on the page. Trying to test parts of it has become a minor specialist interest rather than a main concern in the design of theories. What the reported tests chiefly offer are occasional correspondence between theory and life, or selective historical explanations like that of Mancur Olson noticed earlier. Examples are analysed later in this chapter.

If the purpose is really to understand and predict political behaviour better than politicians or political scientists do, by dismissing much of what they know about people's motivation, it seems absurd to persist after more than thirty years with a type of theory which persistently fails to deliver. At the very least such infertility should have provoked some serious writing about the reasons for persisting in that direction, and for expecting such abstract, axiomatic, universal theory to help rather than hinder political understanding. But we can find none: only the unchanging injunction, from a dwindling proportion of the theorists, to 'wait and see: proof is just around the corner'. We are driven to agree with the philosophers, political scientists, historians, sociologists, lawyers and industrial relations experts who believe that the industry continues partly as a source of dubious arguments for small government (where better liberal and conservative arguments are available) and partly as a recreation which has been, but should no longer be, accepted by the theorists' peers as a payable academic activity.

While public choice theorists have persisted with their assumption of a single motive, there has been an increasing volume of factual research by psychologists and others into people's actual motives, wants, and sources of satisfaction and happiness. A survey and summary of the results of more than a thousand investigations appeared in 1991 in Robert E. Lane's *The Market Experience*. Among Lane's conclusions are these: When members of affluent societies are assured of a basic standard of living, economic factors become much less important sources of happiness and satisfaction (or lack of them) than are family life, friendship, intellectual development, self-reliance and self-esteem. In their economic activities they do not behave with anything like the consistent greed and rationality of economic theory. (Firms often do, but people acting on their own behalf usually don't.) Economic activity still does quite a lot to help or hinder their personal development and happiness – but it does so much more powerfully through their experience of work than through the levels of wealth, income, leisure and consumption that they achieve. Above the breadline, there is very little relation between income and happiness, but a strong relation between happiness and challenging, self-directed, enjoyable work. Lane concludes that 'the economists' ideas that work is the sacrifice or disutility that earns for workers the benefits or utilities of consumption is ... quite false'. (p. 235)

This research has a simple implication for public choice theory. Most critics of public choice theory have argued that economic theory cannot explain political behaviour. The mass of evidence surveyed in *The Market Experience* says that it cannot explain much economic behaviour either: it is basically, psychologically untrue of most individual human motivation.

Before discussing some general qualities of public choice reasoning we consider a couple of samples, chosen because they offer both detailed and very general explanations of government behaviour, and have strong policy implications.

BUREAUCRACY

William Niskanen based his theory of bureaucracy on the assumption that a desire to maximize their budgets sufficiently explains bureaucrats' behaviour. Neither Gordon Tullock's nor Anthony Downs' books on the subject agreed with that, and the facts don't always agree with it. We sketched Niskanen's analysis earlier. Here we notice what he proposed to do about it.

To make bureaucracy more efficient Niskanen suggested three measures. Government bureaus should compete with one another (and where possible with private suppliers) by trying to underbid one another in tenders for government business. When a bureau wins a contract, its chief should be allowed to pocket a proportion of any budget savings the bureau achieves (*Bureaucracy and Representative Government*, pp. 201–9). He should also get his appointment as head of bureau by competitive bidding, probably by offering the politicians who appoint him bigger campaign contributions (to be sourced from budget savings) than his competitors offer them (pp. 202, 207). Since many government outputs can't be measured (pp. 42, 47), and profit-seeking bureaucrats will therefore compete to cut costs by short-changing the customers, who may then recoil against the politicians who order the services, how can the politicians protect themselves? They must appoint monitors. Niskanen has no great faith in the monitors, but does not subject them to his standard analysis. Readers can do so. If Niskanen is right, the monitors must also be bureaus with profit-seeking chiefs. To cut their costs in order to generate budget savings and personal gains, all they need do is monitor less rigorously. They have a further incentive to do that: the people whom they monitor have jobs and personal gains (also at customers' expense) whose retention depends on favorable monitors' reports, so favorable reports should certainly earn a cut of the gains. If bureau chiefs won't cut the monitors in, hostile reports can have them replaced. (Another branch of public choice theory specializes in the 'capture' of monitors.)

The trouble with setting a thief to catch a thief is that they will often do better to join forces. This scheme would put the boldest robbers of the public purse in charge of it, as long as they shared their loot with the politicians. We think public and politicians, even venal politicians, would do better to look for honest, committed, salaried bureau chiefs and have their work reviewed where necessary by honest, committed, salaried monitors. Niskanen strongly disagrees. He thinks honest government is overrated. 'The widespread disregard of some laws and the long-term corruption of some regulatory agencies and local governments often represent a functional accommodation to bad law', and trying to keep people honest takes the monitors' minds off keeping their operations efficient (pp. 192–4). How such puritanical monitors come to exist in a public choice world Niskanen does not explain. He acknowledges that 'the combination of honest government and good government' if it ever does occur is 'twice blessed', but does not appear to think it worthwhile to recruit and train people and design institutions to achieve that double blessing.

Niskanen's argument is pragmatic: dutiful public servants are few, and are apt to be obsessed with honesty rather than efficiency. James Buchanan runs a similar line for more fundamental reasons. His own version of the theory for which he is famous assumes selfish wealth-maximizing behaviour in everyone. If that is changeable, the theory is not curable: any dutiful public service contradicts it. So Buchanan has repeatedly advised against attempts to improve the education, training or selection of public servants, or to nourish a 'culture of service'. He wants an incurably self-serving bureaucracy to be restrained from evildoing by legal and constitutional restraints alone.

RENT-SEEKING

Gordon Tullock's 1967 argument[7] about what has since been labelled rent-seeking was sketched in Chapter 2. If socially unproductive gains (for example from tariff protection) are available from government, many will try to get them. The social costs are the consumption lost by the winners' inefficient use of resources, the lobbying and other costs of the unsuccessful as well as the successful contenders for government favours, and whatever the government spends on deciding and administering, or resisting, the unproductive favours. Those costs may well equal or exceed the winners' gains.

These were intelligent concerns, though less novel than public choice theorists claim – Tullock's originality lay in introducing cloistered welfare economists to relationships long familiar to others. Legislative draftsmen and judges in courts of record spend much of their time worrying about the unintended effects and unnecessary responses which may be prompted by the rules they write. A few critical decisions, for example, have kept gold-digging litigation for professional negligence, and the consequent growth of defensive over-servicing, at much lower levels elsewhere than in the United States. Most European governments manage their trade policies in ways which attract a little less lobbying than occurs in Washington. Governments designing welfare services and entitlements were trying not to invite undesirable responses to the new opportunities long before there was public choice theory. And so on – but it was true that these pervasive facts of life were not reflected in economists' welfare theory, so there was good reason for Tullock's contribution.

We noted that Tullock's paper recognized business as well as government sinners. Firms can seek unproductive gains in a business way by building monopolies, or in a state-aided way by lobbying for tariffs. Government causes social losses by listening to pleas for tariffs, but it also *reduces* social losses by anti-trust action. (The cost of anti-trust action is a social loss but it may prevent bigger losses by deterring attempts at monopoly.) This evenhanded approach has been continued by some welfare and institutional economists, some of whom call the subject 'directly unproductive profit-seeking'. But most public choice work on the subject calls it rent-seeking, defines it as 'the resource-wasting activities of individuals in seeking transfers of wealth through the aegis of the state',[8] and blames government as creator of the rent-seeking opportunities, rather than the rent-seekers themselves who are merely doing what comes rationally.

From tariff and monopoly the theorists have moved on to identify rent-seeking wherever government administers collective marketing or price support schemes; licenses people to practise skilled trades and professions; regulates industry; chooses locations for public enterprises or public goods; or contracts with private suppliers for goods and services. There is mathematical theory, much of it with fairly unreal assumptions, about the propensity to seek rents: the proportions of their turnover or investment or asset value which firms in different situations with different risk aversion, different numbers of competitors, etc., might rationally invest in seeking unproductive gains of various kinds.

As the literature has expanded, some micro- and some macro-absurdities have appeared in it. Case by case, some theorists have extended 'rent-seeking' to include any gain-seeking from government, however productive or not the relevant activity may be. Competitive private tenders to supply productive public goods – schools, offices, roads and bridges – are defined as rent-seeking as the theorists' attention slides from the outcome of the activity to its gain-seeking motivation. Add all such cases together and there may be no remainder of efficient, unwasteful public action. One macro-theory of rent-seeking proposes itself as a sufficient theory of the state. In *Politicians, Legislation and the Economy* (1981) R.E. McCormick and R.D. Tollison declare that all legislation transfers wealth, usually from weaker to stronger contenders for government favour, *and may be assumed to have no other purpose*. Six years later Tollison was even surer that government is about taking wealth from some people ... and giving it to other people ... or put into the terms of this chapter, about rent-protection and rent-seeking.

Most people are taken aback at such a starkly simple (and cynical) view of government. They wonder, well surely government is about something more than organized, legitimate theft? Surely government is about Truth, Beauty, Justice, the American Way, and the production of Public Goods?

And, of course, the rent-seeking theory has answers to these types of questions. Yes, government does produce things in the rent-seeking theory of the state, but these are mere by-products of the fundamental transfers at stake. We thus get our national defense, roads, schools, and so on as an unintended consequence of the competition for wealth-transfers ...

But more importantly, and more scientifically, the rent-seeking theory of government is an *empirical* theory. Not only is it on the front page of the newspapers every day, but there is scholarly empirical support for the theory which is strong and growing. This cannot be said about any other theory of government (such as the public interest theory) of which I am aware. And it is this scientific hallmark (testability) of the rent-seeking theory, which will make it harder and harder to avoid as the best available rational choice explanation of government ... There is an important empirical theory of government extant, and it is the rent-seeking theory.[9]

We can compare Niskanen's belief that 'The US federal government annually transfers around $30 billion to special interest groups other than the poor, the primary purpose of which is to induce around $100 million in campaign contributions'. (*Bureaucracy and Representative Government* p. 207) Similar explanations (on ten times the scale) are offered for the US defence budget. Most of this writing does not merely purport to expose particular American scandals; it is offered as a general theory of democratic government.

Two things are wrong with that (and with much writing like it). First it conveys scientistic illusions about social knowledge. See how it conceives theory. In principle (it implies) theory must explain and predict behaviour by deduction from axioms, which should be as few as possible. In practice that usually means ascribing effects to single causes and behaviour to a single type of motive. Thus Tollison contrasts his rent-seeking theory of the state with a public interest theory of the state as monocausal alternatives, mutually exclusive, one right and the other wrong.

Second, be clear what his theory of the state says. It says there is mounting factual proof that all our roads and bridges, schools and universities, public and academic scientific research (antibiotics, electronics, laser surgery, genetic engineering) and defence forces and policies are 'mere by-products' – explicitly, *unintended* consequences – of plundering misuses of legislative power. It does not say that some of them were accompanied by corruption, it says that none of them was motivated by anything else. Only the 'legitimate theft' was intended, the actual public goods were not. People who disagree with this are first accused of supposing that all government is conducted with godlike altruism. If they insist that actual motives are mixed and variable they are dismissed as forsaking theory and proper science for 'mere description and *ad hoc*ery'.

Students are taught these images of science and of government. Such stuff educates rising numbers of the people we employ to govern us, and tells us not to hope or try to improve their quality. Insistently, explicitly, it tells *them* not to try to improve, except as 'legitimate thieves': to be anything else is irrational. Remember it, reader, as often as you think this book unreasonably angry.

We can attend more calmly to theory which tries to stick to rent-seeking from unproductive activity. Some of it, especially some of its case studies, is valuable, but does not need distinctive public choice assumptions to make it so. Most of it has a selective bias: unlike some of the economists who study unproductive profit-seeking of all kinds, public choice theorists tend to look only for gain-seeking from government. In deciding how much of that is wasteful there is rarely the attention that there ought to be to the imagined alternatives or counterfactuals by which the waste is measured.

For example, not all tariffs reduce output or consumption. But scarcely any theory or case study of rent-seeking by tariff acknowledges even the orthodox exceptions for infant industries, advantages of scale, exchange-rate and balance-of-payment problems, or responsive/corrective uses of tariffs. There are also other objections to the assumption that all trade restrictions waste resources which would otherwise be better used. If depopulating an industrial region or a company town disuses more public and domestic capital than it saves private capital, orthodox economists will not notice the wasteful effects; but protecting the relevant industry, permanently or transitionally, may preserve more real output than it loses. There are conditions, especially in small countries, in which protecting some industries can sustain skills and supply inputs for other industries, profitably in total. Diversity of occupations may also be valued for the variety of work, skills and lifestyles that it offers to a national population.

The theme need not be laboured. Tullock and most other public choice theorists have assumed that the alternative to any tariff is an ideally competitive, efficient supply with full employment and no strategic economic or exchange problems. (Historically it has been the lack of some of those conditions which has occasioned many of the tariffs.) Some of the rent-seeking studies also appear to assume that population can move freely, without cost, between regions and nations, and that there is always an efficient capital market without speculative dealing or public influence on the supply or international movement of money. When opportunity costs are defined thus by reference to ideal rather than actual alternatives, the best available options can be defined as wasteful. We agree with the institutional economists who insist on comparative rather than imaginary measures of economic performance; but those too can be uncertain: which compared cases offer practicable alternatives to each other in particular conditions of time and place? 'In the real world ... measuring inefficiency has a large arbitrary component'.[10]

There is a further reason for that. All economic activity, and the value of products by which 'welfare' is measured, depend on property rights and procedures. Those rights and rules necessarily change from time to time and are the subject of efforts by many interested and disinterested parties to defend or reform them. To define as wasteful a change from one property basis to another may be arbitrary in that it must be based on one basis or the other; and more generally it is either a technical mistake or wilfully conservative to define all law-changing and law-defending activity in a dynamic self-governing society as wasteful. Much of it is a necessary condition of any efficiently adaptable legal system. Writing it off as wasteful is like writing off as wasteful all the immediately-unfruitful elements in private firms' mineral search, research and experimental activities, or policy discussions.

Nevertheless rough work may be better than none, and when it is done on sensible and well-understood assumptions, identifying unproductive rent- and profit-seeking is, we agree, a useful activity. Some public choice theorists contribute usefully to it. But much of their work is distorted by biases *against* government and *for* axiomatic theory. If we now list some effects of the biases it is not to suggest that they all appear in all the work, but they afflict a good deal of it.

Institutional arrangements vary greatly in the opportunities they offer for rent-seeking. The bad cases are often reformable. Put like that, most public choice theorists would agree (except those who depict all government, however designed, as purely predatory). But in practice the longing for universal theory is strong, and we have read many case studies of rent-seeking attracted by particular institutional arrangements in particular (usually local American) conditions, which are then generalized to large classes of institution or policy, or to government generally, when more useful and supportable conclusions would recommend specific local reforms.

Theorists of rent-seeking scarcely ever search the democratic world for its *best* practices and try to generalize principles or policies from those. It is hard to escape the conclusion that most of them do not want there to be any very good government.

There can be considerable independence between the virtues (or not) of public policies, and the opportunities they make for private gain and gain-seeking. Some excellent policies are accompanied by some waste or corruption; some worthless policies make no private opportunities. Some theorists (though not Niskanen, we noticed) tend to judge the public worth of the policies as inverse to the private gain or waste that accompanies them. Some go further to insist that the private gain, not the public output, is the effective purpose of the policies. (That view of government is the mirror-image of the crude Left view of capitalism, which sees profit as its only purpose, the exploitation of labour as its only significant effect, and production as incidental, if reported at all.)

The literature is sometimes clear in principle but less often strict in practice at distinguishing the costs of unsuccessful gain-seeking which –

- are necessary to efficient production;
- may but need not accompany efficient production;
- substantially reduce the efficiency of production; or
- accompany and perhaps motivate unproductive activity.

Only the last fits Tullock's original characterization of the welfare costs of tariffs and monopolies. But in dealing with the other three the literature shows wide variations, often shaped by anti-government prejudice. A notional example will illustrate.

(1) A private housing developer usually chooses his building contractors by competitive public tender, i.e. by considering as many tenders as are attracted by a public invitation to tender. If there are (say) six tenders, the tendering costs of the unsuccessful five are wasted. They may sometimes total more than the successful tenderer's profit on the contract. No public choice theorists, as far as we know, count those costs as rent-seeking waste.

(2) A public housing developer does the same for the same reasons with the same efficient result, because ambitiously she wants to be seen to do her job well, and compassionately she wants to house as many poor families as possible from her fixed capital budget. Some public choice theorists will count the unsuccessful tenderers' costs as rent-seeking waste. Few will believe the account of the woman's or her board's motives in our first sentence above.

(3) The private housing developer, a shrewd operator who knows his business and his builders well, sometimes finds it more efficient to contract

with one builder directly without going to tender. Nobody calls that builder's profit rent.

(4)   The public developer does the same for the same reasons with the same effect. Most public choice theorists will call some part at least of the builder's profit rent. Many will also suppose that the builder must have got his contract by somehow rewarding the developer, and that the developer's subordinates will redouble their rent-seeking efforts to displace her in order to attract such inducements for themselves.

(5)   A corporate board builds itself a luxurious country retreat 'for strategic think-tanking and long-term policy planning'. Senior managers redouble their efforts – and their diversion of corporate and personal resources – in attempts, mostly unsuccessful, to flatter and cajole their way into board seats. Some public choice theorists might report some rent-seeking if the facts were brought to their notice, but very few go looking for such private sector cases. Others would define directors' rewards as market exchanges and perceive no rents at all. None will ascribe the firm's existence and output to the directors' rent-seeking rather than the owners' profit-seeking.

(6)   If the board of a public enterprise does the same, all public choice theorists will report rents, rent-seeking costs and social waste. Some will assert that the rents are the part or sole cause of the enterprise's existence and output.

These discriminations spoil what could otherwise be useful investigative work in (we hesitate to say it) the public interest.

From these samples of theory at work we now turn to some of the theorists' methodological claims.

POSITIVIST PRETENCES

One way in which public choice theorists map what they do employs a distinction between positive and normative theory, a distinction which they relate to the concept of Pareto optimality.

An allocation of resources is said to be Pareto optimal if no change can make anyone better off without making someone else worse off.

If opportunities do exist to make everyone better off, or to make some better off without any loss to others, it is assumed that nobody need oppose such changes, so support for them can be unanimous. Such improvements are movements toward or onto the Pareto frontier. Once a Pareto optimum is achieved it is assumed that no change from it can expect unanimous support because (by definition) any change must disadvantage somebody.[11]

So far, the argument claims to be 'positive' in that it relies on objective observation and logic. It does not require any value judgements or interpersonal comparisons of utility (which many theorists regard as unwarranted guesswork). All the judgements of better or worse off are made by the relevant individuals for themselves and revealed to the observer by their behaviour. In 'Politics without romance' (1984) James Buchanan insisted that the theory of public choice 'is or can be a wholly positive theory, wholly scientific and *wertfrei* in the standard meanings of these terms'.[12]

For any society there can of course be any number of alternative Pareto optima. For example if resources are distributed with perfect equality and nobody can gain without somebody losing, that is Pareto optimal. If a monarch owns everything and his subjects are slaves who own nothing, that also is Pareto optimal if the slaves could gain only at the monarch's cost. In neither condition could a unanimous vote for any change be expected.[13]

To prefer one Pareto optimum to another, or to define a change from one to another as a change for the better or worse, it *is* necessary to make value judgements and perhaps interpersonal comparisons of utility. You may guess that taking some of the monarch's surplus wealth that he never uses, to supply a thousand slaves with better food and clothing, is likely to add more to their happiness than it subtracts from the monarch's happiness (a factual guess). You may decide that the change should therefore be made (a moral judgement). You may want to make it even if the pain to the monarch is greater than the pleasure to the slaves, if your principles of justice (another moral choice) don't require you to total up everyone's subjective 'utility'. If you predict that the slaves would vote for such a change under a democratic constitution which allowed majority decisions about property rights, that may be a factual prediction, but if you believe it justifies making such a change or having such a constitution you are again making judgements of right and wrong.

This is the basis of the belief that quite objective factual conclusions can be drawn about changes which move systems towards or onto the Pareto frontier: if all or some members can be seen to have gained and none have lost, the system's service to its members has clearly improved. But moves *along* the frontier, from one Pareto optimal condition to another, and any other changes that leave losers as well as winners, cannot be identified as changes for better or worse – observers may not be able to identify the direction or net effects of such changes – without applying some principle of justice, or weighing the winners' pleasure from their gains against the losers' pain from their losses.

The theorists' conclusion is that the study of unanimous behaviour and of systems which require unanimous consent to any change can be value-free and 'positive'; the study of non-unanimous behaviour and of systems which allow non-unanimous changes of law or policy is necessarily normative.

That distinction is often accompanied by a distinction between 'allocation' and 'distribution' (or more often, 'redistribution'). The disposition of resources in a Pareto optimal system is called an allocation of resources. Moves towards or onto the Pareto frontier (i.e. changes which make some better use of resources without reducing any individual's resources) may well be achieved by improving the allocation of resources. But changes which take from some members to give to others cannot be defined as improvements (because that would require moral or interpersonal judgements) so they are called *re*distributions. They cannot happen under any constitution which requires that changes be unanimous, because the potential losers would veto them. They may happen without disturbing the Pareto optimum if they come by market 'exchange', for example if technical changes extinguish some firms or some jobs; but if government extinguishes the jobs the losers have cause to complain.

The theorists' general distinction between positive and normative public choice theory may be summarized as follows:

Positive theory deals with –
- the allocation of resources
- constitutions which require that changes have unanimous support
- changes with no losers
- Pareto optimal allocations
- movements onto the Pareto frontiers

Normative theory deals with –
- the redistribution of resources
- constitutions which allow majority rule
- changes with losers, including
- movements along the Pareto frontier from one Pareto optimum to another

Those distinctions relate to the 'macroeconomics' of public choice, i.e. to theory about political systems as wholes. Buchanan certainly meant his claim of value-freedom to apply not only to items in the left hand column, but also to the 'micro' theory of individual political behaviour. That theory reasons its way from postulates about motivation to the likely behaviour of individuals, and consequently of institutions , in a world in which the postulates are assumed to hold. Users of the theory are invited to see for themselves how well its explanations and predictions (i) accord with real political life, and (ii) compare with explanations and predictions arrived at by other means.

Question: What could be value-structured about that approach?

Answer: As Buchanan develops it, at least five things. It seeks to entrench some laws but not others against alteration by majority vote. It distinguishes political processes from outcomes. It gives contradictory meanings at different times to its concept of unanimity. It relies on a tax-collector's distinction between capital and income. It argues that for an important category of laws it is not majority rule but a right of veto for any individual or minority that should count as democratic. Each of these arguments has value premises and the following sections expose some of them to see what the values appear to be.

MEANINGS OF UNANIMITY

The desire for political unanimity seems absurd because real societies are rarely unanimous about anything, least of all the constitution their members would prefer or the particular public goods they would like to pay for. Why bother to theorize about such improbabilities? Critics tend to believe that the main purpose is to justify giving the rich a veto over any transfer of their wealth. We think there is also an ambition to keep the theory value-free. Since it is impossible for any significant social theory to be value-free, those who try too hard to achieve the impossible are driven into ambiguities and contradictions.

If you wish to understand politics as a marketplace for individual exchanges, there are alternative ways of understanding the economic markets which supply your market model. You can focus on the fact that voluntary market exchanges take place under market rules. The individual traders have not usually given unanimous consent to all the market rules. The rules are typically made by state or local governments or representative trade associations. They typically include rules against types of misbehaviour which some of the traders would vote to permit if they had their way. So if your values and social purposes prompt you to understand politics as a market in order to give special importance to its elements of individual exchange, economic markets do not actually give you any ground for requiring that the constitution – the 'market rules' of government – should have every citizen's consent. Some of the rules are likely to be needed to prevent misbehaviour which some of the citizens would otherwise commit, and perhaps vote to deregulate. Moreover a majority of small traders may think it fair to finance the market's administrative costs from a tax on the richest traders rather than on (say) all turnover.

That would not accord with most public choice theorists' values, so they are tempted by an alternative view. Instead of focusing on the provenance of the market rules they choose to focus on the fact that traders in economic markets volunteer to trade there. That is not a universal fact – plenty of people must trade in their local markets or starve – but to the extent that trading *is* voluntary the traders may be assumed to consent to the market rules. It is similarly argued that if people are free to leave their country those who choose to stay may be presumed to consent to the country's laws. The same reservation applies – in practice many people cannot easily emigrate – but for those who can, public choice theorists are not the first to argue that they can be presumed to consent *even to laws they have voted against*. That is the only basis on which it is remotely practical to speak of unanimous consent to the laws; but it has special hazards for public choice theorists. If a millionaire's continuing presence in a country signifies his consent to its laws, including any laws which he votes against, it follows that majority rule may lawfully take away his millions and public choice theorists will have to call that act 'unanimous'. We will presently see that the theorists define justice as compliance with rules agreed to unanimously, so they may also have to call the plunder 'just'.

To avoid those intolerable conclusions the theorists are driven to use different concepts of unanimity for different purposes, especially for defining the respective rights of rich and poor. On pp. 102–3 of Geoffrey Brennan and James Buchanan, *The Reason of Rules* (1985) members of any society are assumed to consent to its rules. 'The mere fact of participation obligates each participant, as if by an explicit promise, to abide by the rules, provided that the participants have a genuine option not to participate if they so choose.' However difficult it might be to emigrate, however a citizen may have voted against the relevant laws, however disadvantaged she may be as (say) a struggling lone parent contending with the rich and powerful for political influence, there is no escape from the obligation to *obey* the laws, which (by a logical slide) public choice theorists call *consenting* to and *agreeing with* the laws:

> To say, for example, that the agreement is nonvoluntary if the bargaining strengths of the parties to it are not precisely equal seems absurdly restrictive. It seems that only in cases of extreme duress or outright coercion does agreement to the rules *not* morally bind the players . . . It is worth making this point clearly so as to guard against the prospect of admitting alien concepts of "justice" through the back door under the cover of the "voluntariness" constraint. In some literature, the "justice" of abiding by an agreement is made entirely contingent on the justice of the status quo, the latter notion of "justice" usually making appeal to the relative income positions of the parties. We emphasize that the voluntariness of agreement is not to be so construed in our conception.

So much for the rights of poor people who disagree with laws which keep them poor. But turn to page 138 for the rights of the rich to veto laws which might reduce their riches – for example

> a collective decision to levy a tax on wealth. In this case, persons who have accumulated wealth have made prior choices under other rules. A change in fiscal rules of this sort violates all criteria of "fairness" and could never lay claim to Pareto superiority [i.e. unanimous support] even as a purely conceptual criterion.

The weak interpretation of unanimity – the one on page 102, the presumption that every member of society consents to its rules – cannot possibly protect capital owners from such horrors. Capital owners must have the strong interpretation, the Pareto test which entitles any citizen to veto any change that threatens his interests.

Should the poor, then, be entitled to veto increases in their tax burdens? Not necessarily – not if we introduce two further distinctions, one between rules and the distributions to which they lead, and one between prospective and retrospective legislation in a novel meaning of those terms. First,

> rules provide the framework within which patterns of distributional end states emerge from the interaction of persons (players) who play various complex functional roles. The precise distributional effects of a change in the rules on any identified person or group at any point in time may be difficult or impossible to predict. A status quo defined only in terms of the rules (the laws and institutions) within which persons act is conceptually very different from a status quo described by a particular distribution of valued goods and claims. . . .
>
> Changes in rules are *prospective* in their distributional implications, whereas changes in observed distributions themselves are necessarily *retrospective*, with reference to the choice behaviour of the persons who act to generate the results. Changes in rules that can lay claim at all to consensual agreement can, at best, modify personal expectations about future distributional patterns. Rule changes cannot modify observed distributions as such . . .
>
> [For example] A collective decision to levy a progressive tax on incomes is a change in fiscal rules. Despite the distributional consequences that might be predicted, such a decision may conceptually be agreed to by all persons in the community, particularly if there is a time lag between the agreement and actual levying of the tax. An individual

would know that if he chose to earn income, this income would be taxed at progressive rates.

The Reason of Rules, p. 138

The ban on taxing capital follows, to complete the refined social morality distilled on this memorable page. If I choose to spend my youth learning a trade which is expected to earn me a particular after-tax income, it is proper for government to change the rules and frustrate those expectations. It is not clear whether that may be done by majority vote as a 'post-constitutional' act; or with my consent given because I fail to foresee the harm it may do me; or with my consent presumed because I have not emigrated; but one way or another it may be done. If on the other hand I spend my youth accumulating capital, or if I inherit capital which my ancestors acquired by industry, luck, war or crime, my expectation that I can enjoy it all, untaxed, for life, without emigrating, must be inviolable. For a majority to overrule me on that issue would not only be 'retrospective', it would also be 'majoritarian' which is defined as undemocratic; what is defined as democratic is for my single veto to overrule any majority.

It is true, as these theorists and many welfare economists believe, that the use of Pareto's concept of efficiency requires no value judgments by those who use it? No. To choose it as one's only criterion of efficiency is a moral choice. To do so for the purpose of avoiding value judgements is another moral choice. To use it to argue for political unanimity and rights of veto is another and quite nasty moral choice – it declares it to be socially efficient for slave-owners to veto the abolition of slavery, for the rich to veto any regulation or reduction of their wealth, for corporate swindlers to veto any strengthening of company law, for the employed to veto any income transfers to the unemployed. It is a poor defence of the theorists' objectivity to say 'We do not necessarily endorse such social arrangements as right or good, we merely recognize in them, analytically, a Pareto optimum as defined'. To draw attention to this and to no other meaning of efficiency is unavoidably persuasive; and the truthfulness of the Paretian test is as dubious as its morality. Because scarcely any economic changes increase everybody's income, Paretians have to insist that changes which increase some incomes without reducing others are improvements which nobody need oppose. (People who oppose them are commonly accused of envy.) The Paretian belief conceals the value judgement that an absolute loss of income does the loser material harm but a proportionate loss does not. That may be objectively false as well as morally disputable. Any increase in a society's total income may pose divisive questions about its distribution: a member's interest in getting a larger or smaller share of the gain is no different in principle from her interest in avoiding a loss. Gains for some but not for others can often cause actual loss to the others. If workers' wages rise, for example, that may hurt the rich by making golf lessons or domestic service more expensive for them. If the rich get richer without reducing poor incomes the poor may still lose in a variety of ways. They may suffer stigma when they can't keep up with prevailing lifestyles. More materially, some supplies are not expandable so if the rich get richer the poor are likely to get absolutely less – for example, as the rich get richer they bid up the price of land so the poor can afford less of it and at worse locations, which often also means less and worse housing. The same may be true of energy as that becomes scarce. It has been true of many necessities in wartime, justifying rationing and price controls – but those would generally be vetoed under a Paretian rule of unanimity. The Paretian decision to count amounts but not proportional shares of income is both value-based and factually deceptive.

PROCESSES AND OUTCOMES

There are similar objections, factual and moral, to claims that distinctions between political 'processes' and 'outcomes', or between rules and outcomes, are quite objective. The distinction between process and outcome is specially slippery. There is an obvious sense in which all processes are outcomes and many outcomes are processes: which is defined as which depends on the moments at which the observer chooses to start and stop the clock. Suppose that a harmful industrial process hurts workers (a process, an outcome) so that reformers begin to agitate (an outcome, a process) to change the law, and parliament changes it. The new law is an outcome which establishes a new process, whose outcomes differ from those of the former law, and in time affect other processes and outcomes in society. Each step can reasonably be seen as both process and outcome, and as having outcomes which are, or affect, processes. Thus a principle that laws should regulate processes but not outcomes is in practice indeterminate: many of the relevant effects can be defined as either or both, at will.

The distinction between rules and outcomes seems clearer at first sight. There is an obvious difference between the rules of poker or tennis and the way individuals choose to play those games and determine their winning or losing outcomes. But in politics the distinction can be less clear. Consider an example at the 'outcome' end of the spectrum: a once-for-all land reform, as in Russia in 1917 or Japan in 1946. One observer can reasonably perceive that the law specified an outcome: a specific pattern and distribution of land ownership. Another observer can just as reasonably see the law creating rules under which land was transferred from one owner to another: the law did not have a million clauses, each specifying a transfer between named owners. Whether the macroeconomic effect or the microeconomic effects are seen as the law's 'outcome' is a matter of choice, and the choice determines whether the law is seen as determining rules or outcomes. Why should it matter? – most rules are designed to affect outcomes and are judged by their actual or expected outcomes; and how directly or indirectly government should try to contrive the outcomes is often a purely pragmatic choice. If fuel is scarce should the law leave it to market 'rationing by price', or ration or license it administratively, or ban some uses of it, or deter its use by taxing it, or tax vehicles according to their engine capacity, or reduce speed limits? All the measures aim at the same outcome, i.e. more efficient use of less fuel. They all have other outcomes too: different effects on individuals' personal and business freedoms and on society's patterns of inequality. In choosing measures a number of principles of efficiency and equity may be brought to bear; there is no special privilege for the principle that laws should determine rules but not outcomes, even when the distinction between them is clear, which it often is not.

Why then do theorists persist with these impractical distinctions? Three reasons suggest themselves, in diminishing order of respectability. First, public choice theorists understandably want the laws to be as clear as possible, and individuals to be as free as possible to determine how to behave within the rules. But in practice that is the same as wanting good rather than bad rules, or wanting the rules to be as few and clear as possible. Rather than relying on the often-unclear distinction between rules and outcomes it would be better to list or categorize, in the light of the theorist's values and technical understanding, the types of behaviour that should and should not be constrained and the rules or kinds of rule that might achieve the most desired and the least undesired constraints.

A second purpose of the distinctions seems to be, as many critics have alleged, to protect established property rights and interests against redistribution. If the distribution of wealth and income is defined as an 'outcome' with which the law and the government should not interfere, efforts to alter the distribution will at least have to be indirect. Changing the rules under which people contend for wealth and income must be done by constitutional means. Many public choice theorists want the constitutional rules to be entrenched against alteration by simple majority vote, whether by requirements of unanimity or by other means. Wealth would indeed be secure if two more of Buchanan's policies were adopted, to ban interference with capital owners' expectations as 'retrospective', and to write tax limits into entrenched constitutions. But there is nothing objective about defining the distribution of wealth and income as an 'outcome'. Money circulates continuously as people earn and save and spend. If you photograph its whereabouts or ownership on a payday the distribution is different from what it was the day before. Whether for analytic or policy-making purposes, only your value-structured purposes can tell you whether to define the distribution of wealth and income as the continuous process of distribution; or as a snapshot of ownership on a particular day; or as the set of aggregates that people get through per week, per year or per lifetime; or as some selection of the innumerable rules which directly or indirectly affect the processes of distribution. It takes two value judgements to decide that the distribution is 'an outcome, not a process', and that the law should not prescribe outcomes.

A third purpose of the distinctions is in effect to reify the Rawlsian veil of ignorance, in the belief that the less people know about the effects of their voting, the more unanimously they may vote. An argument in the final chapter of *The Reason of Rules* appears to claim objective, value-free status for the proposition that there may be unanimous support for entrenching constitutions against majority rule. If political discourse is about rules rather than outcomes (the argument goes) people are less likely to be able to predict the outcomes of their voting. That may calm their fears and attract support for consensual measures, or alternatively it may frighten people into agreeing to least-risk rules, rules which appear to minimize the risk of individual loss. Thus 'an individual can construct a bridge, of sorts, between short-term, identifiable private interest and long-term, nonidentifiable self-interest, which then becomes "public interest".'[14] That consideration might be thought to weigh equally with rich and poor voters. But rich voters have more to lose; they tend to be (or to employ) better-equipped forecasters of the likely outcomes of alternative rules; and they command more means of public persuasion than poor voters do. So it is hard to avoid the suspicion that the less the mass of voters know about the likely effects of their constitutional choices, the easier it may be to persuade them to vote for (or to support by not emigrating) rules which reduce rather than increase capital owners' risks.

The theorists' most breathtaking distinction is between the nature of their own and other people's ideas of public good and communality. Like most public choice theorists Buchanan has consistently denounced all talk of public interest, public good and communal morality as one or all of illusory, arbitrary, authoritarian, and camouflage for individual self-interest.

But without recanting any of that he depicts his own idea of public interest and communal morality as real, objectively observed and democratic:

> Without a shared 'constitutional mentality', without some initial common ground from which discourse can proceed, all argument on constitutional design comes to naught.... The *commonality* of the norm, at least over a large number of persons, is a necessary feature of any operationally useful theory of choice or action that moves beyond the strict individualistic models. Applied to the problem ... of why individuals might be expected to seek out, design, argue for, and support changes in the general rules of the sociopolitical order when, by presumption, such behaviour would be contrary to identifiable self-interest, it is necessary to resort to some version of 'general interest' or 'public interest' as the embodiment of a shared moral norm.
>
> *The Reason of Rules*, pp. xi, 146–7

In the context of Buchanan's writings as a whole the effective distinction seems to be between morals which would expose capital owners' expectations to democratic government, and Buchanan's which would not.

DISABLING THE DEMOCRACY TO DISCIPLINE THE BUREAUCRATS

It is still hard to imagine why the mass or majority of citizens would vote to entrench constitutional rules against themselves, i.e. against majority rule. It is to offer a reason why they might and should do so that Buchanan and other theorists bring together both the 'macro' and 'micro' branches of public choice theory and its 'demand' and 'supply' sides (its theories of voters' and governments' motivation) into a grand historical synthesis and strategic conclusion, as follows.

Public choice 'micro theory' asserts that politicians and (especially) bureaucrats seek to enrich themselves by enlarging their budgets. To that end they raise more taxes, employ more bureaucrats and pay them more than the voters democratically intend. Therefore rules are needed which specify not only how governments must be elected, but also the substantial things which they may and may not do – and these rules need to be entrenched *against alteration by a democratic majority*. This appears to mean that if the democracy wishes to bind its bureaucrats it must do so by binding itself: if it wants its orders to be carried out it must restrict the orders it allows itself to give, and it must entrench the restriction against itself.

That muddled reasoning seems to arise from the theorists' reluctance to 'come out' and identify themselves as open enemies of democracy or at least of universal suffrage. Like the old critics of monarchical misrule who ascribed the misrule never to the king but always to his evil advisers, public choice theorists blame big government not on the people who vote for it but on their bureaucrats who, through their politicians, con them into voting for bigger government than they need, then contrive by bureaucratic machination to make it bigger still. Just as earlier reformers moved to limit royal powers as a way of limiting what evil advisers could induce the king to do, so we should now limit democratic powers, and thus the things which self-serving bureaucrats can tempt the voters, against their true interests, to vote for.

Buchanan argues (probably with the American Constitution in mind) that:

> eighteenth-century wisdom ... imposed some limits on governmental powers. But the nineteenth- and twentieth-century fallacy in political thought was embodied in the presumption that electoral requirements were in themselves sufficient to hold government's Leviathan-like proclivities in check, the presumption that, so long as there were constitutional guarantees for free and periodic elections, the range and extent of governmental action would be controlled. Only in the middle of this century have we come to recognize that such electoral constraints do not keep governments within the implied "contract" through which they might have been established, the "contract" which alone can give governments any claim to legitimacy in the eyes of the citizens.[15]

How does government manage to expand beyond those proper constraints? Buchanan offers a minor and a major reason.

> Increasingly, public choice scholars have started to model governments in monopoly rather than competitive terms. Electoral competition has come more and more to be viewed as competition among prospective monopolists, all of whom are bidding for an exclusive franchise, with profit maximizing assumed to characterize the behavior of the successful bidder. Governments are viewed as exploiters of the citizenry, rather than the means through which the citizenry secures for itself goods and services that can best be provided jointly or collectively.

So much for politicians. Bureaucrats are more numerous and generally more influential –

> Recent developments in public choice theory have demonstrated the limits of legislative control over the discretionary powers of the

bureaucracy. Modern government is complex and many-sided, so much so that it would be impossible for legislatures to make more than a tiny fraction of all genuine policy decisions. Discretionary power must be granted to bureaucrats over wide ranges of decision. Further, the bureaucracy can manipulate the agenda for legislative action for the purpose of securing outcomes favorable to its own interests. The bureaucracy can play off one set of constituents against others, insuring that budgets rise much beyond plausible efficiency limits.[16]

The argument as a whole seems coherent but absurd. Government has got out of hand; that has been caused by the self-interested behaviour of politicians and bureaucrats; it is against the interests of most of the voters and insofar as they have voted for any of it has not been because they actually wanted primary schools or old age pensions or health services or a national opera, it has been because bureaucrats have incited them and played them off against each other. Constitutions specifying how and by whom the legislators should be elected have failed to restrain the growth of government; the need now is for rules, entrenched against amendment by simple majorities, which limit what government is allowed to do. Public choice theory accordingly

> ... raises questions about how governments may be constrained, and about how governments should be constrained. What should governments be allowed to do? What is the appropriate sphere of political action? How large a share of national product should be available for political disposition? What sort of political decision structures should be adopted at the constitutional stage? Under what conditions and to what extent should individuals be enfranchised?[17]

So much for 'Never prescribe outcomes' and, in view of the last question, for justice as 'compliance with rules unanimously agreed by all whom they may affect'. These contradictions seem intelligible only as a strategy to entrench tax limits and capital tax exemptions in the constitution, entrench the constitution against democratic amendment, but pretend that all concerned have agreed both to the tax limits and to their own disfranchisement.

As to 'How large a share of national product should be available for political disposition?' it is interesting to imagine introducing the implied limits at different dates. If the public share had been entrenched when the US Constitution was written, or a century later in the 1880s, that would have prevented much public investment that has been essential to twentieth-century productivity. But if the public share had been entrenched at times when half or more of all new investment was public, as in Britain during

the Napoleonic wars or in some phases of Japan's peacetime modernization, there might since have been more public investment than has actually occurred, or Buchanan would approve. It is stupid to entrench rules
which prevent democratic governments or majorities from responding to
changing conditions.

AUTHORITY AND THE PUBLIC INTEREST

When people speak of public interests or the public good, public choice
theorists often accuse them of wanting to impose their beliefs on others,
authoritatively, without the others' consent. They are also assumed to be
homines economici whose ideas of public good merely disguise their
private interests.

As generalizations the accusations are absurd. In real life people who
speak of public interests or the public good range all the way from selfish
to altruist and from authoritarian through democratic to anarchic. The commonest of all the public goods asserted these days are those of peace, individual liberty, civil rights and democratic government. Our theorists are at
their usual trick of nominating a single selfish purpose as the sufficient
cause and characteristic of what is actually a very diverse array of belief
and behaviour.

In common usage public interests are those which are widely shared or
can best be served by collective action. Since nothing is ever of equal interest to everybody any concept of public interest or public good must be
rough and ready, but it does not follow that we would be better off without
such concepts. It is useful and sensible to talk about a public interest in
peace (though some citizens would profit from war), in defence (though
some might profit from a national defeat), in clean air (though some profit
by dirtying it), in safe streets (though some muggers have contrary interests), and so on. At the same time it is prudent to be sceptical about assertions of public interest, as every hustler insists that the public good will be
served by the widespread use of his particular snake oil; but that does not
make peace, freedom, safe streets, clean air or a cooperative culture any
less desirable.

More ambitious uses of the idea of public good call for more care, and
for some distinctions which have been familiar at least since Plato's
Republic.

First, government can vary from good to bad in its intentions and in its
effects, so Plato was right to insist that citizenship and government are
inescapably moral activities.

Second, Plato thought that good is something to be discovered and known (however imperfectly) rather than felt, desired, chosen, or known by instinct or intuition. We share some of the public choice theorists' objections to that element of Plato's thought; but we don't find their alternative moral foundations satisfactory, and we don't find – either in daily experience or in the history of political philosophy – that people's beliefs about the sources of their morals have any *regular* relation with their beliefs about coercive authority. Most people if they think about it at all seem to think that their morals owe something to each of the sources just mentioned. The proportions of each – i.e. the proportions of 'known', 'learned', 'felt', 'desired' or 'chosen' principles – don't appear to determine people's tolerance of others' beliefs, or attitudes to coercion. People who claim divine or scientific authority for their moral principles (both thought by Buchanan to be specially dangerous) actually range from the most intolerant to the most forgiving and compassionate – from Savonarola to Saint Francis, from the racist designers of the Holocaust to the author of *Child Care and the Growth of Love*. They also range from the most to the least authoritarian – there are religious pacifists and anarchists and scientific pacifists and anarchists. Moreover some of the most intolerant are the most anti-authoritarian, from fear of intolerable government. Even Plato's objections to democratic government were less authoritarian than they are sometimes made out to be. He did not suggest that philosophers had any right or authority to rule over unwilling subjects, he merely advised people to get their government from expert governors for the same practical reason as they got their shoes from expert shoemakers. He was well aware of the corrupting temptations to which governors are exposed, and he proposed drastic upbringing and educational procedures to minimize their self-interests and maximize their benevolence.

All sensible people favour some authority and coercion, for example against murder, theft and drunken driving. Even public choice theorists, when they argue for government by social contract, don't hope to prevent crime by contract with the criminals, they want criminals to be coerced by public authority. They want appropriate authority for judges, military commanders, fire chiefs, registrars of patents and land titles, and perhaps for teachers and parents. Sensible discussions of the uses of authority are not about whether to have any, they are about when, how, by whom, for what purposes and with what safeguards it should be exercised. To support all the regular uses of authority, while using 'authoritarian' as a swearword for whatever uses one opposes, is childish. Some public choice theorists for example think that majority support for censoring pornography is 'authoritarian', but a constitutional limit on taxation, entrenched *against* majority rule, is not.

James Buchanan condemns, as authoritarian, conceptions of public interest or public good which claim to be true and therefore to have some sort of scientific authority. He does not say that all ideas of public good are of this kind, but (except for one of his own, noticed above) it is the only kind he mentions in all but one of his books and readers can reasonably conclude that he thinks most assertions of public good are of this kind. He attacks them without exception or distinction as

> both authoritarian and anti-individualistic ... The authoritarian impera-tive emerges directly from the extraindividual source of valuation of "public good". If "public good" exists independently of individuals' evaluations, any argument against the furtherance of such good because of some concern for individual liberty becomes contradictory. If "public good" exists separately from individuals' preferences, and if it is prop-erly known, it must assume precedence over (although, of course, it could embody) precepts for maintenance of personal liberties.
>
> The "politics as science" paradigm is anti-individualistic because. . . it embodies a definition of "good" in application to the whole community of persons rather than to individual members. In such a definition, how-ever, there need be no crude postulation of some organic unit – for exam-ple, "the state" or "society". Individuals may still be reckoned to be the ultimate units of consciousness; no supraindividual being need be hypothesized. The "good" defined in application to the community remains, nonetheless, supraindividual because individuals cannot ques-tion its independent existence. Implicitly, all persons must agree that what is "good" would be properly promoted if what is "good" could ever be found.

Thus pp. 40–41 of *The Reason of Rules*. It can be compared with the justifi-cation of public interests and norms when they are Buchanan's choice on pp. 146–7. The contradiction is nowhere explained or excused.

In his general hostility to ideas of public good Buchanan may have in mind Plato and Marx, who thought good could be known objectively and were willing to have it enforced if necessary by undemocratic government. But there are not many such scientific authoritarians in democratic societies, whose prevailing ideas of public good tend to put high value on freedom and individuality. On p. 40, as quoted above, Buchanan allowed that ideas of public good 'could embody' such principles – but denounced them nevertheless.

The 'extraindividual' beliefs which seem to be the theorists' real target are those which in Buchanan's words embody 'a definition of good in application to the whole community of persons rather than to individual members'. Those are individuals' beliefs about the moral qualities of whole societies or their cultures or political or economic systems. They certainly include public choice theorists' beliefs, for example the belief that systems of exchange are better than systems of theft. The most important of such beliefs, though least noticed by public choice theorists, are beliefs about the character and quality of the individuals whom societies bring up.

We believe such thought has the highest importance. It has equal value with moral thought about individual character and behaviour: what it is good to be, to love, to do, to work for. In practice – even in the practice of public choice theorists – moral thoughts about individuals and about their societies are inseparable, neither making sense without the other. This belief will be defended later. In contrast to it, public choice theorists of the dominant *homo economicus* school appear to believe in nature to the exclusion of nurture: humans are born to be single-minded self-seeking materialists and there is not much their upbringing or social experience can do about it, except to train and equip them to satisfy their genetically deter-mined desires. (Alternatively any shaping of their minds and morals should presumably be left to their market exchanges with advertisers and other profit-seeking persuaders.) For morals, *homo economicus* has only appe-tites moderated by prudence. It follows that political and economic institu-tions should be designed to prevent theft, facilitate exchanges and perhaps enforce contracts between citizens, but that is all they should do.

Some extremists believe that the same principles of material exchange between self-seeking individuals sufficiently explain relations between lovers, spouses, parents and children, friends and workmates. A spate of journal articles has extended public choice analysis to these areas of domestic feeling and behaviour.[18] Relations between parents and children allow further sinister links to be perceived between altruism and authority, to strengthen the theorists' belief that any concern for others' good or for the common good is likely to be authoritarian and should probably be opposed.

These beliefs offer alternative contradictions. If the individual differ-ences along the spectrum from Savonarola to Saint Francis or from Hitler to the author of *Child Care and the Growth of Love* are genetically deter-mined, it is not promising to assume uniform motivation for most social and governmental behaviour. If on the other hand the differences owe much to the upbringing and social experience of those concerned, public choice theorists face other difficulties. *Homo economicus* may merely be a social creation of a particular time and place, perhaps ephemeral, an unsafe foundation for an axiomatic theory-building industry. If individual character and desires, and thus the political behaviour of majorities, are partly-social creations, their determinants are important. They may be open to concerted conservation or change. If that is so, ideas of public good may deserve attention as formative social forces. It is senseless to condemn such ideas as necessarily authoritarian or unnecessarily 'interventionist'. Families and societies cannot abstain from shaping the character of the people they bring up. One way or another, by action or neglect, they influence individual character, wants and preferences quite unavoidably. It makes sense to debate not whether but how and with what purposes that influence should be used. One purpose may well be to bring up individuals – and thus electoral majorities – with desirable individuality, desirable ideas of freedom and civic obligation, desirable beliefs about the good and bad uses of authority. These are all ideas of collective as well as individual good.

ENDOWMENTS

How do public choice theorists argue for accepting existing inequalities and their causes as fixed facts of life which need not be questioned in theory or attacked in practice? Three main arguments are already familiar in other contexts: the neoclassical economists' explanation of the market distribution of income; the distinction between nature and artifice which Peattie and Rein characterized in the passage we quoted on p. 19; and the scientistic desire to make social theory as parsimonious and universal as Newton's laws of motion.

Economists have traditionally focused on the processes of allocation and exchange in economic life rather than the processes of production. Public choice theorists try to understand government similarly as an arena for innumerable individual exchanges. Both tend to neglect the provenance of two essentials of the business, the people who make the exchanges, and the goods which they exchange. The production of the people, and the production of many of the goods and services which they exchange, are collapsed into the concept of 'endowments', i.e. things which people happen to have. People are endowed (usually in the passive voice to avoid mentioning who or what endowed them) both with personal qualities such as skills and willingness to work and with belongings such as money, land, farms or factories. Acquiring those endowments – i.e. being born, brought up, educated, and inheriting or otherwise acquiring capital property – are processes which have happened before economic analysis begins. But given their distribution, neoclassical economists are happy to explain how the endowments attract income.

For the classical economists the distribution of income was puzzling. They could not decide what determined the shares which went respectively to landowners, capitalists and wage earners. For Adam Smith and for Marx that seemed to be a class problem: what was it about land, capital and labour that determined exactly what proportions their owners would get of the output which they jointly produced?

From the 1860s the marginalists, from whose work neoclassical theory descends, turned the class question into an individual one. They observed that the shares of output which are taken by the contributors to production are not constant but vary with circumstances, so the correct question to ask is how and why they vary. The marginalists answered that question in a practical way. In any current productive process it should be possible to vary the input of one factor of production while holding the others constant, and then to measure the effect of that marginal change on the whole value of output. Add another hectare of land, or another worker, or another unit of capital; when you see what that adds to the whole value of output you know what a unit of that factor is worth. Compare the value of the additional output with the cost of the additional input, and you can judge whether or not to use more of that factor. Efficient producers will adjust their mix of capital and labour until the returns to marginal units of each factor are equal, and equal to their costs.

That is the neoclassic's *scientific* explanation of the levels of rent, profit and wages at any particular time and place if the markets are working efficiently. For some it also justifies a *moral* conclusion that people get what they deserve. The worker earns what his labour contributes to the value of output, the capitalist earns what his capital contributes to it, the landowner earns what his land contributes to it. The enduring popularity of neoclassical theory owes much to the double felicity of its message: by the ordinary forces of supply and demand the factors of production are priced *both* to ensure their most efficient use *and* to pay the contributors to production what they actually contribute to its value.

The limitations of that view of economic life are as familiar as the theory itself. Where market relations work as described they are indeed efficient, they are critically important to general economic efficiency and they are often fair and equitable. But they work as described in perhaps a quarter or a third of economic life. (Half or more of a modern economy's production is done on other principles altogether by households and public services. Within the private sector there are well-known areas of market failure from inequalities of market strength, imperfect information, externalities, market mismanagement, conflicts of interest within firms and so on; and competitive profit-seekers cannot be relied on to deal prudently with resource, environmental or intergenerational problems, or to provide sustenance for many of the people who cannot contribute to production.)

It may be efficient and fair to pay more to people who work hard than to those who don't. It may be efficient though not necessarily fair to pay more to cleverer or stronger or more skilful people. It may be efficient but by some standards it is not at all fair to pay workers and capitalists similarly as producers, although the capital owners don't necessarily work at all but merely permit others to work with their capital. Such distinctions, and the policy questions which they pose, need never be noticed if economic analysis accepts everyone's endowments as given and treats all endowments alike.

These are familiar objections to treating market distributions of income as necessarily fair, even when they do reflect people's contributions to the value of output. Two further objections have special relevance to public choice theory. Many productive endowments are or can be public rather than individual. When government owns land, forests, minerals, undersea resources and so on, or when it owns produced capital like power and gas and water systems, there may often be good reasons for keeping those resources in public ownership and allowing their use, by public or private producers, on terms which majorities or their representatives judge to be efficient, fair, environmentally prudent, and so on. But public choice theory implies that public resources will not usually be used for such efficient, fair or prudent purposes. They will be used instead to enrich the politicians and public servants who have charge of them. So collectively just or prudent policies tend to be impracticable and are better not attempted.

Second, publicly *owned* endowments are not the only public contributions to production. Many private and individual endowments are – partly or wholly – publicly *produced*. Collective action – formal and informal, public and familial, governmental and cultural – does much to shape individual characters, expectations, health, education, inventiveness, productive skills and attitudes to work. It makes little sense to accept those endowments as 'given' *while at the same time attacking and trying to discredit and reduce the public contribution to producing them*. But that is the special contribution of 'dry' economists and public choice theorists to the erosion of their own assumptions, as they work to reduce the size and scope of government, especially the branches of government which help to create and maintain human capital.

In practical terms that means that the theorists ask us to believe that the politicians and public servants who allocate funds to the material infrastructure which private industries need – the roads and bridges, power and water systems and so on – and to the human capital services which private industries need – i.e. people who allocate funds to pre- and post-natal services, child care, child endowment and supporting parents' allowances, school and university and adult education including technical training and retraining, hospital and health services, industrial safety, commuter transport, police, judicial and corrective services, and to all the other public provisions which help to provide industry with a fit and versatile workforce – are doing so for their own enrichment: not just earning pay and promotion by working well, but cheating the voters by spending more than they intend, and exchanging favours for support with interest groups who likewise think of little but their individual enrichment.

In real life the immediate and direct self-interests which obsess public choice theorists are indeed present, and affect behaviour. But most people also see beyond their immediate individual interests to their general interest in living in an orderly, productive and diverse society; and most people are found in fact, when actually investigated, to vote with a range of allegiances and purposes as well as or instead of self-enrichment. But even if their purposes had no elements of altruism, intelligent self-interest would not prompt them to vote for public contributions to their own endowments alone, or to others' endowments only in exchange for support for their own. Adam Smith may have been right not to expect his dinner from the butcher's and baker's goodwill alone. Their self-interest also, perhaps chiefly, prompts them to serve us. But we live longer than Smith's contemporaries did because we know what the butcher's and baker's performance also owes to their education, the regulation of their trades and of other trades whose products they use, the universities and research institutes which developed disease-free milk and meat and all the strains of wheat now in use; and so on.

It might conceivably make sense to imagine a social system of individuals exchanging goods and services with each other, without considering how the individuals and goods and services are produced, if there were known to be no connection between the processes of production and the processes of exchange. But since the system which meets economic demands is the selfsame system which generates many of them, there are triple objections to that separation. First it is simply defective in failing to notice the social construction of much of the freedom and individuality that the theorists treasure. Second, that neglect can lead the theorists to conclusions and policy proposals which would tend in practice to degrade the endowments which they treasure most: the skill, versatility and confident autonomy of their ideal individuals. Third, the neglect arises from a basic mistake about the actual sources of productivity, a mistake which they share with many of their neoclassical and liberal colleagues.

The mistake is an elementary one. Because misconceived government intervention certainly can and sometimes does hinder production, people who have an obsessive dislike of government jump to the conclusion that an *absence* of government must be what *causes* production. Extreme believers in *laissez faire* talk as if the absence of government is the *sufficient* cause of production, as if free trade is all that it takes to generate competitive vigour and economic growth. (The poor third world could soon be rich if that were so.) Public choice theorists appear to believe (1) that least possible government tends to allow the freest and fairest exchanges between individuals, and (2) that more exchange is the sufficient means to more productivity. Both beliefs are half-truths at best. For uninhibited exchanges to take place all sorts of securities and protections have to be supplied by government. And although productivity relies on some exchanges – of work for wages, materials for money, and so on – its main generators are the 'endowments' whose production these theorists deliberately neglect: the individual skills, material desires, attitudes to work, inventiveness, capacities for planning and intricate cooperation, and so on, all of which are partly-social creations and many of which owe some of their provenance to public institutions and services; and second, the accumulated physical and intellectual capital of modern societies, more than half of it possessed otherwise than by private profit seekers: the household capital which equips and maintains workers, the public infrastructure on which private industry depends, the public symbols and services which nourish the feelings of national identity and membership without which (however odd it may seem that it should be so) no society has yet managed to be very productive.

We will explore some of those communal sources of productivity later. Here we draw attention to the contradictions and the values of thinkers who take endowments as given, celebrate some of them (such as individual skill, enterprise and autonomy) as the most valuable of human attributes, and work tirelessly to weaken the processes which produce them.

Public choice theory may incorporate the values and the contradictions which this chapter has alleged. But the simplest objection to it is still that it ain't true. Most of its leaders have long acknowledged that people do not generally behave as the theory assumes and predicts. How do believers reconcile a continuing faith in its explanations with the frequent failure of its predictions?

6 Public Choice: Living with Failure

The purpose of assuming that political behaviour has simple and constant motivation was to build a universal theory of political behaviour – the sort of theory that might work if the pursuit of wealth were as unvarying as (say) the force of gravity.

The attempt has clearly failed. Most of the public choice theorists who nevertheless persist with the work accommodate to the failure in one of two ways. They become eclectic, selecting and reporting examples or aspects of behaviour which spring from rational egoism and not those which don't; or they try to adapt public choice theory and analysis to the facts of mixed motivation. To explain what is wrong with each of those responses, we first summarize yet again the three main reasons for the failure: (1) the diversity and changeability of much political motivation, and (2) the complexity of social causation, which together dictate (3) the unavoidable selectivity of most social theory and explanation.

EXPLAINING DIVERSE, UNSTABLE, COMPLEX BEHAVIOUR

Diversity

Political motivation springs from mixtures of nature and nurture. It can vary from one activity to another: people often bring different values and purposes to bear as they act or vote about different issues, for example about religion, taxation and environmental policy, and about issues which do and issues which don't touch their own material interests. Motivation varies from culture to culture, from person to person and group to group within cultures, and over time within cultures. It varies with people's correct or incorrect, self-verifying or self-defeating beliefs about what their options are. Both about what is possible and about what is desirable people are sometimes open to persuasion. Cultures change, sometimes by concerted effort, to shape changing values and expectations in all or some of their people. The current revolution in women's opportunities is an obvious example. The green revolution is another.

Complexity

Social activity, causally speaking, is like a seamless web. For institutions and social processes to work as they do, the necessary conditions and their causal antecedents are innumerable in at least three respects. First, there are innumerable ways for investigators to 'name the parts', i.e. to ascribe identities to parts and qualities of the web, and thus allow questions about relations between the parts. Second, innumerable conditions have to be present for systems and processes to work as they do; observers can rarely know them all or focus on more than a few of them; so they must decide which to focus on, which to neglect, which to assume to be constant in the conditions or for the purposes of the question in hand. Third, each present condition may have a history – converging chains of cause and effect which it may or may not be important to trace for the purpose in hand.

Selectivity

However perfectly objective an investigator's observations and rigorous his or her reasoning, s/he must still *choose* what pattern of identities to impose on (or 'perceive in' or 'select from') raw life, and which of their relationships and antecedents to study. Of most things worth investigating, total knowledge is impossible. Theorists have to choose promising identities, models and simplifications, and investigators have to choose what questions to ask and what types of answer to look for, in the light of their purposes. Those are social purposes of one kind or another – even the 'purest' theorists distinguish valuable from trivial work, and most of their tests (except for various kinds of intellectual beauty) are related to the value of the social action or understanding to which the knowledge may lead, however directly it leads there (as with most applied research) or indirectly (as with some pure theory). Selection is unavoidable because of the complexity of life and, whether intentionally or not, it cannot help generating knowledge more useful for some people and purposes than for others. That is the irreducible sense in which all social science of any complexity is value-structured, however objective its observations or rigorous its reasoning. If one investigator relates certain rates of local morbidity to ingestion of a poison, another relates it to an industry's failure to contain its wastes, another relates it to government failure to regulate the discharge of wastes, another relates it to prevailing norms which tolerate those failures, another to the parenting and schooling which implant those norms, and another to the economic pressures which encourage those parental and educational failures, the six – though truth-tellers all – have encouraged their readers to recognize different causes, ascribe different responsibilities and think of different remedies which are likely to help and hurt different people.

One further methodological choice has often been misunderstood by the more 'scientistic' social scientists. Should investigators look for scientific laws or for historical explanations? Some, anxious to imitate the forms of natural science, have characterized the choice like this: 'Science is nomothetic: it discovers regularities, distils them in laws and models of behaviour and uses them to explain and predict behaviour. History, and other disciplines at the same primitive, pre-scientific stage of development, are idiographic: they describe unique events and explain them by means of eclectic, ad hoc explanations.' In the example of poisoning by polluted water, the plain-brained historian or city engineer explains that the local tanneries are emitting poisons which find their way into the town water supply. The scientist recognizes a case of laws about profit-seeking, externalities and government failure, and dismisses the historian's explanation as mere description and ad-hocery.

That characterization of the two methods and of relations between them is misleading. First, the historian uses a good deal of generalized knowledge in connecting the relevant causes to their effects; and she may also be treating as unique sequences which *are* unique, i.e. bits of behaviour which are not reliably regular. Second, the scientist's laws do not actually enable him to predict or prevent this poisoning; he may be using the investigation to advertise his laws and language (by showing that they 'fit' the case) rather than to fix the water supply. But third, when rightly used the two explanations are not alternatives but complements. We can illustrate their interdependence most simply by turning from poisoned water to the commonest of all economic laws. The 'law of demand' says that *the lower the price of a commodity, the more of it households will tend to buy*. Some exceptions to that can also be expressed in laws – for example it may not hold for inferior 'Giffen goods' or for goods (coffins, general anaesthetics) for which the demand is inelastic. But suppose that dropping the price of carrots fails to sell more carrots one day because the morning paper has carried a health warning against carrots or an alluring new recipe for parsnips, or because it is Hallowe'en and people only want pumpkins, or St. Patrick's day in Ireland and people want green, not orange, vegetables. Or – turning from carrots to other commodities – some people want to be seen to own the world's most expensive dresses, jewellery, cars, houses, works of art. (We suppose that the van Gogh painting for which Alan Bond paid a world record price gave him more pleasure than it would have given him at half the price.) In such cases the law of demand is broken for reasons which can only be grasped in an understanding or historical way.

The choice between law-based and other explanations should properly depend on the nature of the problem rather than the state of the science.

Political behaviour issues from variously unequal mixtures of regular and irregular thoughts, choices, processes and events. Laws can describe and sometimes predict the regular elements in the mix. Only selective explanations can explain and sometimes predict the irregular ones. Moreover some of what appear to be irregularities may issue from regular forces too complex for analysis; some may occur because the regular tendencies of behaviour have been frustrated or overborn by irregular forces; and some may occur because the 'regular' elements themselves have changed, for example because people have changed their minds and habits. It is not only the complexity but also the self-changing propensity of human behaviour that defeats social scientists' efforts to achieve the rigour and universality of Newtonian physics – and leads the less intelligent of them to 'select for regularity', i.e. to interest themselves only in the regular strands of behaviour, the relationships capable of rigorous proof, the probabilities that can be measured statistically, and so on. To answer any question it is rational to prefer more certain to less certain methods. But it is not rational to accept only the law-based and sure-and-certain elements of the answers, or to choose questions about political behaviour chiefly for the certainty with which they can be answered. Both those attempts at certainty can be self-defeating if they lead investigators to neglect any motives and forces which happen to be hard to measure, or to neglect the selective, understanding, explanatory work which may be necessary to establish where any regular tendencies of behaviour are likely (or not) to prevail.

The original, distinctive enterprise of public choice theory was to see what could be discovered by assuming a law that people seek the same individual material gains by their political as by their economic behaviour. How have public choice theorists responded since that law proved to be false? For a fair sample we read the latest decade (volumes 36–65, 1981–1990) of the journal *Public Choice*. Most contributors have responded in one of two ways: (1) by selectively reporting elements of behaviour which conform to the law and not those which don't, or (2) by accepting that people may derive 'utility' from other things than wealth and egoism. Since the latter amounts to accepting a traditional understanding of mixed and variable motivation it is hard to see why this second group are still public choice theorists, or what they see as distinctive about the public choice approach. In practice two things tend to distinguish them from political scientists and historians: they retain a steady prejudice against government and look for histories and explanations discreditable to it; or they do traditional open-minded work but translate it into public choice jargon. We will not support these conclusions here with classified lists of the 800-odd articles and comments concerned. Instead, examples of each type of response can illustrate what we mean, and any sceptical readers can read the journal volumes to judge for themselves how apt or not our characterization is.

PROTECTING THE LAW

The principles are simple. Search political behaviour for self-interested motivation, report that motivation alone, and let it sufficiently explain the activity concerned. Relax that rule and report altruistic or disinterested motivation only when it has had perverse or self-defeating effects. Don't report regulations, redistributions or reforms which serve their public purposes successfully; or if you do, show that outcome to have emerged from some compromise or equilibrium of self-interests.

There is of course plenty of political behaviour which *can* be sufficiently explained in those ways and the best public choice writing, like the best crime writing or muckraking journalism, sticks to those suitable subjects. Even when political outcomes cannot be sufficiently explained by reference to self-interests alone, it may be possible, by shifting the focus of inquiry, to stick to the self-interests without descending to biased or untruthful reporting. If, for example, the prime movers of a political campaign are plainly disinterested (freemen campaigning for prisoners' rights, whites for black rights, men for women's rights, and so on) but the politicians are by choice or necessity unprincipled office-seekers, the inquiry can focus on the politicians, who may be shown to do nothing but trade favours for support. If on the other hand politicians are doing their honest best to improve the safety, efficiency or environmental performance of an industry, but have to cope with the lobbying and propaganda of hostile interests, the *Public Choice* article can focus on the motivation and behaviour of the interest groups, especially if they manage to frustrate or pervert the government's good intentions.

Good examples of these devices can be found in the journal's few articles on environmental policy. There are very few – it is an awkward subject for public choice theorists because for every self-interested environmentalist defending her own neighbourhood from pollution there tend to be a dozen disinterested defenders of whales, Antarctica or the conditions of life for future generations. The few articles whose primary subject is environmental policy say nothing of the motivation of the prime movers of environmental reform. They treat the reformers as an interest like any other, but chiefly explore conflicts between the materially interested parties: the target industries, their employees, neighbouring landowners, consumers whose budgets may be affected by policy-induced price changes. We learn for example how one American attempt to reduce coalburning sulphur emissions was hijacked: instead of a cheap and efficient switch from dirty coal produced by eastern mines using union labour to clean coal from western mines using non-union labour, the eastern mining interests persuaded the politicians to require expensive 'scrubbing' by all coal users on terms which continue the use of eastern coal and may even (over time, on certain assumptions) make for dirtier air than the unreformed policies would have done. Other contributions recommend market-linked incentive devices for pollution abatement and waste processing. These and similar useful pieces help to explain the levels and instruments of control that have been adopted in some particular cases. But they cannot do it as well as uninhibited political scientists and investigative journalists can do, as long as they deliberately ignore the motivation and strategies of the environmentalists. (One article in our sample notices their strategy, but none explores their motivation.) The outcomes of public-interest initiatives cannot be satisfactorily explained by reference to the resisters and interested parties alone, without relation to the strength and motivation of the mostly-disinterested prime movers. But to give equal attention to the self-interested and disinterested parties would make nonsense of the 'rational egoist' law. So would fair reporting of fair samples of the many successful environmental reforms that have been achieved.

In the Western world a main rival of the environment, for political attention and legislation through the 1980s, was the women's movement. It got even less attention in *Public Choice* (one item in about eight hundred), we suppose for the similar reason that too many of the protagonists are driven by concern for other people's welfare as well as or instead of their own. The one article, about a few correlates of American women's political participation, offered statistical support for the existence of some already-familiar political tendencies of single women, married women, working mothers, educated women and Protestant fundamentalists in the US at a particular date. But of the nature, driving force and moral and institutional progress of the movement, or the respective roles of women and men in it, *Public Choice's* contributors had nothing to say through the 1980s.

The principles of selection employed by those who protect the law of 'rational egoist utility maximization' by discarding all contrary evidence may help to maintain the public choice industry and its scientistic pretensions, or to discredit government, but they do not belong in honest science.

RELAXING THE LAW

The better alternative is to discard the law of rational egoism and study the actual motivation of political behaviour. In 1984 Gordon Tullock suggested that 'the tendency to completely overlook the public interest legislation and public interest motive ... should ... be changed. I do not, of course, want to argue that public interest is the dominant motive in politics, but it is a motive.'[1] In his Presidential Address to the Public Choice Society in 1986 Dennis Mueller suggested 'that we in public choice should rely more on behaviorist psychology to explain and predict individual behavior in prisoners' dilemma situations, and less on game theory.' Psychology is better than game theory at explaining 'the ubiquitous performance of cooperative behavior by individuals ... in situations in which the non-cooperative strategy would appear optimal from a strictly rational egoist perspective.'[2] In 1988 A.J.C. van der Kragt, R.M. Dawes and J.M. Orbell concluded that the altruism which some people display in some games is not determined rationally by their own or the sum of their own and others' benefits – their cooperation has to be explained by some other means.[3] Later that year William Riker noticed first the 'sentimental attachments that encourage people to transcend personal interests in the pursuit of the formal goal of the larger group', and second, that 'slight changes in institutions can result in gross changes in outcomes'.[4]

A rational response to these discoveries would be to discard the assumption of universal rational egoism and study, wherever necessary, actual motivation – i.e. return from public choice theory to mainstream political science, history, psychology, management studies, or whatever. But some practitioners try to rescue the industry by one or both of two methods. They amend public choice theory to admit mixed motivation. We think that makes the theory vacuous or unoriginal, for reasons argued earlier. Or they do ordinary history or political science, often in an over-simplified and under-researched way, but report it in public choice jargon in public choice journals where it normally escapes scrutiny by historians or political scientists as editors, referees or readers. We offer one example of the first device and two of the second.

PSYCHOLOGY

In the presidential address cited above, Dennis Mueller describes how people learn to consider each others' interests and cooperate, thus making rational egoism only one of their modes of behaviour. 'We learn not to steal, to line up and wait our turn, to follow the rules and do what is expected of us'. Experiments show that our cooperative habits survive into adult life, but irregularly – for example we often respond differently, over time, to repetitive situations. There follows a paragraph of collective self-analysis so perceptive and unguarded that it deserves to be quoted in full.

> Except for the choice of words, all of the above is, I am sure, fairly obvious. One is almost embarrassed to make these observations were it not that so many of us who work with rational egoist models continually build our models on assumptions that ignore these truisms from psychology and everyday life. What accounts for our reluctance to make assumptions about individual behavior which allow for conditioned behavior patterns? I think there are at least two explanations. First, we suffer from what those who study innovative activity call "the not-invented-here bias". Any hypothesis not developed from within the rational egoism paradigm is viewed with suspicion. Second, even if we give some credence to these alien hypotheses, we fear that to add them to our analytic models would detract from their rigor, make them more difficult to analyze, might even lead to that most brutal and humiliating of all criticisms, the criticism that our models are *ad hoc*. Let me try to some extent to deal with both criticisms.[5]

He first resorts to algebra. Suppose that cooperative people have a measurable quantity of concern for others' interests. Call the quantity θ; it can vary from nil (0) to ranking others' interests equally with one's own (1).

> Now assume, in situations in which there are n individuals in a prisoner's dilemma, ... that each individual maximizes an objective function, which is a weighted sum of his/her utility and the utilities of the other $n - 1$ individuals in the group. That is, each maximizes

$$0_i = U_i + \theta \sum_{j \neq i}^{n} U_j \qquad (1)$$

> where U_i and each U_j are dependent on the actions of all n individuals. ... [F]rom the perspective of a rational egoist, only two values for θ can be justified. If the actions of the other individuals are contingent on i's actions, i.e. they cooperate if i does, then i sets $\theta = 1$. If not, then i sets $\theta = 0$ ... If i is a pure rational egoist maximizing 0_i, it is very difficult to conceptualize a θ other than zero or one ... But if we think of i as an individual responding, on the basis of prior experience, to the stimulus of being in a prisoners' dilemma situation, then θ could easily take on

values between zero and one. What I propose is that we think of θ not as a parameter to be chosen by an individual, but as one which is characteristic of an individual or a group.

What that and the preceding pages of the address say – and *all* that they say – is that people may be generous and cooperative instead of being rational egoists if they have been conditioned to be so. This appears to have devastating implications for public choice theory. Not only is its basic behavioural assumption unreliable, but political motivation is inherently unstable. It can vary from person to person and from society to society and may well be changeable by collective educational action. It cannot support *any* universal theory of the determinate kind public choice theorists seek.

How can the industry survive? Mueller proposes – explicitly, absurdly – that the *quantity* of such conditioning or consequent propensity to cooperate can be 'estimated from observable data' in each case, and the equation will then enable experts to predict people's behaviour better than they could have done without it.

There is no suggestion that rational egoist motivation might also need to be conditioned (perhaps by liberal doses of public choice theory?). Mueller simply asserts without evidence or argument that 'man is naturally base'; all cooperative or altruistic behaviour is socially conditioned; but it may well be that the societies which survive best are those which condition their members to be most cooperative. Mueller does not explain why naturally base people should implant such virtues in each other, or alternatively why people who work so hard as parents and teachers to implant such virtues should be assumed to be naturally base.

Mueller proposes that 'the principles by which cooperative behavior is learned can be studied and used to predict cooperative behavior. Hypotheses can be derived and tested with experimental data using standard statistical tests.' The hypotheses will have the form of equation (1) above. There are more tricks on the way to this conclusion. Altruism always 'can be' explained as the selfish pursuit of conditioned psychic rewards for altruistic behaviour – so 'the application of Occam's razor dictates maintaining a purely egoistic assumption regarding human behaviour if that suffices, as would appear to be the case.' (The opposite nonsense, that altruism 'can be' sufficiently explained by ethical preference or instinctive generosity, so there is no need to resort to egoism, would spin William of Occam in his grave at similar velocity.) The assumption that all natural impulses are 'base', and all cooperative impulses conditioned by repetitive reward and punishment, seems to have been chosen not because it rests on predominant evidence, or promises well for human self-study and improvement, but because it suits the public choice industry: if mixed motivation *has* to be accepted as a fact and explained, 'going to behaviorist psychology is less of a methodological leap for a social scientist who works with rational egoist models than going to some competing sociological–psychological theories.'[6]

We return to the central proposition that a person's or group's cooperative propensity can be estimated quantitatively from observation of their past conditioning or behaviour, and fed into a utility-maximizing equation, whose use will enable its user to explain and predict their behaviour better than he or she could otherwise have done. That is bad reasoning and its algebraic expression tends to make it worse. For political, explanatory or forecasting purposes, propensities to cooperate can't usefully be reduced to simple quantities of simple dispositions. What moralist, politician, scientist and forecaster need to know is which individuals or groups will cooperate *by what means* with *which* others for *which* purposes. As people deliberate between alternative purposes, strategies and alignments, the quantity of their cooperative propensity or conditioned altruism is interesting only to those who also know what actual purposes can enlist those propensities. A conditioned propensity to cooperate or to sacrifice self to others does not by itself determine the amount of cooperation or sacrifice to be expected – the most cooperative people don't cooperate with enemies or unacceptable purposes, or by unacceptable means, so even the quantity of the cooperative propensity – Mueller's θ – is likely to vary with circumstances. To the extent that the complicated behaviour of large numbers can only be understood by means of simplifying and generalizing, the traditional ways of discovering the dominant beliefs and intentions in most of the people's heads seem more promising than any attempt to understand mental relations between people – their exchanges of meaning, belief, intention – as quantifiable relations between symbolized 'propensities to serve self' and 'propensities to serve or cooperate with others'. Put simply, if people don't seek wealth alone you need to know what they seek instead; merely knowing by what degree their greed is reduced won't by itself suffice to predict what they will think and do.

Mueller's presidential address is one of the most elaborate and authoritative attempts to adapt public choice theory to the facts of mixed, including some cooperative and altruistic, motivation. He claims that his proposal would enable public choice analysts to combine 'both the rigor of mathematical modelling and the realism of assuming only egoistic motivation'. But his proposed model is flawed in theory and useless in practice. In theory no value can ever be given to his θ without subjective value judgments, likely to differ from one analyst to the next, of the relative weight to be given to different modes, objects and acts of cooperation. That would be compounded by the practical difficulties of research and estimation in arriving at a value of θ in real-life cases. Until the substantive aims of the political actors are known, and their ordering and potential conflicts and harmonies known, the equation is useless for any practical purpose. When they *are* known the equation does nothing to improve the use of the knowledge; it merely translates some dependent elements of it into symbolic language, sometimes harmfully. For example to achieve 'rigour' it requires simplifications which depict human thinking and choosing as more mechanically determined and merely reactive than we believe they are. Meanwhile Mueller's disposal of all altruism as self-seeking is doubly unhelpful. It is probably false; and if true it would not help to predict behaviour – analysts are offered no way of distinguishing material from altruistic egoism, i.e. no way of knowing when to expect acquisitive behaviour motivated by greed, or generous behaviour motivated by psychic hedonism, or irrational cooperation motivated by conditioned dispositions, or any mix of the three. The theory has become quite indeterminate: it can explain anything (after a fashion) but predict nothing.

MORALS

So much for adapting public choice theory to admit mixed motives. The journal also prints case studies of mixed motivation. The wisest paper printed during the 1980s (in our opinion) is part theory, part social analysis. Omitting what it says about social science, here is part précis, part free translation of what it says about society:

> Some market failures and government failures arise partly from people's immorality: from a lack of informal, internalized principles of behaviour which, for short, we may call social norms. In business, reliably honest and truthful behaviour can minimize administrative and transaction costs and reduce uncertainty. If it works reliably, voluntary good behaviour is the cheapest way to discipline corporate externalities, and to restrain consumer demand for antisocial goods. As with business, so with government: a culture of honest, responsible service can do more, more economically, for the quality of government than can be achieved in the absence of such culture by the most elaborate, expensive, time-consuming, second-guessing, report-writing systems of hierarchical surveillance and accountability. In business and government alike, some norms complement and strengthen the institutional arrangements, and

some replace them or reduce the need for them. If only for purposes of wealth and efficiency we should study how such norms are generated, maintained and enforced.

Many institutions contribute to the task. As examples, consider families and professional associations. Families implant beliefs, values and motives in children. Because they are life's first lessons and come from powerful, loved and loving parents, through many daily hours over many years, norms learned in childhood tend to be the most durable. Some social scientists see families as transmitters of society's values to children, but parents are more active than that – they create and select values as well as transmitting them. But some families perform the function better than others. Good parenting tends to come with (among other things) long-lasting marriages, low stress, and divisions of labour which allow parents and children plenty of time together. Those helpful conditions tend to accompany specialization and interdependence between spouses.

Through the qualities which it builds into the workforce, good parenting helps market efficiency. But how does market efficiency affect the conditions for good parenting? Economic growth and increasing specialization at work tend, in a number of ways, to hinder wholesome specialization and interdependence at home. As real wages rise, so do the opportunity costs of time spent with children. As both parents go out and earn, and share the housework when they are at home, children get less parental time and attention. With less shared experience and time together, parents and children know each other less well and grow less understanding and tolerant of each other. Parents both earning and (often unequally) houseworking suffer more stress and become economically independent of each other, so more marriages break up. Rising income finances more public and market substitutes for parental care, and other extra-familial temptations. As both parents at work encounter competitive, individualist, acquisitive market values, those infect the values implanted at home at the expense of honesty, fidelity, cooperation and regard for others. As the quantity and quality of parenting thus decline, children are less well trained as parents in their turn, and the decline continues. There are of course some countervailing, helpful effects of economic growth on family life, but they have less force; the net effect of market growth tends to be 'the erosion of precisely those features of the family that give it such potential: frequent and durable interaction between skilled, tolerant and understanding parents and children'.

Professional associations have, and purport to enforce, codes of ethics. Ethical behaviour is often consistent with their members' material interests. Demand for their services depends on public trust in them, and some norms serve both the professionals' and their clients' interests – for example, high qualifications which restrict entry tend to increase members' incomes but also the quality of their work; the ban on advertising can serve their clients' as well as their own interests; and the codes usually have some pure public-interest elements. But the codes are imperfectly effective. The concern to keep the profession's image spotless motivates members to accept genuinely good codes – but it can also deter them from taking public action against offenders. Effective peer review is also inhibited by some general values which market systems encourage: freedom, individualism, privacy and property rights.

Thus families and professional associations have shortcomings as moral agents, and do less than they could for the efficiency of business and government. Other moral agents – governments, educational institutions and the media – suffer similarly, in varying degrees, from effects of the market economy on the formative influences which they exert.

Market growth thus raises some of the costs of implanting and maintaining the moral standards on which market efficiency depends. Increasing specialization at work gives people less common experience and sense of interchangeability; that can reduce empathy, feelings of community, and the desire to deal helpfully and non-instrumentally with one another. Business life, with profit necessary for survival and income as the measure of success, obliges people to act in self-interested ways even if they would prefer to act otherwise. The emphasis on competition and excellence reinforces individualist values of meritocracy and inequality. There are of course some counterfailing forces. Competition encourages suppliers and salespeople to deal helpfully with their customers. Well-managed firms encourage their employees to cooperate with each other. Some of the moral influence of churches, educational institutions, government agencies and the media continues to be wholesome. But the contrary influences are strong, and – most important – the productive and self-destructive propensities of market capitalism seem to be inseparable. The degrading influences are not avoidable by-products of the system, they issue from its central working principles. The only way to reduce their force may be to reduce the market sector share of the mixed economy. A smaller market sector might be both more efficient and more socially responsible.

Conclusion: We should reconsider economic efficiency as our test of market or government failure. If we have only that criterion, we too easily choose partly-self-defeating policies which enhance business or government efficiency in the short run but directly or indirectly inhibit the development and maintenance of human qualities and norms which are conditions of the highest efficiency, and independently valuable for other reasons. The question 'What is the proper role of norms in a market society?' should be replaced by 'What is the role of the market in a society which wants to consist of truthful, caring, trusting people?'

Thus Gordon S. Bergsten, in 1985, in a *Public Choice* article 'On the role of social norms in a market economy'.[7] Three questions: How did argument so absolutely hostile to public choice assumptions and theory get into *Public Choice*? How did such familiar argument – wise, salutary, important, but mostly unoriginal – get into a learned journal supposedly devoted to original work? And why is the original nine times as long as our précis, though it says little more than the précis does about social and economic life?

A first answer to all three questions is some use of jargon. Bergsten can write briskly and clearly, but does not always choose to. Where the précis has children learning 'from powerful, loved and loving parents' the original says 'Not only is the affective component of the relationship likely to be more pronounced, but in addition the power resource asymmetry is greater as well.' But that achieves barely half of the necessary ninefold expansion and, to be fair, it is not representative: much of the article is in plain language.

The idea that capitalism erodes moral standards has been familiar in prose and poetry since medieval times. That the erosion is self-destructive because capitalism depends on the morals which it erodes is a main reason for the growth of business regulation. It was argued in a thorough theoretical way by Fred Hirsch in *Social Limits to Growth* (1976). It is an important message which bears repeating wherever deregulation is contemplated. We can imagine offering it to *Public Choice* – but only to persuade them to close down or change direction, and without much hope of acceptance. How did Gordon Bergsten make such a familiar and hostile message seem both new and acceptable?

The answer is in the bulk of the article which the précis omits. The omitted material can be summarized as follows. Think of morals as market goods. (This seems to us to be unhelpful. Generally speaking, morals are not demanded by consumers or supplied in response to demand. They may have costs but they don't have prices. The impulses which prompt people to behave well and encourage others to do so, and to think what the principles of good behaviour ought to be, are unlike the impulses which underlie demand, supply and pricing in real markets.) Thinking of a 'norms market' seems unlikely to improve our understanding of moral thought and behaviour; but it allows Bergsten to depict a trio of related markets, each with its explanatory economic theory. Economic markets are understood, and their market failures identified, by Normative Economic Theory (NET), otherwise known as welfare economics. Political markets are understood, and their market failures identified, by Normative Economic Theory of Politics (NETP), otherwise known as public choice theory. Norms markets are understood, and their market failures identified, by Normative Economic Theory of (Social) Norms (NETN). This Normative Economic Theory of Norms, though relatively young, has already discovered the technical advantages of honesty and trust in business. But NETN is flawed. It has not yet provided (i.e. translated into public choice jargon) an economic explanation of the supply of the necessary norms. Bergsten's paper repairs that flaw. It takes some familiar economic stresses which afflict modern marriages, and the familiar ambivalence of purpose of professional associations, and translates them into marketable NETN jargon.

We do not think that the translation, or the notion of a norms market, adds anything useful to our understanding of the sources, functions or value of moral thought and behaviour, or the interrelations of the moral and economic elements of modern life. But the substantive social understanding summarized in our précis shows Bergsten to be a most intelligent, generous and compassionate thinker. Perhaps the pretentious translation of his sensible message was done to get it into *Public Choice* not for rational egoist purposes of academic self-advancement, but to sow some self-doubt in the only language that the faithful take seriously. It has to be the language rather than the logic that gets to them. Bergsten concludes by professing to find it ironic 'that economic analysis, assuming as it does rational economic man, and married as it has been for so long to the market, ... should help us not only identify failures of market and non-market institutions, but also help us trace the causes of these failures back to the market and to rational economic man. Orthodox economic analysis is indeed a subversive science.' However attractive, the implication is untrue. Economic analysis adds little to the commonsense knowledge that honest business is usually more efficient than dishonest. Economic analysis does not explain why parents choose the norms they do and try to make their children honest, industrious and generous to others. It does not explain why indoctrination in childhood is most durable. It cannot relate the supply of norms to a demand for them (as economists understand demand) in any truthful way. All it has done in Bergsten's article is to explain some (but by no means all) of the modern hindrances to good parenting. 'Orthodox economic analysis' actually makes nonsense of the notion that moral thought, persuasion and behaviour can be sufficiently understood as trade goods, demanded and supplied like carrots in a vegetable market in quantities determined by marginal costs and prices.

AFFECTION

A final example of translating wisdom into jargon, though a longer paper, can dealt with more briefly.

Public choice theorists have long worried about what they call the 'paradox of voting'. (It is not a paradox for anyone else.) For rational egoists the costs of informing themselves about the issues and going to the poll are likely to be greater than the individual material gains to be expected from voting. So why do people vote? Or engage in a great many other communal activities which rational egoists, who want only individual gains, would avoid?

In 1989 in an article called '"Relational goods" and participation: Incorporating sociability into a theory of rational action',[8] Carole Uhlaner describes in familiar terms how people like to belong, participate, work together, achieve good things for their communities, share one another's joy when they work together. Many people do *not* want to leave the action to others then enjoy the gains as free riders; the action itself is what they most enjoy. Working, contributing, organizing, demonstrating, attending rallies for good causes, they 'do not wish simply to "identify with" a group, but wish to be included'. Uhlaner is as right about real people as Bergsten is, and more comprehensive: for example where Bergsten focuses on the economic conditions for good parenting and neglects other emotional, intellectual or cultural conditions for it, Uhlaner really does see people 'whole' and describe their mixed motivation in a perceptive and comprehensive way. No more devastating disposal could be imagined of the notion that people can be sufficiently understood as rational egoists, or their behaviour sufficiently explained or predicted by deduction from their economic interests alone.

So what is *this* smasher doing in *Public Choice*?

Uhlaner says that the whole array of sociable motivation and behaviour that she so faithfully describes can be sufficiently understood as a pursuit of 'relational goods'. People who want to work together to improve the world for themselves or others simply want sociable relations like other people want money or bread and butter. In seeking the desired human relations they can be rational egoists like anyone else – 'relational goods do not depend on or imply altruism'. By this simple device the public choice faith is made whole again. It is only necessary to avoid noticing that the theory has become vacuous ('people seek what people seek'), indeterminate, and useless for prediction, with no means of explaining or predicting *what* people want, or when they will opt for material or relational goods, or for what mix, or which relational goods; or what conditions dispose them to which choices. It may have been to divert attention from these difficulties, or from the suspicious simplicity of defining giving and taking alike as 'egoist', and collapsing such diversely selfish, cooperative and altruistic purposes into the single concept of 'relational goods', that Uhlaner followed her admirable opening page about human sociability with thirty pages of algebra and games theory about the (still indeterminate, unpredictable) pursuit of the relational goods.

SCIENTISTIC AMBITIONS

In real life, political motivation is both passively and actively variable. It is observed to vary over time in changing conditions, from person to person, group to group and culture to culture. And within some natural limits – limits which seem to be obstinate but are hard to chart in detail – it can be changed by persuasion and collective choice and action. A 'science' which assumes it to be constant, despite a generation of non-proof and disproof, is irrational if its real purpose is scientific discovery.

No doubt some well-intentioned people still write and use public choice theory because it is an accepted academic activity and they enjoy its algebra or other intellectual attractions, or see it as a way of criticizing overgrown government. But as will be argued in a final chapter we do not believe that public choice theory has a fraction of the depth, wisdom, realism or coherence of the traditional liberal, conservative or social-democratic discussions of government. From Locke and Mill through Popper to moderns like Rawls, Hampshire and Williams, liberals have been better critics of unnecessary or unaccountable government. From Plato through Burke to moderns like Oakeshott, Kristol and Moynihan, conservatives have understood human nature and needs and their social dependence – and the slow growth, complexity and fragility of the civilizing institutions – as no public choice theorists have done. From Owenites through Fabians to Tawney, Holland, Nove, Michael Harrington and others, democratic socialists have worked to distinguish the necessary from the unnecessary cruelties and injustices of capitalism, and to develop the law, the public sector and the welfare arrangements which civilize mixed economies and restrain their inequalities. Feminist and environmentalist theories set out the reasons and purposes of movements many of whose political achievements defy public choice expectations. They assume and have proved in practice that action for the benefit of third-world women, unborn generations and other strangers is possible and worth working for. And modern technicians of voting systems and behaviour, like the commercial pollsters led by Gallup or the Nuffield team of electoral analysts led by Butler, know much more about their subject than public choice theorists do. Moreover all these schools of thought are aware of the large elements of self-interest in political behaviour and alert to detect them; none of them sees voters or politicians as godlike or reliably impartial, as public choice stereotypes accuse them of doing.

In contrast to those honorable traditions it seems fair to call the public choice argument not only unconvincing but also disingenuous. Its leaders frequently acknowledge that its original behavioural assumption is not true and does not generate reliable predictions – yet they persist with it. They claim positive, value-free objectivity for much of their work, but base it on the belief, which is wholly moral or arbitrary, that individual material greed is natural and rational but other human aspirations are not. They say that 'communal values' are logically impossible but build their own constitutional programme on what they admit are communal values of their own. Though conceding that its factual basis is often false they continue to recommend a belittling, degraded and degrading view of the potentialities of human purpose and democratic government. If there was ever an element of respectable scientific ambition in the attempt to build a universal theory of political behaviour on the assumption that its motivation is simple, constant and wholly selfish, there has been no excuse for it for many years now.

One critic who shares many of these objections to public choice theory nevertheless thinks it can be rescued. In *Democracy, Bureaucracy and Public Choice: Economic Explanations in Political Science* (1991) Patrick Dunleavy offers to rescue it by supplementing Niskanen's model of bureaucratic motivation with one of his own. Niskanen argued that a desire to enrich or magnify themselves by maximizing their budgets sufficiently explains bureaucrats' behaviour. Dunleavy cites the abundant evidence that, for most of them, it does not. Wherever it does not, he believes their behaviour can be sufficiently explained instead by their liking for a particular kind of organization. 'Rational officials want to work in small, elite, collegial bureaus close to political power centres. They do not want to head up heavily staffed, large budget but routine, conflictual and low status agencies.' (p. 202) So they work at reorganizing their departments to have the desired qualities, for example by privatizing or contracting out to other agencies as many of their functions as they can. This, which he calls 'bureau shaping', is Dunleavy's rival model, and he sets out the conditions which may determine bureaucrats' choices between budget maximizing and bureau shaping strategies.

The main public choice belief survives. Bureau shapers are assumed to be no more interested than budget maximizers are in improving the world for anyone but themselves. 'Without positing an other-regarding or ideological commitment by officials to their bureau or its mission, a good deal of evidence suggests that self-interested officials have strong preferences about the kind of work they want to do, and the kind of agency they want to work in.' (p. 201) The evidence is that they prefer one way of working to another, not that they necessarily prefer either to their social commitments or public duty. But by a leap for which little or no evidence is offered, they are assumed to choose policies purely for the type of organization that the policies will justify. Thus they govern not for public purposes or even to attract votes, but for their private pleasure.

But about selfishness the book is sometimes inconsistent. Dunleavy writes here and there as an acute observer of real life, including the complex motives and mixtures of commitment and self interest to be found in public services. But when he writes about theory rather than life he usually reverts to the public choice assumption that behaviour can be sufficiently explained and predicted as strictly self interested. That is also the only behaviour which the book calls 'rational'. Rational is made to *mean* effectively selfish. It is never used in its normal instrumental meaning to describe, for example, rational ways to relieve poverty or improve health services.

So we have four reasons for not joining Professor Dunleavy's rescue mission.

The pervasive mistake about motivation hinders rather than helps the understanding of political and administrative behaviour.

The mistake is moral as well as factual. Depicting selfish behaviour as the universal and the only rational kind of behaviour effectively recommends it and discourages better behaviour.

Might is not right. On the book's last page Dunleavy observes ruefully that when 'a significant body of work has accumulated in any field of science, after a time external queries about the usefulness of that entire approach must get shrugged off. Within any sphere of knowledge development, what becomes used on a large scale is by definition being found useful.' So were witchcraft, Say's Law and the justifications of slavery 'found useful', in their day, for their ignorant or evil purposes.

The last page also reiterates the author's scientific beliefs. 'The gains made by public choice theory in extending the scope and methods of debate and research in political science towards new forms of logically and mathematically informed reasoning are in my view now undeniable.' Despite forty years of failure he still hopes to explain conscious, reflective human behaviour with its changing purposes, and the conflicts and cooperation and choices those purposes prompt, by means of axiomatic/deductive reasoning which proceeds mathematically from fixed assumptions about a very few of the many springs of human action. As in other social sciences we think the attempt is mistaken.

Part Three

7 What to do Instead: How to Mix a Mixed Economy

Insofar as the theories we have discussed have practical effects they are chiefly on decisions which affect the structure and regulation of mixed economies. (There is a telling account of those effects in Peter Self, 1993.) If the theories are rejected, how should we think instead about the design of mixed economies? How should citizens, politicians, public servants and press approach the innumerable detailed decisions and the occasional strategic choices – or in the ex-communist world the crowding, bewildering strategic choices – by which they help to shape their economic systems? Our argument opened with a commonsense view of the motives at work in political life. We now add some commonsense considerations which people of all persuasions may do well to keep in mind when thinking about the mix of mixed economies.

There can be no universal prescription. The 'best' mix must vary with local resources and circumstances. No mix can be best either for everyone's material interest or for everyone's vision of social good, so the collective choices must often be disagreed and arrived at through conflict and compromise. But in arriving at them we think the citizens will do well to have in mind the following questions and considerations rather than any fixed preference for public or private enterprise, or bigger or smaller government.

MODES OF PRODUCTION

Economists usually see the mixed economy as mixing two modes of production – private enterprise and public enterprise – with corresponding market and governmental methods of resource allocation and decision-making. The facts of life and the purpose of our argument prompt us to add, as a third mode of production, the production which is done within households and voluntary associations without formal payment and unrecorded in most national accounts. There are two common ways of estimating that unrecorded flow of work and output.[1] The output (of meals cooked, clothes laundered, children minded, repairs done, mileage driven, etc.) can be observed, and valued at what commercial suppliers would charge for the same goods and services. Or hours of work can be observed and valued at current wage rates for similar work. Each method has drawbacks and both have elements of arbitrary selection and valuation. But as applied by most practitioners they estimate unpaid work and output at somewhere between 33 and 45 per cent of all work and output in developed economies. Add the output of public enterprise and it becomes clear that private enterprise does barely half of all production – slightly more than half in Japan and the US, slightly less than half elsewhere. We noted earlier that there does not appear to be any regular relation between public/private proportions and measured national income – the US and Sweden with respectively the smallest and largest public sectors have at times run level as the richest countries per head. But recent evidence suggests that the amount of the household share may affect real standards of living: some countries which look poorer than others when conventionally measured look richer when household capital and output are taken into account.[2]

A mixed economy should accordingly be seen as mixing not two but three modes of production: public enterprise, private enterprise and unpaid work in households and voluntary associations. They have different characteristics and need different relations with government. Public policies affect their efficiency, their shares of capital resources and their roles in the economy as a whole. Policymakers should keep all three in mind. But that is not encouraged by prevailing theoretical models – however else they differ, neoclassical and marxist and postkeynesian models are all models of a single capitalist mode of production with varying amounts of market failure and government intervention.

This chapter therefore offers an alternative model, or image, of a modern mixed economy. It recognizes the three modes of production and the need for intelligent government of each of them. In doing so it indicates a range of considerations which (common sense suggests) should bear on public decisions about economic structure and ownership.

We may begin with a brief reminder of the view of complex motivation that was sketched in our first chapter.

People want material goods and services. Besides the goods and services themselves, they want their production and distribution to serve other purposes too: purposes of freedom, security, enjoyment, self-expression, sociability, equality or inequality, justice, and so on.

People have many shared and many conflicting interests and values. Individuals' material interests and their values and purposes often influence each other but don't always or necessarily determine each other.

People both shape and are shaped by their culture. Their culture does a good deal to shape their economic activity, and some of the economic activity is designed to have effects on the culture. People work to sustain or change the culture – for example, to influence each others' wants and values – for both selfish and unselfish reasons. Economic theories are among their means of persuasion.

Most production needs some organization. Simplifying, the types of organization or modes of production can be classified as private, public and domestic. Private enterprises earn for their owners, and range in scale from transnational corporations to individual tradespeople, artists and professionals. Public enterprises range from armies and space agencies to kindergartens, and in our classification include independent non-profit enterprises like churches and universities. In the domestic sector we include unpaid work in charities and voluntary associations as well as in households.

Mixed economies can thus produce for a wide range of purposes besides individual financial gain. It would be unworldly to depict households as motivated only by love, public enterprises only by duty and private enterprises only by profit – mixed motives including plenty of self-interest operate in all sectors. Nevertheless public and domestic work offer more opportunities than the private sector usually can for people who like best to work as reformers, researchers, teachers, in caring occupations, or at economically marginal arts and crafts and charities which many households enable some of their members to practise. Whatever the individual motivation, the three sectors have different institutional capacities. Households can employ unpaid or informally paid workers as private enterprises can't. Public enterprises can produce for multiple economic and social purposes. Private enterprises may give their customers excellent value for money, but it does usually have to be for money: profit-seeking producers can't usually behave much more generously than their competitors do. Even 'satisficing' or 'under-optimizing' (earning enough to survive, but less than you ruthlessly could) can be difficult these days, as less rapacious firms become vulnerable to takeover by the more rapacious. There is value in the diversity of individual motivation and institutional capacity which the three sectors offer.

Each mode can affect the others' performance. Private industrial progress may depend on public education and research. There may be less public inefficiency where there is private competition or standard-setting, and the possibility of privatizing lazy public services. There may be less or more or different domestic slavery if housewives have the option of going out to earn. Labour is less exploited where government pays incomes to the unemployed. There is less financial exploitation of private tenants where poor households can rent public housing, and less bureaucratic oppression of public tenants where there are private alternatives. And so on – a pure capitalist model of a modern economy may even misrepresent the private sector which it *does* model, by neglecting the other sectors' effects on it.

The following sections sketch some characteristics of each mode of production, what each needs from government, what each contributes to the other two, and the roles of market and government in apportioning resources between them.

HOUSEHOLDS

As producers, households do three basic things. They produce people and do a good deal to determine their potential productivity. They produce between 35 and 45 per cent of all material goods and services. And they distribute income, in cash and kind: unearned incomes to children and other dependants, and hard-earned though often inadequate incomes to housewives and other household workers and carers. Households provide the main income of up to 30 per cent of affluent societies' members, many more than receive their main incomes from pensions or other government transfers.

Households thus produce all the people, more than a third of their goods and services, and nearly a third of their incomes. The capital, space and equipment with which they do it have obvious economic importance.

Through the twentieth century household productivity has grown as spectacularly as public and private productivity. Technical progress allows the public and private sectors to pay higher wages for shorter hours of work. That gives earners more money and time at home. The money buys more domestic equipment; technical progress improves and cheapens the equipment; more and better equipment make each houseworking hour more productive. Living standards rise, or given standards are maintained by shorter hours of work so that it becomes possible to keep house *and* go out and earn, with a further increase in household income.

Household productivity depends on, among other things, the capital and the money income available to the household, and within those financial limits it depends on household choices about what to produce at home and what to buy ready-made. How families of economic rationalists might approach their investing, working and spending choices is explored by Jonathan Gershuny in *Social Innovation and the Division of Labour* (1983).

Besides affecting households' access to space, capital and equipment, public policies also affect the amounts of paid and unpaid work which household members are able or required to do. Examples: Increasing public employment to provide more child care may increase private employment by freeing more parents to go out and earn. Reducing public employment by deinstitutionalizing physically and mentally handicapped people may also reduce private employment as workers return home to care for their kin, or it may stress and overload carers who can't afford to stop earning. There are good social and therapeutic reasons for some of the deinstitution-alization of the aged and the mentally ill, but not for as much of it as the shift to the Right has forced for tax-cutting reasons. The main economic effect is a shift from paid to unpaid care, and from most efficient to less efficient use of carers' labour. Many women suffer trebly, tied to wearying dependants and deprived of the incomes they might otherwise earn and the company they might otherwise enjoy at work.

Parents may also bear double burdens if, in home-owning societies, buying the house requires that both of them earn whether they like it or not. Rates of interest and repayment on housing loans have varied widely enough over time and from country to country to double or halve the repayment rates required of young homebuyers. There are parents, almost always mothers, who want paid work but can't find it near enough to home or child care, and others who want to stay with their children but have to earn to keep the mortgage at bay. The constraints arise wholly or partly from governments' housing, banking, planning and other policies. Influ-encing the amount of paid and unpaid work which household members must do, and the resources available to them, is a function of government which rarely gets the attention it deserves where government is dominated by men.

Both the household choices and the constraints on them vary widely. Consider a familiar range of households from richest to poorest, with their domestic productivity determined partly by their means and partly by their preferences.

Some rich households have town and country houses with billiard rooms, music rooms, flats for servants, stables for horses, gardens, pools, tennis courts, cars and boats. Some use that gear energetically, others don't. Other rich choose to live in penthouses, eating out, exercising at gymnasia and sports clubs, consuming chiefly commercial services and recreations, producing very little of what they consume.

Among middle-income households there are schoolteachers' families with modest house and garden, one old car, bikes and camping gear, chess and chequers and Scrabble boards, bookshelves with dictionaries, encyclo-paedias, histories, art books, nature studies, poetry, children's books and tattered cookbooks, doing nearly everything for themselves. Less intellec-tual but equally energetic households equip themselves with workshops, vegetable gardens, electronic games, derelict houses or vintage cars to recondition with their own hands. Lazier households spend their money on smarter clothes and cars and frozen dinners and spend their leisure watching sport, televised on week nights and live at weekends.

An American or Australian worker's family may have a garden full of old cars and a house full of teenagers, friends, videos, electronic sound and fast food. With different options a Scottish worker's family may rent a tower flat, do comparatively little except cooking and school homework there, and look for company and recreation at pubs and clubs away from home.

Among lone parents, one wants to share child care in a commune; another wants a house and garden of her own, however poor – a place for children who get home before she does, a place from which no landlord can shift them.

Some retired couples live on where they brought up their children. Others move to trouble-free apartments, retirement villages, cottages, caravans.

One single person with a busy working and social life may want a capacious apartment, another may be content with a bedsitter. Some less successful singles have even less capital: old men who spend their nights in hostel beds, their days on park benches and their pensions on take-away food and drink.

With economic growth, households move up that 'option ladder'. As income grows, less of it is committed to basic food and shelter and more is left for discretionary spending and saving, including investment in household capital. Households become both freer and – to the extent that they choose to be – more productive.

The upward progress and the widening choices owe much to market forces. But they also depend, especially for their household distribution and total productivity, on government. Apart from the more general public contributions to technological and economic growth, the main public contributions to household productivity are in three areas: the distribution of income; public investment in the infrastructure and services on which households depend; and the financial and housing policies which affect consumer credit and the supply, tenure and ownership of housing.

It takes some money income both to buy or rent housing and household equipment and to make much use of it – domestic production needs fuel, raw materials, maintenance and so on, besides well-fed workers. Full employment policies and public incomes to the old, sick and unemployed, and income supplements to households with children all extend the number of households who can produce satisfactory living standards for themselves.

Besides money income, households need public services: water and power supplies, telephone connexions, roads, drainage and sewerage where appropriate. Most need to live in reach of jobs, shops, schools, health and other services. Most of those are provided by public investment or by private investment which depends on public infrastructure.

In thus noting that household productivity requires some money income and public services, we are reminding readers of the obvious. The reminders have accordingly been short. It is less usual and therefore takes longer to argue, next, that governments need to correct a fundamental inefficiency in the very nature of housing and capital markets.

All rich societies have some households too poor to house themselves at acceptable standards. All governments see some duty to help them. The means vary: public housing, rent subsidies, rent controls, purchase subsidies, tax concessions. Those are commonly accepted as social policies with economic costs. Some of them, especially the tax concessions and other aids to homebuyers, help more well-off households than needy ones. Those are criticised as weak-kneed political concessions to affluent voters. Where their effects are regressive, i.e. where they increase inequalities, we agree with the criticism.

But that is different from arguing as many economists and public choice theorists do that whether or not its effects are socially desirable, government intervention to increase the supply of housing necessarily reduces economic efficiency and growth because it diverts capital resources from productive to unproductive investment. Three things are wrong with that belief. First it defies experience: for half a century now, the fastest economic growth, as conventionally measured, has been accompanied by high housing investment, stimulated by government to exceed what unaided market forces would provide. Second, the conventional measure of growth which excludes household output is indefensible: households produce more than a third of all material goods and services and housing is a main part of the capital with which they do it. Third, it is precisely in the economists' meaning of efficient that it *cannot* be efficient to leave the supply and distribution of housing to unaided market forces. To see why this is so, we may begin by recalling why the market allocation of other capital resources is thought to be efficient.

In economic theory, household members own the means of production – land, labour and capital – but make them available for firms to use. They trade their resources to firms in factor markets, where firms bid competitively for the resources. The firms which win the resources by offering the highest prices for them – the highest rent, interest, dividend or wage – are those which manage to produce the most or best output from least input. It is that pure productive efficiency which enables them to outbid competitors in the factor markets for the resources they need, then outsell competitors in the retail markets. Thus the hidden hand does its work: households' individual earning, saving and spending choices determine how a society's productive resources are used, and get them used with maximum competitive efficiency. Of course in real life there are many market failures and inefficiencies, but to the extent that competitive bidding for capital funds and thus for productive resources is efficient in the way the theory describes, it is because *the producers who can use the capital most profitably, and can therefore bid highest to get it, are those who can make the most productive use of it and thus add most to the national product.*

But that cannot be true of housing capital.

The productive use which a household can make of its capital – its house, garden if it has one, workshop, car, domestic equipment, hobby and recreational gear and so on – is *not* linked to the ability to pay for the capital. The household's ability to save up or borrow capital funds depends on something else altogether – it depends on what its members inherit or earn from paid employment. The capacity to get household capital thus depends on their productivity at work in business or for an employer, *not* on their potential productivity with the domestic capital. The reason is obvious and simple – the goods produced with household capital don't sell for money, so they don't earn the means to buy the household capital. If you ask your banker for a loan to buy a business, she wants to know how profitable the business will be. But if you ask for a loan to buy a house or a family car she doesn't ask how productive the house or car will be, she still wants to know about your wage or business income because it is from that, not from the output of the house or car, that you will have to repay the loan.

There is thus no necessary link between the ability to use household capital and the ability to get it. Of course most well-off households can get what they want, with or without mortgage loans and consumer credit. There are important elements of market efficiency in their individual judgements of how much of what sort of domestic capital they think it worth while to pay for. There may sometimes be some rough correspondence between the capacity to earn plenty of income and thus pay for household capital and the energy to use the capital productively. But wherever young or low-income households can't get capital which they could use productively, there is some lost productivity, and economists have no present means of comparing the loss with the gain from the alternative non-housing use of the resource. Within the housing market, with no reliable market mechanism to link the available capital to the willing labour, it is not hard to find cases of obviously inefficient allocation. At one extreme may be a family with a disabled breadwinner or none, whose one able adult gives all her time to the care of bright energetic children. They could do all sorts of things for themselves, some of which would spin off benefits for society, if they could afford the capital and running costs of well-equipped housing in reach of good schools and services. But poverty has them in a succession of rented flats, passively watching television most of the time because there is no garden or shed or games room, there are bans on pets, musical instruments, ball games and other aids to skill and self-expression, and without secure tenure each forced change of address can force another change of schools and friendships and some further attrition of the children's confidence in themselves and in friendship itself. At the other extreme are affluent couples and singles occupying a lot more real estate than they need or make much productive use of. If economists came across two *firms* like that, one labour-rich but producing very little for lack of capital and the other with a full capital outfit mostly idle for lack of labour, they would holler 'market failure' and consider how government should act to repair whatever gross fault in the economic system was causing such inefficient allocation of resources.

How extensive may the market failure be? The competition for resources is not only between households. In open land and capital markets households compete with business and government bidders for the bank loans and the good locations. If there is no link between the individual households' ability to get capital and their ability to use it productively, there is no reason to expect the total allocation to the housing sector as a whole to be efficient; and if the division of resources between housing and business is not efficient, the allocation to business cannot be efficient. If household products are agreed to be products, a rigorous theorist must see that a theory which is mistaken about housing allocation must also be unfit for its prime task of modelling the efficient allocation of capital to business users. Competent theory would indicate a need for government to intervene if it wished to maximize the national product, perhaps by adjusting market allocations to the extent necessary to equalize marginal productivity between household and household, and between the household and business sectors.

Practice is more convincing than theory. Does high housing investment in practice inhibit economic productivity and growth? No, the historical evidence suggests the opposite.[3] Since 1945 countries which have invested the highest proportions of GNP in housing, always with substantial public aids, have generally had the highest rates of measured economic growth, and with only a partial exception in Japan the housing aids have preceded and helped to stimulate the growth, not merely followed it. Moreover the additional housing was presumably improving household productivity, so those countries' real growth may well have been ahead of their measured rates.

That fast economic growth often accompanies high housing investment should not be surprising. Housebuilding has good multipliers. It stimulates other investment both up and down stream, i.e. in building supplies and in furniture and household equipment. It can be a sparse user of imports so it need not worsen the exchange problems which some fast-growing economies have had. Good housing helps to keep workers happy and healthy. For many, the possibility of owning their housing is a main incentive to save, so some (unmeasured but probably substantial) proportion of housing investment is at the expense of consumer spending rather than alternative investment – nobody knows how much of it is actually 'diverted from other productive uses'. The German and East Asian 'economic miracles' suggest that housing investment may well have stimulated more other investment than it 'diverted'.

To summarize: In open markets (subject to all necessary financial regulation) business capital tends to go in correct proportions to those who will make most productive use of it. Household capital does not. Unaided market forces cannot be expected to allocate resources most productively either between housing and other uses, or between household and household. So there is good reason for government to regulate and augment the market allocation of housing capital, to at least the extent necessary to allow poor households, and many young households before much saving has been possible, to house and equip themselves well enough to put their willing labour to productive use.

The means by which governments may do this are many and various, from specialized housing banks and general financial regulation through public planning and infrastructure, public housing, agreements or joint ventures with private housing developers or cooperatives, mortgage and rent assistance to households, child care and other support services. Historically there have been plenty of wasteful, oppressive and regressive housing policies, culminating in the disastrous deregulation of the US housing finance institutions. But the disasters are well known and documented. No democracy need repeat them. They are outnumbered by solidly successful policies which have assisted the housing of much of the population and also the economic growth of much of north-western Europe, Canada, Australia and East Asia since 1945. It is simply absurd to depict those successes as chiefly benefiting their government administrators or minorities of affluent households, rather than the large majorities, including many of the poorest households, who in fact benefited from them.

It is time to discard two mistaken beliefs: that housing investment necessarily subtracts from economic growth, and that public intervention in housing is usually incompetent or perverse. In fact, households tend to have most need of new capital and the most productive uses for it when they have least means of getting it, early in household life. It is the necessary capital for more than a third of all production. But the market links between getting it and using it are quite imperfect. For economic as well as social reasons people need their governments to conduct active planning, housing and housing-finance policies, to provide domestic production with rather more and better-distributed resources than unaided market forces would allow.

PRIVATE ENTERPRISES

Private enterprises produce about half – or if household production is ignored, more than three quarters – of a modern mixed economy's goods and services. They constitute its biggest single mode of production and are vital to its efficiency. Market relations, when they work as they should, offer the best assurance of consumer choice and sovereignty, and they can contribute much to the efficiency of public and household as well as private production. Together the competitive private and market elements of the mixed economy contribute vitally to its freedom, inventiveness, adaptability and extraordinary productivity.

Those virtues of market capitalism are common knowledge. So are its equally famous shortcomings. It has been common to balance the virtues and vices and settle for the system because the available alternatives – command economies, primitive economies, the many failed attempts at utopian settlements – are in practice worse. But one good effect of the final discredit of the command economies should be a change in the focus of debate. Instead of debating whether capitalism or socialism is best we should think what mix of public, private and household production would be best (for particular societies in particular circumstances with their particular patterns of common and conflicting interests, and so on); and what can be done to make each mode work as well as possible. In that spirit, what are the conditions in which private enterprise does best – what does it need from the other modes of production and from government, and how should its scope in a mixed economy be determined?

From households, private enterprises chiefly need fit, willing and honest managers and workers. In developed societies households have to support children through ten to twenty years of formal education; family upbringing is a main source of attitudes to work and earning; resourceful households with active recreations seem likelier than others to bring up resourceful workers; they also contribute much of whatever built-in honesty and cooperative capacity their children have. The more skilful and versatile the workforce needs to be, the greater the public and private sectors' need for a well-housed, well-equipped, well-educated household sector.

From public enterprises the private sector needs most of the formal education of its workers, professionals and managers; the basic research on which much of its technology is built; varying amounts of applied and developmental research; much generation, storage and retrieval of information by census and statistical services, libraries, archives, legal records, mapping and resource-survey and land-title services; many professional and advisory services, especially to farmers and other small businesses; the standard infrastructure of roads and bridges, rails, ports, airports, power, gas, water, sewerage and telecommunication networks, and varying quantities of public transport. Power and transport costs and public transport efficiencies affect the performance of a great many private industries. In many developing and developed countries private producers also depend on public supplies of steel, coal, forest timber, and storage and handling facilities for farm products. In most developed countries the private arts are supported and subsidized by state theatres, orchestras, opera and dance companies, art galleries and craft centres, music and drama and art schools.

From government, private enterprise needs general and specialized law and order and quick and accessible commercial courts; some regulation of industrial relations and working conditions; helpful trade policies and international trading and exchange arrangements; and a great deal of regulation of industrial safety, waste disposal, commercial and consumer credit, truthful labelling and so on – regulation which business may dislike but which serves it in one or both of two necessary ways. By protecting workers and consumers it helps to keep free enterprise acceptable to democratic majorities; and between firm and firm it restrains types of competition from which honest enterprises need to be protected – for example competition by fraud and deception, industrial espionage, sabotage or corruption, and by products which undersell their competitors only because they are defective or dangerous in ways which buyers can't detect at the point of sale.

Many individual operators – professionals, tradespeople and small businesses – gain more than they lose when government helps with their quality controls. Public authorities license or certify doctors, vets, pharmacists, nurses and other health workers, lawyers, accountants, engineers, architects, teachers, air pilots, ships' officers, drivers and machine operators of many kinds. In many countries they also license or certify other skilled operators (plumbers, electricians, mechanics) and dealers whose competence and probity their clients can't always judge for themselves (stockbrokers, builders, estate agents, casino operators). Critics from Old Left and New Right often agree in denouncing these licensing arrangements, especially for the learned professions, as nothing but self-serving monopolist devices to restrict entry and competition in the ´professions and inflate their prices. Some of them, especially those which originated in the professions' own associations, do some of that. But to suppose that that is all that they do is to miss a valuable public service to the efficiency of the private operations. Public certification, which often adds little to the costs of the relevant training procedures, saves each and every client from having to investigate the competence and probity of the available professionals, and saves the professionals the costs of advertising and private certification to reassure (or deceive) the customers. Licensing can of course be misused, but that calls for reform rather than indiscriminate deregulation.

Bigger enterprises which need incorporation need more basic things from government. As noted in an earlier chapter, they need their corporate existence and the powers and safeguards which allow investors to trust them with their money. The public company is the great invention which links the efficiency of large-scale organization to the efficiency and freedoms of the market. The necessary regulation is not 'bureaucratic intervention', it is an absolute condition of corporate existence. But the economic and technological growth which corporate organization has made possible has had a strong tendency to increase the amount and complexity of the necessary regulation, and to make its quality increasingly important.

Regulation can be difficult. It needs to be well designed and its administration suitably staffed, and it needs to be adaptable to changing needs. The best regimes have been deft at enlisting the interests which they regulate, at building controls into firms' own procedures, at getting private lawyers and accountants to police private firms in the ordinary way of their business, and at minimizing the adversary element in regulation (or at seeing that it sets good performers against bad, rather than both against the regulators). James Landis' design of the long-lived US Securities and Exchange Commission is a famous example, which has done much to rescue US business from the anarchy of the States' chartering rules.

Some regulators have of course been ineffective, needlessly obstructive, or captured by the people they are supposed to regulate. Their shortcomings encourage deregulation, often when the need is to improve rather than dismantle the regulation. Many business people want less regulation of their own activities; some governments agree because they hope to save money; predators encourage both expectations. Disasters have followed, most spectacularly in the US Savings and Loan institutions. Corporate business has millions of people handling trillions of other people's money in the owners' absence. Its rules may often need revision or replacement, but simply deregulating it is no different from deregulating burglary.

The best regulation is done by experienced, incorruptible people who want private enterprise to prosper but who understand the kind of government it needs in order to do so. National public services in Scandinavia, Japan, Germany and France have been very good at it, the Swedes and Japanese specially good at adapting it promptly to changing needs. Tens of thousands of local health, building, vehicle and other inspectors and licensing officers in all developed countries do their work satisfactorily. Most of that success goes unremarked, while advocates of general deregulation focus on a few celebrated US cases, some of them long past, of regulators who were captured or legally outmanoeuvred by the industries concerned, often because they were required to regulate private railroads and utility monopolies which Europeans have controlled more effectively by public ownership.

One condition of economic and business efficiency needs special attention because of shortcomings in the prevailing theory and practice of the English-speaking countries. Capital markets play a vital role in the allocation of productive resources, but we believe they need specially strong and careful public management and have not lately been getting it. We argued earlier that unregulated housing and housing-finance markets have an intrinsic inefficiency. That is a special case of a more general inefficiency in modern capital markets. Since Adam Smith's time three developments have complicated the simple efficiency of firms bidding competitively for the use of the citizens' savings. Limited liability and the separation of corporate ownership from control can make opportunities for directors to gain by operating against rather than for their firms' and shareholders' interests. A high proportion of savings are now collected from their owners and allocated to their ultimate users by banks and other profit-seeking financial intermediaries. And new technology allows instantaneous exchange and transmission of funds from any part of the world to any other. Together these three conditions allow, and sometimes encourage, a number of ill effects of unregulated market competition for capital funds.

Financial intermediaries borrow money and on-lend it to other enterprises. They don't produce anything tangible themselves, but justify their existence by organizing the available funds for use by the productive firms and households to whom they lend. That services does indeed justify their existence, but because of a particular characteristic of competition *between intermediaries* – as opposed to the primary lenders or ultimate users of capital – they can only do it well under public regulation. Intermediaries may borrow then lend, or they may undertake to lend, then borrow, typically from other intermediaries. They compete with one another. Whichever intermediaries get the business, much the same ultimate users will borrow the money in the end. So when intermediaries compete, the winning bids don't necessarily come from the most productive users as in a classically efficient market. Some simply come from the most imprudent bidders. In a simple capital market without intermediaries each borrower (steel-maker, shoemaker) wants just so much debt and bids accordingly. Their bids are limited by their estimates of the quantity and price of steel or shoes they will be able to sell. But financial intermediaries compete, basic-ally, for shares of the business of transmitting a given supply of funds to a given demand for them. The capacity to repay is with the final borrow-ers rather than the intermediaries. Some intermediaries may be more efficient than others – better at containing their internal costs and at lend-ing wisely – but their profit tends to depend more on their volume of busi-ness, i.e. on their market shares. That encourages ambitious bidding, and for some of the individuals who determine the bids there is also a seduc-tive asymmetry of risks. Handling other people's money, they can often link their rewards as directors to the profit or market share they achieve, but there are no equivalent penalties (actual personal losses) for corporate losses. So some intermediaries, especially newcomers with little to lose, want all the funds they can get, and bid accordingly. Others, defensively, have to follow.

Of course bids are limited by judgements of the rates of interest at which on-lending will still be possible. But those judgements are not quite like the judgements which guide individual firms' demands in a simple market. They are judgements of the rates of interest which *all* borrowers can be made to pay without significantly reducing the aggregate demand for funds. If all borrowers have to pay the same inflated rates, sanguine inter-mediaries can hope for a somewhat inelastic demand for their funds, partly because the cost of money can be passed on in product prices much as a general rise in (say) oil or steel or labour costs could be, and partly because if productive borrowers can't be found, speculative or asset-trading bor-rowers probably can.

There are thus treble possibilities of trouble – from higher interest rates, some depressive and some inflationary effects of higher business costs, and some riskier lending mostly for less productive purposes. It would take another book to detail all the distortions to be expected, the reasons for expecting them, and the various ways in which government can act to avert them. Here we merely list baldly some common ill effects if the business is not suitably regulated, as evidenced in three recent histories.

OPEC

The Organization of Petroleum Exporting Countries (OPEC) raised the world price of oil in 1973 and again in 1979 so that the value at annual prices of an unchanged volume of petroleum exports rose from about US$20 billions to $120bn in 1974 and $200bn in 1979. The OPEC proprietors could not spend much of that on imports so they accumulated large foreign cash balances. What to do with all that money? Western banks, competing for shares of it, accepted it at substantial rates of interest although for much of it they had no borrowers who could make sufficiently productive use of it to generate the revenue to service and repay such debts. Some of the money found productive borrowers, in the West and elsewhere, but most of it went to other users. It financed takeovers, often loading the taken companies with excessive debt. It financed other asset trading, chiefly in real estate, liberally enough to inflate the asset prices and bring good speculative returns (to some, for a time) without adding anything to real productivity. And it was lent to Third World and East European governments, or government-guaranteed enterprises, on the assumption that the governments, most of them dictatorships, would have the power and will to service debts from taxation if necessary. Some of that money financed public or private investments, some profitable and many not. Quite a lot was stolen by corrupt individuals. Much, especially in East Europe, was used to subsidize consumption to buy a few more years of submission by increasingly resentful and disbelieving populations. Brutal levels of debt now burden those people and their new governments. If they pay, their political and economic reforms are in danger; if they don't, their Western aid and the Western banking system are in danger. Ironically, the parties in no immediate danger are the primary lenders, the OPEC owners. If they themselves had done the imprudent lending and now faced the consequent losses, there might be a case for trusting to market discipline. But an effect of leaving the management of the market to unregulated intermediaries has been to shift the threatened losses to the other depositors in Western banks and the poor taxpayers of the Third World and Eastern Europe, people who did nothing to cause the trouble and whom it is neither just nor productive to punish for it.

What should have happened instead? When OPEC forced unrequitable exports on the world, a rational international regime would have recognized that some necessary loss must be accepted in fair proportions by exporters and importers alike. If the Western banks accepted all that they could on-lend for viable productive investment, that should lower interest rates and expand the demand for funds by making more marginal and long-term projects viable. Interest rates to depositors should have fallen accordingly; and the large surplus of funds which could still not be lent in a commercially viable way should not have been accepted on an interest-bearing basis at all. If the OPEC owners would not give it or lend it interest-free as Third World aid, Western banks should have accepted it only on terms which would let its real value dwindle in inert, non-interest-bearing deposits. But any such strategy required an international regime of some sort. If the leading governments had agreed, they already had much of the necessary machinery in their central banks' powers, the International Monetary Fund (IMF) and the (mostly unused) emergency powers provided for long before in the General Agreement on Tariffs and Trade (GATT).

The destructive misuse of the OPEC surpluses was an effect of, among other things, competition for market shares by insufficiently regulated financial intermediaries.

Hot money

The post-war international financial system included fixed rates of exchange between national currencies, and many national controls on the quantity and purpose of exchange transactions. Most governments and central banks also exercised considerable control over the quantities, general purposes and interest rates of bank lending within their national economies. Those controls were relaxed step by step, with the main international ones finally discarded in the 1970s.

Thus freed, many financial institutions switched resources from productive to other uses. They financed corporate takeovers from foreign as well as domestic funds, adding to national as well as corporate debt problems. They financed other speculative asset dealing, especially in real estate. And they began to gamble on the fluctuations of the international exchange rates. Large surpluses of footloose money, much but by no means all of it from OPEC, moved restlessly around the world in search of tax havens, the best short term interest rates, and gamblers' gains from the fluctuating exchange rates. Exchange rates ceased to reflect real trading balances or domestic purchasing power; especially in small national currencies they reflected the speculators' gambling expectations of each other. Their distortion and instability added to the troubles of genuine trade and investment. Altogether the new financial freedoms appear to have done much more harm than good. Some of their effects can be illustrated from one small country's experience.

Australia, 1980–90

Through the long postwar boom Australia had steady economic growth, very full employment, generally low, slow-growing inflation, real interest rates near to zero, a swift advance of home ownership from below 50 to above 70 per cent of households, and a large increase of manufacturing. The manufacturing had discriminate protection and was mostly for Australian consumption rather than export, but there was good reason to believe that without it, protected where necessary, employment and the standard of living and the rate of immigration must all have been lower.

The Reserve Bank controlled foreign exchange transactions. Australians could normally buy foreign currency only for purposes of trade, travel or family support. They could not borrow, lend or invest abroad except for trade-linked purposes. The government monitored foreign investment in Australia. It welcomed and protected new industrial investment, but forbade or limited foreign acquisition of financial institutions, newspapers and broadcasters, air transport, real estate, mineral rights and enterprises. Within Australia the markets for business, housing and public capital were roughly segregated by public ownership of about half the banks, and extensive regulation of them all. Trading banks could pay no interest on cheque accounts, and had to hold prescribed proportions of their assets in government deposits or securities at interest rates determined by government; lend on overdraft at regulated rates; and comply with Reserve Bank requests as to the quantities and directions of their lending. Savings banks could pay interest to depositors but must lend most of their assets to government or for housing, all at regulated interest rates. Life insurance companies were induced by tax concessions to lend specified proportions to government, and they could not normally invest abroad.

Between 1980 and 1985 successive governments deregulated the system, except for some licensing and prudential requirements. Foreign banks were allowed to operate in Australia. Banks could deal freely in foreign exchange and (at least in public) the Reserve Bank stopped managing the exchange rate as it had done since fixed rates ceased in 1971. Australian institutions could pay and receive what interest rates they liked, and borrow, lend or invest for any purpose, anywhere in the world.

This general liberation has done the opposite of everything its designers promised. They had predicted that floating the dollar would allow market forces to correct automatically any tendency towards exchange disequilibrium. In fact Australia's net annual payments deficit soared from $2bn in 1980 to $16bn in 1990. The deregulators predicted that any speculative dealing in foreign exchange would tend to reduce fluctuations and stabilize values. They assumed that gamblers would speculate on future trade-based values, but they were soon speculating on other speculators' behaviour as the speculative flows swelled to ten times or more the volume of trade-linked payments, and the Australian dollar fluctuated as never before – from

59 to 90 US cents in a single year. The deregulators predicted that open boundaries would expand the capital available to Australian industry. In fact foreign investment in Australia shifted sharply away from direct investment toward short term lending and the purchase of existing assets: 60 per cent of it had been direct through the 1970s, about 15 per cent was direct by 1985. At the same time some Australian investment shifted abroad so that the proportion of available funds actually used by the Australian business sector fell from about 45 to about 30 per cent. Through the first five deregulated years new manufacturing investment was steadily reduced by financial and tariff changes which the deregulators predicted would expand it. Within the finance industry the deregulators predicted that competition would cut banks' interest rates and profit margins. In fact most of the established banks increased their profits, and nominal and real interest rates rose to be among the highest in the world, and in Australia's history: real interest on safe loans averaged 1 per cent from 1945 to 1980, and 7 per cent from 1985 to 1990. Those rates helped to shift available funds from equity investment to lending and from productive investment to asset trading. They caused much farm and small business failure. They shifted housing funds from poorer to richer buyers. They did nothing good, except for rentier lenders.

The intermediaries' competition for funds was not the only cause of the high interest rates. Increasingly, government acted to keep them high for a macabre reason best explained by economist and financial journalist Tom Fitzgerald. As deregulation allowed the annual exchange deficit to increase, the deregulators introduced

the fateful government policy of raising interest rates so as to encourage a general, non-designated inflow of volatile foreign money in order to bridge the rapidly widening payments gap while also attempting to sustain the exchange rate. The Treasury's own Statement No. 2, tabled with the 1982 Budget, said that the substantial increases effected in interest rates 'were needed to finance the larger deficit on current account'. Nothing like this had ever been done before ... When interest rates are high, the compounding effects can be deadly. Rates of around 15 per cent were paid on the necessary borrowings to cover [the 1982] deficit of $9bn, and the debt remained to be serviced continuously and rolled over in future years. Every one billion dollars borrowed at 15 per cent compounds to two billion dollars in five years ... Suddenly we were in serious trouble: in the space of two years, the forces of drug addiction had taken a strong grip. The high interest rates have a triple adverse effect on the balance of payments: they lift the exchange rate, so boosting imports and weakening exports; they bring in funds which have to be serviced at exceptionally high interest rates by payments overseas; they deter industrial investment at home. This is how the need for artificially inducing short-term funds to bridge the deficit feeds rapidly on itself.

It would have taken an exceptional disciplinary effort to have kicked the habit in the first few years. But the Labor government's dash for total deregulation of the financial and foreign exchange markets in 1983 ... virtually closed off the prospects of an escape. With interest rates left as the only monetary weapon for inflation control and with a freely floating dollar, the deadly reciprocating-engine mechanism was operating.

Thus was a great national tradition suddenly destroyed ... The Department of Treasury and its ministers were primarily responsible. I am not aware of another case of economic miscalculation to compare with it.

Tom Fitzgerald, *Between Life and Economics*, 1990, pp. 45–6.

Fitzgerald and others had warned, in advance, of each of those dangers. As we write in 1993 the leaders of the national government and opposition still defend the general deregulation and support the desperate policies to which it continues to drive them.

Anyone who thinks that world conditions made the Australian troubles inescapable should compare the Swedish performance in comparable circumstances. The Swedish currency was another small one, more vulnerable than the Australian because Sweden had more than twice the Australian proportion of its economic activity involved in foreign trade. From late in the 1960s it also experienced a decline in household saving and a rising propensity to spend on imports, which made its exchange pressures at least as severe as the Australians'. In those conditions the Swedish government and central bank determined broad allocations between government, housing, business at home and Swedish business abroad. They regulated or influenced most domestic interest rates and some of the rates at which Swedish banks lent abroad when they were allowed to lend abroad. Specialized government-controlled institutions did most mortgage lending for housing, farming and shipping. A joint public/private export bank financed Swedish export sales, often on long and easy terms. Most private sector financing was done by strictly regulated commercial banks with government and trade union representatives on their boards, but to supply various kinds of credit which those banks did not supply, the biggest single lender to business was the publicly owned Swedish Investment Bank. Permission was required for most Swedish investment abroad, and for foreign investment in Sweden. As foreign exchange became scarce, most new Swedish investment abroad was required to be financed from abroad. An outstanding quality of the government of the financial system as a whole was its adaptability. Steady purposes were (as they still are) served by flexible methods and institutions. When the structure and methods of control are outmoded the Swedes are quick to update or replace them, recognizing that most systems of financial control tend to be eroded and evaded over time, and need frequent attention.

Misgivings about Sweden's welfare arrangements should not divert attention from her productive performance. Manufacturing, export, employment and economic growth prospered through four decades under that tight financial management. One feature of the regime which was unremarked – and inexplicable – by most orthodox market economists was the extent to which very free trade in goods was maintained only by very strict management of the trade in money.

Summary

Private enterprise needs many inputs from public and household producers; it is not helped if government starves those producers of resources as recommended by 'crowding out' theorists.

Within the private sector government must create and regulate suitable corporate powers and regulate many particular markets. It must control the financial system. If competently done, more may be gained than lost by regulating exchange rates and transactions, interest rates and quantities and broad directions of lending, and it may often pay to make special financial provision for farmers, manufacturers, exporters, and industries which need unusually risky or long-term funding. None of these measures need reduce, and most can enhance, competition and productive and allocative efficiency in the private sector. (Rigorous theory is available to support the practical need for financial management, if not necessarily the measures suggested here. See Colin Rogers, *Money, Interest and Capital: A study in the foundations of monetary theory* (1989) and Alan Kirman, 'The intrinsic limits of modern economic theory: the Emperor has no clothes', *Economic Journal* 99 (Conference 1989) pp. 126–39).

Given their necessary conditions private enterprises can be splendidly productive and market relations can allocate many resources with great economy and sensitivity. The independence of self-employed people and the ease of entry into a thousand lines of small business have value, in freedom and self-reliance and personal satisfaction, above and beyond their economic advantages. It is to defend and improve, not belittle, the services of private enterprise to a productive economy and a free society that we put such emphasis on its necessary conditions, of which one is pervasive and quite complicated good government.

PUBLIC ENTERPRISES

Public enterprises need most of the things which private enterprises need: good human resources from households and educational services; public infrastructure and services; effective regulation; access to capital; and so on. Those which operate in an ordinary market way may differ from many of their private equivalents only in receiving more decisive attention from their owners. Rules of audit, business morality and executive reward tend to be stricter under government ownership (though there have been exceptions), and governments can replace corporate boards and executives more economically than private shareholders or corporate raiders can usually do. In conflicts with hard-bargaining labour, public directors may have on the one hand more capacity to compromise than some private employers can afford – but on the other hand, more power to resist if their governments back them.

Public enterprises which are not under, or only partly under, market discipline have more distinctive problems. Some are market operators who are required to serve other purposes as well as profit. Some are monopolists, or suppliers of public goods which can't be charged for. To keep such enterprises efficient and attentive to their customers' wants there are things which managers can do, things which governments can do, and things which may need to be done about governments.

Public managers can do most of the things private managers can: keep the purposes of the enterprise clear and as widely shared as possible; articulate them into economical and accountable working tasks; attract and hold good people throughout the organization; arrange for their training and retraining; make career paths for them; engage their proud, generous, sociable, *interested* propensities, as well as their acquisitive ones, in the enterprise; devolve working arrangements and quality controls, as far as the work allows, to those doing the work; think incessantly how to economize the non-productive labour of supervision, accounting and administration; see that key members have opportunities to stand off and think about the enterprises' purposes, processes, products ... and so on through the modern management manual. Depending on the nature of the industry, its managers may also take care to buy cheap and sell dear. They may judge what work to do 'in house', what to buy in or contract out, which suppliers and contractors to keep continuously employed (for one kind of economy) and which to discipline with frequent competitive tendering (for another kind). Depending on the nature of the work they may have to make or join in making many judgements about reconciling the multiple purposes of the enterprise or deciding what relative weight to give to each. They must cope with political masters who may vary, over time, from wise to stupid and from statesmanlike to squalid in the uses they want to make of their public enterprises. These are all familiar aspects of public business management in the many well-managed public enterprises to be found around the world. Many of those well-managed examples have not had the research and reportage which they deserve and which could contribute to public managers' education. The management schools' elaborate analyses of private corporate success are not yet matched by many equivalent studies of public success.

Government's first duty to its public enterprises is to design their legal structures. Market competitors (manufacturers, airlines) may do best as ordinary companies with public instead of private owners. Enterprises which are monopolists (power, water, post and telecommunications) or have multiple and non-profit purposes (schools, hospitals, research institutions) also need corporate forms which allow businesslike management at arms length from government. To the extent that they are not under effective market discipline their boards of directors must discipline them. That calls for some differences between private and public boards. Private enterprises whose executives' survival depends on market performance can perhaps afford to be directed by self-recruiting, self-perpetuating executive groups. Public enterprises without effective market discipline cannot afford that directive structure, as a general rule. Their boards of directors must be both legally and humanly able to discipline their executives. They must therefore not be 'executive clubs'. Though they will often act in solidarity with their executives there must nevertheless be some distance, formality, and where necessary tension, between the executives and the people who hire and fire them and monitor their performance. Politicians don't have time to do that work properly. Their public servants often lack appropriate experience for it. Both are inhibited if their only access to the organization is through the executives whose performance is in question. If government has misgivings about the performance of one of its enterprises, the relevant Minister should be in a position to talk independently with the enterprise executives, with the non-executive head and members of the board, and with representatives of employees and customers. A suitable legal structure can allow that. It still won't promise good performance unless the political and business culture and a vigilant press and public ensure that board seats go to appropriately skilled and motivated people, rather than as rewards to superannuated politicians and public servants, or 'business friends'.

There are various formal and informal ways for government to give policy directions to its enterprises without interfering in their day-to-day management. They range from informal agreement, through conditions attached to public capital allocations, to formal government participation in enterprises' forward planning. The formal arrangements may need to be safeguarded by established conventions of government and board behaviour where – as with universities and public broadcasters – government funds activities which need intellectual independence including real freedom to criticize government. However hard that sounds in theory it has been done well enough in practice, especially – with occasional lapses – through the British model of public broadcasting and university funding. It ought to be possible to apply the same model to newspaper ownership, to give private press barons some public competitors.

Public enterprises can be kept honest and accountable and encouraged to be efficient by the formal and informal means listed earlier: appropriate corporate design, audit and reporting requirements, press and academic scrutiny, occasional parliamentary or congressional investigation, and more positively by good directors and managers of whom the world now has plenty if government will look for them. In democratic societies with reasonable culture and conventions of business and government behaviour there is no longer any need or excuse for tolerating scandalous or seriously inefficient public enterprise. (But there would be daily scandals in a 'public choice' society whose business and government were motivated by nothing but individual acquisitiveness.)

It is thus not too hard these days for public managers to manage well, and to be accountable to government and public in ways which need not hinder their efficiency. The third requirement of government is that it make good strategic decisions about the scope and funding of the public sector. In that, the recent Western record is patchier. The reasons sketched above in Chapter 2 need not be repeated at length. If the main competition between political parties is to cut taxes, and if that is legitimized by prevailing Right theories, three linked consequences are likely. Governments won't capitalize or fund their enterprises properly. They will sell off any they can, for the profligate purpose of spending capital directly or indirectly on consumption. And in doing so they will often *increase* the *future* costs of government and necessary services. They sell power generators and public office buildings and lease them back; replace public housing investment by private rent subsidies; privatize their oil producers, steelmakers, banks, power and water and sewerage suppliers, air and sea ports, airlines, bus services, telecommunications. Some of those sales trade tax cuts now for tax or price increases later, and many of them also surrender useful means of national economic management. They accord with Paul Samuelson's theory of public goods (that voters and governments will tend to undersupply them). But they don't support a universal theory of public undersupply. The theory and practice of deregulation, privatization and public capital starvation are comparatively recent. Some of their practical effects are already prompting some professional and popular recoil from them. Nevertheless short-term fixes with long-term costs will always be available in one form or another, and there is great need just now for people, press, politicians and public servants to learn, and teach each other, to distrust those temptations as they have done through much of the modern history of the capitalist democracies. What is needed is not an opposite conviction that public enterprise is good and private is bad, or a rigid defence of the existing public sector. What is needed is an open-minded Japanese/Swedish kind of approach to deciding the scope and allocating the resources of the sectors, and adapting them to changing needs. Among other things the mounting scale of environmental problems seems to call for longer rather than shorter sight than in the past, and for more rather than less public influence over the behaviour of both sectors – the reverse of recent trends and New Right recommendations.

DETERMINING THE MIX

No one chapter, or book for that matter, could sufficiently specify all the culture, human capital, enterprise management and public infrastructure and services which are necessary conditions of the highest public, private and household productivity, or how those conditions may need to vary with time and place. This chapter has merely tried to convey a commonsense frame of mind, and some general considerations to keep in mind, as policy-makers attend to each sector's needs. In similar spirit we cannot now prescribe a best mix of ownership and modes of production for a modern economic system, or sufficient principles for arriving at a mix, or for predicting what may emerge from the interplay of the many interests which contend to influence the mix to their own advantage or toward particular conceptions of justice or common good. As before, we can only list some broad considerations for 'mixers' to keep in mind.

Nobody designs a mixed economy from scratch. Even the ex-communist countries which may appear to be doing so start with existing physical, institutional and cultural resources and political capacities which shape and limit their options. For example historical experience has developed plenty of entrepreneurial flair in a proportion of Hungarian peasants, but very little among Russian peasants; the cooperative and state farm sectors are more productive in Hungary than in Russia; Hungary has supplied its village schools with better teachers than Russia has. As a result, Hungary has different and wider options than Russia does as the two debate how best to diversify their agricultural ownership and management. Another example: mature manufacturing, as in Western Europe, has its own momentum, recruiting and training skilled labour and management by well-established means, drawing capital and working resources from established sources, and maintaining technological leadership chiefly by incessant marginal improvements. Such industries can continue to prosper under almost any distribution of public and private ownership. But when East Asia sets out to industrialize quickly without those established advantages, its first generation of steelmakers, shipbuilders, railroads and other industries with large capital needs and long lead times may need to be created by public investment, and there may also need to be unusually heavy public investment to build up the physical infrastructure necessary for private manufacturing growth. And so on – any going economy at any particular date has its particular accumulation of physical and human capital, and built-in options and restraints.

Within the constraints, questions of economic mix might be simplified as apportioning shares. What proportion of resources should be allocated by administrative decisions and what proportion by market processes? What proportion of all production should be done by households' unpaid labour? And how should paid production be divided between the public and private sectors?

Market and administrative allocation are rarely simple alternatives. Some administrative allocation – for example of uniforms to soldiers – does replace market choice. But much administrative allocation – for example to create money, law and order and public infrastructure – *increases* the scope for private enterprise and market choice. Public education enhances private capacities to choose. When public housing is built by competitive private tender there is political allocation of capital, market competition to produce the goods, then administrative allocation to needy tenants, which may increase their capacity to spend on market goods. Some public airlines, shipping lines, banks, Xray and pathology and other services have been created not to replace market supplies but to keep private suppliers competitive and extend consumers' market choices. And so on – there are quite intricate relations between patterns of market and administrative choice on the one hand and proportions of public, private and household production on the other. (Simple-minded market ideology has sometimes prompted quite self-defeating efforts to 'enlarge market freedoms' by reducing public spending.)

National differences in household productivity reflect differences of culture, inherited urban structure, public policy, inequalities of wealth and income. We earlier compared Norwegians doing more for themselves in capacious houses and gardens with Sweden's apartment-dwellers using more commercial and public services. With hindsight the difference now seems to have been more political than cultural The Swedish Social-Democrats' urban and economic theories favoured rented housing in compact cities for purposes of socialist communal life and capitalist labour mobility; but since the 1970s democratic and market pressures have forced a change toward more home ownership and house-and-garden forms.

Comparisons between compact European and sprawling Australian or North American cities – between, say, Amsterdam and Melbourne – prompt three other observations of interest to policymakers. First, people don't always have rigid preferences for particular urban and housing forms; instead they recognize and enjoy what particular cities do best. Australians who live in European cities seem to enjoy their dense urbanity and live as centrally as they can afford. European migrants to Australia have been observed to choose, on average, bigger suburban gardens than the natives do. Second, cities of both kinds have better and worse ways of adapting to inequalities of wealth and income. Most Amsterdamers now enjoy richer or poorer versions of a common lifestyle. So do most Melbourne households. But it was not always so. The Dutch poor once crowded into tenements with little space or privacy and less plumbing: you could tell class from class at home or on the street. The twentieth-century working class progress to respectable self-contained apartment life was a product of economic growth but it also took public investment, urban policy and housing subsidies. Melbourne's working class had crowded into industrial slums for a century while their betters retreated to segregated house-and-garden suburbs; then when growth and technology made it practicable for workers also to own houses and gardens and cars, helpful government banking and housing policies enabled most of them to do so very quickly, and to share what became a classless suburban lifestyle.

In big cities such policies may depend on some deliberate restraint of land prices. Zoning can free housing land from commercial competition; public housing can take its own land out of the market, and offer cheap housing options which also restrain private rents and prices; rent controls, if properly employed, can restrain prices and rents without the ill effects predicted in economics textbooks; some governments acquire and bank development land then oversupply the market or supply it at regulated prices. If land is cheap people may buy more of it, extending their cities and having to pay more for longer runs of pipes and wires and transport. Experts think that wasteful, and it can worsen the isolation of some outer-suburban housewives and single parents. But it happens only if market and democratic demand make it happen, and the household preferences for space despite its costs have been found to be obstinate, and often knowledgeable: the uses of the private space do appear to contribute to happiness and productivity.

For many households the benefits depend partly on what public provisions accompany the private land. As our third observation, some unpublished Australian research (by Dr Ian Halkett of the South Australian Housing Trust) offers an important moderator to both sides of the debate about urban density and household space. Are public parks and gardens, playgrounds and playing fields, community and craft centres, music centres, public libraries and so on satisfactory substitutes for private house and garden space and equipment? Some are, to some degree; but the public and private facilities are often complementary, each improving the use of the other. People with room to ask friends home tend also to socialize more away from home. People with room for workshops at home go to more craft classes. People with back yards for trailer boats use public launching ramps. People with live music at home go out to more concerts. People with room to keep dogs go out for more walks. And so on – an important quality of the public and household capital available for use by unpaid labour is how they fit and complement each other. Thoughtful government can help them to fit. Coherent policies did so, for example, in many of Britain's postwar New Towns; piecemeal policies failed to do so, even with similar housing designs, where urban growth took the form of unsupported housing estates. A symmetrical conclusion: public spaces and services can't sufficiently replace private housing space and equipment, and generous housing provisions don't remove the need for complementary public provisions.

In one way Amsterdam and Melbourne are misleading indicators of the range of urban and housing choice. Modern cities – especially those which include some ancient quarters – need not have the even texture all over that those two tend to have. Where might Amsterdam add garden suburbs, Melbourne develop a Bayswater and a Left Bank? Ideally any big city should offer its people a full range and diversity of housing and neighbourhood options. For that purpose, market forces are ideal in principle; but in practice, as argued earlier, housing markets are defective and need public help, and many elements of urban structure can only be decided by government. Transport and utility engineers, Treasury officers and other rigorous single-purpose planners can rarely be trusted with them.

Different societies and groups within them will continue to contend, for the usual interested and disinterested reasons, for different urban, housing, mortgage-lending and hire-purchase policies. The debates should be recognized as being about household productivity, as determined by house-holds' access to space, capital, credit and public infrastructure and services.

As to the mix of public and private enterprise, there are many things which obviously do best in public, independent or private ownership. There are standard public services which it would be difficult or pointless to privatize, and activities which use such public powers and sometimes subsidies that outside North America they are generally public: railways, commuter transport, sea and air ports, canals and navigable rivers, general hospitals. Religion and education generally do best in public or independent non-profit ownership. In the private sector there is a vast range of independent self-employed trade and professional people and artists whom it would be pointless to turn into public employees, and small businesses it would be pointless to nationalize. In corporate business there are some particular activities which should usually be private because public enterprises have rarely done them well: farming, building, retailing, the fashion trades.

That leaves five kinds of business to argue about because they can go well enough in either kind of ownership: coal, oil and metal mining; large-scale manufacturing; utilities (power, gas, water, sewerage, telecommunications) which have elements of natural monopoly; broadcasting and other media; and banking and finance.

Those have been publicly owned at particular times and places for a variety of reasons: to supply public goods, to keep dangerous trades out of private hands, to control monopolies, to start new industries, to prevent foreign takeover and removal of existing industries, to maintain uncompetitive firms for purposes of defence, foreign exchange or regional employment, and to provide necessary services to the private sector. Public enterprises can be financed to take longer views and do riskier research and development than any but the biggest private firms can usually afford, and they can operate with multiple purposes as well as or instead of profit – for example to build up under-used, unprofitable capacity for use in wars or emergencies, to give workers more secure jobs and homes than private employers might do, or to work with expensive standards of conservation and environmental care.

Besides those particulars, policymakers have sometimes had in mind two more strategic purposes: to improve the means of national economic management, and to reduce inequalities. The postwar British nationalizers thought that public coal, steel and transport monopolies could be used to support and influence private industries by better means than the traditional regulation and tariff. In practice British governments did not do much of that, but 'trading control' has worked in other cases. Defence contracts are used to nourish local rather than foreign firms, or to create employment in particular regions. Governments which own forests can control private timber and paper milling by contract. Governments which own mineral resources can control their private mining and use by contract. Governments which own a lot of city land (as in Stockholm, or some New Towns) can impose city planning by contract rather than regulation. And strategically, governments which aim to manage levels of employment chiefly by influencing the volume and directions of investment may do so more surely the more of the investment is their own. Finally there is the oldest and best socialist reason for public ownership: to reduce inequalities of wealth. Nowadays it also tends to reduce inequalities of income, by paying better wages than the worst private wages at the bottom of the income scale, and limiting what executives can take at the top.

Those strategic purposes call for as big a public sector as possible, and the heavy industries are the obvious candidates for public takeover. It is in big corporate business that the type of ownership has generally had least effect on efficiency, but most effect on the scope for business misbehaviour. There is a cogent social-democratic or 'market socialist' case for public ownership of most mining, steelmaking, carmaking, shipbuilding and shipping, heavy land transport, aircraft manufacture and major airlines, and telecommunications, to be exercised in corporate forms with continuing competition where appropriate, but with effective public control of environmental standards and executive pay and behaviour.

Less sanguine observers fear that the more enterprises government owns, the harder it may be for good government to keep them all efficient and attentive to their customers, and the easier it may be for bad government to starve them of resources and persist with inefficient or oppressive policies for mistaken theoretical reasons, pork-barrelling or tax-cutting reasons, or any other bad government reasons.

An opposite policy of maximum private ownership may hope to maximize the outstanding virtues of market capitalism: incessant, inventive attention to customers' wants, and pervasive material incentives for productive work and management. It can be doubly economical: competitive pressures may motivate people to cut unnecessary administrative and supervisory activity more reliably than people under administrative discipline do; and where market allocation of resources works as in theory it should it is the cheapest and most efficient method of allocation. Maximum private ownership maximizes the number of directors and executives who can enjoy private business freedom and speed of action and high executive rewards, and it can recruit some of them with their valuable skills to the ranks of capital owners.

The potential disadvantages of having everything possible done by private enterprise are just as obvious: maximum inequalities of wealth and income; more potential for boom and slump and financial instability; more abuse of monopolist and other sources of market strength; a competitive premium on environmental degradation; broadcasting fragmented by advertisements and designed to encourage commercially exploitable wants and values; a pervasive encouragement of acquisitive rather than other purposes in life. It is also likely, as argued by Robert E. Lane in *The Market Experience* (1991), that the more pervasive competitive market forces are, the more consumer sovereignty will prevail over care for the conditions and satisfactions of work; and a mass of modern evidence says that for most people in rich countries – once employed and above the breadline – their experience at work is more important to their happiness and satisfaction with life than their levels of income, consumption or leisure are. More public ownership does not guarantee that more care will be taken to make work interesting and satisfying, at some cost to consumption if necessary; but public ownership and regulation do at least create the possibility of making deliberate collective choices to give some balance to people's interests as workers and as consumers, choices which the evidence suggests could improve life significantly – but which unhindered market forces do not allow.

The divisions of labour between the sectors may well have many of the above effects, as their critics and defenders claim. But the effects are likely to be much modified by other causes, especially the quality of culture, human capital, public infrastructure and business regulation with which the sectors operate. If (say) the 'mixes' of Sweden, Japan and Argentina are compared, the different sector shares of national activity appear to have less effect on productivity than do the different public and household services they enjoy, the law and enforcement under which they work, and the welfare and redistributive policies which accompany them. Because government and public enterprise are commonly lumped together in 'the public sector' it is worth emphasizing that although a bigger private sector leaves less room for public *production*, if its virtues are to keep ahead of its vices it needs more *government*, especially because the bigger private sectors are bigger chiefly because they include monopolist industries and franchised private utilities, the private activities which tend to need most public supervision. Distrust of government, however well-founded, is not necessarily a good ground for privatization. Good performance in either sector depends a good deal on good government (though the effects of bad government may differ: plunder and exploitation in ill-governed private industries, inefficiency and contempt for customers' wants in ill-governed public industries). In Russia and East Europe the most radical reformers, who want most capitalism soonest, are understandably driven by their experience of poor public enterprise under worse government. But savage lessons await attempts to introduce unregulated capitalism into degraded cultures, under governments which may be virtuously democratic at the top but know next to nothing of what it takes to keep capitalism clean and honest, and have few appropriate human resources for the task.

In the West, despite continuing pressure to privatize and deregulate, a number of things may prompt some increase of both government and public enterprise through the coming decades. Economic growth has increased discretionary saving and spending capacity, with effects which make it harder to control inflation and unemployment; government needs some new levers. As more countries industrialize, tougher competition to sell manufactures may prompt more government intervention. Small countries with vulnerable trade and exchange balances may be driven to assist their export and import-replacement industries. Mounting environmental problems demand national and international action, most of it by or at the behest of governments. And some national and international financial systems are in a mess from which only government can rescue them.

In the longer run there may be questions, difficult to predict, about productivity and the future of work. If there are no technical solutions to mounting resource and environmental problems the rich countries may be driven to make do with less artificial energy, private motoring, synthetic materials, paper, industrial and agricultural and household chemicals, and a general return to more labour-intensive production. Alternatively, technical advances may allow abundant clean electricity to power automated capital-intensive industry, labour-saving household equipment and private cars for all, in an economy so productive that if people still worked a forty-hour week for forty years there would be paid employment for only a fraction of those who wanted it. Whether the need is to ration resources or to ration work, there is likely to be some further shift in the balance between individual exchange and collective choice: between market and government.

Thus even without any concern for greater internal or international equality there may be some reversal of the privatizing, deregulating trend and some return to more active public direction of the mixed economies. The need for it has been acknowledged in some influential places. The *Economist* of 6 January 1990 announced that the 1980s experiment with floating exchange rates had failed, and it was time to return to pegged rates. In a number of strategic papers[4] the Japanese government proposes stronger public economic leadership, and better housing and welfare provisions. The European Community continues to elaborate its business and environmental regulation, and to include charters of workers' and welfare rights in its terms of economic association. The Savings and Loan disaster is driving the US government to re-regulate financial institutions, and powerful voices are joining David Aschauer's and Robert Heilbroner's in ascribing America's economic slowdown to a serious shortage of public investment. Mrs Thatcher is replaced, and some Australian leaders begin to doubt that a level playing field is fertile ground for manufacturing growth or survival.

If more active public direction is accompanied by some revulsion from the fashionable greed of the 1980s, the improved means of economic management may be used with some care for equity as well as economic efficiency and environmental prudence.

Of course such improvements may not happen, or not comprehensively enough to be effective. Formidable financial interests, political combinations and theoretical beliefs oppose them. Among the theories are those discussed in this book – but even for champions who want virile capitalism red in tooth and claw we think there are better guides to how to get it.

THEORY FOR MIXED ECONOMIES IN CHANGING TIMES

If mixed economies are perceived as they have been sketched in this chapter, to include:

- public, private and household modes of production, with
- intricate trade and interdependence between them,
- each contributing some intermediate and some final goods to the production and distribution of market and public and household goods and services,
- with each mode of production needing its appropriate kind of government, and
- the system as a whole needing some public management of its distribution of wealth, income and welfare and its levels of employment, inflation and environmental damage,

what sort of theory do governments and their electors need, to enlighten their economic policy-making?

Could there be a rigorous comprehensive theory of such an economy, i.e. of our actual, real-life economy? Could our three-sector social-democratic political economy, with its distributional and welfare concerns and its intergenerational environmental prudence, be modelled in a formal axiomatic/deductive theory with the mathematical and other qualities of the neoclassical theory of a pure capitalist economy?

Such a comprehensive model could perhaps encourage people to attend to all three modes of production and their interrelations and distinctive needs, and to search the whole system for the direct and indirect effects of public action or inaction in any compartment of it. The comprehensive branches of neoclassical theory, especially general equilibrium theory, have helped to stimulate understanding of that internal interdependence. But although they stimulate it they do not themselves supply it. Economic life is too complex, conflict-ridden and irregular for the behaviour of whole national systems to be reliably modelled and predicted by formal deductive means.

Instead, comprehensive neoclassical theory tends to have one incompetent and one competent use.

Incompetent users treat the competitive market model as defining optimum performance, and believe that real economic performance should be made to resemble it as closely as possible, chiefly by removing hindrances to its doing so. Policy should aim at as much competition as possible, the freest possible trade, the least possible regulation, and (with encouragement from many public choice and some social choice theorists) the least possible public goods.

Competent neoclassical theorists, by contrast, have developed their general models to specify with increasing rigour the conditions which would have to be present for real life to behave as modelled. A number of the conditions are plainly impractical, but real life can still be described by differentiation from the model, which can be a useful time-saver. The mistake of idealizing the model and expecting life to imitate it can be avoided by a number of means. All students learn that the simple competitive model does not hold where there are significant externalities, increasing returns to scale, imperfect information or unsatisfactory distributions of wealth and income. Second-year students learn from the theory of second best that while *any* of the perfect conditions is missing, change in the direction of the perfect set may not improve performance; the second best performance is not necessarily achieved by the nearest imitation of the best. (Reducing government while market failures continue may offer examples.) And when the model is elaborated to specify the conditions in which it could notionally operate in stable equilibrium, the necessary conditions multiply in number and impracticality, to include for example the following:

- The economy must be static, with all relevant variables pertaining to the same point in time, or it must at least be 'stationary', with a number of key features constant through other changes.
- It has producers and consumers but no government.
- The number of producers and consumers remains unchanged over time, and so does the number and quality of products.

- There is no time-lag between production, sale and consumption of a product, or between those processes and their effect on the price system.
- There is no uncertainty – buying and selling intentions are always realized.
- The only information flowing between actors in the system is price information.
- There are no indivisible resources or products, no indefinitely increasing returns to scale, no externalities. In economists' jargon, isoquants are continuous and concave upward.
- Each consumer has a definite order of preference.
- Consumers maximize utility, producers maximize total profit.

More dynamic versions have other impossible conditions, such as present prices for all future goods.

Besides listing those conditions, theorists explore the effects of relaxing some of them, usually one at a time. To relax all the impractical and undesirable ones at once – i.e. to return to real life – is to abandon hope of reliable self-equilibration. Thus the general equilibrium theorists' rigorous specification of the conditions necessary for automatic self-adjustment don't define either an ideal or a practicable system. Instead they indicate some likely market failures and intrinsic uncertainties, and they define complex needs for government. A few of the theorists, notably Kenneth Arrow, go on to suggest how to meet the need for government. But for that purpose they have to reason from social values and from local knowledge of actual industries, markets and institutions, rather than from the formal theory of general equilibrium.

The more sophisticated the neoclassical economists' general theories become, the less surely they purport to model or predict the behaviour of national economic systems as a whole. And those theories, for the most part, model only one mode of production, and assume actors motivated by simple and uniform purposes. It is even less likely that formal deductive methods will succeed in predicting the behaviour of systems in which three different modes of production, driven by partly different motivation, must have some of their strategic allocations and prices decided by political choices: frequent, contested and imperfectly predictable choices, which are not wilful 'interventions' in the system but working parts of it.

In those real-life conditions governments attempt variously modest or ambitious economic strategies. The strategies may be based on plenty of measurement and detailed economic analysis. But any whole strategy – even the most abstinent and market-reliant – must still be compounded of very diverse elements, ranging from choices of social purpose and estimates of the political support for them, through guesses about business, labour and consumers' responses to particular conditions and uncertainties, to surer expectations of (for example) tax yields, normal propensities to spend and save and invest, and the dependable performance of many established industries and public services. However serviceable the economist's standard toolkit may be with many of those components, we do not believe that the comprehensive understanding which people and their governments need to have of their mixed economies is likely to be improved by attempts at rigorous mathematical modelling of such economies as whole systems.

It is wrong to judge theory by its formal qualities rather than its performance: to put the highest value, as some academic economists do, on the most abstract, general and determinate kinds of theory. The activity of a mixed economy as a whole does not have the unity or uniformity which could make such theory useful. It has to be understood instead by the various philosophical, political, technical and common-sensical means which have contributed to this chapter's sketch of the subject. Diverse kinds of behaviour demand diverse aids to understanding. Every advanced economy has substantial elements of conflict *and* cooperation, voluntary exchange *and* coercive organization, consumer choice *and* collective choice, market allocation *and* political allocation; and it cannot function without building controversial principles, disputed and changed from time to time, into many of its laws and institutions. Its policy-making may be informed by a great deal of comparatively objective measurement and analysis, but the choices remain political and many of them cannot be either reliably predicted, or judged to be optimal or not, by formal theoretical means alone, or by the crude public choice assumption that 'all men are base' and their actions exclusively self-serving.

The longing for theoretical rigour nevertheless dies hard. But it is far from rigorous, logically speaking, to try to understand the diverse organization, motivation and activity of a mixed economy by the use of unified, determinate, monomotivational theory of a 'high and pure' kind. There is more promise in the (currently unfashionable) tradition of historical and institutional economic thought. And there is a critical need to grasp *why* there cannot be agreed, value-free or purely technical criteria of optimum performance of an economic system. A modern social democracy has an irreducibly political economy. To manage it or merely to understand how it works, the chosen concepts and categories and simplifications – the very categories of thought – need to be related both to the diverse facts of economic life and to the social purposes of understanding it, however disagreed those purposes may be.

8 How to Think Instead: The Resources of Political Theory

This chapter recalls the traditions of thought which public choice theory seeks to replace. Whatever you want to know about government, we think you can find out more and understand it better without monocausal blinkers. Whatever your social purposes, we think they can be better served within the established intellectual traditions, or by inventive thought of like insight and complexity, than by exclusively economic simplifications of politics.

What follows is familiar to political theorists. It is here to introduce their work to readers unfamiliar with it: to any people in business or government, or economists unacquainted with other disciplines, who are in danger of accepting the public choice misrepresentations of the purposes and potentialities of government.

The conventional labels – conservative, liberal, socialist, feminist, green – each stand for a changing miscellany of ideas. Each tradition has internal disagreements, and ideas which are often muddled, misused or otherwise degraded. But we will try to distil some of the best that each offers.

CONSERVATIVES

Most conservatives have limited faith in human nature. People may have noble potentialities but they are also vulnerable, easily persuaded, morally unreliable, capable of aggression and dishonesty. They fear death and strangers, are often uncertain what to do or inept at doing it, and tend to be at their worst when insecure. If they are to lead peaceful, productive, civilized lives they need to be kept in order and protected from each other by pervasive government.

People also have a lot to learn. Some of the learning is collective: the culture and institutions which order civilized life have been accumulated over centuries by incessant, detailed trial and error and a kind of institutional natural selection. And there is individual learning: it takes family, school and government fifteen or twenty years to teach a child what it needs to know merely to live safely in a modern society, and those years must also implant whatever capacity the adult has for love, friendship, fun, cooperation, work and duty, qualities equally important for the individual's and the society's wellbeing.

What sustains civilized life and economic productivity is a very complicated structure of rules, habits, beliefs and – especially – mutual expectations. Some rules and expectations are formal, embodied in laws and institutions. Many are informal: social codes, routines, habits, know-how. People know their roles as spouses, parents, children, friends and enemies, citizens, soldiers, workers, shoppers, players, spectators, and so on. They learn what is expected of them and what to expect of others. That is not necessarily oppressive. A good society's rules and norms tell people how to get the legitimate things they want, and define wide areas of behaviour as areas for choice, diversity, originality, individual self-expression. If the rules are judged to be just or unjust they will also accord with Plato's understanding of politics as a moral activity. People can realize their noblest (or vilest) human potentialities in their public roles as citizens and governors.

But to be happy and productive they must first feel safe. They need law and order, safe streets and stable money, and the informal rules and expectations also need to be reasonably dependable. How can I spend years in training for a trade or profession, perform at my best, hope for profit or promotion, marry to raise a family, and enjoy golf and bridge and gardening, if job requirements are unpredictable, there are no performance standards, there are no marriage contracts but only passing sexual attachments, people have no obligations to the children they beget, everybody cheats at golf and bridge and most of the nurserymen's seed packets are falsely labelled? It is foolish to talk of rules as necessarily cramping freedom and enterprise: reliable rules are conditions of freedom and enterprise. The more time I feel compelled to spend watching my back and defending my patch, the less I have left for work, recreation and joy in life.

Besides social anxieties there are personal ones. People worry about the meaning of life, about mortality, about their individual insignificance in the vast human antheap. So they like to belong, to be part of entities more significant than themselves: to be members of family, neighbourhood, class, church, nation; and to join firms, teams, regiments, clubs and associations. Recall Chester Barnard's waterworks engineer, Mr A, whose very individuality was constituted by his membership of family, church, state, nation, profession and enterprise.

Some people fear death and what may follow it. Some find life depressingly meaningless. Many need watching, or they misbehave. God is always watching, His love and will give meaning to life, He may perhaps overcome death. So religion can combine social discipline with individual consolation. For agnostics, mortality and personal insignificance have to be ameliorated by other means. People locate themselves in chains of membership and cause-and-consequence. They research their ancestors, learn their local and national histories, act together to conserve valued landscapes and buildings. 'We are stewards of our heritage, trustees for our heirs as our forebears were for us. Our children's children will tread these pathways, watch sunset and moonrise over these landscapes, refresh their spirits by these granite streams, enjoy the same poems and the same village pubs, revere the great cathedrals as human masterpieces: love as we have loved, in the world and in the ways that we preserved for them.'

Intelligent conservatives nevertheless don't want to bring history to a stop. Continuous change is needed to prevent catastrophic change. If change is blocked, the needs and pressures for it bank up until they burst destructively. But although change is necessary, life is only safe, productive and enjoyable if *most* of it is predictable at any moment – if property will be protected, banks will pay, trains will run, lights respond to the switch, workers come to work. Only if I can rely on other people doing their jobs can I give my whole attention to doing mine. Given that mutual confidence, the system is resilient. It can cope with many small upsets. If the power fails one day, or the trains don't run or a bank suspends payment, people can focus on that problem to solve it or limit the damage, confident that the rest of life will proceed as usual. Similarly, people can plan and carry out reforms quite successfully if they don't try too many at once. To change a rule or routine they need to be able to see how the new arrangement works and what it does to the rest of the system, in time to reverse it if necessary. If they try to change too much at once, too many people have to learn too much too quickly. There is too much uncertainty about what will work as planned, what will work as usual, and what will not. There may then be catastrophe from either or both of two causes. Too many people, feeling suddenly uncertain, unsafe or unwatched, may switch from their regular work to securing their property, hoarding, hiding or running away, or (as after some natural disasters) raping and looting. It may take military force to restore order and if so it is likely to be an inferior, degraded order. Second, if the old order has been damaged deliberately, as by the French or Russian revolutionaries, the leaders who plan to replace it with a Utopia won't succeed, because people cannot suddenly learn whole new divisions of labour and rules of behaviour any more than they can trade one language for another overnight. If the frustrated revolutionaries have the means they may apply increasing force and terror in attempts to *make* the recalcitrant citizens comply with the plan – attempts which must be self-defeating, if only because Utopian plans never include living permanently under terror.

There is thus both a practical and a scientific basis for the conservative distrust of too-rapid change. In practice if people are deprived of a slow-built, dependable structure of rules and expectations they are driven to behave wildly, defensively, uncooperatively: civilization breaks down. Scientifically, if too much of the structure is disturbed at once it becomes impossible to predict how people will actually respond, beyond knowing that they will not learn a whole new set of rules and expectations in a day. What is unpredictable is unplannable, so revolutionary intentions are never fulfilled, and the (also unpredictable) effects of failing to fulfil them are usually chaotic, violent and undesirable.

If strong government is needed, who should supply it? Conservatives used to favour government from above with authority from some other source than the consent of the governed: the will of God, the divine or hereditary right of kings, the property rights of aristocracies. Governors should be independent of the governed so that they don't have to court popularity. But if they don't have to answer to their subjects, what will motivate them to govern well? Plato wanted them to have a moral education and live in communal poverty to minimize conflicts between their material interests and their public duties. Others have hoped to preserve them from temptation by the opposite method of keeping them independently rich, usually as landowners. Some have hoped that religious faith would make them good governors, others that a strict military education would do it. The history of ruling houses and classes has not shown any of those expectations to be very reliable. But a more general concern for the quality of a society's artistic, intellectual, technical, moral, religious and military leadership has more to be said for it. Conservatives tend to think the quality of elites matters more than other people think it matters, so everyone has an interest in elite children getting more than their pro-rata share of educational and cultural resources.

Liberals tend to think such things can be left to the market. Socialists tend to oppose all educational privileges, earned or unearned. Both those attitudes have elements of hypocrisy. Most liberals want the competence of their neurosurgeons to be established by public certification rather than creative marketing. Most socialists want their neurosurgeons to have had a more selective and expensive education than the mass of workers have. Only conservatives tend to be wholly honest about the importance, for everyone's sake, of the moral, intellectual and practical qualities of leaders and ruling classes.

Since democracy set in, most 'conservative' parties and governments have actually been defenders of capitalist democracy more aptly characterized as liberal. But strands of conservative thought persist. Some Catholics want Catholic laws about sex and marriage. Disciplinarians want compulsory military service and tougher criminal and juvenile courts. Gentler concerns for the way people and their values are shaped by their upbringing prompt policies of censorship, old-fashioned education, and support for family life and home ownership. Many strands remain – mixing sometimes with similar strands from the Left – of the belief that economic activity needs pervasive government. Society is like a body, an organic whole. All its members have obligations to each other. So compassionate conservatives have sometimes run more protective economic policies and more generous welfare and employment policies than do liberals with greater faith in market forces.

Critics from Left and Centre attack the conservative tradition for its neglect or denial of political and economic equality and often of political and religious liberty. Whatever the conservative philosophers intended, their work has lent authority to many rapacious and oppressive regimes and ruling classes. It has been used to justify aggressive war, slavery, the burning of heretics, the subjection of women, class and racial exploitation, and crude thought control. Nevertheless, however imperfect or misused their work has been, the best conservative thinkers have had some special strengths. They have insisted that government is a 'moral person' with the obligations which that implies, rather than a utility or a market place. They have understood, better than anyone before modern psychology, the social construction of individuality and individuals' values and perceptions of the world. They have understood, as many churches have also done, what institutions can do for the psychological support and consolation of their members. They know what civilized life and productivity owe to the quality of slowly grown, complex structures of custom and mutual expectation and trust. They are not always right in expecting rapid change to cause social breakdown and unintended violence, but when it does so they understand better than anyone else *why* it does so – better, for example, than those who simply complain that 'our leaders betrayed us' or 'we were smashed by the CIA and the multinationals'.

To call public choice theory conservative, as its critics do, is usually unfair to conservatism. Conservative thinkers know at least as much as public choice theorists do about the sins which governors and governed commit when public power is misused for private purposes. But instead of seeing it as the behaviour to be universally expected of rational people, conservatives are inclined to see it as sin and to believe that virtuous alternatives can spring – to some degree, at least some of the time – from the same human nature. They see, as public choice theorists can't really afford to see if their theory is to be as rigorous and universal as they would like, that particular manifestations of human nature can owe a good deal to the culture and institutions of time and place and even to the character of government. Above all, conservatives have understood two things better than anyone else has: how the quality of leadership in the broadest sense can affect the quality of a society's life; and what membership – in collectives from family, firm and neighbourhood to church, nation and race – can mean to human beings, for good or ill, above and beyond any benefits which membership may bring in the way of alliances and exchanges to advance individual material interests.

Readers who have not done so may care to read the conservative philosophy scattered in a disorderly way through Edmund Burke's *Reflections on the revolution in France* (1790); Anthony Trollope's novel *The American Senator* (1877) and Joyce Carey's novel *To be a Pilgrim* (1942); Michael Oakeshott's essays in *Rationalism in Politics and Other Essays* (1962) and *On Human Conduct* (1975); and, especially for French and German traditions, Noel O'Sullivan's *Conservatism* (1976). Robert Nisbet's *Conservatism: Dream and Reality* (1986) is a brief introduction to American Conservatism. P.W. Buck (ed.) *How Conservatives Think* (1975) is a brief anthology of British conservative writing, including the best four pages of Burke. The best forty pages of Burke appear in a more comprehensive Anglo-American anthology, Russell Kirk's *The Portable Conservative Reader* (1982).

SOCIALISTS

Socialists have theorized how capitalism could be improved by partial socialist reforms; what form a wholly socialist economy might take; how it might be achieved politically by revolution or evolution; how nearly equal a socialist society might be; how far it might develop the cooperative potentialities of human nature; and how to harness individual self-interest to collective purposes, or tame it by banning exploitive forms of ownership and employment.

One way to order socialist theory is along a spectrum from fantasy to realism about motivation. Some socialists have been as unrealistic in imagining a wholly cooperative society as public choice theorists are in imagining a wholly selfish one. Between those extremes are social democrats who claim to think of 'men as they are and institutions as they might be' and debate how much economic activity actually needs to be done in a private capitalist way, how much can be done as well or better by households or public enterprises, how much could be done by 'capitalist cooperatives' with ordinary business motivation but with widely shared profits to combine capitalist production with socialist distribution of wealth and income. It is these pragmatists, who want to expand the more egalitarian sectors of the mixed economy and reduce, regulate and civilize its necessary capitalist sector as far as can be done without significant loss of productivity or personal freedom, whose thought contrasts most sharply with public choice theory in both its realism and its moral purposes.

Some of the best ideas came early, before Marx managed to discredit thought about socialism as Utopian and replace it by the endless, obsessive, socialist analysis of capitalism. The forgotten work of the early nineteenth century is only now being rediscovered, chiefly by women because some of the best of it was written by women. Kathryn Gargett first reminds us why it was reasonable for the earliest socialists to think quite boldly about alternatives to capitalism. Before 1850,

> capitalism had not yet proved a resounding success. The organization of industry was as haphazard and disorderly as it was enterprising and inventive. Manufacturers were no better at spreading the risks than they were at sharing the profits ... Nor was there any attempt to diminish instability by controlling production. It was the workers who talked about cooperation and combination. [With violent boom and slump, no joint stock or limited liability, and many bankruptcies], capitalism was not yet efficient and had risks for worker and manufacturer alike. Consequently there was room for social critics, such as those who wanted Owenite communities, to think outside capitalism without looking as dotty as they would now. It was also a time when it was possible to think outside class interests, a freedom as important for the right as it was for the left. Owen thought his ideas would help manufacturers as much as workers.[1]

While French Utopians mostly theorized, in Britain and the US Owenites and others experimented. The experiments were quite informative. They discovered that good housing, schooling and factory management could turn thieving country bumpkins into serviceable and satisfied workers – but could not transform their natures as radically as Owen had hoped, to work only for love of the work and one another. Cooperative settlements would not work but cooperative firms *would* – some that Owen founded survive still, and innumerable producers', consumers' and financial cooperatives have prospered since.

Of the greatest interest now, in the age of the 'welfare society', is the *scope* of socialist theory before Marx. Because the leading theorists included Anna Wheeler, Fanny Wright, Emma Martin and Flora Tristan, socialist thought was about home life and work and marriage as well as capitalist industry or replacements for it. Between them the women assembled a list of aspirations which still seem apt nearly two centuries later, for a cooperative economy with personal freedom, self-government and a tolerable life for men and women and children, young and old, at home as well as at work. Most of them wanted democratic government, decentralized cooperative ownership and organization of industry, market relations between co-ops and their customers, and patterns of domestic life, upbringing, education and equal marriage which could serve the double purpose of equalizing men and women, and bringing up cooperative people. Women might well do different work from men, but it could be equally regarded and rewarded.

Socialist thought thus aspired to four dimensions of equality: class equality at work, class equality at home, sex equality at work and sex equality at home. But a tragic effect of Marx's capture of the movement, and the rising role of male trade unions in it, was to dismiss three of the four dimensions from most socialist thought for a century. Equality came to mean equality only among men at work, with paid employment the only meaning of work.

The original breadth of mind and democratic intent of pre-Marxist socialist thought survived in some parliamentary Social Democratic and Labour parties and Fabian intellectual groups. It is that reformist tradition, rather than the revolutionary Marxist tradition, which deserves attention now as being relevant to the tasks of government in both the non-communist and the ex-communist countries. But before focusing on its resources it is worth noticing *what* it was in Marxist thought that contributed (insofar as intellectual causes contributed) to the practical disasters of communist dictatorship.

Marx had theoretical reasons for banning gradualist, reformist approaches to capitalism, and for deferring serious thought about what should replace it until the revolution to replace it was under way. But the effect of the ban in practice was nihilist. Socialists should prepare to abolish existing political, economic and social institutions without deciding what should take their place. One crucial effect of that has not, as far as we know, been noticed by the historians of the movement: the lack of a socialist plan quite unbalanced the analysis of capitalism. If you don't know what new structure you want you can't know how much, or which parts, of the existing structure you should destroy. A socialist plan, however provisional and adaptable, would have enabled the revolutionaries to look over the existing political, economic and social institutions and say 'this and this we can use, so preserve them; this we need but must reform; this is incurable and must be replaced; this won't be needed, so it can go.' And from that sort of practical thought quite a different theoretical analysis of capitalism might have emerged.[2]

But without that basis for discriminate analysis and action, what prevailed was another ill effect of the obsession with capitalist ills rather than socialist intentions. Marx had seen many existing institutions exploited or perverted for capitalist purposes. But with no basis for deciding which of the infected institutions would recover naturally once private capital ownership ceased, which of them could be reformed by socialist government, and which were genuinely incurable, what came to prevail instead was a plague mentality: *all* infected tissue – everything capitalism had touched – must be surgically removed, burned and buried.

Examples:

Market relations had worked to capitalists' advantage and left the old and infirm and unemployed to starve for lack of income – so market relations were 'essentially capitalist' and must be abolished. (Constructive socialists might have said 'Socialist society will want efficient enterprises and consumer sovereignty; as long as *big* business is publicly or cooperatively owned, and the old and unemployed are supplied with income, market relations will be fine.') Marxists saw private ownership of the means of production as the essence of capitalism, so resolved to abolish it. (Constructive socialists might have decided to redistribute ownership and revise its legal meaning, as part of a plan to have a corporate sector in public and cooperative ownership alongside plenty of privately owned and conventionally motivated family farms and small businesses.) Marx had observed that bourgeois marriages enslave women and transmit capitalist property, so some intellectuals concluded that a socialist society should do without marriage. (Constructive socialists would have considered how a socialist society should support love, family life and household productivity, and bring up children to be cooperative adults; and would have decided accordingly what reform of existing marriage laws and household economics might be needed.) In Marx's day the cooperative movement had failed to revolutionize the ownership of all land and industry, so Marxists wrote it off. (Constructive socialists, considering how land and industry could best be owned in a socialist society, might well have seen plenty of scope for cooperatives and learned from the existing ones how best to establish and manage them). Above all, because Marx saw peasant and bourgeois majorities outvoting socialist workers in some French elections he dismissed representative democracy as a capitalist device. So when a democratic majority elected a revolutionary socialist assembly to draft the Russian socialist constitution in 1918, Lenin could get away with abolishing it overnight.

Local democracy took a little longer. Though Marx had condemned representative democracy he approved of direct local democracy, and it worked quite well in many of Russia's local-government soviets for a while after the revolution. But by 1922 the dictatorship had suppressed the last of it. So in the world's first socialist economy, what should replace the private ownership of the means of production? Representative national and local democracy had been dismissed as bourgeois. Cooperatives and mass share ownership were dismissed as petit-bourgeois. Only the national dictatorship could claim (however falsely) to be proletarian. And having dismissed market relations between enterprises as capitalist, resources would have to be allocated and outputs distributed by central planners. Thence came the command economy.

Among Marx's reasons for not planning ahead were two elements of his materialist determinism. Socialism was historically inevitable, so it was something to be predicted rather than deliberately planned. And – somewhat inconsistently – it should not be designed by bourgeois thinkers conditioned by capitalist society, it should be designed by proletarians in the heat of revolutionary action. In fact that condemned it to be designed in haste, during a civil war, by the same socialist leaders – bourgeois men conditioned by capitalist society – who had refused to think ahead about it. For a few disastrous months they tried to have workers manage factories and nobody manage families. Without any proper preparation for either experiment, both failed. Manufacturing virtually ceased, some bands of homeless teenagers roamed the streets, and for want of forethought about socialist industry or family life the dictators resorted to patriarchy at home and bureaucracy backed by terror at work. (Significantly, the workers' opposition to both was led by Kollontai, the only woman on the Central Committee, and it cost her her position there.) The point we wish to make is that the disaster of the communist dictatorship and command economy, insofar as it had intellectual causes, owed something to the presence of a 'vacant set' – a blank where the socialist alternative ought to have been – not just in the preparations for revolution but in the basic Marxist analysis of capitalist society.

A modern analogy is relevant as we turn to the merits of social-democratic theory. What an obsession with capitalist ills could do once, an obsession with communist ills may do now. It has always been right to oppose communism in its actual form of dictatorship and command economy. But it has usually been wrong, and often disingenuous, to oppose every democratic reform from the age pension to school milk as another fatal step *toward* communist dictatorship and command economy. The East's retreat from those two horrors is inspired by the West's achievements, but those were not in fact achieved by raw capitalism with minimal government. Raw capitalism with minimal government was what inspired the original Marxist revulsion. What is attracting the East back to the fold is the social-democratic transformation of raw capitalism into the modern mixed economy which does only half its work in a capitalist way, has learned by experience to suffuse that half with quite elaborate public supports and regulation, and for the other half has developed much of the best of the pre-Marxist socialist programme. The civilizing elements of the mix have lately been attacked, and some of them dismantled, by the privatizing and deregulating shift to the Right. They are attacked by 'dry' economic theory, and by the economic theories of politics which are the subject of this book. And for the simple-minded they can again be attacked as socialist now that the East's collapse has proved that 'socialism doesn't work'. It will be ironic if obsessive hatred of the communist perversion of socialism should drive Russia back a hundred years to embrace the raw capitalism, minimal government, pervasive corruption and barbarous poverty which inspired the dictatorial version of socialism in the first place.

It will also be a pity if the valuable elements of Marxist theory are thrown out with the bathwater. Marx made theoretical mistakes about the supposed self-limiting and self-destructive tendencies of capitalism. He misjudged democratic government and its economic capacities. But he also had some valuable economic insights; and it will always be salutary to analyse productive activity with an eye for the surplus value it creates, the forces which determine who gets what shares of that value, the necessity and justice (or otherwise) of those arrangements, and possible reforms or replacements of them. It will be another irony if such a furiously scientistic positivist comes to be remembered chiefly for the wholesome moral implications of his work.

The reform of capitalism and creation of modern welfare and redistributive services can be seen as a movement in socialist directions, but it had diverse origins in a double sense: the ideas and projects came from a wide range of sources from socialist to conservative; and for many of the reforms the necessary majorities were similarly diverse. Who (for example) supported drastic new public controls of US banks in the 1930s and 1990s? Conservatives and communists did, to protect poor savers from rich bankers. Liberals did, to strengthen the capitalism they believed in. Democratic socialists did, to strengthen public control over the uses of private credit. And so on – the example could be multiplied many times: not many of the measures which have reformed or replaced elements of raw capitalism can be credited exclusively to one type or group of reformers. But we can set the socialist contributions into context by sketching reformist traditions of three or four broad kinds, all of which continue to confound public choice expectations.

The first is common to all reformist traditions: the simple desire for good government, and in one's own occupation, good work and good conscience. An example – which could fit as well under our conservative, liberal or socialist headings – is faultlessly documented in Oliver MacDonagh's *A Pattern of Government Growth 1800–1860: the Passenger Acts and their Enforcement* (1961). Historians had tended to accept a model of early industrial reform in which concerned individuals detected bad practices which needed reform; campaigned to persuade public and politicians of the need; prevailed against conservative resistance; and finally persuaded government to legislate, whereupon reform happened, and prospered as long as it did not develop bureaucratic arthritis. On the contrary, MacDonagh discovered, it was often with the arrival of the bureaucrats, rather than the change of law, that effective reform began. In the nineteenth century much British passenger shipping, especially of poor emigrants, was cruelly dangerous to the life, health and savings of the passengers. Reformers got eight regulatory Acts passed over thirty years, with next to no effect. Then in 1833 one inspector was appointed, experimentally, to see what he could do. Robert Low, a half-pay naval lieutenant, started work at Liverpool. In twenty reports in his first eighteen months he told the national government what was wrong with the traffic, the law and its administration. Bit by bit his advice was taken; better Acts provided for more inspectors whose advice produced still better Acts. No public choice expectations were fulfilled. The reformers' aims were achieved. Passengers were effectively protected, at negligible public cost. The inspectors were not captured or corrupted by the shipowners. Nor were the responsible Ministers or the legislature. None of the people who conceived, enacted or enforced the reforms had any pecuniary interest, except the inspectors in their modest wages. The public action benefited only the poor passengers it was meant to benefit. It revealed, among other things, 'that much ... of the new administrative system was presented and accepted as a-political ... and that lobbies and interests (even very powerful ones, as in the case of coal mines or the mercantile marine) might be emasculated by the mere establishment of a field executive. [And] the whole process required little more than that men should have reacted reasonably to established facts, and with reasonable compassion for the sufferings of others.' (pp. 8–9) Public choice theorists should read MacDonagh's book and hang their heads in shame – but not because he happens to have lit on an unusually innocent case. In the patient modern development of the institutions of civilized life – in education, health, housing, local government, public libraries, museums, art galleries and information services, pensions for the aged and infirm and unemployed, prison reform, navigational aids, road and bridge building and all the other public achievements which public choice theorists seek to discredit – there have been many more 'impurities' than there were with the nineteenth-century Passenger Acts. Issues *have* been politicized. Class and sectional interests *have* often prevailed. Successful reforms *have* advanced some reformers' careers. Good projects have been blocked and worse have succeeded. But the impurities don't support the theory that individual self-interest alone has animated (and by implication corrupted) the civilizing achievements. On the contrary the mixtures of motive which have converged in those achievements reinforce the case for direct, open-minded, real-life investigation of the historical processes and possibilities of institutional reform and development. Even the reforms which had no particular socialist character were achieved in many cases by people and methods which encourage the socialist expectation that – with due exceptions and precautions – quite a lot of compassion, duty, altruism, cooperative spirit and pride in good work can be enlisted in good causes, often with genuinely good effect.

That was just as well, because capitalist problems were demanding, and economic growth was allowing, many new public activities. There were measures (pensions, health insurance) to care for people whom capitalist activity did not sufficiently support. There were measures (national parks, subsidized arts) to provide luxuries and graces which market forces would not provide. There were measures (factory acts, pure food and drug laws) to protect people from harm capitalists might otherwise do them. There were measures (roads and bridges, universities and research institutes) to do for the private sector what it could not afford to do for itself. And – specially interesting for our present purpose – there were measures to make the capitalist mechanisms themselves work better. We can instance two English economists, quintessentially liberal and pro-capitalist in intent, whose work convinced them that capitalist efficiency required the use of some socialist devices.

J.A. Hobson thought that capitalist instability and unemployment arose from under-consumption. Left to themselves market forces distributed too much income to owner-investors and too little to worker-consumers. Capitalists responded by trying to get the state to seize foreign markets and investment opportunities for their surplus output and savings. As a liberal free-trader in the 1890s Hobson wanted the state to respond instead by helping labour to bargain for a higher wage share, and by welfare and income transfers, as far as might be necessary to bring investment and spending into equilibrium. The measures which kept capitalism fully employed would also make it more equitable. By the 1930s Hobson feared that the threat of those wholesome policies was turning the capitalist establishment against democracy; he wanted more determined redistributive policies, was a leading supporter of the Labour Party and wrote sympathetically of socialist alternatives.

Different theory led J.M. Keynes to similar conclusions about effective demand in the 1930s. His language remained more liberal and pro-capitalist than Hobson's but his strategy was more socialist. Perhaps for that reason no 'Keynesian' government has ever actually applied it. He did not favour the fine-tuning of consumers' income and spending power that was practised in his name after his death. Instead he proposed to stabilize demand by stabilizing investment, which he wanted to do by 'socializing' investment to the point where three quarters or more of it would be public or publicly directed.[3] (To the extent that it was publicly rationed and directed, Japanese investment through the 1950s and 1960s may have come closest to his prescription.) Left Keynesians – Joan Robinson, Thomas Balogh, Michal Kalecki – went further. They predicted correctly that if demand management were used to maintain full employment in democratic conditions there would be rising inflation unless there were also some social restraint of wages. They also predicted, more accurately of some workforces than others, that workers would not tolerate such restraints unless they applied fairly to capitalist incomes too. Thus a line of reasoning which had begun as a pure capitalist corrective arrived at conclusions hostile to one of the most treasured capitalist freedoms.

There remains socialism for its own sake: the impulse of many theorists and members of the Socialist, Social-Democratic and Labour parties of Europe and the Commonwealth to move their mixed economies in socialist directions for socialist reasons: to reduce inequalities of wealth, income, household space and capital, esteem, civil rights and access to legal process, economic opportunity, access to desired public goods and services and influence over their provision; by those means to distribute positive individual freedoms with greater equality; to have as much productive capital as possible in public, cooperative, household or non-profit ownership, and only as much as may be necessary for productive efficiency in unequal private ownership; to run as much economic activity as practicable on non-exploitive principles, and only as much as may be unavoidable on unequalizing 'big capitalist' principles. The necessary inequalities might still be substantial. But their scale should be moderate enough to allow everyone who wished to do so to share a common lifestyle. In Richard Tawney's words 'What is repulsive is not that one man should earn more than others, for where community of environment, and a common education and habit of life, have bred a common tradition of respect and consideration, these details of the counting house are forgotten or ignored.'

How far to go in which of those directions, and by what means, is of course widely disagreed among democratic socialists. No country has gone as far as most socialists want. How far that is the fault of the socialist idea, the conservative resistance, or the people's wisdom or folly, can be disputed without end. But our present subject is not the practical achievements but the theory which accompanied them.

That theory converges from Left and Right. The two streams might be characterized as repentant Marxism and repentant liberalism, each driven by bitter experience of the unrepentant originals. From the Left came Marxists and other outright enemies of private capitalism whose values and political judgement made them democrats and gradualists rather than red revolutionaries. Their most famous text was Edouard Bernstein's *Evolutionary Socialism*, published in 1899 by a leading theorist of the German Social Democratic Party, the biggest socialist party in the world at the time. Bernstein could see that with manhood suffrage the party was increasing its numbers in the Reichstag at each election, it was linked to the dominant trade union organization, and it represented workers whose real income was rising with economic growth, slowly but undeniably, as Marx had insisted it could not. Something was therefore wrong with the analysis which predicted the perpetual immiseration of the workers. With industrialization steadily increasing the working class proportion of the electorate, perhaps it was also wrong to reject representative democracy. Bernstein still argued for a full socialist transformation of the economy, but to be done step by step by parliamentary means, and with quite hard-headed assumptions about the motivation of socialist work and management. Ninety years later another body of theory with similar intent – to propose principles and institutional forms for some sort of market socialism to replace the communist command economies – has been reviewed by Wlodzimierz Brus and Kazimierz Laski in *From Marx to the Market: Socialism in search of an economic system* (1989).

The approach from the liberal side – the socialist intent to take the mixed economy as far as practicable in more equal and cooperative directions – has classics worth reading still, especially Richard Tawney's *The Acquisitive Society* (1921) and *Equality* (1931, with additions in the fourth edition of 1952). Ross Terrill, distilling Tawney's constructive vision from all his works in *R.H. Tawney and his Times: Socialism as Fellowship* (1973), found 'a view of socialism not as efficiency, or order, or the symmetry of a perfect social machine, or even of abundance, but of a right order of social relationships, the ... goal of which is human fellowship'. Tawney was nevertheless quite practical about the motivation of work and the dilemmas of organization. If coal mines are nationalized as recommended by a 1919 Royal Commission, will mine managers 'have as much freedom, initiative and authority in the service of the community as under private ownership? ... It is possible to conceive an arrangement under which the life of a mine manager would be made a burden to him by perpetual recalcitrance on the part of the men at the pit for which he is responsible. It is possible to conceive one under which he would be hampered to the point of paralysis by irritating interference from a bureaucracy at headquarters. In the past some managers of "cooperative workshops" suffered ... from the former: many officers of the Employment Exchanges are the victims ... of the latter.' (*The Acquisitive Society*, 209–10) The Royal Commission had proposed a workable course between them, avoiding both.

Modern books which try to base realistic estimates of democratic socialist possibilities on realistic assumptions about economic and political motivation include C.A.R. Crosland, *The Future of Socialism* (1957), Stuart Holland, *The Socialist Challenge* (1975), Hugh Stretton, *Capitalism, Socialism and the Environment* (1976) and Alec Nove, *The Economics of Feasible Socialism* (1983).

FEMINISTS

The feminist and environmental movements have a double relation to the 'rational egoist' theories. The theories are no help to the movements, and the progress achieved by the movements is decisive evidence against the predictive power of the theories.

The women's movement has persuaded men to surrender some at least of what *homines economici* would not have surrendered; and far from having constant motivation as rational egoists, feminists have managed to *change* many women's motivation, and persuade them not to accept as constants but to *choose* what natures and aspirations to have. And they choose diversely.

Two centuries ago in most of what are now economically developed countries women could not expect to vote or run for office, be educated as men were, own property while they had fathers or husbands alive, earn in any but menial occupations, decide freely whom to marry and whether to have children, sue for divorce, keep their children if separated, or expect police protection from domestic violence if it stopped short of murder or maiming. They now have those rights, if not all with full equality. In achieving or resisting the changes plenty of self-interests have operated, and economic growth was a condition for some of them. But by themselves such economic explanations cannot sufficiently explain the changes. Employers, and male workers in some industries, may have seen advantages for themselves in admitting more women to the workforce; but it was against the material interest of most men to end the male monopoly of rich and powerful occupations in government, business, law, medicine, academia and the 'labour aristocracy' of skilled trades. Polls and introspection suggest that most of the men who support the new equalities have been persuaded chiefly by sympathy and considerations of justice, and/or by ranking the quality of relations with women above the material gains to be had by continuing to exclude or exploit them. If men were ever rational egoists, women have changed quite a number of them; at the very least they have induced them to narrow the scope for egoist behaviour and expand the scope for just, affectionate or conscientious behaviour.

Public choice defenders may argue that there has merely been an addition to the political population: including women in the system has increased the number of contenders but they may all be assumed to contend as rational egoists on public choice principles. It is an unsatisfactory defence. Rational egoist assumptions could not have predicted and cannot explain why women were enfranchised, or why there was then a pause of half a century or so before the next radical changes; or why women divide as they do about the kind of society, and gender roles, that they want. These 'instabilities' may explain why there is so little notice of women's political activity in the public choice literature.

There is of course plenty of self-interest in the women's movement and the resistance to it, and some divisions of the movement work to improve women's wealth and income partly by persuading women to act more like rational egoists than they have customarily done. But even those *advocates* of rational egoist behaviour want to *change* women's natures and aims. The central point is that for both feminists and the conservative women who oppose them, women's motivation is problematical; it is believed to be changeable; some feminists hope that men's motivation may also be changeable. So motivation is not assumed to be stable, it is a main subject of debate, choice and action.

Since Simone de Beauvoir's *The Second Sex* appeared in 1949 the debate has been wide-ranging and quick-changing. What does not change is the perception that women have everywhere had less power, money and freedom than men. The debate is about why that has been so, the possibility of changing it, and whether and how to change it. Many of the questions addressed by feminist writers can be simplified as questions about paired alternatives: alternative analyses pointing to alternative directions of change.

Have men dominated women because of their biological natures alone? Or have a few natural differences – women's child-bearing, men's physical strength – enabled men to impose the rest of the differences, which amount to most of the differences, by social arrangements which could be changed by collective choice? If the latter, how much of the difference is maintained by custom and institutional force, i.e. by external constraints on women, and how much is built into their personalities and preferences by their upbringing, then self-imposed?

Whether men's nature dictates their gender relations directly, or indirectly through their design of the formative beliefs and institutions which shape both sexes' characters and expectations, what alternatives would male nature allow? Men have been persuaded to give women the vote and admit them to government and the professions; could they be persuaded to cooperate in further reforms? Through the 1980s some of the best-selling feminist books treated men as incorrigible: 'all men are rapists, all women have been raped', dominance and submission are incurable, the poor best hope for women is in as radical a separation as possible. Other feminists thought that message, like other crime fiction, sold so well chiefly because it was novel and sensational. Why had 'domineering rapists' allowed women to vote, to get equal pay in some occupations, to become professors and judges and prime ministers, to win Nobel prizes? To depict women as natural victims was insulting to women as well as men, and discouraged further reform.

Some feminist philosophers wonder whether men and women can have the same understanding of themselves, each other, and their relations with each other. Shared understanding is difficult, or in a certain sense unfair, because languages and their meanings are mostly male creations. The word 'freedom' stands for the kinds of freedom men want, ideas of equality are about particular equalities and inequalities that men have thought important, and so on. Women experience life differently and value its elements differently, but are disadvantaged because the language in which they have to think is biased against them and unsuitable for the work they have for it – all powerless groups suffer because the powerful make the languages.

There is argument about the distinctive values and capacities of women and men, whatever the cause of the differences. Should feminists celebrate the peaceful, conciliatory, nurturant character of women and think how it might contribute to the reform and better government of society? Or should those 'soft' values be seen as causes and effects of defeat and submission, and women try instead to 'imitate the action of the tiger' and match men's strength and confidence in battling for equality with them? What mixtures are possible, for example of men's strength with women's values? Is it ridiculous to think of fighting hard to achieve a less combative society? (Several women heads of government have fought wars.)

The different analyses underlie different programmes: what should the women's movement aim for in practical politics?

Left feminists want to eliminate gender inequality in the course of reducing all inequalities. Right feminists want women to get their fair share of existing inequalities, i.e. their fair share of top jobs, high pay, capital wealth. Both have generally wanted more equal relations within households, and doubted if that could ever be consistent with the traditional household division of labour. The Left suspect the Right of wanting a female class structure to allow successful women to exploit unsuccessful women as domestic servants. The Left meanwhile have not been relieved of much housework by their working class partners, or (through most of their history) offered equal pay by their partners' labour unions.

An articulate movement has developed, called third-wave feminism by some of its members and anti-feminism by its feminist critics, which values the traditional division of labour for a number of reasons. It gives women command of a realm in which they have natural advantages over men. It avoids the stress of trying to earn, keep house and raise children all at once. It provides the best care for children, which promises the best adults. It keeps neighbourhoods alive and helpful through the working day. It claims not to be against women's interests, because half the children who benefit from it are girls and the other half may become more workable partners if they are brought up by well-supported mothers rather than by neglect, commercial or communal care, or broken homes and step-parents. There are wider social benefits: better parenting now reduces the need for police and social workers later. Women with these conservative aims are not necessarily conservative about the means to them. They may want better local resources and support services for households. They may want measures, including new provisions for re-training and re-entry, to enable parents to stop earning for five or ten years without loss of occupational status or opportunity. Some want government to put strict new obligations on fathers. And they want parenting to be recognized and paid as a valuable and respected occupation: people who choose to stay home to do it well should not be despised or taught to think less of themselves, least of all by champions of women's interests.

Common to all this thought is the belief that women's and men's understanding of themselves and their relations with each other can be changed, to some degree at least, by new thought and collective action. As they change, they develop new aims, rules and elements of motivation in their political, social and economic life. Thus motivation is not something to be assumed, it is a subject of research, re-education and choice. But such efforts would be futile, and the substantial changes achieved already could not have happened, if political motivation were as uniformly selfish and stable as public choice theory must assume it to be if it is to be the axiomatic, predictive science it aspires to be. The changes already achieved, many of them led by women and supported by men who could not expect to benefit individually from them, indicate that the public choice assumptions were wrong and the reformers' hopes were not all futile.

The most interesting argument, however, is no longer about the degrees of selfishness, sympathy or altruism which motivate the distribution of social costs and benefits. A broad division of the women's movement believes as some communitarian philosophers do, and as Carole Uhlaner asserted in the *Public Choice* article on 'relational goods' cited earlier, that the most important object of individual desire, political action and social research is not the distribution of social benefits and costs to atomistic individuals, it is the quality of relations between them: working, loving, liking, hating, housekeeping, child-rearing, playful, sporting, social and political relations of every kind.

These ideas of social dependence can coexist with ideas of individual autonomy if one function of individual autonomy is a freedom to prefer some kinds of social relation to others. Some people look for relations of power and submission, cruelty and suffering. Some want independence, non-entanglement, free choice and freedom from obligation: market relations between autonomous individuals as in public choice theory. (Perhaps that theory depicts a particular personality type, rather than a basis for a general political theory.) Some people want loving, friendly, trustful relations; many want them to last and welcome mutual dependence as encouraging that. 'Well-rounded' people may want some of all these types of relation: perhaps love at home, contract at work and brutal competition in sport. Some of these preferences are selfish: people want their own relationships to be enjoyable and their own teams to win. Others are more disinterested or sociable: people want to know that there are good relations all over, to constitute a good society and perpetuate it by bringing up good citizens.

It may be these different types of personality and attitudes to human company that attract people to the individualist or communitarian philosophies which are discussed later in this chapter. Here the purpose is to notice that the division between atomistic and communitarian ideas tends to coincide with a particular division in feminist thought. All feminists, including the most individualist, think it matters how people are brought up. Whether gender differences are wholly or only partly due to nurture, they certainly owe *something* to it, and any revolution in gender relations needs to include a revolution in the way girls and boys are conditioned and taught to regard themselves and each other. To that extent, because they perceive that people are shaped by as well as shaping their societies, all feminists are communitarians – feminism has no equivalents of the traditional (male) liberalism which interests itself only in the political relations of fully-formed autonomous adults without asking how such adults are produced. But there are feminist disagreements about the *kinds* of adult, and adult relations, that a gender-equal society should try to shape, and those disagreements are easily linked to disagreements between individualist and communitarian philosophies. Whether for logical reasons or for reasons of temperament and sensibility, unisex aspirations tend to go with philosophical ideas of individualism, self-interest and social contract, and 'special value' feminists tend to be communitarians with moral rather than (or as well as) contractual ideas of justice. The common ground and the differences between the two approaches are exemplified in the work of two contemporary philosophers.

In 'Justice and Gender'[4] and 'Reason and Feeling in Thinking about Justice'[5] Susan Moller Okin argues for a strict unisex programme: 'gender is incompatible with a just society'. She uses the philosophical devices of social contract and (in a limited way) the 'veil of ignorance'. If people had to negotiate a constitution and social structure before they knew what their own capacities and social situation would be, modern contractarian philosophers argue that they would agree on arrangements as equal and fair-to-all as possible, to minimize the hardships they would suffer if fate should land them at the bottom of the heap. Thus a principle of justice is derived, without overt moral premises, from self-interest. But the contract is only a notional agreement; it is real, present people who are actually invited to consider what they would agree to behind the veil of ignorance; and Okin doubts if it would be either possible or fair to reach such an agreement in a divided society:

A number of feminist scholars have argued in recent years that, in a gender-structured society, women's and men's different life experiences in fact affect their respective psychologies, modes of thinking, and patterns of moral development in significant ways. Special attention has been paid to the effects on the psychological and moral development of both sexes of the fact, fundamental to our gendered society, that children of both sexes are primarily reared by women. It has been argued that the experience of individuation – of separating oneself from the nurturer with whom one is originally psychologically fused – is a very different experience for girls than for boys, leaving the members of each sex with a different perception of themselves and of their relations with others. In addition it has been argued that the experience of *being* primary nurturers (and of growing up with this expectation) also affects the psychological and moral perspective of women, as does the experience of growing up in a society in which members of one's sex are in many respects subordinate to the other.... [But] if principles of justice are to be adopted unanimously by representative human beings ignorant of their particular characteristics and positions in society, they must be persons whose psychological and moral development is in all essentials identical. This means that the social factors influencing the differences presently found between the sexes – from female parenting to all the manifestations of female subordination and dependence – would have to be replaced by genderless institutions and customs. Only when men participate equally in what has been principally women's realm of meeting the daily material and psychological needs of those close to them, and when women participate equally in what have been principally men's realms of larger scale production, government, and intellectual and creative life, will members of both sexes develop a more complete *human* personality than has hitherto been possible ... I conclude that ... we cannot complete such a theory of justice until the life experiences of the two sexes have become as similar as their biological differences permit.[6]

In *Equality and the Rights of Women* (1980) and *The Grammar of Justice* (1987) Elizabeth Wolgast disagrees both with that view of gender, and with the rational egoist assumptions of that view of justice. The philosophical 'derivation of a just state from self-interest is a long, ongoing tradition of attempts to derive moral rules or principles of justice from self-interest, of attempts to show that being moral must in some way be reducible to doing what is to one's benefit.' In that tradition atomistic individuals are seen as contracting with each other to create society: 'for such creatures communal life has to result from rational self-interest.... The man at the center of such a theory "is the man who benefits from others' compliance, not the man who leads the life of virtue by complying himself."'

Connected with [the individual's freedom to act, to express himself and pursue his interests] is the importance of competition.... In the state of nature competition was perfectly free but threatening; in a society it can be made orderly and peaceful, and thus it becomes the normal mode of human interaction.

But when this picture is applied to society, anomalies appear. In such a society the elderly and frail must compete with the young and strong, men compete with their childbearing wives, the handicapped compete with the well endowed. Correspondingly, the economy of the community is seen as an *n*-person game in which each player plays against all the others to maximize his advantage. The problems of this picture have not deterred social and economic thinkers from using it, even though it is at center a picture of ruthless egoism and unconcern for others.[7]

Wolgast wrote before Okin and did not refer to her work, but Okin's reasons for wanting to abolish gender are in the tradition Wolgast describes. To enable women to get equal benefits, she wants to produce fairer competition between women and men, and easier agreement on rules for equal treatment, by conditioning them to be as alike as possible.

In *Equality and the Rights of Women* Wolgast reminds us that uniformly equal treatment would have some very unequal effects, because equal rights are not the only important rights.

> Some rights depend on individual differences, on accidents of fortune, on talents, or on other features that distinguish people. These rights are special or differential ones; among them are the right of a blind person to use of a white cane, the right of a veteran to burial at public expense, the right of an indigent to government assistance, the right of a fatherless child to public support. Many rights are of this kind. They are not rights for everyone but rights only for those who qualify, and most of them have a presumptive basis in needs ... The two kinds of rights, equal and differential (or special), work quite differently. With regard to an equal right, taking a person's individual qualities into account may constitute discrimination. But with special rights, they *must* be taken into account, for these rights are based on human differences.[8]

Can any single principle justify rights of both kinds? Wolgast thinks not. We reason from different foundations to rules appropriate to different problems – 'we have many "just making" reasons, and they can lead to a certain amount of moral uncertainty when we must choose among them. But the complexity is not optional.' The alternative of a single principle and uniform rules can work perversely or tyrannically – 'true equality is safe only where there is uniformity ... a perfectly egalitarian society needs to prevent differences appearing, or to squelch them.'[9] Okin has since argued for just that uniformity.

What does this account of justice imply about gender?

Since our societies, especially the most free and equal of them, are laced with rights of both kinds, and with both uniform and discriminating laws and policies – and need to be: they would be less free and equal if they were not – Wolgast sees no good reason to insist that all the law and practice of gender be of the equal-and-uniform kind and none be of the special or differential kind. Feminists should freely consider which uniformities and which differences would be most desirable for their own sakes – for women, children, men – and (at least as important) what range of lifestyles, and sameness and difference, should be open to individual choice.

The unisex ideal may hope to produce better people than present men and women. (Okin hopes to see 'members of both sexes develop a more complete human personality than has hitherto been possible'.) But that hope may prove to be as illusory as some other dreams of transforming human nature have been; and in practice most unisex reforms are designed to have women behave more like men. That may be appropriate if it is on rational egoist principles of justice that women seek equal power in business, government and intellectual life. But if at least half the reason for wanting it is to empower women to improve those activities by bringing distinctive qualities and capacities to bear on them, the distinctive qualities should not be discarded on the way to the top. The argument applies more generally to society as a whole. Many gender roles have been profoundly unjust, but they don't all *need* to be. Wherever difference and complementarity can be fair, and people want them, they may contribute valuably to the quality and variety of life and love. And if one purpose is to reform men, they may respond better to feminine women made influential by just reforms than to women who aspire to much of their unregenerate masculine nature.

To the extent that just relations can be achieved with an appropriate mixture of uniform and differential rights and culture, women can have wider choices than uniform androgyny would allow. There is more than one tolerable way for two people to divide the work of earning and keeping house. Wolgast agrees with Margaret Mead and others that bearing and bringing up children is 'a fair part of what life is about', to be embraced and enjoyed, not dismissed as a chore to be minimized. Western men should do much more of it. That can be good for men, good for women's work loads and career opportunities, probably good for the children. But there is more than one way to do it, with similar or distinct parental roles, and the tolerable ways of doing it, including different divisions of labour, should be open to parents' choice.

It is at least possible, finally, that biological differences impose more differences of temperament and specific capacity than unisex theorists suppose, and that women might be further disadvantaged, and society more unruly, if women lost all differential rights and opportunities. Wolgast quotes the biologist Mary Midgley on the human species –

> We are fairly aggressive, yet we want company and depend on long-term enterprises. We love those around us and need their love, yet we want independence and need to wander. We are restlessly curious and meddling, yet long for permanence. Unlike many primates, we do have a tendency to pair-formation, but it is an incomplete one, and gives us a lot of trouble.[10]

Feminine characteristics may do more than we realise to limit the trouble, and may be harder to change than unisex theorists hope. They may also contribute to both sexes' joy in life.

Thus four advantages are claimed for 'special value' feminism. Biology may impose some differences which it would be harmful to suppress. A free society should allow its members to decide and negotiate their roles, including (if they wish) divisions of labour. Some of women's distinctive qualities are socially valuable and will be more so as sexual equality increases their influence. And – subject to fair shares and just rights – some sex and gender differences can contribute to the joy and interest of life.

> In the absence of a compelling reason against them, it seems reasonable to suppose that sex roles in some form or other are tolerable. What is needed is not their abolition or their amalgamation to a single androgynous role, but adjustments within them. In many respects adjustment is needed to make the roles more similar. [Many present differences are falsely based, unjust, and must go.] But to say that grown women are generally somewhat easier with children than men, somewhat more expressive of feelings, more understanding of others' feelings, more demonstrative, and somewhat less competitive, is not clearly false. Nor are the consequences for sex roles clearly negligible. Some differences between the sexes, their nature, temperament, and roles, may actually be a nice thing.[11]

These are not anti-feminist arguments. Their aims overlap with the unisex aims and they support plenty of genderless fair sharing. But in a broad way *Equality and the Rights of Women* is about relations between equality as traditionally defined and sought by men and the quality and value of human relations as understood by women, the two considered as rival or twin foundations for a feminist programme.

Okin's and Wolgast's are not the only feminist philosophies. Main divisions and directions of contemporary feminist thought are discussed by Lynne Segal in *Is the Future Female? Troubled Thoughts on Contem-*

porary Feminism (1987). Ethical argument about the kind of society for which women do or ought to strive, including argument about relations between ethics of justice and ethics of care, is collected by Cass Sunstein in *Feminism and Political Theory* (1990). The clearest reasons why public choice or other monocausal economic theories of politics could not predict, explain or help women's twentieth century achievements can be found in *Women's Claims: A Study in Political Economy* (1983) as Lisa Peattie and Martin Rein describe how supposedly permanent facts of human nature and motivation have been unfixed, and opened to individual choice and collective action, by the women's movement.

ENVIRONMENTALISTS

Public choice analysts have investigated quite a lot of environmental policy-making. As noted earlier, their case studies typically focus on the motivation of the self-interested contenders: direct sufferers from physical or financial ill effects of environmental degradation, profit-seeking industries, workers whose jobs are at risk, vote-seeking politicians, rival bureaucrats: Hamlet without the prince. There is little or no explanation of the motivation of the prime movers of most environmental vigilance and reform, the multitude of researchers, writers, activists, subscribers and voters for environmental reform who expect no material benefits for themselves from the policies they battle for, or whose individual shares of any communal benefits will be trifling compared with their commitments of time and energy. Many know that their real incomes will decline along with everyone else's if their full programme of economic and environmental restraint is implemented. Public choice analysts usually treat them as interested parties like any others. There is nothing wrong with treating them so if the purpose is to analyze not the motivation of the parties but their interplay, and the working of the political system, in arriving at environmental policies; any political scientist or journalist with that purpose might treat them so. But it is not honest to claim that such studies confirm the public choice assumption that all the parties' behaviour could be predicted from knowledge of their individual material interests.

As in case studies, so also for the green movement as a whole. Two arguments are offered for believing that environmental concern, even when apparently disinterested, is still economically motivated. It is said to be class-based. And any disinterested opinions are likely to be ineffective because strongly organized and motivated business lobbies are expected to prevail over the diffuse opinions of the general public.

There are three objections to the belief about class. First it may have been true in the US but has not been true everywhere. The most dramatic and effective conservationist action in Australia was by a builders labourers' union which used its industrial muscle to block or relocate more than three billion dollars worth of developmental investment in the 1970s. In Norway the early political leaders of the green movement were the Labour Party and its electors. Second, there is plenty of evidence that class attitudes to environmental issues are not fixed. Acid and radioactive rain have affected opinions in every class in north-western Europe. There is some evidence that Australian environmental values relate more to generation than to class, because people now under forty had lots of environmental education at school and most people over forty did not. Third, the original American argument does not actually support public choice assumptions. It says that disinterested action to protect the environment, especially in the long term, is commoner in the middle than in the working class. It is a logical mistake to assume, from that, that middle class people have material self-interests in conservation. If the rich are found to be more generous than the poor are to heirs and strangers, that may show that the rich behaviour is class-related but it does not show that it is self-interested.

The argument about concentrated and diffuse interests uses a logical mistake to arrive at a false prediction. Public choice theorists and others have observed that in some business and regulatory conflicts, the small numbers in particular firms or industries can prevail politically over the larger numbers of their customers because the few are well organized and strongly motivated while the many are unorganized, and less intensely concerned by marginal changes in the price or quality of goods or services which represent only a small fraction of each individual's spending. Does that model predict the likely relations between environmentally offensive industries and the diffuse public support for environmental protection? Not in principle, because experience of conflicts between intense and diffuse self-interests creates no presumptions about conflicts between self-interested and disinterested or beneficent parties. And not always in practice: some European elections have been swung by green voters, some materially interested in the green issues but some not. The Australian swings have been on issues of forest conservation, sand mining and uranium export which did not touch the swinging urban voters' material interests, while the defeated loggers and miners were rich, organized and articulate. When people bring moral concerns to bear in politics they sometimes act with more passion than they would ever bring to conflicts about marginal changes in their tax rates or consumer prices.

We noticed earlier some implausible attempts to rescue the 'rational egoist' assumption by simply re-defining unselfish behaviour as selfish. Unselfish people are said to be seeking psychic satisfaction for themselves as selfishly as others seek money for themselves; it doesn't matter whence they seek 'utility' as long as they seek it, and that they do seek it for themselves is part of the investigator's definition of any human action. Common sense or honest science observes that in environmental politics there are typically some people with profits or jobs at risk, some of them with and some without principled beliefs independent of their material interests. There are people with broad concerns for prosperity and full employment in the long run, some of them with and some without material interests in those prospects. There are some defending their own environmental benefits, some defending others' benefits, some concerned with the economic or environmental welfare of strangers and generations unborn. There are deep ecologists defending the welfare of animal and vegetable species for their own sakes rather than for human use. To ignore or abstract from the differences between those purposes by lumping them together as rational egoist utility-seeking – but then to pick out and report only, selectively, the genuinely self-seeking ones, as nine out of ten *Public Choice* articles do – is neither honest nor promising science.

Environmentalists of course have to contend with individual, corporate, national and generational selfishness – and some would add, species selfishness. Their main means of doing so has been to awaken and mobilize a range of contrary purposes in large numbers of people. Some of the purposes are non-economic without necessarily being unselfish – aesthetic preferences, for example. Some are disinterested – people campaign for benefits to be enjoyed by other people, not themselves. Some are generous, foregoing consumption or other pleasures for the benefit of others, including other species or human generations. The purposes change as perceptions of the problem do, and perceptions have changed a good deal through recent decades.

In *Post Environmentalism* (1990; called *Sustaining the Earth* in the US) John Young notices a likeness between a common pattern of development of individual environmental consciousness and the changing concerns of modern environmental theory. Thirty years ago Rachel Carson's *The Silent Spring* (1962), Paul Ehrlich's *The Population Bomb* (1962) and other loud alarms shocked people into anxious states of mind and called for revolutionary changes of purpose in industrial societies. A stream of technical and scientific writing followed, about the extent of depletion and spoiling of the world's natural resources and the physical action needed to conserve them. Diverse proposals all called for drastic economic restraint – but at whose cost? And what political, educational or other action could make it happen? Zealots urged humankind to forget all other political divisions and concerns and unite to Save The Planet. Others argued that far from being forgotten, traditional conflicts must become more acute. Any effective environmental reform must affect different occupations and lifestyles differently, and cut some people's incomes and freedoms more than others'. It would no longer be plausible to claim that government faces a natural market distribution of income with which it need not interfere. So environmental reformers need to integrate their concerns with the traditional concerns of politics. They need to show how alternative green reforms, or none, might affect existing moral and material interests, and look for alliances accordingly. In this view the task is not to replace existing political organizations but to green them. Thus was born the continuing tension between greening the old political parties, and withdrawing from them to work through new Green parties instead.

Some Right theorists thought that the way to conserve over-used common resources was to get them into private ownership. Some Left theorists thought that public ownership offered surer conservation and fairer rationing. Many environmental economists believed that the hidden hand could be re-educated to do the job. They built theory and practice on the idea that environmental misuse is a kind of market failure: it simply signifies that available resources are not being used in the way that would maximize human satisfactions. The failure happens because some resources (air, water) are ownerless and unpriced, and some products (pollution) are unpriced externalities of productive processes. Economists should price the externalities and shadow-price the 'free' resources. They could then supply government with cost-benefit analyses of alternative kinds of corrective action to restore efficient market conditions. Firms could be taxed to simulate payment for free resources, and required to internalize the external costs they cause. Emission taxes and quotas, 'pollution banks' and other devices could motivate producers and consumers to make the most efficient use of available resources. Cost-benefit analyses could be (though in practice they rarely were) refined to incorporate values for equitable distribution between individuals and between generations. Analysts developed dubious but ingenious methods of shadow-pricing. Land prices upwind and downwind of offensive industries were said to indicate what people were prepared to pay to avoid particular hazards; medical and life insurance spending was said to indicate the price of life; and so on. With life, clean air, aesthetic values, etc., priced into product prices and into GNP, firms could continue to maximize profit and government could continue to adopt the policies that would maximize GNP. The interests of future generations could be discounted, like other futures, at current interest rates. Thus it almost seemed as if the necessary collective self-restraint could be motivated by ordinary individual self-interest: only the prices need be reformed, not the people.

There was predictable criticism of that approach from the usual critics of undue faith in market forces. Poverty, forced unemployment and inequitable distribution cannot really be abolished by smart taxing and pricing. They have not been when they arose from other causes, and won't be when they arise, perhaps more severely, from environmental causes.

Meanwhile the green movement has diversified, with its divisions embracing many spiritual, aesthetic and ethical values as well as material survival. Far from being disposable by shadow pricing, most of its concerns are intrinsically uncertain and controversial. There is no knock-down way to decide whether or how far to gamble on new technology, for example on the invention of new sources of clean energy. Meanwhile the possible ways of economizing energy range from some which would stop the rich wasting it to some which would freeze the poor to death. Wilderness can be conserved to be enjoyed by many, by few or by nobody. Even agreed goals may occasion disagreement about the speed and cost at which to try to achieve them. 'The environment', Young observed, 'seen first as a technological and scientific problem, then as an economic and political one, has become a philosophical and ethical one.'

Philosophical discussions of environmental policy may begin with a traditional distinction between intolerable and merely undesirable behaviour, or between duty and virtue. Kant distinguished perfect from imperfect duties. A perfect duty is a categorical obligation: thou shalt not kill, for any price. Imperfect duties are matters of virtue rather than rule and may depend on circumstances: don't be rude unless unreasonably provoked. On that principle the purposes of public policies may be seen as of, roughly, three kinds. There are perfect duties: it is forbidden in any circumstances to kill, steal, enslave people, employ children in coalmines. There are imperfect duties, or virtues: it is desirable to reduce pollution *wherever possible*, to prevent *unreasonable* invasions of privacy, to *economize* energy. Many of these policies concern behaviour whose desirable and undesirable elements can't be entirely divorced: we can't have air, land and sea transport without *some* risk, so the question is how much. Third, there are policies which although they may incidentally restrain some bad behaviour are chiefly informative aids to efficiency: weather forecasts, regular weights and measures, the rules of the road, and the many industrial and commercial regulations which chiefly tell people what to expect of each other, and of government, in their daily business.

There are environmental policies of all three kinds. There are strict rules against directly endangering life. There are measures to reduce risk, restrain pollution, encourage green values. And there are comparatively neutral aids to efficiency such as land-use plans for new neighbourhoods which tell you where to build if you need to emit noise or smoke, where to live if you want to be among other households, where the shopping centre will be, where the schools and parks and playgrounds will be. Policies thus range from the purely moral to the purely convenient. At any point along that line they may range from consensual to bitterly disputed, and the disputes may have varying elements of conflicting material interest and moral or aesthetic disagreement. It is a mistake to insist that all policy-making has only one of those diverse characteristics, or that similar principles should guide all of it from the strictly moral to the merely convenient.

For environmental policy some simplifications of a more helpful kind are suggested by Mark Sagoff in *The Economy of the Earth* (1988). He begins with four distinctions: between citizens and consumers, values and preferences, public and private interests, and (more obscurely because it refers to problems in the philosophy of science) between virtues and methods. As a consumer you shop according to your individual preferences. As a citizen you join in debating and determining principles of social order and government. Your citizen's views may accord with your individual preferences on some issues but not on others, and when they do coincide the preferences may have influenced the moral ideas or the moral ideas the preferences, or both may have been derived from the society around you. We cannot expect to understand you if we suppose that your judgements of good and evil express *either* nothing but individual desires and aversions *or* nothing but godlike detachment and benevolence. If you are intelligent you will recognize both those potentialities in yourself and therefore in the politicians and public servants who represent you in government. You will not think that good government can be sufficiently ensured by defining those officials' powers and methods in advance; it is also prudent to choose officials with appropriate virtues.

Government should certainly meet many of its people's needs. But it is also the process by which they discuss and decide what their collective values and goals should be – values and goals which must certainly conflict with some of their individual wants and interests. Does the idea of collective values which may conflict with individual interests imply an illiberal belief in uniformity? No – in any society, however free and pluralist, there have to be innumerable policies, like the criminal law and the rule of the road, which embody dominant values and impose no-option rules. Liberal democracy merely promises everyone a share in deciding them. Following

Kant, Sagoff's approach 'makes individuals the ultimate sources of policy – but it submits policy to their judgment rather than deriving it from their preferences. This view treats people with respect ... insofar as it regards them as thinking beings capable of discussing issues on their merits. This is different from regarding people as bundles of preferences.' This does not encourage policy-making by cost-benefit analysis or by shadow-pricing moral considerations – 'we do not decide to execute murderers by asking how much bleeding hearts are willing to pay to see a person pardoned and how much hard hearts are willing to pay to see him hanged'. Nor should rights to pollute be decided that way.

Nevertheless non-economic goals often have economic costs, and it is sensible to deliberate about them with their costs and practicality in mind. There are also public issues which are rightly decided by market or market-like means. (Where should public services be located to serve most of their clients most conveniently?) So there is plenty of scope for experts, including economists, to help environmental policy-makers to be as well informed as possible about the economic costs and interrelations of the goals they have in mind, and the efficiency of alternative ways of achieving them. But that does not mean that the policies should be derived from individual preferences, or by balancing their economic costs and benefits alone. Many of them should be chosen for ethical or aesthetic reasons, and it is those ethical and aesthetic considerations, *not* their economic benefits, that should be balanced against their economic costs. 'What separates these questions from those for which markets are appropriate', Sagoff argues, 'is this: They involve matters of knowledge, wisdom, morality, and taste that admit of better or worse, right or wrong, true or false – and these concepts differ from that of economic optimality. Surely environmental questions – the protection of wilderness, habitats, water, land, and air as well as policy toward environmental safety and health – involve moral and aesthetic principles and not just economic ones. This is consistent, of course, with cost-effective strategies for implementing our environmental goals and with a recognition of the importance of personal freedoms and economic constraints.' (p. 45) This argument connects with a more general one about human nature, citizenship and government. As Sagoff sums it up and relates it to liberal political philosophy:

> Social regulation reflects public values we choose collectively, and these may conflict with wants and interests we pursue individually. It is essential to the liberty we cherish, of course, that individuals are free to try to satisfy their personal preferences under open and equitable conditions. It is also part of our cherished conception of liberty that we are free to

choose societal ideals together and free to accomplish these ideas in ways consistent with personal and political rights through the rule of law.

Social regulation most fundamentally has to do with the identity of a nation – a nation committed historically, for example, to appreciate and preserve a fabulous natural heritage and to hand it on reasonably undisturbed to future generations. This is not a question of what we *want*; it is not exactly a question of what we *believe in*; it is a question of what we *are*. (p. 17)

As to what we are, individually and collectively, a sophisticated debate is in train among liberal and communitarian philosophers. It is the subject of the remainder of this chapter. Meanwhile a short but comprehensive history of environmental thought and a lucid analysis of its ethical problems can be found in John Passmore's excellent *Man's Responsibility for Nature* (1974). A thorough survey of contemporary environmental theory, and especially of relations between the physical problems and the social problems of 'voluntary scarcity' and environmental management, is Allan Schnaiberg's *The Environment: From Surplus to Scarcity* (1980). What the environmental policies and practices of a sustainable society might actually be is suggested by Michael Jacobs in *The Green Economy* (1991).

LIBERALS

If government is not by God's command, or by hereditary right of monarchs or aristocrats, or by simple conquest and subjection, what *should* its foundation be?

One liberal manifesto dates from 431 BC in Pericles' account of the freedom, self-government and civic virtues of Athens as reported (or imagined) in Thucydides' *History of the Peloponnesian War*. A century later Aristotle proposed a great act of faith in human nature. People are born not just with material appetites but with high moral and intellectual potentialities. A good society should enable its citizens to realize the best of their potentialities. One of them is for good government, so everyone should participate in it: 'political government is government of free and equal citizens'. Aristotle believed that the adult potentialities are present in the child as the oak is in the acorn. To grow to the full, both need appropriate conditions. He was a liberal individualist in wanting people to discover and fulfil their own potentialities, not anyone else's programme for them. But his ideal community was also sociable and egalitarian. People could not be free, think for themselves or command their own life choices without a sufficient standard of living, which it was society's business to enable them to earn. They should regularly eat together, both to see that the poor got sufficient nourishment and to encourage sociability and political discussion. Aristotle managed to be both an individualistic and a social or communitarian liberal.

Those and other Greek and Roman theories of citizens' rights and governments' duties were available to the philosophers of the Enlightenment who set out in the seventeenth and eighteenth centuries to justify the English, American and French revolutions against arbitrary government, and to propose principles of secular, responsible government and citizens' rights over or against government. Most of them built on the twin foundations of natural law and social contract. The first was a Christian idea and the second had some Christian authority so they might allow secular principles of government to coexist peacefully with the still powerful established churches.

Natural law is discoverable by human reason; contracts to be valid must be voluntary; both ideas assume a basic civic competence in people. An imagined contract between citizens and government entitled the citizens to determine the form and powers of government. In particular it allowed them to entrench, as prior to government and independent of it, individual rights defined by natural law, including rights to life, liberty and property, with which government might therefore interfere – if at all – only by consent and due process. Liberal theory ever since has been concerned with two purposes and the relations between them. One is to entrench particular rights, usually including some property rights and personal freedoms, against interference *by* government though in practice they depend *on* government. The other is to establish some consensus for orderly government among people who – as the glory of liberal society – differ widely, and must always be free to differ, not only in their material interests but also in some of their deepest moral beliefs.

Natural law and social contract were useful devices for those purposes, but they were fanciful inventions. For sceptical moderns, could liberal theory come down to earth, to rest on nothing but present facts and the citizens' wants? There were already strands of utilitarianism in Hobbes' and Locke's thought in the seventeenth century. The next century saw the further development of Hobbes' simple psychology of pleasure and pain as the motivators of all behaviour. In France Helvetius proposed that the only aim of government should be the greatest happiness of the greatest number of its citizens. In England Hume and then Bentham stripped that principle of any remaining association with natural law, social contract, past history or communal identity. 'Nature' said Bentham in his *Introduction to the Principles of Morals and Legislation* (1780) 'has placed mankind under the governance of two sovereign masters, pain and pleasure. It is for them alone to point out what we ought to do, as well as to determine what we shall do. On the one hand the standard of right and wrong, on the other the chain of causes and effects, are fastened to their throne.' Those assumptions were not necessary to Bentham's many schemes for legal, administrative and constitutional reform, which owed more to simple considerations of efficiency. He made no actual calculations of pleasures and pains. Items of natural law and individual right were smuggled back into the argument, for example to insist that everybody's pains and pleasures should count equally. But throughout, Bentham was an individualist: he saw all interests as individual and put no value on the quality of relations between people, or on a society's general structure or culture except as they satisfied individual interests. He also had a split mind about economic and other interests. With some of the economists of the time he believed there was a natural harmony of economic interests: most of government's economic controls should be dismantled. Between people's other interests there were real, sometimes irreducible conflicts: public action might well be needed to reconcile or adjudicate those conflicts and to protect the citizens from one another.

The utilitarians became democrats for practical reasons: nobody had natural political rights, but government was unlikely to attend to the interests of people it did not represent. John Stuart Mill wanted to extend the franchise to women, and to workers as soon as they were well enough educated to vote rationally. In other respects, in his early writing, he took the liberal theory of government to its minimalist extreme. Government's business was to protect the citizens from foreigners and each other; it should not try to improve them, or protect them from themselves. But his timing was paradoxical. Liberal theory and practice had succeeded in clearing away a great deal of traditional privilege, religious oppression, parliamentary corruption and inequity, obsolete legal practice, and complicated and often inefficient trade controls. Those achievements seemed amply to justify a pragmatic theory of minimal government. But the theory was perfected just as history was outdating it. As Mill was developing it through the 1830s and 1840s, a flood of reports were exposing both the cruelties of industrial capitalism and its growing needs for public support. Liberals contributed to the first effective factory acts, restrictions on women's and children's employment, provisions for public health, public investment in water supply and sewerage, road networks; in Europe, rail and inland navigational networks; and in Europe and the US, public provisions for technical and higher education and research. When Mill's minimalist masterpiece *On Liberty* was published in 1859, Germany and the US – Britain's leading industrial competitors – were about to develop policies of tariff protection, higher education and research and public transport investment some way ahead of their British equivalents.

Three trends were obsolescing the minimalist view of government. People needed – and as the franchise extended, were demanding – protection from capitalist dangers and cruelties. Private capitalism needed public infrastructure whose volume and cost increased steadily with mechanization and technical progress. And economic growth was generating a surplus – for the mass of people, the world's first surplus above minimal subsistence – whose distribution and use were open to choice. By act or omission government could not help influencing the distribution of the growing surplus, and many of its possible uses (mass education, higher education and research, old age pensions, public hospitals, public housing, public libraries and museums and art galleries, national parks, public playing fields) required public investment or income transfers.

Mill was one of the first to adapt liberal theory to the new needs but the most original transformation, which did much to rescue liberal theory from the banality and internal confusions of utilitarianism, was the work of the Oxford philosopher T. H. Green. Encouraged by classical Greek and modern German philosophers, Green gave new depth and attraction to the creed of individualism by insisting on its moral dimension. The moral implications of individual autonomy were inescapable: citizens as voters, and governments on their behalf, could not help acting justly or unjustly, morally or immorally, selfishly or generously. For Green that was not regrettable. Where utilitarians saw 'morality' as nothing but appetite moderated by prudence, Green thought that the capacity for moral thought, discrimination and action was the highest human capacity. But to exercise their moral faculties people had to be free to choose, and self-reliant as choosers. They must be genuinely free, not merely in law but also in practice, to choose between options actually open to them. Many important options were open to individual choice; some (like reforming the law or deciding on war or peace) were open only to collective choice. For the full realization of the highest human faculty and the central liberal ideal, people must make their own individual choices rather than having them imposed by government or economic poverty, and they must take part in their societies' collective choices rather than having them imposed by unrepresentative government.

Green distilled these thoughts into a distinction between negative and positive freedom. Negative freedoms depend on an absence of interference. Free thought, speech, publication, assembly, worship, migration, trade, and enjoyment of property and privacy may require some law and order but beyond that they simply require non-interference by the abstinent government of the early liberal ideal. It was understandable that such an ideal should have been conceived through two centuries of struggle to dismantle the manifold oppressions of monarchical, aristocratic and ecclesiastical rule and the pervasive but increasingly obsolete and self-defeating regulation of trade and industry. But in the new industrial economy of Green's world most of those negative freedoms were useless to the mass of people who worked to daily exhaustion, slept in bare tenements, had no choice but to spend their subsistence wages in the only way that could keep them alive, and being illiterate could know very little about the political issues of the day.

To be individuals truly free and responsible for their own material and moral choices, people need some basic economic resources, an educated understanding of the world in which they act, and a share in the collective choices which shape that world. It is in the nature of those advantages that no individual can have them unless others also have them; and to have any of them is to have not only an individual advantage but a share in common goods which can only exist communally.

In practice Green's principles thus encouraged liberal governments to enlarge their citizens' effective freedoms by any means that worked, and to extend the freedoms to as many citizens as they could. That defined as liberal most modern public health and welfare and economic infrastructure: measures which add to the choices open to citizens, and to the number of citizens to whom they are open. Green was equally interested in people's capacity to know their options (unknown options are not real options) and to choose wisely and well. While he was at work in the 1870s the debate about England's first compulsory education Act posed a critical question (for liberals) about relations between negative and positive freedoms. Could it possibly be right, or liberal, for a government to force unwilling parents to force unwilling children to school? Yes (said Mill, Green, and the liberal Prime Minister Gladstone) – without education a person has fewer options in life, less capacity to know them all and choose and use them well, and less understanding of the value of education as a liberator. Green also thought that ignorance reduced people's moral understanding, and therefore their realization of their highest human potentiality. Gladstone thought, among other things, that an uneducated Britain would be out-produced and consequently out-gunned by imperial Germany – the first compulsory education Act arose directly from a Board of Trade inquiry into the sources of Germany's growing industrial productivity. That sounded pragmatic but concealed a principle: education serves common as well as individual purposes. A society is likely to be more productive and interesting to live in if its members are able to develop their full intellectual potentialities. Life is richer and more interesting for me as well as for my neighbour if my neighbour is educated and skilful. So because it may both *free him* and *enrich me*, my altruism can join with my self-interest in voting to finance a school from my taxes, and to force my neighbour to go to it. Compulsory education could thus enlarge the individual freedom of the children concerned, it was a condition of national freedom in the simplest meaning of the term, its contribution to productivity could extend the material conditions of independence to yet more of the population, and it could enrich the lives even of those who might continue to pay for their own education without compulsion.

Green remained a liberal, with a presumption in favour of private enterprise and market relations wherever they would work tolerably. He specially valued the moral effects of people being responsible for their own welfare wherever possible. But they cannot be responsible for things they cannot control, and they are unlikely to act responsibly if the conditions of their upbringing and life make it too hard to develop industrious and responsible qualities of character.

Mill eventually went further than Green, though still not very far, in openly socialist directions. In successive revisions of *Principles of Political Economy* and in posthumously published *Chapters on Socialism* (1879) he imagined what might now be called market socialism. If without confiscation corporate business was by degrees purchased for its workers until most firms were workers' cooperatives, capitalist motivation might be joined to socialist distribution. As internal conflicts between capitalist and worker gave way to cooperative teamwork within firms motivated by competition between them, Mill hoped that the habit of cooperation might spread to other social spheres and institutions. Even without such socialist afterthoughts his final view of the proper functions of government was, like Green's, pragmatic and quite extensive.

With help from Mill, Green had restored to liberal philosophy the link between individual and community which Hume and the utilitarians had jettisoned. Freedom is a doubly social creation: family, educators, culture and government all have to contribute *both* to the production of the autonomous, self-reliant individual, *and* to the range and variety of political, social and economic opportunities which make the capacity to choose worth having. Individual freedom is a partly-communal creation.

There followed a generation of liberal, Fabian and social-democratic thinkers – including some like the economist J.A. Hobson who was a liberal free-trader in the 1890s but a socialist supporter of the Labour Party by the 1930s – who are hard to classify as exclusively liberal or socialist. In the US the pragmatic philosophers, the great jurists of the Harvard Law School, a generation of inventive newspapermen, and Presidents from both parties made liberalism a progressive, constructive creed, the protagonist rather than opponent of big government. Few theorists of any note on either side of the Atlantic followed Herbert Spencer in sticking to a minimalist view of government and opposing the whole direction of twentieth century progress. In Britain, paradoxically, the Liberal Party which had a parliamentary majority for thirteen years to 1918 was five years later a spent force, never to govern again. In 1937 in his *History of Political Theory* George Sabine concluded that 'liberalism has tended to disintegrate either in the direction of conservatism or in the direction of socialism'. With longer hindsight it might now be seen to have captured both of them. But not for minimal government – the conservative and social-democratic regimes of the twentieth century have been liberal in Green's positive rather than Spencer's negative meaning of the word.

Few members of those governments may have read Mill or heard of Green. The main force that has rejoined the liberal concern for freedom and individuality to an interest in community has been historical experience rather than theory. Modern productivity has created economic needs, and social opportunities for concerted action, to which all the Western democracies have responded in varying degrees but in broadly similar ways.

Postwar debates

Some strict individualism and some preference for minimal government survived into the twentieth century in some branches – especially the Austrian branch – of neoclassical economic theory. Von Mises and von Hayek expressed philosophical objections to notions of distributive justice based on anything other than existing property rights and endowments. They opposed most attempts to make public economic policies either masterful or moral. The philosopher Karl Popper elaborated Burke's objections to revolutionary change and applied them to almost any ambitious social planning. All this writing was directed against Marxist theory and communist practice; von Mises and von Hayek also opposed a good deal of the public activity in the mixed economies. As 'Austrians' they were centrally concerned with problems not of motivation but of knowledge: the uncertainties at which business decisions have to guess, the complexities of economic activity which are too great for government to master, the difficulties of prediction which make forward planning unreliable. With many of their conclusions, and the use and misuse of their arguments by others, we do not agree; but for readers interested in the intellectual resources of the liberal Right, Friedrich von Hayek's *The Road to Serfdom* (1944) and *The Constitution of Liberty* (1961), and Karl Popper's *The Open Society and its Enemies* (1946), have much greater depth and intelligence than their equivalents in the public choice literature.

Those ideas were not widely popular through the long boom after the Second World War. Interest in them revived with the end of the boom and the general shift to the Right in the 1970s. At the same time the old liberal differences about relations between individual and community revived with the publication in 1971 of John Rawls' *A Theory of Justice*.

Perennial problems of liberal philosophy occupy the discussion of Rawls' work. Liberals are necessarily pluralists – people only need freedom if they differ in their interests and principles of belief and behaviour. But given their differences, how can a free society avoid falling apart in conflict and disorder – or how can it ensure that majorities don't abridge some freedoms, oppress some minorities, and rank some freedoms above others to their own advantage? What reasoning can distinguish freedom itself, embodied in individual rights, from all the other interests and conceptions of good which contend with one another in a free society?

In one way or another most liberal theorists have begun by making distinctions between right and good, or between justice and morality. The values which they want to protect at all costs, and enforce on or guarantee to everybody, they call matters of right and justice. The values they would allow people to disagree about they call matters of good and morality. The purpose of the distinction is to insist that right and justice are prior to goodness and morality and must prevail over them. Thus a person may have a right to behave immorally, and it may be just to uphold that right. But what reasoning can distinguish the privileged values from the optional ones, prove that the privileged ones are superior, and justify entrenching them in constitutions? By what reasoning can liberals distinguish right from good, justice from morality? To give justice its priority, the two must be established independently of each other: rights and justice must not be supported because they are good or lead to good outcomes; they must have foundations independent of the foundations of morality.

The classical philosophical attempt was made in the 1780s by Immanuel Kant. Freedom is real only if there is choice: not just opportunities for choice but real acts of choice. Kant distinguished the chooser from the things chosen – the 'subject' from the 'objects' of choice – and focused on the chooser. The chooser is free only if he exercises an autonomous will. He is not free if his choices are dictated by his appetites, or by habits or traits of personality instilled into him by his upbringing or his society: to the extent that those forces determine his choices he is not a chooser, he is a mere transmitter of physical or social forces: a transmitter of causes, not a cause himself, and therefore not free. He is free only to the extent that his will is the original, uncaused cause of his choices and actions.

To the extent that a man exercises a free will, his choices are irreducibly moral. He can blame nothing and nobody else for their moral quality and effects. Notice the implications for public choice theory. *Homo economicus* or any other 'rational egoist utility maximizer' is not free at all, he is a creature of compulsive appetite, a mere automaton. Alternatively if such people *are* free their egoism and greed are not fixed in their nature but *are* free choices which they do not have to make and for which they therefore bear full moral responsibility.

Kant was well aware of the presence and force of appetites and social conditioning. Their effects were such that people could not hope to distinguish their free selves from their conditioned selves by introspection. The presence in each person of an element of autonomous will had to be established indirectly by a kind of reasoning that made it a transcendental or metaphysical idea. But if you believe in it, the political implications for liberals are clear. Justice consists in realizing and ensuring the citizens' freedom, i.e. their nature and potentiality as choosers. To entrench anything else but that in a constitution is to *reduce* their freedom. Only if their will can operate independently of any coercion or conditioning – independent of any cause except itself as a free deliberative will – are they truly free. It follows that 'society is best arranged when it is governed by principles that do not presuppose any particular conception of the good, for any other arrangement would fail to respect persons as beings capable of choice'.[12] So constitutions and principles of right and justice should be amoral. Except for protecting freedom itself, they should be merely political constitutions, and principles of justice should be merely procedural. They should neither dictate nor depend on any ideas of social good, they should simply ensure the citizens' rights to choose. Nothing in Kant's argument suggests that free citizens will or should choose selfishly, or prefer selfish to cooperative or communal lifestyles. Nevertheless because it sets right before and above good, and because in practice such rights are exercised by people plentifully influenced by appetites and social conditioning, Kant's highly moral conception of freedom can be thought to justify what critics from Right and Left of it see as the traditional, squalid, class-biased liberal licence for unrestricted greed and exploitation: what matters to liberals is not how much evil people do to each other, but that they can freely choose to do it.

Through four decades from his first paper in 1951 John Rawls worked to repair one weakness in Kant's argument, one liberal misuse of it, and one unresolved conflict in traditional American aspirations.

Kant's 'subject' or autonomous individual will is not something that can be observed in action or discovered by introspection. No socially conditioned eye can disentangle it (if it exists at all) from the appetites and conditioning by which it is affected or with which it coexists. So Kant's will has to be posited or imagined as a metaphysical notion in which modern, rational people may find it hard to believe. To anchor it in reality, Rawls invites people to imagine what principles of government they would choose to live by if they had to choose them in advance, behind a veil of ignorance, not knowing what their own social roles, capacities or situations might be: whether rich or poor, powerful or powerless, clever or not, and so on. In that situation which Rawls calls 'the original position' he expects that reasonable people would agree to have institutions which allowed the greatest freedom consistent with equal freedom for all; and for other goods than freedom he expects that they would be risk-averse and agree to a radical limitation of material inequalities. Though people in the original position do not know what their interests, tastes or moral preferences will be in the real world, they do know about basic human needs for food, shelter and income. Because Rawls thinks they will fear poverty more intensely than they desire wealth, he expects them to agree to a principle of distributive justice which he calls 'the difference principle': inequalities should be limited to those which, by the behaviour they motivate, actually improve the income of the poorest.

Why that revolutionary rule? People in the original position don't know what natural or social assets they will have in real life, so they face a lottery, and its risks convince them of its random injustice: 'distributive shares are decided by the outcome of the natural lottery; and this outcome is arbitrary from a moral perspective. There is no more reason to permit the distribution of income and wealth to be settled by the distribution of natural assets than by historical and social fortune.' Faced with the risks of that lottery, reasonable people take out insurance; they agree in effect 'to regard the distribution of natural talents as a common asset and to share in the benefits of this distribution whatever it turns out to be.'[13] Compare Marx's principle 'from each according to his ability, to each according to his need'.

Thus Rawls offers equal freedom to everyone, a radical limit on material inequalities, and a resolution of the endemic conflict in American life and thought between the principles of equality and freedom; and he suggests that these principles of justice should be agreed by all reasonable people quite independently of their differing and often conflicting material interests, moral principles and conceptions of social good.

Ideas of good (as opposed to right) are the second main subject of *A Theory of Justice*. Just as Rawls has proposed a rational foundation for justice, so he proposes a rational foundation for ideas of good, including moral good. Good, he argues, is a purely descriptive word. Things are good if they perform their functions well: a good spade, a good dinner, a good mashie shot. So are people in their various roles: a good bricklayer, a good mother, a good bridge-player. But what distinguishes a good *person*? A good person is one who is good at carrying out a good life plan. A good life plan is one which is well designed to serve good ends. The ends which people want to achieve are determined by three things. First, their desires (which may include affections, desires to be loved and well-regarded, to enjoy the pleasures as well as the material advantages of human association; desires are not all greedy or antisocial). Second, their capabilities: to be good, life plans need to be achievable by the people concerned in the circumstances in which they find themselves. Third is the Aristotelian principle that 'human beings enjoy the exercise of their realized capacities (their innate or trained abilities), and this enjoyment increases the more the capacity is realized, or the greater its complexity.' Why is that so? 'Presumably complex activities are more enjoyable because they satisfy the desire for variety and novelty of experience, and leave room for feats of ingenuity and invention. They also evoke the pleasures of anticipation and surprise, and often the overall form of the activity ... is fascinating and beautiful. Moreover, simpler activities exclude the possibility of individual style and personal expression which complex activities permit or even require, for how could everyone do them in the same way?' (pp. 426–7)

We still lack a principle of good to distinguish good from bad desires. Why is a life devoted to (say) good government or life-saving science better than a life devoted – with full Aristotelian skill and enjoyable complexity – to cruelty or crime? To this fundamental question some philosophers give utilitarian answers: what is good is what causes the greatest happiness to the greatest number. Others invoke moral intuitions, emotional indicators or religious revelations or commands, i.e. sources of moral principle other than rational self-interest. Rawls avoids both those options. His principles of justice, already established as prudent self-interest for people uncertain of their individual fortunes, allow him to depict morality as prudent self-interest too. The principles of justice will suffice to tell good desires and ends from bad. Behind the veil of ignorance, the citizens have decided for self-interested reasons to pool their individual endowments for social use, to 'share one another's fate'. So 'a good person is one who has to a higher degree than the average the properties which it is rational for citizens to want in one another.' Those properties include all the standard virtues which need to be instilled into and cultivated by the people if the principles and institutions of a just society are to be secure and function well. So 'the fundamental virtues are among the broadly based properties that it is rational for members of a well-ordered society to want in one another.' (pp. 435–6) Thus four hundred and thirty seven pages of argument have arrived at the 'golden rule' that it is in your interest to do unto others as you would have them do unto you. It doesn't require any special moral principle, command from God, or actual goodwill toward others except by way of exchange.

The theories of justice and goodness are thus built on rational individualist foundations. Logically speaking, individuals are the prime movers: they constitute society, and they act in it according to their diverse interests and moral principles, under no constraints except those to which with prudent self-interest they have willingly agreed. Those elements of the theory may appear to accord with public choice theory, but the rest does not. A prohibitive difference between markets and political systems is spelled out on p. 360 of *A Theory of Justice*; and in the two principles of justice, in the account of moral goods in Part Three of the book, and in response to criticism since, Rawls has emphasized that his theory not only introduces a radical principle of equality, it also allows (and Rawls expects) most citizens to enter voluntarily into plenty of cooperative activity, to constitute communities in which they enjoy and value their membership, and to encourage virtues of affection and compassion in the common culture they develop together. Between individualists and communitarians Rawls thus occupies a conciliatory middle position, having reasoned his way from individualist premises to quite sociable conclusions. In the words of his most savage critic, 'Rawls's innovation is to incorporate the maxims of contemporary social welfare into the fundamental principles of political justice.'[14] In Rawls' words 'The social system is not an unchangeable order beyond human control but a pattern of human action. In justice as fairness men agree to share one another's fate.'[15]

Just as this chapter cannot do justice to Rawls' argument, it cannot do justice to his critics either. What follow are the briefest indications of some practical difficulties with the theory of justice; a principled objection from the liberal Right; and some argument from those, including the present authors, who think that perhaps Rawls, and certainly some of his followers, underestimate the necessary contribution of moral intuition and community life to individual identity and freedom. We also think that unanimous, nonmoral or neutral principles of justice are impossible.

Practical difficulties
People in Rawls' original position know that there will be material inequalities in the real world and that they will dislike being poor. We do not agree

that everyone in that position would therefore be risk-averse. First there are likely to be some gamblers. Second there are likely to be some who think they may value the challenge and interest of a diverse, unequal, competitive society above whatever value they put on the minimum income which is guaranteed by the difference principle. So in the original position as described, we do not think *all* reasonable people would agree to limit inequalities. Even if they agreed to do so they could never agree how to go about it. It is nearly impossible to know what inequalities will actually get the poorest people the highest incomes. The analysis of direct and indirect social causation depends on so much valuing and selecting of the causal chains to be traced, the conditions to be accepted as fixed and those to be treated as variable, the human acts to be treated as choices and those to be treated as mere transmitters of other forces – and so on – that there could be no agreed knowledge of how much of which inequalities were necessary to maximize the poorest people's incomes. Moreover the matter is usually open to manipulation, especially by the richest of those concerned. To maximize the poorest incomes, the best available executives need to manage public and private business as well as they possibly can. What rewards will induce them to do that? As argued earlier, *they* currently decide what to take. How would a Rawlsian republic decide it? On the one hand psychological and managerial wisdom suggest that top people want the top rate whatever it is. Its distance above the rest has not appeared to affect performance; for example the recent escalation of executive 'take' does not seem to have brought generally better performance. Nor should it in economic theory: income changes can have both income and substitution effects. (More pay per unit of work may motivate more work – or by making a desired income available for less work it may motivate less.) On the other hand executives have developed a group capacity to manipulate the prevailing rates and would be well placed to extort whatever they saw fit as the price of their best performance. What practical use is the difference principle if analysis can't determine *what* inequalities will do most for the poorest incomes, or be proof against manipulation by interested parties?

The principle of 'equal freedom for all' also has practical difficulties. Unanimous agreement about its implementation seems impossible. To agree how to contrive equal freedom for all, people have to agree the value judgements which rank freedoms in relation to each other: will all the people have *this* freedom, or all have *that* (incompatible) one? This freedom which only half the people will actually use, or that one which the other half will use? Will all have free speech (to make instructional pornographic films), economic freedom (to market them), and personal freedom to walk safe streets by day and night? People cannot even agree whether or not those freedoms are compatible, let alone which of them to prefer if they are not; and each is valuable to different groups. Thus although people on the Left may applaud Rawls' principles, his theory does not help to reduce the technical or political difficulties which social-democrats have always had in trying to apply them.

Libertarian objections

In *Anarchy, State and Utopia* (1974) Robert Nozick offered a more ruthless version of John Locke's seventeenth-century argument that rights to property are prior to government. However unequally property may be owned, no principle of justice should allow government to interfere with it: 'there is no moral outweighing of one of our lives by others so as to lead to a greater overall *social* good. There is no justified sacrifice of some of us for others' (p. 33). If you believe that (which Nozick no longer does), you will not accept that Rawls' difference principle should limit the amount anyone may own, or allow the rich to be taxed for the benefit of the poor.

Philosophical objections

Some philosophers do not think it possible, even by reflective abstraction, to strip away everything that appetites and experience have contributed to a person's character, and still leave an 'unencumbered self' able to exercise a pure, 'uncaused' will. A will as unencumbered as that would have too vacant a mind to will anything. One cannot actually think of oneself existing at no time, in no place, with no past and no experience of human company, yet capable of inventing principles of public justice and private morality for an as yet unknown society, and (hardest to imagine) still interested enough to invent such things. It is to avoid these impossibilities that Rawls invites ordinary worldly people, rather than abstractions, to decide what distributive principles they *would* support *if* they could set aside their particular interests and moral beliefs. He expects that self-interest would prompt them to choose his low-risk principles of equality and difference. Why would the losers from those rules – the people who would otherwise benefit from greater inequality – then support the rules in the real world in full knowledge of their personal costs? It could only be for moral reasons, from a generosity, or a preference for compassionate social principles, that they were not asked to show behind the veil of ignorance. Rawls claims to write for the real world, with reformist intent. Why introduce the device of the veil of ignorance? It allows a pretence that the proposed principles could attract unanimous, exclusively self-interested support. What use is that fiction if the principles have no hope of unanimous self-interested support in the real world, and even majority support for them must depend on some at least of the citizens having benevolent moral natures? Rawls is really asking his readers and imagined citizens a straightforward moral question: what would be fair distributive principles for government to impose in the real world of unequal endowments and conflicting interests? The egalitarian principles which he suggests could only appeal to the moral sense of many of his readers. The goods to be achieved by the proposed principles are not different in kind from the other goods that people disagree about in pluralist societies.

In this view, the ideas of good which underlie people's moral principles also underlie their beliefs about the political rights people should have and the desirable functions and limits of government. Liberal efforts to distinguish 'good' from 'right' – i.e. to distinguish behaviour which government should be allowed to regulate from behaviour it should leave alone – are like any other efforts to distinguish more valuable from less valuable goods. Freedom is good and life is good – which good should prevail in deciding whether people should be free to murder? Liberals value some freedoms above other goods, including some freedoms above other freedoms. In doing so, and in trying to give operational meaning to such vague principles as 'equal freedom for all' or 'all freedoms that do not interfere with other freedoms' they differ from other moral thinkers only in detail. In democratic societies nearly everyone wants the traditional freedoms of speech, assembly, worship, privacy, movement, due process of arrest and trial, and so on. Hardly anyone wants to free the citizens to murder, rape, enslave, injure, rob or defraud one another. Detailed differences arise mostly in particular areas of business, educational and sexual activity. When they do, liberals should argue like anyone else for their values, but without trying to privilege some of them as right rather than good, i.e. as prior, different in kind, or spuriously unanimous.

There remains a cluster of ideas about relations between individuals, their societies and their freedoms which are variously labelled social liberal, Aristotelian or communitarian. We will try to combine them in a composite sketch of a liberal Aristotelian communitarian pluralist social philosophy.

COMMUNITARIANS

An opening summary: People live in communities which do much to both form and free their members. Societies have histories, cultures, institutions, in which many ideas of good are incorporated. Though much influenced by those ideas, people continue to reflect on them, disagree about them, criticize and revise them. Like other liberals, communitarians put high values on individuality and the two conditions of freedom: the *scope* for choice and invention, and the *capacity* to choose and invent. Where other liberals tend to think people are freest when least influenced by others, communitarians think it takes a lot of history and collective action both to develop the complex society that offers a great diversity of options, and to bring up individuals with confident, skilful capacities to think and choose for themselves. Though mostly developed by communitarian liberals, these ideas offer equally good philosophical foundations for conservative, socialist, feminist or environmental theory. With that happy capacity they make a fitting conclusion to our argument.

'Hardly anyone', we said a page or two back, 'wants to free people to murder, rape, enslave, injure, rob or defraud one another.' Imagine three approaches to avoiding such misbehaviour. A liberal wants government to bar those freedoms because they endanger more valuable freedoms. A communitarian wants society to bring up people with built-in moral principles which restrain them from evildoing; the law is just a back-up, to restrain anyone whose upbringing fails to stick. An Aristotelian wants people to do without bad behaviour because they have no use for it: it has no place in the enterprise of living life to realize their highest human potentialities.

Modern Aristotelians update Aristotle's aristocratic principles by extending them to everybody, and to ordinary life. Since his time an economic revolution has made most work tolerable and a lot of it interesting; and forty hours of it suffices to support eighty waking hours away from it for other enjoyable activities. The new productivity has also enabled everyone to be literate, better informed about the world than Aristotle could be, and acquainted at the touch of a switch with the highest arts. So everyone, not just a leisured upper class, can realize high human potentialities. The idea of individual potentiality is not metaphysical. It rests on what human beings have done, practical imagination of what more they might do, and judgements about the desirability of their diverse possibilities.

Human beings are a double mix, of lower and higher nature, and of nature and nurture. We are creatures 'between beasts and gods', with elements of animal nature and appetite, but also reflective, inventive and moral capacities above those of other species. In our natures there are diverse potentialities – for cruel and destructive behaviour, for innocent breadwinning and recreation, for love and friendship, and for high intellectual, artistic and political achievement. The limits which our genetic nature imposes on those developmental possibilities are uncertain, but within whatever they are, the most important task of science, art, philosophy and government is to develop the self-understanding and the social arrangements which will allow the members of society to realize, exercise and enjoy their highest potentialities. That is already a moral requirement and it calls for further judgements, individual and collective, as to which potentialities are 'high', which are compatible with which, and by what principles and procedures any conflicts between them should be resolved.

High potentialities are not confined to high life as they seemed to be in classical Athens; they are present in everyone's daily life. Household production, recreation and family life see many of the worst cruelties, the dullest drudgery, the saddest emptiness and aridity of life – and also the most welcome security, the most absorbing and satisfying activity, the deepest, richest, least selfish, most enduring love, and for good or ill a large part of everyone's character formation. The extreme potentialities for good and evil are inspiring and appalling. To live family life better rather than worse is at least as important as to have better rather than worse artists, philosophers and politicians – so much so that a good deal of today's art, philosophy and politics is designed to enable or inspire people to live private life well, and to encourage them to think for themselves how to live it best given their individual passions and potentialities. One utilitarian idea which communitarians welcome is thus the 'affirmation of ordinary life'. But they insist that its quality depends on more than the utilitarian satisfaction of desires. It depends also on the nature of the desires: the quality of the people's aspirations, and their will and capacity to live up to them.

What does that mean in practice? What will an individual make of the raw materials she has to work with: her innate potentialities and limitations, her family and social situation, the opportunities to learn from others, the confidence with which she learns from experience and picks and chooses among the conflicting moral ideas her society offers her? In developing a character for herself and a capacity to decide her own directions she will face opportunities of, morally speaking, four general kinds.

First there are opportunities to get on (or drop out) by crime or other bad behaviour. If she has wholesome Aristotelian ambitions those temptations won't occur to her. If she has communitarian moral principles she will resist them if they do occur to her. If she has neither of those self-restraints she needs to be deterred by fear of detection and punishment, and all societies have law, police and informal social sanctions for that purpose. The Aristotelian option is the best: it costs neither the individual nor the community anything. The second costs the community nothing – instilling good morals into people is at least as cheap in the long run as instilling bad morals or none. The more those two can reduce the need for coercion, the better – policing costs money and makes opportunities for further evil in the dangerous powers police and prison staff have to have.

Second, there is a vast range and variety of innocent work and recreation open to our representative citizen: occupations from Accounting to Zoo-keeping, recreations from Archery to Zen contemplation. Much of what she elects to do in those areas may accord well enough with rational choice or utility-maximizing theories. Nevertheless moral thought will have contributed to the law and custom that define what activities are permissible, and to regulating many of them. She herself may have moral reasons among others for her choices; and her relations with workmates, acquaintances and strangers in the course of her daily activities will owe some of their value, and the joy or pain they cause her, to the moral qualities of everyone's behaviour and of the prevailing social norms and institutional arrangements.

Third, there are relations with kin, friends, lovers, comrades in arms, sometimes business partners: anyone on the other end of her climber's rope. These relations cannot be sufficiently explained or valued by the elements of self-interested exchange which many of them contain. That is specially true of her loves. Introspection, our knowledge of the people we know best, and much of the world's best art agree that most humans have an even more imperative need to love than to be loved. Happily or miserably they often love other creatures – people, pets, pop stars they've not actually met – who don't love them in return. Some loves are possessive or oppressive. Some include or have some likeness to desires. Others are better described as acts of will, as love is defined by some Christian philosophers. Some are difficult to describe at all by anyone who insists on strict distinctions between facts and values. Above all many are generous, self-sacrificing if necessary, genuinely willing the good of the loved rather than the lover. The most important of all the qualities of life for a great many people are the affectionate qualities of their loves, friendships and family life.

Fourth are the goods with which Aristotle was most concerned: the highest capacities for art, science, philosophy and government. They are judged to be highest for a number of reasons. They are the capacities which most decisively differentiate humans from other species. They are the most difficult skills calling for the highest intelligence and moral discrimination. They are the most influential in ordering other goods and shaping a society's law, education and public institutions. Aristotle thought that to excel in these occupations was to realize one's humanity to the fullest. We may think that friendship and family life can also realize the best in us, and (in bringing people up) can do much to generate the capacities that Aristotle celebrated. Both ideals can be compared with James Buchanan's and

Gordon Tullock's ideal of a society whose artists, scientists, philosophers, politicians, public servants and voting citizens use their high capacities and public powers chiefly for private enrichment, restrained only by rules against theft and capital taxation.

How liberal are the communitarian and Aristotelian ideals? How free in practice are societies in which such ideals prevail? Do they aim to impose an authoritative vision of good on a censored, conformist society, as some of their critics fear?

Communitarians think it a gross mistake, which many liberals make, to suppose that people are freer the less they have been influenced by others. People need plenty of teaching – by family, school, friends, employers, fellow workers and daily experience of life – to discover and develop their faculties, including their deliberating and choosing faculties. Individual independence and self-reliance are partly social, perhaps chiefly social, creations. They are of course optional creations – students can resist liberating lessons, teachers can teach oppressively – but the remedy for that is to reform, not abolish, the education. It is also to keep the teaching plural. Plenty of parents, teachers and pastors teach people to resist oppressive government. Quite a lot of law, public services and public education are there to free young people from oppressive parents, churches or employers. The traditional liberal education, one of the glories of western civilization, is designed above all to develop people's capacity for self-reliant reflection, judgement and choice. To the extent that it also teaches them not to murder, rape, enslave and so on, it merely conveys prohibitions which liberals of all persuasions want to enforce. But in introducing pupils to as wide a variety as possible of 'the best that has been thought' including the best contradictions and disagreements – in making them read Aristotle as well as Plato, Machiavelli as well as Aquinas, Locke as well as Hobbes, Burke as well as Rousseau, Marx as well as Mill, Keynes as well as Hayek, Taylor as well as Rawls, and for half a century now quite a lot of non-Western art and comparative religion – it not only avoids telling its apprentices what to think, at its best it rewards them chiefly for the quality and originality of what they think for themselves. It does also try to instil some privileged values, like honesty and mutual respect, but high among them (once again) are the values put on freedom, originality and intellectual self-reliance. As rising proportions of young people stay longer at school, popular versions of that curriculum are developed with the same liberating and enabling purposes, with attention to life skills, problem-solving skills, and current political and moral controversies including questions of international and environmental ethics.

Liberal education and the independent, individually-directed research which accompanies some of it are one source of democratic societies' capacity for self-criticism and debate about what is good. They feed other sources as they supply talent, research and argument to a free press and to salaried opposition politicians and back-benchers doing their professional best to convince the citizens that the government, and often enough the social principles it stands for, could be bettered. In a society with unequal distributions of wealth and private power it is not likely that freedom, self-criticism and social progress will be improved by cutting these public resources. If education is only for those who can pay for it, research resources go only to those with private patrons, the courts are accessible only to those who can pay counsel and afford appeals, and members of the legislature need private incomes or paymasters, individual freedom and social criticism are likely to fare worse than they do now.

Three recent books relate this communitarian critique to actual institutions. In *Whose Keeper? Social Science and Moral Obligation* (1989) Alan Wolfe defends the communitarian emphasis of Scandinavian institutions against the individualism underlying comparable institutional structures and practices in the United States. In *The Good Society* (1991) Robert Bellah and his co-authors depict a general malaise in American society and a need for change in the formative institutions of 'family, school, community, corporation, church, state and nation'. In *The Moral Commonwealth: Social theory and the promise of community* (1992) Philip Selznick focuses on recent philosophical and theoretical debates in the social sciences about the need for a communitarian change of direction in modern societies. All three link philosophical to social analysis in proposing communal institutions which would encourage more equal and cooperative societies while respecting diverse values.

The practical reasons why freedom and individuality are partly social creations overlap with psychological and philosophical reasons. Some of those are argued simply by Michael Sandel in *Liberalism and the Limits of Justice* (1982), and most originally and elaborately by Charles Taylor in *Sources of the Self: The making of the modern identity* (1989). Philosophers of this school argue that Kant's, Rawls' and others' idea of an 'unencumbered self' is a mistake. A human self is constituted partly by its bodily existence but of necessity also by its experience, moral intuitions and social environment. Learning is something which the self does, but it also transforms the self. Individuals have self-knowing, self-critical, self-changing capacities just as liberal societies do. When a person learns or decides that some things are good and some bad, and thereafter sees them as good and bad, the disposition to recognize their moral 'colour' in that way becomes an element of the person's character, a quality of the self. It becomes a quality of Kant's and Rawls' 'subject', the chooser, the will itself which decides – among other things – what itself should *be*, as well as what it should believe and do.

Some philosophers may still insist that for a self to have attributes – skills, purposes, moral opinions – there must be a subject, a self which 'has' those things, a will which decides to have them. Otherwise who or what is it that possesses them? There are complicated answers to that question but we think a simple answer will do. The verb 'to have' does not require a subject separate from its object, nor does our way of thinking about the parts and attributes of any complex entity require it. A horse 'has' a head, body, legs and tail. No independent fifth entity exists to 'have' those parts; what 'has' them is the whole which they constitute. We can imagine a headless or tailless or legless horse; but we do not look into a vacant stable and think here must be a horse without four of its parts. When a person has, i.e. owns, a horse, the subject is different from the object. When a person has a brain, a club foot or a sweet disposition, those are parts of the whole. When a person has one purpose one day but a different purpose next day, friends who dislike the change may say 'You're not yourself today' and friends who like the new purpose or think it more coherent with the person's other purposes may say 'This is the *real* you'. The difference is not significant. People certainly change. They can also change their purposes or strategies, on occasion, without changing their character much. Whether a particular change of belief or disposition is best understood as a change in the self or as an unchanged self choosing to act differently is a question of degree, interpretation, opinion; it may often depend on value judgements of the relative importance of the similarities and differences between the two phases. Judgements one way or another cannot entitle philosophers or constitution-makers to distinguish the citizen's 'real' self which wills (as free, or as agreeing with all other citizens' wills) from the actual characteristics and dispositions of the citizen's will (as unfree because conditioned by society, or as deserving less power or protection because in disagreement with others).

Thus ideas of goodness and attitudes to it are part of everyone's character: part of the subject self which makes up its mind (for example) what political rights it thinks people should have, what kinds of behaviour government should regulate and what kinds it should not. Ideas of good underlie thought about right and justice just as necessarily as they underlie thought about censorship, sexual behaviour, education, or any of the other subjects which liberals want people to be free to disagree about. Freedom itself is a concept with irreducible moral elements. Moral thought has to decide whether the absence of external constraint or the presence of an internal capacity to choose is the mark of the freedom that matters. There can even be moral uncertainties about the internal capacity to choose. Imagine for example two people, for convenience a woman and a man, one more fair-minded than the other. In living her life the woman's more scrupulous moral character and reasoning constrain her to choose her behaviour from a narrower range of options than the less scrupulous man is prepared to consider. This is partly because the woman acknowledges a greater individual responsibility for her choices: she makes them freely, and answers for them. The man is prone to blame 'human nature', 'necessity' or 'social pressures' for any of his choices that harm other people, and he believes those excuses himself. Thus one person reduces her options because she sees herself as freer and more autonomous; the other allows himself to choose from a wider range of options because he sees his will as less free, more naturally and socially constrained. Only a moral judgement can decide which of the two should be regarded as more free, or the relative value that should be put on the external freedom to choose from wider options, and the internal conviction that one's choices are free and one's own.

How are ideas of good arrived at?

This is not the place for the classical philosophical discussions of the question. But whatever their nature, such ideas reach us from particular sources or are conceived in particular circumstances, and their sources in that practical sense are important to anyone interested in relations between individuals, their communities, their freedom and their ideas of good. They are specially relevant to the liberal claim to distinguish 'right' as prior and superior to 'good'.

Charles Taylor distinguishes internal from transcendent goods. The first arise in particular social systems or situations, the second go with being human. Families, institutions, societies are organized in particular ways which require particular kinds of behaviour based on particular ideas of good, to function well. What is good behaviour in a bank or an air traffic control office might not be so good in an art school or a field hospital. What is good in a family may not always be good in government. Charles I was said to be a good father but a bad king. Those judgements refer to virtues specific to family life and government. As a person Charles was brave but deceitful. Courage is a virtue and deceit is a vice in kings and beggars alike and in friends and enemies alike. Regardless of the purposes they happen to be serving they are thought to be transcendent moral qualities of humans in any circumstances.

Ideas of good reach us from many sources: parents and teachers, the law, the rules and practices of institutions and associations, art and history. We reflect on particular ways of behaving; on the quality of life in particular families, associations, societies; on others' arguments past and present. We judge details: a good thought, a good action. We judge what we perceive as wholes: whole lives, whole societies, whole processes of growth and change. We judge parts and wholes in relation to each other. It is from all this experience – not from a single source or by reference to a single principle or authority – that we distil our ideas of what it is good to be, how it is good to live, what it is good to do in a general way and in particular circumstances. We do not do it only by reference to our material interests, or only as we are taught by a single authority, or only by reasoning of Rawls' kind, or only by emulating people we love or admire. We distil wisdom from all these sources. Their diversity does not necessarily cause confusion. Plenty of coherent personalities reason their way to coherent ideas of good and principles of action in this eclectic way.

In studying existing ideas of what is good, political philosophers do well to pay special attention to exotic societies remote in place and time. To decide what people and societies should desirably be like, it helps to know what they could possibly be like. Nobody can know exactly how our genetic nature limits our moral and social potentialities – much ideological disagreement springs from different estimates of what humans could or could not inspire, educate or force each other to be and do. The best though still imperfect guide may be to learn as much as possible about the diversity achieved so far: the social arrangements and collective norms that have existed, or been tried and failed. Few people foresaw the capacity for genocide, not just by impersonal bombing but face to face by tens of thousands of executioners in mass, assembly-line exterminations, that this century discovered. When the medieval historian Richard Southern heard it said that there could never be much productive work or invention without competitive financial incentives he recalled that the eleventh and twelfth century revolutions in science, farm accounting and productivity were mostly conceived and carried out by celibates sworn to poverty. In *Patterns of Culture* (1934) the anthropologist Ruth Benedict compared the economies, social structures and ideas of good of three indigenous western American societies. A secure farming community ran on love and conformity. A tribe hunting over disputed territory exalted cruelty and the warrior virtues. The Kwakiutl, fishing in safe, abundant waters, invented capitalist values and the ostentatious waste of wealth.

We need not suppose that travellers from any of those or other unlike cultures would necessarily have regarded the others with uncomprehending disapproval. However conditioned, people still in varying degrees see and think for themselves. When people look into their own minds and feelings and consider their own and others' experience of life – experience known directly, and vicariously from books and arts – most of them conclude without needing to be told that in ordinary circumstances love is better than hate, kindness better than cruelty, friendship better than enmity, fidelity better than betrayal, peace better than war but (when occasion demands) courage better than cowardice, and so on. Conceptions of those traditional virtues and vices vary between individuals and cultures, but they also overlap a good deal. Many of the judgements do not seem very different in kind from other qualitative judgements – that health is better than sickness, repletion better than hunger, interest better than boredom, most laughter better than most tears. Adam Smith's *Theory of Moral Sentiments* (1759) has scarcely been bettered as a description of the sympathy with others' joy and suffering that people feel, often as 'factually' as they feel their own joy and suffering, much as they feel heat and cold. People also recognize many goods and evils much as they recognize colours (for which individual eyesight also varies). As the matters for judgement shade off into more difficult or disagreed issues, as selfish concerns complicate them and as different goods conflict with one another, the judgements bear more resemblance to the moral judgements of the philosophers' fact/value split: the "oughts" that cannot logically be derived from any "is". The moral, valuing faculties that are then brought to bear are variously called intuitions, emotional responses, self-interested rationalizations, considerations of prudence or mere caprices.

By what means can one idea of good be compared with another, or one society with its prevailing ideas of good be compared with another? Many moderns have been taught that the only scientific way, which would be the only valid way, to compare one good with another would have to be factually based and independent of the ideas to be compared: 'deductive arguments proceeding from premises that are true, necessary and external to all history'.[16] For people who believe that those would be the only valid tests but are impossible, because there is no logical way from 'is' to 'ought', it seems to follow that ideas of good are mere subjective feelings, or masks for material interests or bids for power. How do people live with that 'moral vacuum'? Some conclude to 'look after number one' as carefree hedonists. Some are depressed, find life meaningless and living pointless.

Taylor proposes other bases of comparison between ideas of good: 'practical explanations of their merits that are fully internal to human history, non-deductive in structure, seeking coherence and fit between theory and our deepest and most indispensable beliefs about ourselves'.[17] Ethical views may not be hard to compare when one succeeds another, perhaps resolving difficulties in the first and incorporating its ideas of good into some more coherent scheme. We have already noticed some examples. The classical Greek ideal of citizenship had an internal inconsistency: it based its idea of good on universal human potentialities but then, chiefly for economic reasons, denied that its idea of good was available to women, slaves or other manual workers. Modern Aristotelians resolve the difficulty by extending the ideal to everyone. Who would now want to return to minority citizenship and 'minority humanity'? But there is a new difficulty. Not everyone can realize what Aristotle proposed as the highest human potentialities – there is neither room nor talent for everyone to be an original artist, philosopher or politician. That difficulty is resolved by the affirmation of ordinary life. In modern economic conditions, high ideals of family life and love, and work and recreation to the limit of each individual's capacities, become plausible. Having conceived the expanded vision and gone some way toward realizing it, who would argue for a return to slavery, the subjection of women, and minimal support for children as the unwilled consequences of our sexual nature?

Like liberal ideas of justice, these ideas do relate to what people can have – but only instrumentally, as material means which affect what they can choose to *be* and *do*. Besides appropriate shares of wealth, income, food, shelter and so on, communitarians want forms of organization which offer satisfying roles to the people in them. Besides short hours and good pay, workers want to be able to contribute to the purpose and arrangement of their work. Besides protection from neglect or maltreatment, children need loving, stimulating, liberating family life. Besides equal access to education they need the kinds of education and recreation that discover and develop their best potentialities. Thus where liberals want to distribute economic output in some fair way, communitarians also want it produced in fulfilling ways, which may not always be how market forces would arrange it. Where liberals judge tax, welfare and other non-market distributions by the shares people get, communitarians judge them also by the human relations involved in the distributive procedures.

These arguments converge on the conclusion that our social experience does much to constitute our individuality, reasoning powers and ideas of good, which in turn constantly re-shape our social arrangements and the ideas of good which they incorporate. Since ideas of good are inescapable we should be explicit rather than evasive about them. Areas of neutrality may be contrived institutionally for particular purposes, to provide impartial judges and auditors and umpires, but even those are supposed to be ruled by high moral principles, not by none.

It is to avoid having government or political philosophy favour any one idea of good against others, and thus limit the citizens' freedom to differ, that liberals want to set right above good, and entrench rights in purely procedural constitutions and principles of justice which do not incorporate or depend on ideas of good. Communitarians think that confuses a proper desire for free speech and fair procedures in deciding what institutions it would be good to build, with the different and mistaken idea that the laws and institutions can then be built without incorporating any ideas of good. In fact many institutions, in the most liberal society, have to incorporate particular, often disagreed, ideas of good. And liberals like everyone else want to pick and choose between good and bad freedoms and restraints. They have no right to privilege their particular list of goods as rights required by justice, while belittling conservative, socialist, feminist, environmentalist or any other lists of desired freedoms and restraints as merely subjective 'moral preferences' or 'ideas of good' of inferior status.

By consensus, by majority, or by governmental or bureaucratic choice, better or worse ideas of good, including better or worse freedoms and restraints, have to be built into the structure and practice of innumerable social institutions. Since there are no neutral options, communitarians want the ideas of good to be explicit and widely discussed as important. Where some liberals fear that too much debate about moral principles may be divisive or may encourage ambitions to have government enforce some illiberal 'one true good', communitarians hope it will deepen and sophisticate everyone's moral thought and lead to more and better-based consensus or more respectful and better understood differences. Far from necessarily reducing either freedom or consensus, the heart of the communitarian argument is that this approach is more likely to enhance them.

If any reader wants a conclusion to this chapter and book, it is this. We did not set out to persuade you to accept our own positive beliefs. Your beliefs about economic and social policy are your own. They express your values and practical understanding of how the world works. Unavoidably, the values and practical understanding colour one another to some extent. But we think neither is likely to be improved by use of the public choice and other theories we have attacked: whatever society you aspire to build, with whatever pattern of conservative, liberal, social-democratic, communitarian, feminist and environmental qualities, the traditions of thought which go by those names offer better guides to action, or starting points for new thought.

Notes

CHAPTER 1: MOTIVES

1. James M. Buchanan, 'The Pure Theory of Government Finance: A Suggested Approach', *Journal of Political Economy* 57 (1949) pp. 496–505; Kenneth Arrow, 'A Difficulty in the Concept of Social Welfare', *Journal of Political Economy* 58 (1950) pp. 328–46; Paul A. Samuelson, 'The Pure Theory of Public Expenditure', *Review of Economics and Statistics* 36 (1954) pp. 387–9.
2. D.C. Mueller, *Public Choice*, Cambridge University Press, 1979 and *Public Choice II*, 1989; H. van den Doel, *Democracy and Welfare Economics*, Cambridge University Press, 1979; R. Sugden, *The Political Economy of Public Choice: An Introduction to Welfare Economics*, Oxford, Martin Robertson, 1981; B.S. Frey, *Democratic Economic Policy: A Theoretical Introduction*, Oxford, Basil Blackwell, 1983; J. Bonner, *Politics, Economics and Welfare: An Elementary Introduction to Social Choice*, Brighton, Sussex, Wheatsheaf Books, 1986; I. McLean, *Public Choice: An Introduction*, Oxford, Basil Blackwell, 1987; D. Reisman, *The Political Economy of James Buchanan*, College Station, Texas A&M University Press, 1990; D. Reisman, *Theories of Collective Action: Downs, Olson and Hirsch*, London, Macmillan, 1990; P. Dunleavy, *Democracy, Bureaucracy and Public Choice: Economic Explanations in Political Science*, New York, Harvester Wheatsheaf, 1991.
3. *The Theory of Moral Sentiments* VII, ii, 2.14.

CHAPTER 2: A VERY SHORT HISTORY

1. *Journal of Political Economy* 57 (1949) pp. 496–506.
2. *Journal of Political Economy* 58 (1950) pp. 328–46.
3. Reprinted in James M. Buchanan, *Fiscal Theory and Political Economy: Selected Essays* (1960).
4. *Fiscal Theory and Political Economy*, pp. 83, 85.
5. *Review of Economics and Statistics* 36 (1954) pp. 386–9.
6. *World Politics* 12 (1960) pp. 541–63.
7. *Journal of Political Economy* 65 (1957) pp. 135–50.
8. The same, pp. 135–8.
9. The same, pp. 139–40, 148.
10. *Social Research* 29 (1962), For the quotations that follow, see the following footnote.
11. The same, pp. 1, 3, 5, 6, 23–5, 33.
12. *Journal of Political Economy* 67 (1959).
13. The same, pp. 576–7, 579.
14. *Journal of Political Economy* 69 (1961) pp. 192–9.
15. James M. Buchanan, *Liberty, Market and State* (1986) pp. 19–27.
16. *The Calculus of Consent* p. 252.

17. Reprinted in R. A. Musgrave and A.T. Peacock, *Classics in the Theory of Public Finance* (1958) pp. 108–9.
18. Charles K. Rowley, 'The Calculus of Consent', in Charles K. Rowley (ed.) *Democracy and Public Choice: Essays in Honor of Gordon Tullock* (1987) pp. 42–3.
19. *Journal of Political Economy* 72 (1964) pp. 87–8.
20. *American Economic Review* 2 (1962) pp. 1217–18.
21. John Crecine, *The American Political Science Review* 63 (1969) p. 182.
22. This chapter is not criticizing the work it lists, though this sneer strains the rule; but instead of offering evidence for his theory Niskanen asks readers to test it by their own experience. Our experience includes teaching students in British, American and Australian universities and service in state and city planning offices, in efficient public housing and industrial development enterprises and in inefficient ones, in clubs and camps for hard-up children, in disease and infestation control in the US forest service, in various research activities and in armed services in war. All those activities are bureaucratic in Niskanen's definition. Our observation of our own and others' motivation does not agree with Niskanen's, though we have of course encountered bad bureaucratic behaviour here and there. We have also worked in the private sector as wage workers, self-employers and as entrepreneurs, meeting different kinds but not really different magnitudes of bad behaviour. After the generalized insult to us and our kind on p. 34 of *Bureaucracy and Representative Government* it was a comfort to learn from the following pages that *some* good intentions are found in the public services, though Niskanen thinks they do much the same harm as bad intentions do.
23. *Western Economic Journal* V, 3 (1967) pp. 224–33.
24. See Note 2 to Chapter 1.
25. Ronald H. Coase, 'The problem of social cost', *Journal of Law and Economics* 3 (1960) pp. 1–44.
26. Robert W. Hahn, 'The political economy of environmental regulation: Toward a unifying framework', *Public Choice* 65 (1990) pp. 21–47.
27. William M. Landes and Richard A. Posner, 'The Independent Judiciary in an Interest Group Perspective', *Journal of Law and Economics* 18 (1975) pp. 875–901. The passage quoted is from p. 877.
28. Dennis C. Mueller, *Public Choice II* (1989) p. 286.
29. The same, pp. 214, 213.
30. G.M. Anderson and P.J. Brown, 'Heir Pollution: A Note on Buchanan's "Laws of Succession" and Tullock's "Blind Spot"', *International Review of Law and Economics* 5 (1985) pp. 15–23; Kenneth Arrow, 'The Place of Moral Obligation in Preference Systems' (1967), reprinted in his *Collected Papers* vol. 1 (1984); 'The Organization of Economic Activity: Issues Pertinent to the Choice of Market versus Non-Market Allocation' (1970), reprinted in his *Collected Papers* vol. 2 (1984); 'Gifts and Exchanges', *Philosophy and Public Affairs* 1 (1972) pp. 343–67; 'Social Responsibility and Economic Efficiency', *Public Policy* 21 (1973) pp. 303–17; 'Taxation and Democratic Values: A Case for Redistributing Income'. *New Republic* 171 (2 November 1974) pp. 23–5; 'A Cautious Case for Socialism', *Dissent* 25, 4 (1978) pp. 472–80; 'Two Cheers for Government Regulation', *Harpers* 262 (1981) pp. 18–22; Keith G. Baker, 'Public Choice Theory: 'Some Important Assumptions and

Public Policy Implications' in Robert T. Golembiewski and others (eds) *Public Administration: Readings in Institutions, Processes, Behavior, Policy* (3rd edn, 1976) pp. 41–60; Brian Barry, 'Some Questions about Explanation', *International Studies Quarterly* 27 (1983) pp. 17–27; Norman P. Barry, 'Unanimity, Agreement, and Liberalism: A Critique of James Buchanan's Social Philosophy', *Political Theory* 12, 4 (1984) pp. 579–96; William J. Baumol and Wallace E. Oates, *The Theory of Environmental Policy: Externalities, Public Outlays, and the Quality of Life* (1975); Gerhard Colm, 'In Defence of the Public Interest', *Social Research* 27 (1960) pp. 295–307; Thomas R. DeGregori, 'Caveat Emptor: A Critique of the Emerging Paradigm of Public Choice', *Administration and Society* 6 (1974) pp. 205–28; C. Dyke, 'The Question of Interpretation in Economics', *Ratio* XXI, 1 (1983) pp. 15–29; Norman Furniss, 'The Political Implications of the Public Choice-Property Rights School', *American Political Science Review* 72 (1978) pp. 399–410; Victor Goldberg, 'Public Choice – Property Rights', *Journal of Economic Issues* 8 (1974) pp. 555–579; Robert T. Golembiewski, 'A Critique of "Democratic Administration" and its Supporting Ideation', *American Political Science Review* 71 (1977) pp. 1488–507; Scott Gordon, 'The New Contractarians', *Journal of Political Economy* 84, 3 (1976) pp. 573–90; Robert Graftstein, 'The Public Choice Theory of Constitutions', *Social Science Quarterly* 62 (1981) pp. 199–212; Russell Hardin, 'Constitutional Political Economy – Agreement on Rules', *British Journal of Political Science* 18 (1988) pp. 513–30; Michael James, 'Classical Liberalism, Public Choice and Political Leadership', *CIS Policy Report* 4, 1 (1988) pp. 1–5; Mark Kelman, 'On Democracy-Bashing: A Sceptical Look at the Theoretical and "Empirical" Practice of the Public Choice Movement', *Virginia Law Review* 74 (1988) pp. 199–273; Steven Kelman, '"Public Choice" and Public Spirit', *Public Interest* 87 (1987) pp. 80–94; Charles P. Kindelberger, 'On the Rise and Decline of Nations', *International Studies Quarterly* 27 (1983) pp. 5–10; C.B. MacPherson, 'Market Concepts in Political Theory' *Canadian Journal of Economics and Political Science* XXVII, 4 (1961) pp. 490–7; Gerald Marwell and Ruth Ames, 'Economists Free Ride, Does Anyone Else? Experiments on the provision of public goods IV', *Journal of Public Economics* 15 (1981) pp. 295–310; Max Nieman, 'The Virtues of Heavy-Handedness in Government', *Law and Policy Quarterly* 2 (1980) pp. 11–34; Alessandro Pizzorno, 'On the Rationality of Democratic Choice', *Telos* 63 (1985) pp. 41–69; John Plamenatz, *Democracy and Illusion: An examination of certain aspects of modern democratic theory* (1973) Chapter 6, pp. 148–79; John Quiggin, 'Egoistic Rationality and Public Choice: A Critical Review of Theory and Evidence', *Economic Record* 63 (1987) pp. 10–21; Robert B. Reich, 'Why Democracy makes Economic Sense' *New Republic* 3, 596 (19 December 1983) pp. 25–32; Warren J. Samuels and A. Allan Schmid, 'Polluter's Profit and Political Response: The Dynamics of Rights Creation', *Public Choice* 28 (1976) pp. 99–105, and Samuels' contributions to his and James Buchanan's 'On Some Fundamental Issues in Political Economy: An Exchange of Correspondence', *Journal of Economic Issues* IX, 1 (1975) pp. 15–38; Amartya Sen, *Collective Choice and Social Welfare* (1970); 'The Impossibility of a Paretian Liberal' (1970), 'Behaviour and the Concept of Preference' (1973), 'Rational Fools: A Critique of the Behavioural Foundations of

Economic Theory' (1977), 'The Moral Standing of the Market' (1985), 'Social Choice and Justice: A Review Article [of vol. 1 of Kenneth Arrow's Collected Papers]' (1985), and other papers collected in *Choice, Welfare and Measurement* (1987); 'Economic Methodology: Heterogeneity and Relevance' *Social Research* 56, 2 (1989) pp. 299–329; and 'Individual Freedom as a Social Commitment', *New York Review of Books* XXXVII, 10 (14 June 1990) pp. 49–54; J.F.J. Toye, 'Economic Theories of Politics and Public Finance', *British Journal of Political Science* 6 (1976) pp. 433–47; and Gordon Tullock, 'The General Irrelevance of the General Impossibility Theorem', *Quarterly Journal of Economics* 81 (1967) pp. 256–70.

31.   Thomas R. DeGregori, 'Caveat Emptor: A Critique of the Emerging Paradigm of Public Choice', *Administration and Society* 6, 2 (1974) pp. 219–20.

CHAPTER 3: PUBLIC GOODS

1.   Paul A. Samuelson, 'The Pure Theory of Public Expenditure', *Review of Economics and Statistics* 36 (1954) pp. 387–9.

2.   Richard Titmuss, 'The Social Division of Welfare' and other essays in *Essays on the Welfare State* (1958).

3.   *Journal of Political Economy* 58 (1950) pp. 328–46.

4.   For a survey of the industry see Amartya Sen's entry, 'social choice', in J. Eatwell, M. Milgate and P. Newman (eds) *The New Palgrave: A dictionary of economics*.

5.   Anthony Downs. 'In Defence of Majority Voting', *Journal of Political Economy* (February 1961) pp. 192–9.

6.   Robert B. Reich, 'Why Democracy Makes Economic Sense', *The New Republic* 3, 596 (19 December 1983) pp. 25–32.

7.   David Alan Aschauer, 'Is Public Expenditure Productive?', *Journal of Monetary Economics* 23 (1989) 177–200; 'Does Public Capital Crowd Out Private Capital?', *Journal of Monetary Economics* 24 (1989) 171–188; *Public Investment and Private Sector Growth*, Economic Policy Institute, 1990; 'Infrastructure: America's Third Deficit', *Challenge* 34, 2, March/ April 1991, 39–45. See also Kevin T. Deno, 'The Effect of Public Capital on US Manufacturing Activity, 1970 to 1978'. *Southern Economic Journal* 55, 2, 1988 and Alicia H. Munnell, 'Why has Productivity Growth Declined?', *New England Economic Review* January/February 1990, and 'How does Public Infrastructure Affect Regional Economic Performance?' in *The Third Deficit: The Shortfall in Public Capital Investment*, Federal Reserve Bank of Boston Conference Series 34, 1991.

8.   *Challenge* 34, 2 (March/April 1991) p. 39.

CHAPTER 4: PUBLIC ENTERPRISE

1.   An Australian Minister of Finance, reluctant to finance the re-equipment of public airlines, asked why his government should lose votes by taxing people

to buy public assets, so that the opposition could win votes by promising to cut taxes which they could do by selling the assets. Better cut the taxes yourself by flogging everything saleable, and leave your successors to lose votes by raising taxes because there is nothing left to sell. We hereby register The Peter Walsh Doctrine of The Bare Cupboard.

CHAPTER 5: PUBLIC CHOICE: THE ATTEMPT

1. Dennis C. Mueller, *Public Choice II* (1979) p. 1, and *Public Choice II: A revised edition of Public Choice* (1989) pp. 1–2.
2. Geoffrey Brennan and James M. Buchanan, 'Is Public Choice Immoral? The Case for the "Nobel" Lie', *Virginia Law Review* 74, 1988, p. 180.
3. Geoffrey Brennan and James M. Buchanan, *The Reason of Rules: Constitutional political economy* (1985) p. 51.
4. William A. Niskanen, *Bureaucracy and Representative Government* (1971).
5. Michael Pusey, *Economic Rationalism in Canberra: A Nation-Building State Changes its Mind* (1991).
6. Peter Self, 'What's Wrong with Government?', *The Political Quarterly* 61, 1, 1990, p. 24.
7. Gordon Tullock, 'The Welfare Costs of Tariffs, Monopolies and Theft', *Western Economic Journal* V, 3 1967, pp. 224–33.
8. J.M. Buchanan, R. Tollison and G. Tullock (eds) *Toward a Theory of the Rent-Seeking Society* (1980) p. ix.
9. Robert D. Tollison, 'Is The Theory of Rent-Seeking Here to Stay?', in Charles K. Rowley (ed.) *Democracy and Public Choice: Essays In Honor of Gordon Tullock* (1987) p. 155.
10. Douglass C. North, 'Rent-Seeking and the New Institutional Economics', in Charles K. Rowley (ed.) *Democracy and Public Choice* (1987) p. 163.
11. Not necessarily. Some theorists count 'psychic income'. If the rich voluntarily give to the poor, both may be better off if the utility the rich derive from feeling generous exceeds the utility they lose by doing without the money. The Pareto frontier will be reached and giving will cease when the marginal utility of the next dollar equals the marginal utility of giving it away. In this form the theory says next to nothing. It abandons the determinate motivation of *homo economicus*, allows that any mixture of self-seeking and altruism may operate, and loses any predictive or explanatory power: it merely says that what people do must be what it pleases them to do. But notice that the argument still purports to be 'positive' – it assumes that the rich decide for themselves what balance of money and warm glow they prefer, and the theorist still does not have to compare their satisfaction at giving a dollar with the poor's satisfaction at getting it.
12. James M. Buchanan, 'Politics without Romance: A Sketch of Positive Public Choice Theory and its Normative Implications', first published in 1979 and reprinted in James M. Buchanan and Robert Tollison, *Theory of Public Choice II*, University of Michigan Press, 1984, p. 12.
13. Theorists may argue that either of these extreme distributions would offer the population little incentive to work. In the perfectly equal society everyone

might gain by introducing some incentive inequalities and therefore producing more for everyone. Similarly the monarch might grow even richer by freeing his slaves and paying them incentive wages to produce more for him and themselves. Those could both be unanimous decisions in favour of changes towards or onto the Pareto frontier. But in each case some member(s) of society would have to accept immediate losses as means to future gains, which means that the society takes a switchback route to the Pareto frontier, i.e. a route whose initial direction is non-Paretian. There is opportunity here for quite a clutch of journal articles to specify, and perhaps disagree about, the conditions necessary for such contingent and sequential changes to count as Pareto-positive. The conditions include for example discount rates for risk and for deferred utility, rates which are of course subjective and may vary from member to member so that no interpersonal comparisons are required. There are questions of periodization: the Pareto-positive status of the whole change-set may depend on the choice of starting and finishing dates. It may require some suspension of the Lipsey/Lancaster second-best theorem to establish that a change which has not yet brought the society to the Pareto frontier is a change 'away from' or 'toward' that frontier. In Chapter 5 of *The Reason of Rules* (1985) James Buchanan notices that the ultimate direction of a first change may not be known until later changes in the sequence have been decided, and it can be seen whether the first change made opportunity for further change toward or away from the Pareto frontier. He could have extended the argument to questions of 'no loser' unanimity, as follows. If the population has a normal age distribution, some members of the group which accepts immediate losses as means to eventual gains may not live long enough to enjoy the gains. Can the change-set then be accepted as unanimous with no losers? The potentialities of these questions may well run beyond journal articles to a monograph or two. The sole purpose of this footnote is to illustrate the autogeneration of pointless tasks, in the logical manipulation of monomotivated automata in uninteresting imaginary worlds, which characterizes much of the public choice literature. We have however spared readers the algebra in which such argument is often expressed.

14. *The Reason of Rules*, p. 139.
15. 'Politics without Romance', p. 15.
16. 'Politics without Romance', p. 19.
17. 'Politics without Romance', pp. 15–16.
18. There may be some tendency for public choice theorists to be more selfish than average, whether because their theories encourage it or because selfish people are attracted to this kind of theory. But there are certainly individual exceptions – like King Charles I, generous husbands and fathers however mistaken about government – and we are tempted to present one of them as evidence against his own professed beliefs. Readers will recall Mr A, the waterworks engineer whose seven codes of conduct were described by Chester Barnard in the passage quoted earlier from pp. 267–8 of *The Functions of the Executive*. In similar spirit we present Professor B, happily married father of three, tenured at the University of X, a well-regarded public choice theorist. He recognizes obligations which we suspect would rank, if tested, in this order: to children, to spouse, to students, to colleagues, to

democratic government, to his church (surprisingly there *are* some Christian public choice theorists who believe they get some of their values from what Buchanan, who is *not* our Professor B, condemns as extraindividual sources), and to his nation. We know him as a decent, affectionate, industrious man. He gives more time to his students than strict career-advancement would allow. Though his university is not in the very first rank, nor his salary its very highest (so there would be scope for further ambition) he stays put, welcoming his tenure partly because it frees him to teach better, and to spend more time with his family, than the sticks and carrots of publish-or-perish insecurity used to allow. It also means that he need never again force wife and children to move house and sever their local links and friendships. One of Professor B's most attractive shortcomings is some inability to take himself too seriously. He enjoys taking the same light-hearted deflationary view of other people, especially pompous colleagues. He is Christian by conversion and presumably has some sense of sin. He is mathematically gifted and enjoys doing the algebra in which most of his published work is expressed. Those last three characteristics are the only reasons we can see for his being a public choice theorist at all. That he *is* one should amuse him even more than it distresses us, because nothing makes his professed beliefs about human motivation quite as absurd as does the evidence of his own self and life.

CHAPTER 6: PUBLIC CHOICE: LIVING WITH FAILURE

1. Gordon Tullock, 'A (Partial) Rehabilitation of the Public Interest Theory', *Public Choice* 42, 1, (1984) p. 89.
2. Dennis C. Mueller, 'Rational Egoism versus Adaptive Egoism as Fundamental Postulates for a Descriptive Theory of Human Behaviour', *Public Choice 51*, 1 (1986), pp. 3–23.
3. *Public Choice* 56 (1988) p. 233.
4. *Public Choice* 57 (1988) pp. 247–57.
5. *Public Choice* 51, 1 (1986), p. 6.
6. The same, p. 15.
7. *Public Choice* 45 (1985) pp. 113–37.
8. *Public Choice* 62 (1989) pp. 253–85.

CHAPTER 7: WHAT TO DO INSTEAD: HOW TO MIX A MIXED ECONOMY

1. For reviews of the many estimates that have been made of the amount and value of unmarketed domestic work and output, see Richard Rose, 'Getting By in Three Economies', in J-E Lane (ed.) *State and Market: The politics of the public and the private*, London, 1985, and Luisella Goldschmidt-Clermont, *Unpaid Work in the Household*, ILO Geneva, 1982.
2. See for example the Japanese/Australian comparisons by Ian Castles in 'Living Standards in Sydney and Japanese Cities: A Comparison', in Kyoko

Sheridan and others (eds), *The Australian Economy in the Japanese Mirror*, 1991.
3. Evidence up to the 1970s is reviewed in Barbara Ward, *The Home of Man* (1976), and Orville F. Grimes Jr, *Housing for Low Income Urban Families: Economics and Policy in the Developing World* (1976).
4. See for example *International Trade and Industrial Policy in the 1990s – Towards creating human values in the global age*, MITI, 5 July 1990; and the discussion in Leon Hollerman, *Japan Disincorporated: The economic liberalization process*, Hoover Institution Press, 1988, Chapter 5.

CHAPTER 8: HOW TO THINK INSTEAD: THE RESOURCES OF POLITICAL THEORY

1. *Women as social critics in England, 1820–1850* (1983) an unpublished BA thesis in the University of Adelaide, pp. 1–2.
2. The role of imagined alternatives in causal analysis is discussed at greater length in H. Stretton, *The Political Sciences* (1969) pp. 238–69, 432–4, and in L. Orchard and R. Dare (eds), *Markets, Morals and Public Policy* (1989) pp. 252–9, from which parts of the present chapter are drawn.
3. For this view of Keynes' intentions see A.H. Meltzer, 'Keynes's General Theory: A different perspective', *Journal of Economic Literature* 19, 1981, 56; J.A. Kregel, 'Budget Deficits, Stabilization Policy and Liquidity Preference, Keynes's Postwar Policy Proposals', in F. Vicarelli (*ed.*) *Keynes's Relevance Today* (1985); and Colin Rogers, *Money, Interest and Capital* (1989) Chapter 10 and p. 288.
4. Susan Moller Okin, 'Justice and Gender, *Philosophy and Public Affairs* 16, 1 (1987) pp. 42–72.
5. Susan Moller Okin, 'Reason and Feeling in Thinking about Justice', in Cass R. Sunstein, (ed.) *Feminism and Political Theory* (1990) pp. 15–35.
6. *Philosophy and Public Affairs* 16, 1 (1987) pp. 69–72.
7. Elizabeth Wolgast, *The Grammar of Justice* (1987) pp. 15, 18–19.
8. Elizabeth Wolgast, *Equality and the Rights of Women* (1980) pp. 41–2.
9. The same, pp. 43, 54.
10. The same, p. 117.
11. The same, pp. 124–5.
12. Michael J. Sandel, 'The Procedural Republic and the Unencumbered Self', *Political Theory* 12, 1 (1984) p. 85.
13. John Rawls, *A Theory of Justice* (1971) p. 101.
14. Allan Bloom, *Giants and Dwarfs* (1990) p. 319.
15. *A Theory of Justice*, p. 102.
16. Martha Nussbaum, reviewing *Sources of the Self* in *The New Republic* 202, 15, 9 April 1990, p. 33.
17. The same.

Works Consulted

Anderson, Gary M. and Brown, Pamela J., 'Heir Pollution: A Note on Buchanan's "Laws of Succession" and Tullock's "Blind Spot"', *International Review of Law and Economics*, 5 (1985), pp. 15–23.

Arrow, Kenneth J., 'A Difficulty in the Concept of Social Welfare', *Journal of Political Economy*, 58 (1950), pp. 328–46.

Arrow, Kenneth J., *Social Choice and Individual Values*, Yale University Press, New Haven, 1951.

Arrow, Kenneth J., 'The Place of Moral Obligation in Preference Systems', 1967 (reprinted in Arrow, Kenneth J., *Collected Papers of Kenneth J. Arrow, Volume 1: Social Choice and Justice*, Basil Blackwell, Oxford, 1984).

Arrow, Kenneth J., 'The Organisation of Economic Activity: Issues Pertinent to the Choice of Market versus Nonmarket Allocation', 1970 (reprinted in Arrow, Kenneth J., *Collected Papers of Kenneth J. Arrow, Volume 2: General Equilibrium*, Basil Blackwell, Oxford, 1984).

Arrow, Kenneth J., 'Gifts and Exchanges', *Philosophy and Public Affairs*, 1 (1972), pp. 343–67.

Arrow, Kenneth J., 'Social Responsibility and Economic Efficiency', *Public Policy*, 21 (1973), pp. 303–17.

Arrow, Kenneth J., 'Taxation and Democratic Values: A Case for Redistributing Income', *New Republic*, 171 (2 November 1974), pp. 23–5.

Arrow, Kenneth J., 'A Cautious Case for Socialism', *Dissent*, 25 (1978), pp. 472–80.

Arrow, Kenneth J., 'Two Cheers for Government Regulation', *Harpers*, 262 (1981), pp. 18–22.

Arrow, Kenneth J. and Kurz, Mordecai, *Public Investment, the Rate of Return, and Optimal Fiscal Policy*, Resources for the Future, Johns Hopkins University Press, Baltimore, 1970.

Aschauer, D.A., 'Is Government Spending Stimulative?', *Contemporary Policy Issues*, VIII, 4 (1990), pp. 30–46.

Aschauer, D.A., 'Infrastructure: America's Third Deficit', *Challenge*, 34, 2 (March/April 1991), pp. 39–45.

Atkinson, Anthony B., 'James M. Buchanan's Contributions to Economics', *Scandanavian Journal of Economics*, 89 (1987), pp. 5–15.

Baker, Keith, 'Public-Choice Theory: Some Important Assumptions and Public-Policy Implications', in Golembiewski, Robert, Gibson, F. and Cornog, G. (eds), *Public Administration: Readings in Institutions, Processes, Behavior, Policy*, 3rd edition, Chicago, Rand McNally, 1976.

Barnard, Chester, *The Functions of the Executive*, Harvard University Press, Cambridge, Mass., 1968 (c1937).

Barry, Brian, *Political Argument*, Routledge & Kegan Paul, London, 1965.

Barry, Brian, *Sociologists, Economists and Democracy*, University of Chicago Press, 1978.

Barry, Brian, 'Some Questions about Explanation', *International Studies Quarterly*, 27 (1983), pp. 17–27.

Barry, Brian and Hardin, Russell (eds), *Rational Man and Irrational Society*, Sage, Beverly Hills, 1982.

Barry, Norman P., 'Unanimity, Agreement, and Liberalism: A Critique of James Buchanan's Social Philosophy', *Political Theory*, 12 (1984), pp. 579–596.

Baumol, William J. and Oates, Wallace E., *The Theory of Environmental Policy: Externalities, Public Outlays, and the Quality of Life*, Cambridge University Press, New York, 1988 (c1975).

Beauvoir, Simone de, *The Second Sex*, Cape, London, 1953 (c1949).

Bellah, Robert, Madsen, Richard, Sullivan, William, Swidler, Ann and Tipton, Steven, *The Good Society*, Alfred Knopf, New York, 1991.

Benedict, Ruth, *Patterns of Culture*, Houghton Mifflin, New York, 1934.

Bergsten, G.,'On the Role of Social Norms in a Market Economy', *Public Choice*, 45 (1985), pp. 113–37.

Berle, A.A. and Means, G.C., *The Modern Corporation and Private Property*, Macmillan, New York, 1940 (c.1932).

Bernstein, E., *Evolutionary Socialism*, Schocken Books, New York, 1961 (c1899).

Bloom, Allan, *Giants and Dwarfs*, Simon & Schuster, New York, 1990.

Bonner, John, *Politics, Economics and Welfare: An Elementary Introduction to Social Choice*, Wheatsheaf Books, Brighton, 1986.

Borcherding, T.E., Pommerehne, W.W. and Schneider, F., 'Comparing the Efficiency of Private and Public Production: The Evidence from Five Countries', *Zeitschrift für Nationalökomonie/Journal of Economics*, Supplement 2 (1982), pp. 127–56.

Brennan, Geoffrey, 'The Buchanan Contribution', *Finanz Archiv*, 45 (1987), pp. 1–24.

Brennan, Geoffrey, 'Politics *with* Romance: Towards a Theory of Democratic Socialism', in Hamlin, Alan and Pettit, Philip (eds), *The Good Polity: Normative Analysis of the State*, Basil Blackwell, Oxford, 1989.

Brennan, Geoffrey and Buchanan, James M., 'The Normative Purpose of Economic Science: Rediscovery of an Eighteenth Century Method', *International Review of Law and Economics*, 1 (1981), pp. 155–66.

Brennan, Geoffrey and Buchanan, James M., *The Power to Tax: Analytical Foundations of a Fiscal Constitution*, Cambridge University Press, 1980.

Brennan, Geoffrey and Buchanan, James M., *The Reason of Rules: Constitutional Political Economy*, Cambridge University Press, 1985.

Brennan, Geoffrey and Buchanan, James M., 'Is Public Choice Immoral? The Case for the "Nobel" Lie', *Virginia Law Review*, 74 (1988), pp. 179–89.

Brennan, Geoffrey and Pincus, Jonathan, 'Rational Actor Theory in Politics: A Critical Review of John Quiggin', *Economic Record*, 63 (1987), pp. 22–32.

Brus, W. and Laski, K., *From Marx to the Market: Socialism in Search of an Economic System*, Oxford University Press, 1989.

Buchanan, James M., 'The Pure Theory of Government Finance: A Suggested Approach', *Journal of Political Economy*, 57 (1949), pp. 496–506.

Buchanan, James M., *Fiscal Theory and Political Economy: Selected Essays*, University of North Carolina Press, Chapel Hill, 1960.

Buchanan, James M., *Public finance in democratic process: fiscal institutions and individual choice*, University of North Carolina Press, Chapel Hill, 1967.

Buchanan, James M., *Demand and Supply of Public Goods*, Rand McNally, Chicago, 1968.

Buchanan, James M., 'What Kind of Redistribution do We Want?', *Economica*, 35 (1968), p.185–90.

Buchanan, James M., *The Limits of Liberty: Between Anarchy and Leviathan*, Chicago University Press, 1975.

Buchanan, James M., *Freedom in Constitutional Contract: Perspectives of a Political Economist*, Texas A&M University Press, College Station, 1977.

Buchanan, James M., 'Why does Government Grow?', in Borcherding, T. (ed), *Budgets and Bureaucrats: The Sources of Government Growth*, Duke University Press, Durham, NC, 1977.

Buchanan, James M., *What Should Economists Do?*, Liberty Press, Indianapolis, 1979.

Buchanan, James M., 'Politics without Romance: A Sketch of Positive Public Choice Theory and its Normative Implications', 1979 (reprinted in Buchanan, James M. and Tollison, Robert (eds), *The Theory of Public Choice II*, University of Michigan Press, Ann Arbor, 1984.)

Buchanan, James M., *Liberty, Market and State: Political Economy in the 1980s*, Wheatsheaf Books, Brighton, 1986.

Buchanan, James M., *Economics: Between Predictive Science and Moral Philosophy*, Texas A&M University Press, College Station, 1987.

Buchanan, James M., 'The Constitution of Economic Policy', *American Economic Review*, 77 (1987), pp. 243–50.

Buchanan, James M., *Explorations into Constitutional Economics*, Texas A&M University Press, College Station, 1989.

Buchanan, James M., 'Socialism is Dead but Leviathan Lives On', John Bonython Lecture, Centre for Independent Studies, Sydney, 1990.

Buchanan, James M. and Samuels, Warren, 'On Some Fundamental Issues in Political Economy: An Exchange of Correspondence', *Journal of Economic Issues*, IX (1975), pp. 15–38.

Buchanan, James M., Tollison, Robert and Tullock, Gordon (eds), *Toward a Theory of the Rent-Seeking Society*, Texas A&M University Press, College Station, 1980.

Buchanan, James M. and Tullock, Gordon, *The Calculus of Consent: Logical Foundations of Constitutional Democracy*, University of Michigan Press, Ann Arbor, 1962.

Buchanan, James M. and Wagner, Richard E., *Democracy in Deficit: The Political Legacy of Lord Keynes*, Academic Press, New York, 1977.

Buck, Philip W., *How Conservatives Think*, Penguin, Harmondsworth, 1975.

Carey, Joyce, *To Be a Pilgrim*, Michael Joseph, London, 1942.

Christainsen, Gregory B., 'James Buchanan and the Revival of Classical Political Economy', *Challenge*, 31 (1988), pp. 11–15.

Coase, Ronald H., 'The Problem of Social Cost', *Journal of Law and Economics*, 3 (1960), pp. 1–44.

Colander, David C., (ed), *Neoclassical Political Economy: The Analysis of Rent-Seeking and DUP Activities*, Ballinger Publishing, Cambridge, Mass., 1984.

Coleman, Alice, *Utopia on Trial: Vision and Reality in Planned Housing*, Hilary Shipman, London, 1985.

Colm, Gerhard, 'In Defence of the Public Interest', *Social Research*, 27 (1960), pp. 295–307.

Connolly, William, *Appearance and Reality in Politics*, Cambridge University Press, 1981.

Crosland, Anthony, *The Future of Socialism*, Macmillan, New York, 1957.

Daniels, N., 'Justice between Age Groups: Am I My Parents' Keeper?', *Health and Society*, 61 (1983), pp. 489–522.

DeGregori, Thomas R., 'Caveat Emptor: A Critique of the Emerging Paradigm of Public Choice', *Administration and Society*, 6 (1974), pp. 205–28.

Domberger, S. and Piggott, J., 'Privatization Policies and Public Enterprise: A Survey', *Economic Record*, 177 (1986), pp. 145–62.

Douglass, R., Mara, G. and Richardson, H. (eds), *Liberalism and the Good*, Routledge, New York, 1990.

Downs, Anthony, 'An Economic Theory of Political Action in a Democracy', *Journal of Political Economy*, 65 (1957), pp. 135–50.

Downs, Anthony, *An Economic Theory of Democracy*, Harper Row, New York, 1957.

Downs, Anthony, 'Why the Government Budget is Too Small in a Democracy', *World Politics*, 12 (1960), pp. 541–63.

Downs, Anthony, 'In Defence of Majority Voting', *Journal of Political Economy*, 69 (1961), pp. 192–9.

Downs, Anthony, 'The Public Interest: Its Meaning in a Democracy', *Social Research*, 29 (1962), pp. 1–36.

Downs, Anthony, *Inside Bureaucracy*, Little, Brown, Boston, 1967.

Dunleavy, Patrick, *Democracy, Bureaucracy and Public Choice: Economic Explanations in Political Science*, Harvester Wheatsheaf, New York, 1991.

Dyke, C., 'The Question of Interpretation in Economics', *Ratio*, 25 (1983), pp. 15–29.

Elster, Jon and Hylland, Aanund (eds), *Foundations of Social Choice Theory*, Cambridge University Press, 1986.

Fitzgerald, Tom, *Between Life and Economics*, Australian Broadcasting Commission, Sydney, 1990.

Floyd, R.H., Gray, C.S. and Short, R.P., *Public Enterprise in Mixed Economies: Some macroeconomic aspects*, Woodhead Faulkner, 1985.

Frey, Bruno, *Democratic Economic Policy: A Theoretical Introduction*, Basil Blackwell, Oxford, 1983.

Furniss, N., 'The Political Implications of the Public Choice-Property Rights School', *American Political Science Review*, 72 (1978), pp. 399–410.

Galbraith, John Kenneth, *The Affluent Society*, André Deutsch, London, 1977 (c1957).

Gargett, Kathryn, *Women as Social critics in England, 1820–1850*, Unpublished BA Honours thesis, University of Adelaide, 1983.

Gershuny, Jonathan, *Social Innovation and the Division of Labour*, Oxford University Press, 1983.

Gifford, A. and Kenney, R.W., 'Socialism and the Revenue Maximizing Leviathan', *Public Choice*, 42 (1984), pp.101–6.

Goldberg, Victor, 'Public Choice – Property Rights', *Journal of Economic Issues*, 8 (1974), pp. 555–79.

Golembiewski, Robert T., 'A Critique of "Democratic Administration" and its Supporting Ideation', *American Political Science Review*, 71 (1977), pp. 1488–507.

Goldschmidt-Clermont, L., *Unpaid Work in the Household*, ILO, Geneva, 1982.

Goodin, Robert, *Political Theory and Public Policy*, University of Chicago Press, 1982.

Gordon, Scott, 'The New Contractarians', *Journal of Political Economy*, 84 (1976), pp. 573–90.

Graftstein, Robert, 'The Public Choice Theory of Constitutions', *Social Science Quarterly*, 62 (1981), pp. 199–212.

Green, Thomas, *Lectures on the Principles of Political Obligation and other writings*, Cambridge University Press, 1986 (c1880).

Grimes, O.F., *Housing for Low Income Urban Families: Economics and Policy in the Developing World*, World Bank/Johns Hopkins University Press, 1976.

Hahn, Robert W., 'The Political Economy of Environmental Regulation: Towards a Unifying Framework', *Public Choice*, 65 (1990), pp. 21–47.

Hamlin, Alan, 'Public Choice, Markets and Utilitarianism', in Whynes, D. (ed), *What is Political Economy?*, Basil Blackwell, Oxford, 1984.

Hardin, Russell, *Collective Action*, Johns Hopkins University Press, Baltimore, 1982.

Hardin, Russell, 'Constitutional Political Economy – Agreement on Rules', *British Journal of Political Science*, 18 (1988), pp. 513–30.

Hayek, Friedrich von, *The Road to Serfdom*, University of Chicago Press, 1975 (c1944).

Hayek, Friedrich von, *The Constitution of Liberty*, University of Chicago Press, 1961.

Head, John, *Public Goods and Public Welfare*, Duke University Press, Durham, NC, 1974.

Heilbroner, Robert, 'Lifting the Silent Depression', *New York Review of Books*, 24 October 1991, pp. 6–8.

Hindess, Barry, 'Rational Choice Theory and the Analysis of Political Action', *Economy and Society*, 13 (1984), pp. 255–77.

Hindess, Barry, *Choice, Rationality and Social Theory*, Unwin Hyman, London, 1988.

Hindess, Barry (ed), *Reactions to the Right*, Routledge, London, 1990.

Hirsch, Fred, *Social Limits to Growth*, Routledge & Kegan Paul, London, 1976.

Hirschman, Albert, *Exit, Voice and Loyalty*, Harvard University Press, Cambridge, Mass., 1970.

Hirschman, Albert, *Shifting Involvements: Private Interest and Public Action*, Martin Robertson, Oxford, 1982.

Holland, Stuart (ed), *The State as Entrepreneur: New Dimensions for Public Enterprise: The IRI State Shareholding Formula*, Weidenfeld and Nicolson, London, 1972.

Holland, Stuart, *The Socialist Challenge*, Quartet Books, London, 1975.

Hollerman, L., *Japan Disincorporated: The Economic Liberalization Process*, Hoover Institution Press, 1988.

Ignatieff, Michael, *The Needs of Strangers*, Chatto & Windus, London, 1984.

Jacobs, Michael, *The Green Economy*, Pluto Press, London, 1991.

James, Michael, 'Classical Liberalism, Public Choice and Political Leadership', *Centre for Independent Studies Policy Report* (Sydney), 4, 1 (1988), pp. 1–5.

Kelman, Mark, 'On Democracy-Bashing: A Sceptical Look at the Theoretical and "Empirical" Practice of the Public Choice Movement', *Virginia Law Review*, 74 (1988), pp. 199–273.

Kelman, Steven, '"Public Choice" and Public Spirit', *Public Interest*, 87 (1987), pp. 80–94.

Kindelberger, Charles, 'On The Rise and Decline of Nations', *International Studies Quarterly*, 27 (1983), pp. 5–10.

Kirk, Russell (ed.), *The Portable Conservative Reader*, Penguin, Harmondsworth, 1982.

Kirman, A., 'The intrinsic limits of modern economic theory: The Emperor has No Clothes', *Economic Journal*, 99 (1989), pp. 126–39.

Kregel, J.A., 'Budget Deficits, Stabilization Policy and Liquidity Preferences, Keynes's postwar policy proposals', in Vicarelli, F. (ed.), *Keynes's Relevance Today*, University of Pennsylvania Press, Philadelphia,1985.

Kukathas, Chundrun and Pettit, Philip, *Rawls: A Theory of Justice and its Critics*, Polity Press, Cambridge, 1990.

Landes, William M. and Posner, Richard A., 'The Independent Judiciary in an Interest Group Perspective', *Journal of Law and Economics*, 18 (1975), pp. 875–901.

Lane, J-E (ed.), *State and Market: The Politics of the Public and the Private*, Sage Modern Politics Series, vol. 9, Sage Publications, London, 1985.

Lane, Robert, *The Market Experience*, Cambridge University Press, 1991.

Larmore, Charles, *Patterns of Moral Complexity*, Cambridge University Press, Cambridge, 1987.

Lindblom, Charles, *Politics and Markets*, Basic Books, New York, 1977.

Locksley, Gareth, 'Individuals, Contracts and Constitutions: the Political Economy of James M. Buchanan', in Shackleton, J.R. and Locksley, G. (eds), *Twelve Contemporary Economists*, Macmillan, London, 1981.

MacDonagh, Oliver, *A Pattern of Government Growth 1800–1860: The Passenger Acts and their Enforcement*, Macgibbon & Kee, London, 1961.

MacPherson, C.B., 'Market Concepts in Political Theory', *Canadian Journal of Economics and Political Science*, XXVII (1961), pp. 490–7.

McCraw, T.K., *Prophets of Regulation*, Harvard University Press, Cambridge, Mass. 1984.

McCormick, R.E. and Tollison, R.D., *Politicians, Legislation and the Economy: an inquiry into the interest-group theory of government*, Kluwer, Boston, 1981.

McLean, Iain, 'Review Article: Some Recent Work in Public Choice', *British Journal of Political Science*, 16 (1986), pp. 377–94.

McLean, Iain, *Public Choice: An Introduction*, Basil Blackwell, Oxford, 1987.

Marwell, Gerald and Ames, Ruth, 'Economists Free Ride, Does Anyone Else? Experiments on the Provision of Public Goods, IV', *Journal of Public Economics*, 15 (1981), pp. 295–310.

Mayo, Elton, *The Human Problems of Industrial Civilization*, Macmillan, New York, 1933.

Meltzer, A.H., 'Keynes' *General Theory*: A Different Perspective', *Journal of Economic Literature*, 19 (1981), pp. 34–64.

Meyer, R., 'Publicly Owned versus Privately Owned Utilities: A Policy Choice', *Review of Economics and Statistics*, 57 (1975), pp. 391–9.

Meyers, Diana T., 'Review of James Buchanan's *Liberty, Market and State*', *Economics and Philosophy*, 3 (1987), pp. 351–61.

Millward, R., 'The Comparative Performance of Public and Private Ownership', in Roll, Eric (ed.), *The Mixed Economy*, Macmillan, London, 1982.

Millward, R., *Public Sector Economics*, Longman, London, 1983.

MITI, *International Trade and Industrial Policy in the 1990s: Towards Creating Human Values in a Global Age*, Japanese Government, 1990.

Monsen, R. and Downs, Anthony, 'Public goods and private status', *Public Interest*, 23 (1971), pp. 64–76.

Mueller, Dennis, *Public Choice*, Cambridge University Press, 1979.

Mueller, Dennis, 'Mueller on Buchanan', in Speigel, H. and Samuels, Warren (eds), *Contemporary Economists in Perspective*, JAI Press, Greenwich, Conn., 1984.

Mueller, Dennis, 'Rational Egoism versus Adaptive Egoism as Fundamental Postulates for a Descriptive Theory of Human Behavior', *Public Choice*, 51 (1986), pp. 3–23.

Mueller, Dennis, *Public Choice II: A revised edition of* Public Choice, Cambridge University Press, 1989.

Newman, Oscar, *Defensible Space: Crime Prevention through Urban Design*, Macmillan, New York, 1972.

Nieman, Max, 'The Virtues of Heavy-Handedness in Government', *Law and Policy Quarterly*, 2 (1980), pp. 11–34.

Nisbet, Robert, *Conservatism: Dream and Reality*, Open University Press, Milton Keynes, 1986.

Niskanen, William, *Bureaucracy and Representative Government*, Aldine-Atherton, Chicago, 1971.

Nove, Alec, *The Economics of Feasible Socialism*, Allen & Unwin, London, 1983.

Nozick, Robert, *Anarchy, State and Utopia*, Basic Books, New York, 1974.

Nussbaum, Martha, 'Aristotelian Social Democracy', in Douglass, R., Mara, G. and Richardson, H. (eds), *Liberalism and the Good*, Routledge, New York, 1990.

Oakeshott, Michael, *Rationalism in Politics and Other Essays*, Basic Books, New York, 1962.

Oakeshott, Michael, *On Human Conduct*, Oxford University Press, 1975.

Okin, Susan Moller, 'Justice and Gender', *Philosophy and Public Affairs*, 16 (1987), pp. 42–72.

Okin, Susan Moller, 'Reason and Feeling in Thinking about Justice', in Sunstein, Cass (ed.), *Feminism and Political Theory*, University of Chicago Press, 1990.

Olson, Mancur, *The Logic of Collective Action: Public Goods and the Theory of Groups*, Harvard University Press, Cambridge, Mass., 1965.

Olson, Mancur, *The Rise and Decline of Nations*, Yale University Press, New Haven, Conn., 1982.

Olson, Mancur, 'Towards a Mature Social Science', *International Studies Quarterly*, 27 (1983), pp. 29–37.

Olson, Mancur, 'Why Some Welfare-State Redistribution to the Poor is a Great Idea' in Rowley, Charles (ed.), *Democracy and Public Choice: Essays in Honor of Gordon Tullock*, Basil Blackwell, Oxford, 1987.

Olson, Mancur, 'Economy, Logic, and Action: Interviewed by Richard Swedberg', *Society*, 27 (1990), pp. 71–81.

Orchard, Lionel, 'Public Choice Theory and the Common Good', in Orchard, Lionel and Dare, Robert (eds), *Markets, Morals and Public Policy*, Federation Press, Sydney, 1989.

O'Sullivan, Noel, *Conservatism*, J.M. Dent, London, 1976.

Passmore, John, *Man's Responsibility for Nature*, Duckworth, London, 1974.

Peattie, Lisa and Rein, Martin, *Women's Claims: A Study in Political Economy*, Oxford University Press, 1983.

Pier, W.J., Vernon, R.B. and Wicks, J.H., 'An Empirical Comparison of Government and Private Production Efficiency', *National Tax Journal*, 27 (1974), pp. 653–6.

Pizzorno, Alessandro, 'On the Rationality of Democratic Choice', *Telos*, 63 (1985), pp. 41–69.

Plamenatz, John, 'Neo-Utilitarian Theories of Democracy', in Plamenatz, John, *Democracy and Illusion: An Examination of Certain Aspects of Modern Democratic Theory*, Longman, London, 1973.

Popper, Karl, *The Open Society and its Enemies*, Routledge & Kegan Paul, 1946.

Pryke, Richard, *Public Enterprise in Practice: The British Experience of Nationalisation over Two Decades*, Macgibbon & Kee, London, 1971.

Pryke, Richard, *The Nationalised Industries: Policies and Performance Since 1968*, Martin Robertson, Oxford, 1981.

Public Choice, vols. 36–55, 1981–1990.

Pusey, Michael, *Economic Rationalism in Canberra*, Cambridge University Press, 1991.

Quiggin, John, 'Egoistic Rationality and Public Choice: A Critical Review of Theory and Evidence', *Economic Record*, 63 (1987), pp. 10–21.

Rawls, John, *A Theory of Justice*, Oxford University Press, 1971.

Rawls, John, 'Justice as Fairness: Political not Metaphysical', *Philosophy and Public Affairs*, 14 (1985), pp. 223–51.

Rawls, John, 'The Idea of an Overlapping Consensus', *Oxford Journal of Legal Studies*, 7 (1987), pp. 1–25.

Rawls, John, 'The Priority of Right and Ideas of the Good', *Philosophy and Public Affairs*, 17 (1988), pp. 251–76.

Reich, Robert, 'Why Democracy Makes Economic Sense', *The New Republic*, 3, 596 (19 December 1983), pp. 25–32.

Reisman, David, *The Political Economy of James Buchanan*, Texas A&M University Press, College Station, 1990.

Reisman, David, *Theories of Collective Action: Downs, Olson and Hirsch*, Macmillan, London, 1990.

Rhoads, Steven, *The Economist's View of the World: Government, Markets, and Public Policy*, Cambridge University Press, 1985.

Riker, William H., 'The Place of Political Science in Public Choice', *Public Choice*, 57 (1988), pp. 247–57.

Robson, W., *Public Enterprise: Developments in Social Ownership and Control in Great Britain*, Garland Publishing, New York, 1985 (c1937).

Rogers, Colin, *Money, Interest and Capital: A Study in the Foundations of Monetary Theory*, Cambridge University Press, 1989.

Roll, Eric (ed.), *The Mixed Economy*, Macmillan, London, 1982.

Romer, Thomas, 'Nobel Laureate: On James Buchanan's Contributions to Public Economics', *Journal of Economic Perspectives*, 2 (1988), pp. 165–79.

Rose, Geoffrey, 'Reflections on the Changing Times', *British Medical Journal*, 301 (3 October 1990), pp. 683–7.

Rose, Richard, 'What if Anything is Wrong with Big Government', *Journal of Public Policy*, 1 (1981), pp. 5–36.

Rose, Richard, 'Getting by in Three Economies: The Resources of the Official, Unofficial and Domestic Economies', in Lane, J-E (ed.), *State and Market: The Politics of the Public and the Private*, Sage Modern Politics Series, vol. 9, Sage Publications, London, 1985.

Rose, Richard, *Public Employment in Western Nations*, Cambridge University Press, 1985.

Rosenblum, Nancy (ed.), *Liberalism and the Moral Life*, Harvard University Press, Cambridge, Mass., 1989.

Rowley, Charles K., 'The Calculus of Consent', in Rowley, Charles K. (ed.), *Democracy and Public Choice: Essays in Honor of Gordon Tullock*, Basil Blackwell, Oxford, 1987.

Rowley, Charles K., Tollison, Robert D. and Tullock, Gordon (eds), *The Political Economy of Rent-Seeking*, Kluwer, Boston, 1988.

Sabine, George H., *A History of Political Theory*, Harrap, London, 1937.

Sagoff, Mark, *The Economy of the Earth: Philosophy, Law and the Environment*, Cambridge University Press, 1988.

Samuels, Warren J. and Schmid, Allan A., 'Polluter's Profit and Political Response: The Dynamics of Rights Creation', *Public Choice*, 28 (1976), p. 99–105.

Samuelson, Paul, 'The Pure Theory of Public Expenditure', *Review of Economics and Statistics*, 36 (1954), pp. 387–9.

Samuelson, Paul, 'Diagrammatic Exposition of a Theory of Public Expenditure', *Review of Economics and Statistics*, 37 (1955), pp. 350–6.

Samuelson, Paul, 'Aspects of Public Expenditure Theories', *Review of Economics and Statistics*, 40 (1958), pp. 332–8.

Samuelson, Paul, 'The World Economy at Century's End', in Tsuru, S. (ed), *Human Resources, Employment and Development*, vol. 1, Macmillan, London, 1983.

Sandel, Michael, *Liberalism and the Limits of Justice*, Cambridge University Press, 1982.

Sandel, Michael, 'The Procedural Republic and the Unencumbered Self', *Political Theory*, 12 (1984), pp. 81–96.

Sandmo, Agnar, 'Buchanan on Political Economy: A Review Article', *Journal of Economic Literature*, XXVIII (1990), pp. 50–65.

Schnaiberg, Allan, *The Environment: From Surplus to Scarcity*, Oxford University Press, 1980.

Segal, Lynne, *Is the Future Female? Troubled Thoughts on Contemporary Feminism*, Virago, London, 1987.

Self, Peter, *Econocrats and the Policy Process: The Politics and Philosophy of Cost Benefit Analysis*, Macmillan, London, 1975.

Self, Peter, *Political Theories of Modern Government: Its Role and Reform*, Allen & Unwin, Winchester, Mass., 1985.

Self, Peter, 'What's Wrong with Government?', *Political Quarterly*, 61 (1990), pp. 23–35.

Self, Peter, *Government by the Market? The Politics of Public Choice*, Macmillan, London, 1993.

Selznick, Philip, *The Moral Commonwealth: Social Theory and the Promise of Community*, University of California Press, 1992.

Sen, Amartya, *Collective Choice and Social Welfare*, Holden-Day, San Francisco, 1970.

Sen, Amartya, 'The Impossibility of a Paretian Liberal', *Journal of Political Economy*, 78 (1970), pp. 152–7.

Sen, Amartya, 'Liberty, Unanimity and Rights', *Economica*, 43 (1976), pp. 217–45.

Sen, Amartya, 'Rational Fools: A Critique of the Behavioral Foundations of Economic Theory', *Philosophy and Public Affairs*, 6 (1977), pp. 317–44.

Sen, Amartya, 'Social Choice and Justice: A Review Article', *Journal of Economic Literature*, XXIII (1985), pp. 1764–76.

Sen, Amartya, 'The Moral Standing of the Market', *Social Philosophy and Policy*, 2 (1985), pp. 1–19.

Sen, Amartya, 'Adam Smith's Prudence', in Lall, S. and Stewart, Frances, eds, *Theory and Reality in Development*, Macmillan, London, 1986.

Sen, Amartya, 'Economic Methodology: Heterogeneity and Relevance', *Social Research*, 56 (1989), pp. 299–329.

Sen, Amartya, 'Individual Freedom as a Social Commitment', *New York Review of Books*, XXXVII (14 June 1990), pp. 49–54.

Sheridan, Kyoko, *The Australian Economy in the Japanese Mirror*, University of Queensland Press, 1991.

Sheridan, Kyoko, *Governing the Japanese Economy*, Polity Press, Cambridge, 1993.

Stretton, Hugh, *The Political Sciences: General Principles of Selection in Social Science and History*, Routledge & Kegan Paul, London, 1969.

Stretton, Hugh, *Capitalism, Socialism and the Environment*, Cambridge University Press, 1976.

Stretton, Hugh, *Political Essays*, Georgian House, Melbourne, 1987.

Stretton, Hugh, 'Women and the Future of Work', in Orchard, Lionel and Dare, Robert (eds), *Markets, Morals and Public Policy*, Federation Press, Sydney, 1989.

Sugden, Robert, *The Political Economy of Public Choice: An Introduction to Welfare Economics*, Martin Robertson, Oxford, 1981.

Sunstein, Cass (ed.), *Feminism and Political Theory*, University of Chicago Press, 1990.

Tawney, Richard, *The Acquisitive Society*, Bell, London, 1921.

Tawney, Richard, *Equality*, Allen & Unwin, London, 1952 (c1931).

Taylor, Charles, *Sources of the Self: The Making of the Modern Identity*, Cambridge University Press, 1989.

Terrill, R., *R.H. Tawney and his Times: Socialism as Fellowship*, Harvard University Press, Cambridge, Mass., 1973.

Titmuss, Richard, *Essays on the Welfare State*, Allen & Unwin, London, 1976 (c1958).

Toye, J.F.J., 'Economic Theories of Politics and Public Finance', *British Journal of Political Science*, 6 (1976), pp. 433–47.

Trollope, Anthony, *The American Senator*, Chapman & Hall, London, 1877.

Tullock, Gordon, 'Problems of Majority Voting', *Journal of Political Economy*, 67 (1959), pp. 571–9.

Tullock, Gordon, *The Politics of Bureaucracy*, Public Affairs Press, Washington DC, 1965.

Tullock, Gordon, 'The General Irrelevance of the General Impossibility Theorem', *Quarterly Journal of Economics*, 81 (1967), pp. 256–70.

Tullock, Gordon, 'The Welfare Costs of Tariffs, Monopoly and Theft', *Western Economic Journal*, 3 (1967), pp. 224–33.

Tullock, Gordon, 'A (partial) Rehabilitation of the Public Interest Theory', *Public Choice*, 42 (1984), pp. 89–99.

Uhlaner, Carole, '"Relational Goods" and participation: Incorporating Sociability into a Theory of Rational Action', *Public Choice*, 62 (1989), pp. 253–85.

van den Doel, Hans, *Democracy and Welfare Economics*, Cambridge University Press, 1979.

van der Kragt, A.J.C., Dawes, R.M. and Orbell, J.M., 'Are People Who Cooperate Rational Altruists?', *Public Choice*, 56 (1988), pp. 233–47.

Wagner, Richard E., '*The Calculus of Consent:* A Wicksellian Retrospective', *Public Choice*, 56 (1988), pp. 153–66.

Walzer, Michael, *Spheres of Justice: A Defence of Pluralism and Equality*, Basic Books, New York, 1983.

Walzer, Michael, *Interpretation and Social Criticism*, Harvard University Press, Cambridge, Mass., 1987.

Ward, Barbara, *The Home of Man*, André Deutsch, London, 1976.

Wicksell, Knut, 'A new principle of just taxation', in Musgrave, Richard A. and Peacock, Alan T. (eds), *Classics in the Theory of Public Finance*, Macmillan, London, 1958.

Williams, Bernard, *Ethics and the Limits of Philosophy*, Harvard University Press, Cambridge, Mass., 1985.

Wolfe, Alan, *Whose Keeper? Social Science and Moral Obligation*, University of California Press, 1989.

Wolgast, Elizabeth, *Equality and the Rights of Women*, Cornell University Press, Ithaca, NY, 1980.

Wolgast, Elizabeth, *The Grammar of Justice*, Cornell University Press, Ithaca, NY, 1987.

Young, John, *Sustaining the Earth*, Harvard University Press, Cambridge, Mass., 1990.

Index